THE HOSPITALLERS, THE MEDITERRANEAN AND EUROPE

Professor Anthony Luttrell

The Hospitallers, the Mediterranean and Europe

Festschrift for Anthony Luttrell

Edited by

KARL BORCHARDT
University of Würzburg, Germany

NIKOLAS JASPERT
Ruhr-Universität Bochum, Germany

HELEN J. NICHOLSON
Cardiff University, UK

ASHGATE

[redacted]

Published by
Ashgate Publishing Limited
Gower House
Croft Road
Aldershot
Hampshire GU11 3HR
England

Ashgate Publishing Company
Suite 420
101 Cherry Street
Burlington, VT 05401-4405
USA

Ashgate website: http://www.ashgate.com

British Library Cataloguing in Publication Data
The Hospitallers, the Mediterranean and Europe: Festschrift for Anthony Luttrell
1. Knights of Malta – History. 2. Hospitalers – History. 3. Crusades. I. Luttrell, Anthony, 1932– . II. Borchardt, Karl. III. Jaspert, Nikolas IV. Nicholson, Helen J., 1960– .
271.7'912

Library of Congress Cataloging-in-Publication Data
The Hospitallers, the Mediterranean, and Europe: Festschrift for Anthony Luttrell / edited by Karl Borchardt, Nikolas Jaspert, and Helen J. Nicholson.
p. cm.
Includes bibliographical references and index.
1. Hospitalers. I. Luttrell, Anthony, 1932– . II. Borchardt, Karl.
III. Jaspert, Nikolas. IV. Nicholson, Helen J., 1960– .
BX2825.H68 2007
271'.7912–dc22 2007010255

ISBN 978-0-7546-6275-4

This book has been printed on acid-free paper.

Printed and bound in Great Britain by MPG Books Ltd, Bodmin, Cornwall.

Contents

PART 2: RHODES AND THE LATIN EAST

PART 3: THE MILITARY-RELIGIOUS ORDERS IN THE WEST

Contributors

Authors

David Allen is a graduate of Durham and Cambridge Universities and taught modern history at the University of Birmingham before retiring to Malta in 1999. He has published several articles about the Order of St John's history in early modern Europe and the New World. He is Honorary Associate Member of the Centre for Mediterranean Studies at the University of Leeds.

Carlos Barquero Goñi is doctor in Medieval History by the Autonomous University of Madrid. He has published several books and articles on the Hospitallers in Medieval Spain. His most recent book is *La Orden de San Juan de Jerusalén en Navarra. Siglos XIV y XV* (Pamplona, 2004).

Pierre Bonneaud, licencié en droit, diplômé de l'Institut d'Études Politiques (Paris), diplômé de l'École de Hautes Études de Sciences Sociales (Paris), s'est consacré depuis 1994 à la recherche sur l'ordre de l'Hôpital, en particulier dans la Couronne d'Aragon, au XVe siècle. Il a récemment publié *Le prieuré de Catalogne, le couvent de Rhodes et la couronne d'Aragon, 1415–1447* (Millau, Bez-et-Esparron, 2004).

Judith Bronstein teaches at the Department of General History at the University of Haifa. In 2005 she published the book *The Hospitallers and the Holy Land, Financing the Latin East, 1187–1274*. She has also published several articles on the Hospitallers. Her Ph.D. is from the University of Cambridge.

Jochen Burgtorf is associate professor of medieval history at California State University, Fullerton. He has published several articles on the military orders, co-edited a collection of essays (*International Mobility in the Military Orders*, 2006; with Helen Nicholson) and is working on a book concerning the Templars' and Hospitallers' leadership structures.

Nicholas Coureas is a member of staff at the Cyprus Research Centre, Nicosia. His numerous publications include *The Latin Church in Cyprus, 1195–1312* (1997) and *The Assizes of the Lusignan Kingdom of Cyprus* (2002).

Peter Edbury is a graduate of the University of Saint Andrews (MA 1970; PhD 1974) and since 1977 has taught in Cardiff University where he is now Professor of History. He has written widely on the Latin states in the East between the twelfth and fifteenth centuries, and his most recent major work is a new edition of John of Ibelin's *Livre des Assises* (Brill 2003).

Alan Forey, who is now retired, taught in the universities of Oxford, St Andrews and Durham. He has written seminal comparative studies on the military orders, including *The Military Orders from the Twelfth to the Early Fourteenth Centuries* (1992).

Luis García-Guijarro Ramos is Lecturer in Medieval History at the University of Zaragoza at Huesca. He has researched into various aspects of military and monastic orders in medieval Spain. His publications include *Papado, Cruzades y Órdenes Militares, siglos XI–XIII* (1995), a comparative analysis of the structure of the international military orders and of the role they played in the Latin Church.

Michael Gervers is Professor of History at the University of Toronto, Scarborough & St. George. He is the founder (1975) and director of the "Documents of Early England Data Set" (DEEDS) Project (http://www.utoronto.ca/deeds). Numerous articles and books concern the Hospitallers, especially *The Hospitaller Cartulary in the British Library (Cotton MS Nero E VI). A Study of the Manuscript and its Composition, with a Critical Edition of Two Fragments of Earlier Cartularies for Essex* (1981); (ed.), *The Cartulary of the Knights of St. John of Jerusalem in England: Essex*,. 2 vols, (1982–96); (ed.), *Dating Undated Medieval Charters* (2000).

Bernard Hamilton is Professor Emeritus of Crusading History at the University of Nottingham and the author of many highly-respected books on medieval history, including *The Latin Church in the Crusader States: The Secular Church* (1980), *Religion in the Medieval West* (1986), and *The Leper King and his Heirs: Baldwin IV and the Crusader Kingdom of Jerusalem* (2000).

Nicole Hamonic is a PhD candidate at the Centre for Medieval Studies, University of Toronto. Her thesis is on the Hospitallers in London and Middlesex, and she is currently preparing an edition of the London and Middlesex documents contained in the Hospitaller Cartulary in England (BL Cotton MS. Nero E VI). She has worked as a researcher at the DEEDS Project with Professor Gervers since 2002.

Peter Herde is Professor Emeritus of History at the University of Würzburg. His research interests include both medieval and modern history, particularly the history of Italy and the papacy. Among his publications and editions are *Audientia litterarum contradictarum*, 2 vols (1970) *Cölestin V. (1294); Peter von Morrone, der Engelpapst* (1981) [revised Italian edition 2004], *Gesammelte Abhandlungen und Aufsätze*, 3 vols (1997–2005); *Das Brief- und Memorialbuch des Albert Behaim* (MGH, 2000).

Norman Housley is Professor of History at the University of Leicester, where he has taught since 1983. He has written extensively about the crusades, focusing on crusading activity between 1200 and 1600. Among his recent books are *Religious Warfare in Europe, 1400–1536* (Oxford University Press, 2002) and *Crusading in the Fifteenth Century: Message and Impact* (Palgrave Macmillan, 2004).

Zsolt Hunyadi is Adjunct Professor in the Department of Medieval and Early Modern Hungarian History at the University of Szeged (Hungary). He recently completed his PhD dissertation on *Hospitallers in the Medieval Kingdom of Hungary, c.1150–1387* at the Central European University, Budapest. He also works on papal charters in Hungary prior to 1198.

David Jacoby is an Emeritus Professor of History at The Hebrew University of Jerusalem, Israel. His publications include: *Studies on the Crusader States and on Venetian Expansion* (1989); *Byzantium, Latin Romania and the Mediterranean* (2001) *Commercial Exchange across the Mediterranean: Byzantium, the Crusader Levant, Egypt and Italy* (2005)

Anna-Maria Kasdagli, a graduate of the University of Birmingham (1983). She is employed as an archaeologist in Rhodes by the 4th Ephorate of Byzantine Antiquities (Hellenic Ministry of Culture), since 1986. Her published articles (Greek and English) concern topics ranging from medieval numismatics, epigraphics and heraldry to military architecture.

Benjamin Z. Kedar is a member of the Israel Academy of Sciences and Humanities. His research interests include the history of the Frankish kingdom of Jerusalem, aerial photography and history, expulsion as an issue of world history, and cultural persistence under conditions of total political collapse. His publications include: *Merchants in Crisis* (1976), *Crusade and Mission* (1984) and *The Changing Land between the Jordan and the Sea* (1999), *Franks, Muslims and Oriental Christians in the Latin Levant: Studies in Frontier Acculturation* (2006).

Johannes A. Mol is research fellow at the Fryske Akademy in Leeuwarden and professor in Frisian history at Leiden University. He publishes on the medieval history of the Frisian lands and on the military orders in the Netherlands. Furthermore, he is involved in the development of a parcel-based historical GIS for Friesland (http://www.hisgis.nl).

Gregory O'Malley studied at London and Cambridge, and held a research fellowship at Emmanuel College, Cambridge, from 2000 to 2003. He is the author of *The Knights Hospitaller of the English Langue, 1460–1565* (Oxford, 2005), and has written several articles on the English *langue* of the order of St John and on English contacts with the Eastern Mediterranean in the fifteenth and sixteenth centuries. He now works in industry.

Jonathan Riley-Smith was Dixie Professor of Ecclesiastical History at Cambridge University until his retirement in 2004. He has published very extensively on the Order of St John of Jerusalem, on the crusades and on the kingdom of Jerusalem. His publications include *The Knights of St John in Jerusalem and Cyprus, 1050–1310* (1967), *The Feudal Nobility and the Kingdom of Jerusalem, 1174–1277* (1973), *What were the Crusades?* (1977; 3rd edn, 2002), *The First Crusade and the Idea of Crusading* (1986), and *The First Crusaders, 1095–1131* (1997).

Jürgen Sarnowsky is Professor of Medieval History, Department of History, University of Hamburg (since 1996).His books concern the economic history of the Teutonic Knights in Prussia (1993), the constitutional history of the Hospitallers in the 15th century (2001); England in the Middle Ages (2002); and a Latin-German edition of Enea Silvio Piccolomini's *Historia austrialis* (2005); and is editor of sources in the internet: http://www.rrz.uni-hamburg.de/spaetmittelalter.

Elizabeth A. Zachariadou was Professor of Turkish Studies in the Department of History and Archaeology of the University of Crete from 1985 to 1998. Among her books are *Trade and Crusade: Venetian Crete and the Emirates of Menteshe and Aydin* (1300–1415), Venice 1983; *History and Legends of the Old Sultans, 1300–1400* (in Greek), Athens 1991 (2nd edition, 1999) and she has edited several volumes on the history of the Ottoman Empire.

Editors

Karl Borchardt is Professor for Medieval and Regional History at the University of Würzburg and Research Fellow at the Monumenta Germaniae Historica in Munich. Hospitaller commanderies were already included in his PhD on ecclesiastical institutions in Rothenburg prior to the Reformation (1988). Since then he has published several articles on Hospitallers in Germany and other parts of Central Europe. Further publications include *Die Cölestiner. Eine Mönchsgemeinschaft des späteren Mittelalters* (2006). For seven years he has been editor of the Bulletin of the Society for the Study of the Crusades and the Latin East.

Nikolas Jaspert is Professor of medieval history at the University of Bochum. He has published on medieval Iberia, the crusades and religious orders. He is the author of *Stift und Stadt. Das Heiliggrabpriorat von Santa Anna und das Regularkanonikerstift Santa Eulàlia del Camp im mittelalterlichen Barcelona* (1996) and *The Crusades* (2006) and has co-edited a collection of essays on *Jerusalem im Hoch- und Spätmittelalter* (2002).

Helen J. Nicholson is Reader in history at Cardiff University, Wales, and publishes on the Military Orders, crusades, and various related subjects. Her recent books include *Love, War and the Grail: Templars, Hospitallers and Teutonic Knights in Medieval Epic and Romance*, 1150–1500 (2001) and *The Knights Hospitaller* (2001); and she has edited with Anthony Luttrell the volume *Hospitaller Women in the Middle Ages* (2006).

List of Illustrations

Graph

Maps

Editors' Preface

Anyone who studies the Hospitallers or the history of the late medieval Mediterranean will know Anthony Luttrell either in person or through his numerous publications. Anthony Luttrell's 75th birthday falls in October 2007; it is an established custom in the academic world that this occasion should be celebrated by the publication of a festschrift. As each of the three editors has profited greatly over many years from Anthony Luttrell's expertise and generous friendship, we decided to organise this collection of essays as a mark of appreciation and gratitude. Twenty-one friends and colleagues from ten different countries have been able to write papers in time. In keeping with the nature of the volume and as an expression of the individual contributors' appreciation to its intended recipient, the editors allowed contributors to select their own topic, rather than attempting to impose a structure. The result is a wide-ranging and sometimes controversial collection of papers, whose subjects range from the period of the first crusades in the late eleventh and early twelfth centuries to the beginnings of the Early Modern period in the sixteenth century and even touch upon present-day problems of the military-religious orders. Not only are the Eastern Mediterranean, Cyprus, Rhodes and Malta discussed but also the possessions and problems of the various military-religious orders in their European bases, from the Iberian Peninsula and Ireland in the west to Hungary and the Levant in the east. We know that this is only a small and by no means representative sample of scholars from all over the world who are grateful for all the inspiration and information they owe to Anthony Luttrell. It sheds some light on Anthony Luttrell's remarkable achievement that no single editor felt able to master such a long span of time and so many different geographical and social settings. Michael Gervers has written an introductory essay pointing out some important topics and merits of Anthony Luttrell's research. The three editors wish to thank him and all other contributors warmly for all their work. Our special thanks are due to John Smedley and the editorial staff at Ashgate, who are about to publish the sixth Collected Studies Series volume of Anthony Luttrell's articles, and without whose kind support this festschrift would not have been possible. We hope that it will help to highlight some of the important historical questions where Anthony Luttrell's work has had great influence.

Karl Borchardt, Würzburg and Munich
Nikolas Jaspert, Bochum
Helen Nicholson, Cardiff

Figure A Clerks in the rent office producing the very records of which Anthony Luttrell, and the editors and contributors to this volume have made so much use. Image taken from *Stabilimenta Rhodiorum Militum* by Guillaume Caoursin, Ulm, 1496. Reproduced with kind permission of the Curator of the Museum of the Order of St John.

Introduction

In Honour of Anthony Luttrell

Michael Gervers

It is somewhat humbling to recognize how little is known about the past, despite the centuries that western scholars have devoted to studying it. One may well wonder, then, where the history of the Hospitallers would have been without the dedicated research and publishing of Anthony Luttrell. For the past fifty years Tony has done more to interpret the Order's activities than all those who have gone before him. We hope and expect even more from him in the years to come.

Every one of the 230 articles and host of monographs listed in his bibliography is a reflection of a brilliant academic career which saw him leave Bryanston School in Dorset for Oriel College, Oxford in 1951, whence he graduated in 1954. His last year at Oriel was spent as the De Osma Student at the Instituto de Valencia de Don Juan (Madrid), and from then on the Mediterranean region became his home. The following year found him at the Colegio Mayor Ximénez de Cisneros at Madrid University, supported by the Consejo Superior de Investigaciones Cientificas, while from 1956 to 1958 he was the Rome Scholar in Medieval Studies at the British School in Rome. He completed his studies at the Scuola Normale Superiore in the University of Pisa and in 1959 received the MA, D.Phil. from Oxford. With degrees in hand, he set off immediately to teach. Over the next quarter century he was attached to, or lectured in history at Swarthmore College (Pa.), Edinburgh University, and the (Royal) University of Malta. He returned to Rome for an extended interlude from 1967 to 1973 as Assistant Director and Librarian of the British School.

After 1977 Tony pursued his research, holding one prestigious grant after another. He spent 1977–78 and 1984–85 in the School of Historical Studies at the Institute for Advanced Study, Princeton. The period 1978–79 found him at the Institut de Recherche et d'Histoire des Textes (IRHT/CNRS, Paris), and 1980–81 in the Center for Byzantine Studies at Dumbarton Oaks. From 1982 to 1985 his work was supported by a grant from the National Endowment for the Humanities. Also in 1985, as a Fellow of the Gladys Krieble Delmas Foundation, he carried out research in the Veneto. The Vicente Cañada Blanch Senior Fellowship, which he held in 1986–87, took him back to Spain, while support from the Alexander von Humboldt Foundation brought him to the University of Würzburg in 1987–88. For the two following years he was a Leverhulme Research Officer with the Venerable Order of St John of Jerusalem at Clerkenwell in London, while 1992–93 saw him again in Rome, as the Balsdon Senior Fellow at the British School. He completed 1993 with the IRHT/CNRS, this time at its new headquarters in Orléans.

There has never been a break in his research and writing, and the Knights of the Order of the Hospital of St John of Jerusalem in Rhodes and Malta have been great beneficiaries of his patient examination of their archives. However, the Knights alone were not enough for Tony in Malta. During the 1970s and 1980s, when he lived there with his family for extended periods, he turned the very soil of the island itself in search of clues to its early and medieval history. Two of his five monographs, edited works and collected essays about Malta, are devoted to the excavation of the churches in the casal of Ħal Millieri. These publications attracted considerable interest, in part because so little was known about the history of the island before the Knights. Sumner McKnight Crosby, then head of the Department of Art History at Yale, congratulated Tony 'for his enthusiasm and determination' in publishing *Ħal Millieri: A Maltese Casale, Its Churches and Paintings*, and for having 'given medievalists a new insight into Mediterranean culture'.[1] *Speculum*'s reviewer applauded the method, but questioned the importance of the site: '*Ħal Millieri* marks out ground rules for a serious examination of the archival and material records of a rural settlement in a complex historical site in the Mediterranean. The question now becomes one of determining which sites will in fact repay the scholarly effort invested in them.'[2]

Repaying the scholarly effort was not the point. Archaeology has always been a fascination for Tony, as also a method; and one which he applies to his great advantage and success when working in the archives. This is shown especially by his monograph on the mausoleum and castle at Halikarnassus and by the discovery of the lost papal castle at Sorgues near Avignon, his article on which was published as a book in French translation. The archives, too, are excavation sites, and from the detail comes the historical narrative. 'Among the reasons for [the] relative obscurity [of Hospitaller Rhodes]', wrote Jonathan Riley-Smith, 'are the fact that the sources are so extensive that mining them will be a lifetime's work.'[3] Mining the sources, both archival and archaeological, is precisely what Tony has spent his life doing, and more.

Tony is known not only for his scholarship, but also for his scholarly generosity. All those of us who have come into his ever-expanding intellectual orbit have profited from his sagacity, wisdom, knowledge and encouragement. We are unanimously grateful for his friendship and support. Pierre Bonneaud applauds Tony's 'limitless interest for new approaches and his availability to offer his assistance and help to newcomers in the field of research dedicated to the Military Orders'.[4] Jochen Burgtorf recalls how meeting Tony as an undergraduate led him to his current pursuit: 'Tony ... mentioned a few names, among them Albert of Schwarzburg. Almost twenty years later Albert of Schwarzburg is still on my mind as I work on the prosopography of the Hospitallers' central convent. Little did I know, on that day back in 1988, that Tony Luttrell had just introduced me to my future research.'[5]

1 *The Art Bulletin*, 61/3(1979), p. 482.

2 F.K.B. Toker, *Speculum*, 54/2 (1979), p. 400.

3 *Bulletin of the School of Oriental and African Studies, University of London*, 61/1 (1998), p. 148.

4 Pierre Bonneaud, e-mail, 14 February 2007.

5 Jochen Burgtorf, e-mail, 5 February 2007.

It is not only Tony's intellectual generosity and fervent curiosity that have been shared by friends and colleagues alike, but also the proverbial hospitality of the Luttrell household. So many of us have spent delightful days in their tiny, perfect house on Perfect View, and now on Richmond Place, or in Malta, or wherever his charming wife, Margaret, might be. These can be considered working visits, and to work with Tony is, as Elizabeth Zachariadou recalls, also working with Margaret: '[Tony] volunteered to translate the manuscript of my book, *Trade and Crusade*,[6] from Greek English to English English. He recruited his very nice wife Margaret … Poor Margaret was obliged to work very hard with my text as if Tony's efforts were not sufficient. Both of them wanted to turn it into perfect English.'[7] 'The lifestyle is very English', writes Karl Borchardt, 'only the breakfast is not: a Swiss nanny employed by Tony's parents is responsible for the fact that some kind of "Müsli" continues to be served.'[8] Nicholas Coureas 'was made to dig in the garden'.[9] In another cooperative venture, Tony and Margaret have brought up two fine daughters, Marina and Cecilia, who are both following the family tradition of research, writing, preserving and protecting.

Thankfully, many of the articles in Tony's extensive bibliography are available in Variorum reprints, including one to be published in this, his seventy-fifth year. A recent venture into relatively new territory is the informative introduction to a book on Hospitaller women, co-edited with Helen Nicholson.[10] As critical of his own work as he can be in his reviews of that of others, he describes it as being 'not entirely satisfactory but should be a step forward'.[11] Every one of Tony's publications about the history of the Hospitallers, of Malta and Rhodes, and of related matters in art and archaeology, has always been, and will surely continue to be, innovative and a step forward.

The contributors to this volume, and the many thousands of students and scholars around the globe who know him through his books and articles, fully concur with David Jacoby about Tony's scholarship, and one particularly outstanding omission: 'I told him more than once that he is too much of a perfectionist, that we all eagerly await his synthesis on the Hospitallers, that he is the only one capable of producing it, and that it would be unfortunate, given the huge amount of material he has assembled, if he would not do so. It would be worthwhile, I think, to remind him of our expectations.'[12] We offer this volume to you, then, Tony, in recognition of our appreciation of the high level of scholarship you have set for us, and as a reminder that there is still one more major mountain to scale.

---

6 Elizabeth A. Zachariadou, *Trade and Crusade: Venetian Crete and the emirates of Menteshe and Aydin*, Bibliothèque de l'Institut hellénique d'études Byzantines et post-byzantines de Venise, no. 11 (Venice, 1983).

7 Elizabeth Zachariadou, e-mail, 13 February 2007.

8 Karl Borchardt, e-mail, 6 February 2007.

9 Karl Borchardt, e-mail, 6 February 2007.

10 Anthony Luttrell and Helen J. Nicholson, eds, *Hospitaller Women in the Middle Ages* (Aldershot, 2006).

11 Personal note of 2 February 2007.

12 David Jacoby, e-mail, 6 February 2007.

PART 1
The Crusader Period

Chapter 1

A Note on Jerusalem's Bīmāristān and Jerusalem's Hospital[1]

Benjamin Z. Kedar

On 5 Ramadan 438, a date that corresponds to 5 March 1047, Nāser-e Khosraw, a Persian civil administrator turned pilgrim and traveller, arrived in Jerusalem. In his detailed description of the city we read:

> Jerusalem has a fine, well endowed *Bīmāristān* [hospital]. Many people are given drugs and elixirs. The physicians who are there receive salaries from the endowment for this *Bīmāristān.*[2]

This passage attests to the existence, in eleventh-century Muslim Jerusalem, of a true hospital – that is, a hospital in which salaried physicians attend to patients. Such hospitals, which were exclusively medical institutions, are known to have existed elsewhere in the realm of Islam. For instance, in 872 Ahmad b. Tūlūn, ruler of Egypt, founded a hospital at Fustāt (Old Cairo), each ward of which was reserved for a different illness. In 981 'Adūd al-Dawla, who ruled a large part of the Islamic empire in the second half of the tenth century, built a large hospital in Baghdad; the well-equipped institution, which came to be known as al-'Adūdi hospital, had 24 physicians, whose number in 1068 had risen to 28.[3]

In the realm of Islam, professional medical treatment was also quite commonly available outside of hospitals. The Cairo Geniza, that vast repository of discarded documents written in the Hebrew script that constitutes a major source for the history

---

1 An earlier version of this paper was presented at the symposium 'Medicine and Disease in the Crusades', held in January 2005 at the Wellcome Trust Centre for the History of Medicine, University College, London.

2 *Sefer Nameh. Relation du voyage de Nassiri Khosrau en Syrie, en Palestine, en Égypte, en Arabie et en Perse pendant les années de l'hégire 437–444*, ed. and trans. C. Schefer, (Paris, 1881), p. 21; my thanks to Professor Reuven Amitai for having translated this passage for me. W.M. Thackston's translation locates the Bīmāristān in Jerusalem's eastern part: *Nāser-e Khosraw's Book of Travels (Safarnāma)*, trans. W.M. Thackston, Jr., Persian Heritage Series 36 (Albany, NY, 1986), p. 23. The translation appears to be based on an edition defective at this point.

3 See for instance S. Hamarneh, 'Development of Hospitals in Islam', *Journal of the History of Medicine* 17 (1962), 366–84; M.W. Dols, 'The Origins of the Islamic Hospital: Myth and Reality', *Bulletin of the History of Medicine* 61 (1987), 367–90; L.I. Conrad, 'The Arab-Islamic Medical Tradition', in L.I. Conrad et al., *The Western Medical Tradition, 800 BC to AD 1800* (Cambridge, 1995), pp. 135–8.

of the area between north-western Africa and India – and especially of Egypt and Palestine – in the eleventh and twelfth centuries, amply attests to this availability. 'In the Geniza papers', writes Shelomo Dov Goitein, 'we find a Jewish doctor, and often more than one, in many a little town or large village and occasionally Christian and Muslim colleagues are mentioned as well. The prescriptions preserved indicate that even for humdrum cases of constipation or of the loosening of bowels a doctor was consulted.'[4] In the event of serious illness, even a man of limited resources could benefit from a consultation of several doctors; this happened for instance in Ramle, Palestine, in about 1060.[5] There were oculists, physicians treating wounds, healers specializing in stomach troubles, experts in bloodletting, and professional veterinarians, one of whom treated a donkey that had suffered a dislocation while carrying building materials.[6]

During roughly the same period as that in which the Persian traveller Nāser-e Khusraw described the Jerusalem *Bīmāristān* with its salaried physicians, a rich Amalfitan by the name of Maurus established a *hospital* in Jerusalem, and another in Antioch. So reports the contemporary chronicler Amatus of Montecassino (born ca. 1010) in his *Ystoria Normannorum*, which covers the period 1016–78; the chronicle survives only in an Old French translation dating from ca. 1300.[7] A short, anonymous notice about Archbishop John of Amalfi (ca. 1070–ca. 1082) reports that he made a pilgrimage to Jerusalem, where he was received by Amalfitans who, a few years earlier, had established there two *hospitalia*, one for men and one for women.[8] The Jerusalem-born William of Tyre, writing about a century later, proffers more details: merchants from Amalfi founded a monastery in honour of the Virgin Mary near the Church of the Holy Sepulchre and located there an abbot and monks from their country. A convent was later erected nearby and, finally, a *xenodochium* for pilgrims, healthy or sick.[9]

What was the nature of the Amalfitan 'hospital' in Jerusalem? The eleventh-century West had no counterparts to the contemporary hospitals of the Islamic world,

4 S.D. Goitein, *A Mediterranean Society: The Jewish Communities of the Arab World as Portrayed in the Documents of the Cairo Geniza*, vol. 2: *The Community* (Berkeley, 1971), p. 241.

5 Goitein, p. 254; for the Arabic text (in Hebrew letters) and a Modern Hebrew translation, as well as for the approximate date, see M. Gil, *Palestine during the First Muslim Period (634–1099)*, 3 vols (Tel Aviv, 1983), 3: 61–4 (in Hebrew).

6 Goitein, pp. 255–6. However, the assertion (p. 251) that even eleventh-century Ramle possessed a hospital divided into different wards, appears to derive from an incorrect reading: see Gil, *Palestine*, 2: 214.

7 'Et [Maurus] avoit fert cert hospital en Anthioce et en Hierusalem; o la helemosine de sa ricchesce les soustenoit.' *Storia de' Normanni di Amato di Montecassino, volgarizzata in antico francese*, ed. Vincenzo de Bartholomaeis, Fonti per la Storia d'Italia 76 (Rome, 1935), p. 342. On Amatus see F. Avegliano in *Lexikon des Mittelalters*, vol. 1 (Munich and Zurich, 1977–80), col. 513. For the original Latin title of his chronicle see *Chronica monasterii Casinensis*, in Monumenta Germaniae Historica, Scriptores 7:728.

8 F. Ughelli and N. Coleti, *Italia sacra*, vol. 7 (Venice, 1721), col. 198.

9 Guillaume de Tyr, *Chronique*, ed. R.B.C. Huygens, Corpus Christianorum, Continuatio Mediaevalis, 63, 63A (Turnhoult, 1986) (hereafter WT), 18.5, pp. 815–16.

where salaried physicians regularly attended to patients and medical lore accumulated. It is symptomatic, from this point of view, that when, in the late eleventh century, Constantine the African translated into Latin *The Complete Book of the Medical Art* by ʿAlī ibn al-ʿAbbās al-Majūsī, he omitted the advice to visit hospitals in order to gain medical knowledge, for hospitals in which such knowledge could have been acquired did not yet exist in the Latin West.[10] Should we conclude therefore that the Amalfitan 'hospital' was merely a hospice of the type then current in the West? Possibly so. But an alternative hypothesis – namely, that the Amalfitans were influenced to some extent by the superior medical practice of the Islamic world – is also conceivable.

When the Amalfitans established their Jerusalem 'hospital,' presumably some time after the middle of the eleventh century, they were no newcomers to the Muslim Levant. There is evidence for the voyage of one Leo Amalfitanus to Egypt in 978.[11] The eleventh-century Christian chronicler Yahyā of Antioch reports that when in May 996 the suspicion arose in Cairo that the fire that had consumed 16 warships in the city's arsenal was started by 'Romish merchants from Amalfi', the mob alongside Berber soldiers massacred 160 of the Amalfitans and looted their wares. Other Amalfitans were able to escape.[12] This means that there may have been a colony of perhaps as many as two hundred Amalfitans in Cairo at the time.[13] Two Geniza letters attest to the presence of Amalfitan merchants in Egypt in the mid-eleventh century, while a third mentions a Jewish merchant's voyage from Alexandria to Amalfi, via Constantinople and Crete, in the same period.[14] Indeed, it has been hypothesized that the Amalfitans provided naval assistance during the Fatimid conquest of Egypt in 969, secured a favourable commercial status in return, and thus became predominant among the Latin Christians who traded in the Muslim East.[15] At any rate, it is plausible to assume that the Amalfitans who decided to establish a 'hospital' in Jerusalem were cognizant of the availability of professional medical services in the Islamic world. Indeed, the existence of Jerusalem's *Bīmāristān* could hardly have escaped them.

---

10 See D. Jacquart, 'Le sens donné par Constantin l'Africain à son oeuvre: les chapitres introductifs en arabe et en latin', in *Constantine the African and ʿAlī ibn al-ʿAbbās al-Mağūsī. The* Pantegni *and Related Texts*, ed. C. Burnett and D. Jacquart (Leiden, 1994), p. 79.

11 See A.O. Citarella, 'Patterns in Medieval Trade: The Commerce of Amalfi before the Crusades', *Journal of Economic History* 28 (1968), 544, quoting the *Codex diplomaticus Cavensis*, 1:114–15.

12 C. Cahen, 'Un texte peu connu relatif au commerce oriental d'Amalfi au Xe siècle', *Archivio Storico per le Province Napoletane* NS 34 (1953–54), 62; English translation and commentary in R.S. Lopez, *The Tenth Century: How Dark the Dark Ages?* (New York, 1959), pp. 28–9. According to the Muslim chronicler al-Musabbihi the number of murdered Amalfitans was 107.

13 Cf. C. Cahen, 'Le commerce d'Amalfi dans le Proche-Orient musulman avant et après la Croisade', *Comptes rendus de l'Académie des Inscriptions et Belles Lettres*, 1977, p. 292.

14 Goitein, *A Mediterranean Society*, vol. 1: *Economic Foundations* (Berkeley, 1967), pp. 46, 325, 329. For the approximate dates of these letters see Citarella, p. 544. The letter mentioning the voyage of more than 70 days to Amalfi is translated in S. D. Goitein, *Letters of Medieval Jewish Traders* (Princeton, 1973), pp. 42–5.

15 Citarella, p. 545; Cahen, 'Le commerce', pp. 292–3, 300.

Given that the Jerusalemite al-Muqaddasī, writing in the 980s, reported that in al-Shām (that is, Syria/Palestine) the physicians were generally Christians,[16] one may hypothesize that the Amalfitans hired some Oriental Christian physician(s) to provide professional medical treatment in their new establishment.

This hypothesis is supported by a close reading of the above-mentioned anonymous notice about Archbishop John of Amalfi. The notice reports that in the two *hospitalia* the Amalfitans had erected in Jerusalem some time before the archbishop's arrival, 'infirmi curabantur'.[17] Now, it has been claimed that the term *infirmus* refers to the disabled and the weak (who may, however, also be suffering from some disease), whereas the terms *egroti* and *egrotantes* refer unequivocally to the sick.[18] However, the phrase 'infirmos curare' is biblical; Christ enjoined the Apostles: 'infirmos curate',[19] a charge that has always been understood to mean, 'Heal the sick'. We may therefore conclude that when the anonymous notice asserts that 'infirmi curabantur' in Jerusalem's Amalfitan *hospitalia*, it is the healing of the sick that is being referred to – although, unlike the Muslim *Bīmāristān*, the *hospitalia* did not treat only the sick. Before mentioning the curing of the sick, the anonymous notice spells out that the *hospitalia* were erected 'ad homines et mulieres recipiendos, in quibus et alebantur'. In other words, the primary function of the *hospitalia* was to provide shelter and food for pilgrims from the West. In addition, the sick among them were offered a cure. Writing in the 1170s or early 1180s about the beginnings of the Jerusalem Hospital, William of Tyre makes the same point when he asserts that to the pre-1099 *xenodochium* were gathered both the healthy and the sick (*sanos vel egrotantes*).[20] It should be noted that the earliest reference to sick people in the post-1099 Jerusalem Hospital appears in Albert of Aachen's account that in 1101 a messenger of Count Roger of Apulia – that is, Roger Borsa, Bohemond's brother – brought to Jerusalem 1,000 bezants, one-third of which was earmarked 'in sustentatione hospitalis languidorum et ceterorum inualidorum'.[21] 'Languidus' and 'invalidus' usually mean 'sick' and 'feeble,' respectively.[22]

Ample documentation from the 1180s, much of which has come to light in recent years, leaves no doubt that the Jerusalem Hospital of the Knights of Saint John by that time served, *inter alia*, as a true hospital in which salaried physicians attended to a

16 Al-Muqaddasī, *The Best Divisions for Knowledge of the Regions (Ahsan al-Taqāsīm fī Ma'rifat al-Aqālīm)*, trans. B. Collins (Reading, 2001), p. 153.

17 Ughelli and Coleti, *Italia sacra*, col. 198. Bruno Figliuolo, referring to the same column, quotes mistakenly 'infirmi cenabantur': B. Figliuolo, 'Amalfi e il Levante nel Medioevo', in *I comuni italiani nel Regno Crociato di Gerusalemme*, ed. G. Airaldi and B.Z. Kedar, Collana Storica di Fonti e Studi 48 (Genoa, 1986), p. 591 n. 66.

18 P.D. Mitchell, *Medicine in the Crusades: Warfare, Wounds and the Medieval Surgeon* (Cambridge, 2004), p. 64.

19 Matt. 10:8; see also Matt. 10:1, where 'ut … curarent omnem languorem et omnem infirmitatem' is understood to mean 'to cure every kind of ailment and disease.'

20 WT 18.5, p. 816.

21 Albert of Aachen, *Historia Ierosalimitana*, ed. and trans. Susan B. Edgington, Oxford Medieval Texts (Oxford, 2007) Bk 7, ch. 62, p. 574.

22 See A. Blaise, *Dictionnaire latin-français des auteurs chrétiens*, 2nd edn (Turnhout, 1967), s.v.

large number of patients, and its daily routine resembled in many important respects that of hospitals in the Islamic world and Byzantium.[23] At present, our documentation does not mention salaried physicians, or professional medical treatment in the Jerusalem Hospital at an earlier date.[24] But, as we know, the earliest mention of a phenomenon in the available documentation must not be regarded as constituting proof of that being actually the phenomenon's earliest occurrence. The phenomenon may have occurred earlier; it may have developed gradually. Possibly its earliest form took shape already with the establishment of the Amalfitan *hospitalia*. For these were not erected on a cultural *tabula rasa*. They were established in an area about whose medical services we are quite well informed, by people who were no newcomers to the Muslim Levant.

---

23 See the Latin text edited by B.Z. Kedar, 'A Twelfth-Century Description of the Jerusalem Hospital', in *The Military Orders*, vol. 2, ed. H. Nicholson (Aldershot, 1998) pp. 3–26, reprinted in Kedar, *Franks, Muslims and Oriental Christians in the Latin Levant: Studies in Frontier Acculturation* (Aldershot, 2006), Study X; and the Old French text edited by S. Edgington, 'Administrative Regulations for the Hospital of St John in Jerusalem Dating from the 1180s', *Crusades* 4 (2005), 21–37. The Latin text has been re-edited by A. Beltjens, 'Le récit d'une journée au grand hôpital de Saint-Jean de Jérusalem sous le règne des derniers rois latins ayant résidé à Jérusalem ou le témoignage d'un clerc anonyme conservé dans le manuscrit Clm 4620 de Munich', *Société de l'Histoire et du Patrimoine de l'Ordre de Malte*, 14, Numéro special (2004), 3–79. On some of the professional and ethical deficiencies of this re-edition see R.B.C. Huygens, 'Editorisch Verfehltes zum Hospital von Jerusalem', *Deutsches Archiv für Erforschung des Mittelalters*, 61 (2005), 165–67.

24 Mitchell (*Medicine*, p. 64) believes to have identified the earliest reference to the provision of medical treatment in the Jerusalem Hospital in the text which Wilkinson dubbed 'Work on Geography' and dated to 1128–37. The Latin text, published by de Vogüé, reads: 'In Jerusalem Xenodochium sive Muscomion; Xenodochium grece, latine peregrinorum et pauperum susceptio. Muscomion id est hospitale ubi de plateis et vicis egrotantes colliguntur et foventur.' M. de Vogüé, *Les églises de la Terre Sainte* (Paris, 1860), p. 427. Wilkinson translates: 'In Jerusalem is the Xenodochium or the Nosokomion. The Greek word xenodochium translated into Latin is a refuge for travellers and poor people. Nosokomion is the hospice which cares for the sick people taken into it from the squares and alleys.' J. Wilkinson et al., *Jerusalem Pilgrimage 1099–1185* (London, 1988), p. 200. It should be noted, however, that Wilkinson marks the passage in question with a vertical side line, which, according to his introduction (p. 13), means that he believes it to have been added after the death of Fretellus, who (according to his understanding of P.C. Boeren's introduction to the edition of Fretellus (Amsterdam, 1980)) died in 1157 (p. 12). Moreover, one should bear in mind that Hans Eberhard Mayer, in his review of Wilkinson's book, warned scholars to remember that Wilkinson's 'Work on Geography' is a conjecture, and to abstain from using it as if it had really existed in this form: H.E. Mayer in *Deutsches Archiv für Erforschung des Mittelalters* 45 (1989), 204–5. On the other hand, one should note the similarity of the phrase 'hospitale ubi de plateis et vicis egrotantes colliguntur et foventur' to William of Tyre's statement on the early Jerusalem *xenodochium*, 'ubi tales sanos vel egrotantes colligerent, ne de nocte per vias iugularentur, et in eodem loco congregatis de reliquiis fragmentorum utriusque monasterii, tam virorum quam mulierum, ad cotidianam sustentationem qualemqualem aliquid ministraretur.' WT 18.5, p. 816.

Chapter 2

The Templars, the Syrian Assassins and King Amalric of Jerusalem

Bernard Hamilton

William of Tyre reports that the Master of the Syrian Assassins sent an ambassador to Jerusalem who told King Amalric that the Master had diligently read the New Testament and had become convinced that the Muslim faith was erroneous. He had therefore banned its practice in his dominions, and he and his subjects wished to receive Christian baptism. He made only one condition: that he should be freed from the annual payment of 2,000 bezants in tribute to the Knights Templar. The king was overjoyed. He agreed to this condition and offered to compensate the Templars for their loss of revenue. The Assassin ambassador was given a royal safe-conduct, but as he was about to enter his own territory he was ambushed by a group of Templars, one of whom, Walter of Mesnil, killed him. This led to a confrontation between the Order and the crown. Odo of St Amand, the Master of the Temple, claimed that judgment in this case was reserved to the pope, but despite this Amalric seized Walter of Mesnil and imprisoned him in chains in the royal fortress of Tyre. William of Tyre places these events between Saladin's attack on Transjordan in September 1173 and the death of Nur ad-Din in May 1174.[1] He was in a position to be well informed about them: at the time he was tutor to the king's son and had been commissioned by Amalric to write the history of the kingdom. By the time he wrote this part of it, he had become chancellor and had charge of the royal archive.[2]

News of these events reached England, where they were mentioned by Walter Map in his *De Nugis Curialium*. James Hinton argued that this part of the work was written in 1181–2, but as Christopher Brooke has pointed out, it is impossible to be quite certain that a particular anecdote was not added at a later date.[3] If this story was recorded by Walter in 1182, then it must be independent of William of Tyre, whose *History* was then unfinished and therefore not available in Western Europe.[4]

---

1 William of Tyre, *Chronicon*, 20, 29–30, ed. R.B.C. Huygens, Corpus Christianorum Continuatio Mediaevalis, 63, 64A (Turnholt,1986) [henceforth WT], pp. 953–6.

2 P.W. Edbury and J.G. Rowe, *William of Tyre. Historian of the Latin East* (Cambridge, 1988), pp. 13–31.

3 J. Hinton, 'Walter Map's *De Nugis Curialium*. Its plan and composition', *Publications of the Modern Language Association of America* 32 (1917), pp. 81–132; Walter Map, *De Nugis Curialium. Courtiers' Trifles*, Dist. I, c. 22, ed. and trans. M.R. James, revised by C.N.L. Brooke and R.A.B. Mynors (Oxford, 1983), pp. xxiv–xxxii, 66–9.

4 Edbury and Rowe, *William of Tyre*, pp. 28–31.For further discussion, see p. 26 of this volume below.

Walter reports that the Assassins held discussions chiefly with the Latin Patriarch of Jerusalem, which suggests that he was drawing on a different source, possibly an oral one. The only other writer to mention the Frankish–Assassin discussions is James of Vitry, Bishop of Acre (1216–28) in his *Historia Orientalis*. His account is very like that of William of Tyre, but includes one piece of additional information.[5]

The negotiations between King Amalric and the Assassins have received cursory treatment from most historians. Bernard Lewis says merely that: 'William of Tyre records an abortive approach by the Old Man of the Mountain to the king of Jerusalem, proposing some form of alliance.'[6] Hans Mayer also reports the story told by William of Tyre, but says nothing about the religious content of the negotiations.[7] Marshall Hodgson considers this episode in his history of the Assassin Order and takes the religious dimension of the discussions very seriously, but his treatment is brief.[8] Farhad Daftary mentions William of Tyre's account, but does not discuss it, in his monumental history of the Ismailis.[9] Peter Willey mentions it only briefly in his survey of the archaeology of Ismaili castles.[10] Jerzy Hausinski has examined William's story at more length and takes the religious issues seriously, but largely ignores the political context in which these talks took place.[11] The one writer who shows awareness of the political and religious complexity of the issues involved in these negotiations is Malcolm Barber in his history of the Templar Order, but he is not able to devote very much space to discussing them.[12] This episode needs to be investigated in more detail.

The name 'Assassins' was given by their enemies to the Nizarite Ismailis, a radical Shi'ite group. The term is derived from the Arabic word *hashish*, hemp. Their leaders, it was claimed, supplied this drug to their élite followers and, having made them dependent, coerced them into murdering the victims whom they named. These rumours would seem to have been unfounded, because the Assassins owed their success to excellent coordination of hand and eye, precisely the qualities that would be impaired by drug addiction.[13] The Nizarite movement had been founded by Hasan-i-Sabbah, a Persian Ismaili, who in the years 1078–94 sought to start a revolution in the lands of the Abbasid Caliph on behalf of al-Mustansir, the Fatimid Caliph of Cairo, whom the Ismailis acknowledged as lawful Imam. The Ismailis believed that

5 James of Vitry, *Libri duo, quorum prior Orientalis sive Hierosolimitana, alia Occidentalis Historiae nomine inscribuntur*, I, 14 (Douai, 1597) pp. 42–3.

6 B. Lewis, *The Assassins. A Radical Sect in Islam* (London, 1967), p. 5.

7 H.E. Mayer, *Geschichte der Kreuzzüge*, 10th edn (Stuttgart, 2005), p. 153.

8 M.G.S. Hodgson, *The Order of Assassins. The Struggle of the early Nizari Ismailis against the Islamic World* (The Hague, 1955), p. 204 (cf. pp. 175–8).

9 F. Daftary, *The Ismailis. Their History and Doctrines* (Cambridge, 1990), p. 398.

10 P. Willey, *Eagle's Nest. Ismaili Castles in Iran and Syria* (London, 2005), pp. 46–7.

11 J. Hauzinski, 'On alleged attempts at converting the Assassins to Christianity in the light of William of Tyre's account', *Folia Orientalia* 15 (1974), pp. 229–46.

12 M. Barber, *The New Knighthood. A History of the Order of the Temple* (Cambridge, 1994), pp. 100–5.

13 F. Daftary, *The Assassin Legends* (London, 1994), pp. 88–94; Hodgson, *Order of Assassins*, p. 134.

an Imam had the right to designate his successor, but when al-Mustansir died in 1094, his designated heir, Nizar, was set aside and imprisoned by the ambitious vizir of Egypt, al-Afdal, in favour of his younger brother, al-Mustali, who was married to al-Afdal's sister. Hasan-i-Sabbah refused to recognise al-Mustali as Imam, but continued to give his allegiance to Nizar, claiming to be the *hujjah*, the living proof of the unseen Imam, and his representative. Hasan's followers later claimed that Nizar's infant son had been smuggled out of Egypt and brought to the castle of Alamut, where he lived as the Hidden Imam. Hasan was faced with a practical problem: hitherto he had been able to count on the support of the Fatimid Caliphate in his struggle with the Abbasids, but he was now left with the task of organizing a revolution throughout the entire Islamic world, single-handed.[14]

Hasan sent preachers, *dais*, throughout much of the Muslim world to gain support for the Nizarite cause. They met with considerable success, because there was widespread discontent in both the Abbasid and Fatimid empires about the ways in which the Caliphs were being manipulated by warlords, and many of the new adherents, while looking to Hasan as their religious leader, were the political subjects of other rulers. Hasan also gained control of other castles and their surrounding regions. Most of his subjects were peasants, but from them and from his religious adherents elsewhere he raised troops who garrisoned his castles and formed his armies.[15] He also trained a select group of warriors as assassins, *fidais*. They were not thugs, but religious zealots who were sent on missions to kill some of the political and religious leaders of the Islamic establishment. The *fidais* needed great courage and dedication, for the chances of their escaping after fulfilling their mission was often very slight. The daggers which they used to kill their victims were said to have been ritually consecrated,[16] and Hasan taught that those who died in the service of the Imam would be assured of Paradise. Some assignments involved long-term planning, because the *fidais* had to serve for many years in the retinues of princes before they were trusted enough to approach them closely. Although the *fidais* were few in number, they had a high success rate and inspired considerable fear throughout the Abbasid and Fatimid empires.[17]

The Frankish conquests which followed on from the First Crusade caused confusion among the Muslim rulers of Syria and Palestine. Hasan hoped to profit from this chaos and sent agents there in about 1100, but it was not until the 1130s that the Nizarites were able to establish a permanent power base in the Jabal Bahra. This mountainous region, adjacent to the Crusader states of Antioch and Tripoli, had been partially, but never totally, subdued by the Franks.[18] William of Tyre, writing in the 1170s, says that the Assassins had ten castles in this area and ruled over some

14 Daftary, *Ismailis*, pp. 336–51.

15 Hodgson, *Order of Assassins*, pp. 62–81.

16 Arnold of Lübeck, *Chronica Slavorum*, IV, 16, ed. I.M. Lappenberg in *Monumenta Germaniae Historica, Scriptores* 21: 179.

17 Hodgson, *Order of Assassins*, pp. 82–4.

18 P. Deschamps, *Les châteaux des Croisés en Terre Sainte. III. La défense du comté de Tripoli et de la principauté d'Antioche* (Paris, 1973), pp. 36–43.

60,000 subjects.[19] The Syrian Assassins were governed by masters appointed by and responsible to the Grand Masters of Alamut, who were known to their followers as the Sheikh, or Elder, and to the Franks as 'The Old Man of the Mountains'.[20]

The Frankish rulers of Antioch and Tripoli reacted very differently to these new neighbours. Raymond of Poitiers, Prince of Antioch (1135–49), allied with the Nazirite leader Ali ibn Wafa against their common enemy, Nur ad-Din of Damascus, and both of them were killed fighting against him at the battle of Inab in 1149.[21] This tradition of goodwill was maintained by Raymond's son, Bohemond III, who in 1180 granted the fief of Bikisrail, situated near the northern border of Nizarite territory, to the Order of St James of the Sword. Among the estates of the fief listed in Bohemond's charter was 'the castle of Gerennes with its appurtenances, except for the estates which we have given to the Sheikh of the Assassins [Vetulo Assideorum]'.[22]

Raymond II of Tripoli (1137–52) had lost Rafaniya and much of the surrounding territory in the Orontes valley to Zengi of Mosul in 1137. He took defensive measures by creating in 1144 what amounted to a palatinate lordship centred on Crac des Chevaliers for the Knights of St John. Included in the grant were the lost lands in the Orontes valley, if they could be recovered from the Saracens.[23] In 1151 Zengi's son and successor, Nur ad-Din, sacked Tortosa and although he left no garrison there, the citadel and the other fortifications had been badly damaged and the castellan could not afford to restore them. In 1152 Raymond made the fief of Tortosa into what was in effect a Templar palatinate lordship, which adjoined the small lordship which that Order already held at Chastel Blanc (Safita).[24] Later that year Nizarite *fidais* fatally stabbed Raymond II as he rode through the city gate of Tripoli.[25]

The Nizarites had no quarrel with Christians, and Raymond was the only important Frankish leader to be killed by them before the Third Crusade. It is possible that this was their response to Raymond's foundation of the Templar lordship of Tortosa. Certainly the Templars fought the Nizarites at first, but by King Amalric's reign a peaceful solution had been found. James of Vitry, writing some 50 years later, relayed information perhaps supplied by the Templars: 'For they [the Assassins] were at that time [c. 1173] tributary to the brethren of the Temple, paying them two thousand bezants each year in order to hold securely a certain part of their territory, for [the Templars] had been accustomed to launch many attacks against it because

19 WT, 20, 29, p. 953; Willey, *Eagle's Nest*, pp. 216–45.

20 Lewis, *Assassins*, pp. 97–124; C. Nowell, 'The Old Man of the Mountain', *Speculum* 22 (1947), pp. 497–519.

21 WT, 17, 9, pp. 770–2; Ibn al-Qalanisi, *The Damascus Chronicle of the Crusades*, trans. H.A.R. Gibb (London, 1932), p. 292.

22 H.E. Mayer, *Varia Antiochena. Studien zum Kreuzfahrerfürstentum Antiochia im 12 und frühen 13 Jahrhundert* (Hanover, 1993), pp. 116–17.

23 J. Riley-Smith, *The Knights of St John in Jerusalem and Cyprus, c. 1050–1310* (London, 1967), pp. 55–6.

24 J. Riley-Smith, 'The Templars and the castle of Tortosa in Syria: an unknown document concerning the acquisition of the fortress', *English Historical Review* 84 (1969), pp. 278–88; Barber, *New Knighthood*, pp. 81–3.

25 WT, 17, 19, pp. 786–7.

it was so near.'[26] The English chronicler, William of Newburgh, explained that the normal Nizarite scare tactics did not work against the Templars: '[The Old Man of the Mountain] knew that it was a useless act if one of his servants should by chance kill a Master of the Temple, because the Templars would soon appoint another one who would strive more fiercely to avenge the death of his predecessor.'[27]

Like all Ismailis, the Nizarites distinguished between the literal meaning of the Qur'an and of sharia law and the spiritual truths which they enshrined. They also had inherited a cyclical cosmology which was, in part at least, Gnostic in origin, and they 'worked out a cyclical … view … of religious history, in terms of the eras of different prophets recognized by the Qur'an'.[28] But when they first settled in the Jabal Bahra, the Nizarites conformed to the observances of the sharia and, in the eyes of their Frankish neighbours at least, appeared no different from any other Muslim community.

This changed during the reign of the fourth Master of Alamut, Hasan II (1162–66), who, on the 17th day of Ramadan in 1164, held a solemn assembly at which, speaking as the *khalifa*, the vicegerent of the Imam, he declared that the Day of Resurrection had come. He seems to have intended this to be understood in a spiritual rather than a literal sense. His followers could still experience physical death, but from that time forward they could, while still in this life, enjoy a full vision of God, made manifest through the representative of his Imam, a vision which would continue in Paradise after their deaths. Those who rejected this revelation were damned, because their wilful blindness shut them out, in both this world and the next, from sharing in the contemplation of God. Since a new dispensation had begun, the old dispensation was at an end and Hasan's followers were no longer bound to observe the ritual laws of Islam: the new dispensation was inaugurated with a banquet held in the middle of the fast of Ramadan.[29]

When this happened, the Master of the Syrian Assassins was Rashid ad-Din Sinan, described by William of Tyre as 'a very eloquent man with a keen mind and a good intelligence'.[30] The biography of him by the Ismaili Abu Firas, written in 1324, was largely hagiographical.[31] A more straightforward account is given by Kamal ad-Din of Aleppo (1192–1262) in his biographical dictionary. He reports that Sinan, a native of Basra, was trained at Alamut in the reign of the Grand Master Muhammad I (1138–62) in the company of the future Grand Master Hasan II. When Hasan came to power in 1162 he sent Sinan to Syria as his representative. At that time Abu Muhammad was Master of the Syrian Nizarites, but after his death Sinan was appointed new Master by the Grand Master.[32] The *Bustan*, a contemporary Shi'ite

26 James of Vitry, *Historia Orientalis*, c. 14, pp. 42–3.

27 William of Newburgh, *Historia Rerum Anglicarum*, IV, 24, ed. R. Howlett, Rolls Series 82 (I) (London, 1884), pp. 364–5.

28 Daftary, *Ismailis*, p. 139.

29 Ibid., pp. 386–9; Hodgson, *Order of Assassins*, pp. 148–57.

30 WT, 20, 29, p. 953.

31 S. Guyard, 'Un Grand Maître des Assassins au temps de Saladin', *Journal Asiatique* 7 ser., 9 (1877), pp. 387–489.

32 B. Lewis, 'Kamal al-Din's biography of Rasid al-Din Sinan', *Arabica* 13 (1966), 231–4.

Syrian chronicle, reports that the Syrian Ismailis broke the sharia law in 1165–6, which suggests that Sinan had become Master by that time.[33]

Although some doubt has been expressed by modern scholars about the degree to which the sharia was abandoned by other Nizarite believers after 1166,[34] there is clear evidence about what happened in the case of the Syrian community. William of Tyre reports that Sinan '... put an end to the observances of a false religion, destroying the houses of prayer which they had previously used, abolishing their fasts, and allowing them to drink wine and to eat pork'.[35] This conduct scandalized other Muslims, particularly the devout Sunnite prince Nur ad-Din, who dominated Islamic northern Syria. When the religious changes were first adopted, vigilante groups of Sunni Muslims massacred Nizarite Ismailis living in Nur ad-Din's dominions who had abandoned the observances of sharia law.[36]

In 1166 Sinan's friend and patron, the Grand Master Hasan II, was murdered. He was succeeded by his son, Muhammad II, who continued to uphold his father's theological teaching but abandoned all attempts to promote a world revolution. Since unbelievers were already in outer darkness, he argued, they could be ignored, and he undertook no military activity. Only one assassination ordered by Alamut is recorded during the first 26 years of his reign.[37] Sinan could not adopt a similar pacifist policy because of the hostility of Nur ad-Din, and seems to have broken links with Alamut soon after Hasan II's death. He may have rejected Muhammad II's claim that he and his father were true Imams and of Nizarid descent, not merely representatives of the Hidden Imams.[38] Daftary thinks that the fragmentary surviving evidence supports this view:

> Later Syrian Nizari writings ... make only vague references to what may have been Sinan's teaching. But these writings do not explicitly emphasize the status of the current imam and the manifestation of the unveiled truth in him. On the contrary, their emphasis is on self-knowledge ... as constituting [an] important step towards knowing God.[39]

Certainly in his negotiations with the Franks Sinan acted as an autonomous ruler and did not seek authorization from Alamut. There is much contemporary evidence that his subjects considered him their supreme religious authority during his lifetime, and, indeed, a cult of him was maintained by them after his death, which still survives.[40] His assertion of independence seems to have been viewed unfavourably at Alamut and Kamal ad-Din cites a lost twelfth-century source which records that

33 C. Cahen, 'Une chronique syrienne du VIe/XIIe siècle, le "Bustan al-Gami"', *Bulletin d'études orientales de l'Institut français de Damas* 7–8 (1937–8), p. 136; cf. Hodgson, *Order of Assassins*, p. 186, n. 3; Daftary, *Ismailis*, p. 689, n. 154.

34 Daftary, *Ismailis*, p. 390.

35 WT, 20, 29, pp. 953–4.

36 For example, the attack on the Shi'ites of el-Bab reported by Ibn Jubayr, *The Travels*, trans. R.J.C. Broadhurst (London, 1952), pp. 259–60.

37 Hodgson, *Order of Assassins*, pp. 180–4.

38 Daftary, *Ismailis*, pp. 391–6; Hodgson, *Order of Assassins*, pp. 160–2.

39 Daftary, *Ismailis*, pp. 400–1.

40 Ibid., p. 401; Willey, *Eagle's Nest*, p. 237.

Muhammad II 'sent emissaries a number of times from Alamut to kill Sinan, fearing his usurpation of the headship, but Sinan used to kill them'.[41]

Sinan thus found himself in the unenviable position of being at war with Nur ad-Din, while being unable to call on Alamut for help. Moreover, in the early years of his Mastership he was also at war with the Franks. This was reported by Rabbi Benjamin of Tudela. Joshua Prawer, using the evidence of early manuscripts of his work, has argued convincingly that Benjamin visited the Levant in 1169–71 and was present in the county of Tripoli on 29 July 1170 when a great earthquake occurred.[42] Benjamin writes:

> In the neighbourhood [of Jabala] dwells a people called al-Hashishim. They do not believe in the religion of Islam, but follow one of their own folk whom they regard as their prophet ... They call him the Sheikh al-Hashishim ... Their principal seat is Kadmus ... They are at war with the sons of Edom, who are called the Franks, and with the ruler of Tripolis.[43]

At the time of Benjamin's visit Raymond III of Tripoli was a prisoner of Nur ad-Din and King Amalric was administering the county.[44] It was therefore with him that Sinan opened negotiations. Both William of Tyre and Walter Map emphasize that the Nizarite leader expressed an interest in Christianity, and there is no reason to doubt that this was so. William of Tyre says that Sinan had studied the New Testament, while Walter Map, who had evidently heard the same rumour, supposed that Sinan had obtained the sacred texts from the Latin Patriarch of Jerusalem. That was a false inference, because the county of Tripoli was under the ecclesiastical jurisdiction of the Latin Patriarch of Antioch, who would have dealt with any approach of that kind.[45] But the Syrian Nizarites did not need to obtain texts of the Gospels from the Franks, for, as Marshall Hodgson pointed out, among the Ismailis 'knowledge of the Christian scriptures was a tradition dating back at least to Kirman [d.c. 1019]'.[46] A similar interest in Christian writings was shared by Sinan's successor as Master of the Syrian Nizarites, whom the Dominican Yves Le Breton, the envoy of Louis IX of France, visited in 1250. The Master had a copy of 'Our Lord's sayings to St Peter' and when Yves commented on this the Master told him: 'I am devoted to my lord St Peter', which was the prelude to a cross-purpose discussion.[47] It seems reasonable to suppose that Sinan shared the same kinds of interest in and knowledge of Christianity as the Master of the Syrian Nizarites in Louis IX's day, and that

41 Lewis, 'Kamal al-Din', p. 231.

42 J. Prawer, *The History of the Jews in the Latin Kingdom of Jerusalem* (Oxford, 1988), pp. 191–4.

43 Benjamin of Tudela, *Itinerary*, ed. and trans. M.N. Adler (London, 1907), pp. 16–17.

44 M.W. Baldwin, *Raymond III of Tripolis and the Fall of Jerusalem (1140–1187)* (Princeton, 1936), pp. 10–15.

45 J.G. Rowe, 'The Papacy and the Ecclesiastical Province of Tyre', *Bulletin of the John Rylands Library* 43 (1960–1), pp. 160–89.

46 Hodgson, *Order of Assassins*, p. 176.

47 John of Joinville, *Histoire de Saint Louis*, cc. 462–3, ed. N. de Wailly (Paris, 1868), pp. 164–5; B. Hamilton, 'Knowing the enemy: Western understanding of Islam at the time of the Crusades', *Journal of the Royal Asiatic Society* 3rd ser., 7 (1997), p. 377.

William of Tyre and perhaps other Latin churchmen took this as evidence that he was seriously considering becoming a Catholic Christian. This must have appeared a quite strong possibility because the Nizarites were known to have abandoned the ritual practices of Islam. Nevertheless, these hopes rested on a misapprehension, for the Nizarites understood the role of Christ in sacred history in a quite different way from the learned Frankish clergy. Among the texts preserved by the Syrian Ismailis are some fragments relating to Sinan. In one passage he explains that all the prophets recognized in the Qur'an (which, of course, included Jesus) were manifestations of one divine revelation: 'Do not be misled by the changing of forms. You say so-and-so passed and so-and-so came; I tell you to consider the faces as all one face.'[48]

Although William of Tyre and other clergy may have considered the conversion of the Assassins to be the most important part of the negotiations, King Amalric's priorities may have been rather different. He was planning a joint attack on Egypt with William II of Sicily, scheduled for the summer of 1174.[49] Egypt was ruled by Nur ad-Din's lieutenant, Saladin, who, after the death of the Fatimid Caliph al-Adid in 1171, had restored Egypt to the spiritual obedience of the Abbasid Caliph. He had left the Fatimid princes alive, while depriving them of all political power[50] and in the winter of 1173–4 a group of Egyptian officials in Saladin's service conspired to restore the Fatimid Caliphate and approached Amalric for help. Saladin learned of this plot and in a letter written by his chancellor al-Fadil complained that the Syrian Nizarites were also a party to it.[51] Although the Nizarite movement owed its existence to its rejection, after 1094, of the claims of the Fatimid Calpihs to hold the Imamate, it is possible that Sinan, who acted independently of Alamut after 1166, was willing to co-operate with a pro-Fatimid movement. Certainly the participation of the Syrian Nizarites, who had a network of supporters in Egypt and were skilled in the art of political assassination, would have greatly increased the conspirators' chance of success. The murder of the Nizarite envoy by the Templars in the winter of 1173–4, while this complex set of negotiations with the pro-Fatimid dissidents was taking place, ended the possibility of Assassin involvement. Perhaps as a consequence of this, Amalric's attempt to join forces with the rebels was a fiasco. He sent an official embassy to Cairo, instructing one of its members to contact the conspirators. Saladin's agents informed him of this and he countered by attaching a Coptic Christian as his own official representative to the Frankish embassy, instructing him to pass himself off as a dissident and to arrange meetings between Amalric's agent and the conspirators. Having in this way discovered the identity of

48 Hodgson, *Order of Assassins*, pp. 199–201, 248–50.

49 B. Hamilton, *The Leper King and his Heirs. Baldwin IV and the Crusader Kingdom of Jerusalem* (Cambridge, 2000), pp. 75–6, 86–8.

50 M.C. Lyons and D.E.P. Jackson, *Saladin. The Politics of the Holy War* (Cambridge, 1982), p. 47.

51 Ibn al-Athir, *Kamil al-Tawarikh*, Recueil des Historiens des Croisades, Historiens Orientaux (henceforth RHC Or.) I (Paris, 1872), p. 599; Lyons and Jackson, *Saladin*, p. 67; Lewis, *Assassins*, p. 114.

the conspirators, Saladin had them all executed on 6 April 1174 after the Franks had left Cairo.[52]

The Master of the Temple, Odo of St Amand, would seem to have sanctioned the murder of the Assassin envoy to the court of Jerusalem. William of Tyre describes how, when that envoy

> was about to enter his own territory, he was … set upon by the aforesaid brethren [of the Temple] with drawn swords and they killed him while he had a royal safe-conduct … [In doing so] they were guilty of treason [*lese majestatis crimen*]… it is said that a certain brother [Templar], Walter of Mesnil, a wicked man with only one eye … committed this crime, but with the full knowledge of his brethren.[53]

This murder was intended to wreck the negotiations between the Nizarites and the king. Odo of St Amand had had a distinguished career as a royal official in the reigns of Baldwin III and Amalric before he became a Templar in about 1170 and his rapid promotion as Master of the Order was certainly due to royal influence.[54] He could easily have dissociated himself from the murder of the envoy, but he chose not to do so. When the king demanded that Walter of Mesnil should stand trial for treason, Odo refused, claiming that he had already placed Walter in custody and had referred the case to Rome for judgment. Despite this, Amalric seized Walter by force and imprisoned him at Tyre. As Malcolm Barber has pointed out, although Odo of St Amand was claiming that his Order was exempt from secular jurisdiction, the matter was not so clear cut. For while 'the bull *Omne datum optimum* could certainly be interpreted in this way, the hanging of the twelve Templars around 1166 shows that the king was not prepared to concede this'.[55] William of Tyre reports that the king was intending to seek the opinion of other rulers about how to proceed, but died before doing so.[56]

Odo of St Amand, together with the Master of the Hospital, was partly responsible for the defence of the Kingdom of Jerusalem and cannot have been ignorant of the king's negotiations with pro-Fatimid dissidents, and he must therefore have been aware of the political consequences of killing the Assassins' envoy. The Templars had no objections in principle to making military alliances with Muslims[57] and must therefore have had some other motive for wrecking the negotiations. William of Tyre reported the story in such a way as to imply that the conversion of 60,000 Muslims who lived in the Assassins' lordship was rendered impossible by the Templars, who were reluctant to part with an annual tribute of 2,000 bezants which the Assassins paid them. This is in keeping with the way in which William portrayed the Order in the years after c . 1150: he invariably shows its members as concerned to accumulate

52 Al-Maqrizi, *A History of the Ayyubid Sultans of Egypt*, trans. R.J.C. Broadhurst (Boston, 1980), p. 47; Hamilton, *Leper King*, p. 81.

53 WT, 20, 30, pp. 954–5.

54 Barber, *New Knighthood*, p. 107.

55 Ibid., p. 105.

56 WT, 20, 30, p. 955.

57 For example the Templar Geoffrey Fulcher was one of the chief negotiators of a treaty between the Franks and the Fatimid Caliph in 1167, WT, 19, 18, pp. 887–8.

wealth and power at the expense of the secular clergy.[58] Moreover, he felt particular animosity towards Odo of St Amand, whom he held responsible for the death of his brother Gerard at the battle of Marj Uyun in 1178,[59] and whom he described as: 'A man who neither feared God nor showed respect for his fellow men.'[60] The belief that the military orders were avaricious was quite widely shared, as can be seen from Canon Nine of the Third Lateran Council,[61] though Walter Map was surprised by it: 'Perhaps many lie when they tell these stories about the lords Templar … How they behave at Jerusalem I do not know; here with us they live harmlessly enough.'[62]

It is difficult to take William of Tyre's explanation of this incident seriously. The tribute of 2,000 bezants was quite a substantial sum, which would have provided annual money-fiefs for about seven Frankish knights.[63] No doubt the Templars would have been unwilling to lose this source of income, particularly so soon after the earthquake of 1170, when expensive building repairs were needed to many of their castles; but as King Amalric agreed to indemnify them for this sum it is unlikely to have been an issue.

Walter Map explained the Templars' actions in the following way: '[They] set an ambush by the way and killed [the Assassins' envoy] lest (it is said) the belief of the infidels should be done away and peace and union reign. For the Assassins, they say, are the prime masters of the infidelity and unbelief of the paynim.'[64] This explanation rests on a false premise. Far from being 'the prime masters of the infidelity … of the paynim', the Assassins were so radical in their understanding of the Islamic faith that other Muslims viewed them with misgiving.

What distinguished the Nizarite Ismailis in the twelfth century from all other kinds of Muslim fighting men was their use of assassination as a legitimate form of warfare. Political assassinations took place also in the Catholic world, but they were never considered meritorious religious acts and were regarded as a form of murder, which was a mortal sin. The Templars were committed by their profession to upholding the ideals of Christian knighthood and it is possible that their real objection to an alliance with the Assassins was that they considered such methods of warfare dishonourable. King Amalric and his secular advisers, on the other hand, appear to have been less discriminating about the alliances they formed to strengthen the defences of the kingdom.

The king made his peace with Sinan, disclaiming all responsibility for the murder of his envoy,[65] but serious negotiations between the two sides were never renewed. During the winter of 1173–4 Raymond III of Tripoli was released by Nur ad-Din and

58 Barber, *New Knighthood*, pp. 98–107.

59 Abu Shamah, *The Book of the Two Gardens*, RHC Or. IV (Paris, 1898), p. 202.

60 WT, 21, 28, p. 1002.

61 *Conciliorum Oecumenicorum Decreta*, ed. Istituto per le scienze religiose, Bologna (Bologna, 1973), pp. 215–17.

62 Walter Map, *De Nugis*, Dist. I, c. 22, p. 69.

63 J. Riley-Smith, *The Feudal Nobility and the Kingdom of Jerusalem, 1174–1277* (London, 1973), p. 10.

64 Walter Map, *De Nugis*, Dist. I, c. 22, p. 67.

65 WT, 20, 30, p. 955.

Amalric's regency in the county came to an end.[66] Then, on 11 July 1174 Amalric died, leaving a minor heir, Baldwin IV, for whom, a few months later, Raymond III was appointed regent.[67] Since Raymond III's father had been killed by the Assassins this made it certain that negotiations would not be re-opened with them before the king came of age in the summer of 1176.

By that time the situation had altered radically. The most serious threat to Sinan's independence seemed to have receded when Nur ad-Din died in May 1174 leaving a minor heir and his generals fought each other for power. Within six months, Saladin, who already ruled Egypt, had gained control of Damascus as well and constituted a new threat to Sinan.[68] Nizarite *fidais*, acting on Sinan's orders, made two attempts to assassinate Saladin in 1175–6 and he responded by attacking the Assassin castle of Masyaf in July 1176, but withdrew after a few weeks without having achieved anything. Observers were puzzled by this and offered a variety of explanations; that his army wished to return to Egypt and did not want to become involved in a campaign of long sieges, or that Sinan had threatened Saladin's uncle, the governor of Hama, who persuaded his nephew to withdraw.[69] The real reason seems to have been that Baldwin IV of Jerusalem came of age during this campaign and the truce that Raymond of Tripoli had made with Saladin in 1175 automatically came to an end. The young king led his army in an attack on the Beka'a valley, thus forcing Saladin to come south to defend Damascus.[70] This may imply that Baldwin IV was hoping, by coming to the aid of Sinan, to revive the negotiations that had been stalled since 1174. If that was his intention it bore no fruit. Kamal ad-Din learned from the son of one of Saladin's advisers that the Assassins made a third attempt on his life soon after his return from the Masyaf campaign, and that this led the sultan to open peace negotiations with them.[71] His reasons for doing so are self-evident: his security arrangements had proved incapable of screening him from the Assassins and this increased the likelihood that one of their future attempts would prove successful. Sinan had secured his goal: by making peace with Saladin he had neutralised his chief enemy, but that precluded any fresh negotiations with the court of Jerusalem.

The agreement of 1176 was observed by both parties. The Assassins did not make any further attempt on Saladin's life, and he honoured the alliance by insisting that the Assassins should be included in the peace which he made with Richard I at the end of the Third Crusade.[72] Nevertheless, Saladin was reluctant to invoke the aid of Sinan and his followers. Since he justified his wars against fellow Muslims by claiming that he wished to unite Western Islam in the *jihad* against the Franks, he could not afford to be seen as the ally of the heretical Assassins, who were execrated by the whole of orthodox Islam.[73] Ibn Jubayr, secretary to the Moorish governor of

66 Baldwin, *Raymond III*, p. 14, n. 23.

67 Hamilton, *Leper King*, pp. 84–94.

68 Lyons and Jackson, *Saladin*, pp. 81–4.

69 B. Lewis, 'Saladin and the Assassins', *Bulletin of the School of Oriental and African Studies* [London] 15 (1953), pp. 240–1.

70 Hamilton, *Leper King*, pp. 106–8.

71 Lewis, 'Kamal al-Din', pp. 236–7.

72 Abu Shamah, *Two Gardens*, RHC Or. V (Paris, 1906), p. 77.

73 Lyons and Jackson, *Saladin*, pp. 200–41.

Granada, who visited the Levant in 1184, made no attempt to conceal his distaste for the Assassins, even though they were allied to Saladin at this time; '[On the slopes of the Jabal Bahra] are castles belonging to the heretical Ismailites, a sect which swerved from Islam and vested divinity in a man. Their prophet was a devil in man's disguise called Sinan, who deceived them with falsehoods and chimera.'[74]

It is possible that the Knights Templar, like Saladin, shared a distaste for the Nizarites' methods of warfare and, as a religious brotherhood dedicated to the service of Christ, did not wish to be associated with a group whose behaviour differed so radically from the ideals of the new Knighthood.

74 Ibn Jubayr, *Travels*, p. 264.

Chapter 3

The Old French William of Tyre, the Templars and the Assassin Envoy

Peter W. Edbury

William of Tyre is justly famous as an early and influential critic of the military orders. Scattered through the latter part of his history are several reports of events that detract from the Templars' reputation for probity in seeking the best interests of the Latin East. These range from the Templar greed which delayed the capture of Ascalon in 1153 through to the Christian defeat at Marj Ayun in 1179, for which William held the Templar master, Odo of St Amand, responsible.[1] In some instances alternative accounts of these episodes exist in sources from Western Europe, and, by comparing them with William's version, we can glimpse something of the extent to which William was prepared to denigrate the Order.[2] William's hostility is understandable. As a bishop, he would have resented the orders' privileges, which meant that he and his fellow bishops had lost jurisdiction and income, and, as chancellor of the kingdom and thus a prominent servant of the crown, he would have been fearful of their ever- increasing wealth and military might, which in time was to bring them into a position to challenge royal authority. It is likely, but not certain, that in 1179 William had participated in moves at the Third Lateran Council to curtail their privileges,[3] and perhaps his critical anecdotes were in part an attempt to justify the attack on the orders on that occasion and to discourage people in the West from making further endowments and thus facilitating their growing power.

It is in this context that historians have tried to interpret William's well-known story of the Templars and the Assassin envoy. In late 1173 or early 1174 the leader of the Syrian branch of the Assassins sent an envoy to the king offering to convert to Christianity if the king would agree to remit the annual tribute of 2,000 dinars they were paying to the Templars who controlled Tortosa and other nearby fortresses. King Amaury was delighted by this proposal and expressed his readiness to compensate the Order from his own resources, but then the Templars ambushed and killed the

1 Guillaume de Tyr, *Chronique*, ed. R. B. C. Huygens, Corpus Christianorum, Continuatio Medievalis, 63, 63A (Turnholt, 1986) (hereafter WT), 17:27 (pp. 798–9), 18:9 (pp. 822–3), 19.11 (p. 879); 20.29–30 (pp. 953–5), 21.28 (p. 1002).

2 H. Nicholson, 'Before William of Tyre: European Reports on the Military Orders' Deeds in the East, 1150–1185', in *The Military Orders,* vol. 2: *Welfare and Warfare*, ed. H. Nicholson (Aldershot, 1998) pp. 111–18.

3 P.W. Edbury and J.G. Rowe, *William of Tyre: Historian of the Latin East* (Cambridge, 1988), p. 128; M. Barber, *The New Knighthood: A History of the Order of the Temple* (Cambridge, 1994), p. 107.

envoy as he was returning. The king demanded satisfaction, but the master, Odo of St Amand, refused, saying that he had enjoined a penance on the chief culprit and was sending him to the pope – in other words the master was making it clear that, thanks to the papal exemptions, the king had no jurisdiction. King Amaury, however, took matters into his own hands; he had a group of armed men enter the Templar house in Sidon and arrest the man; he was then taken to Tyre and incarcerated. William concluded his account by noting that Amaury had to exculpate himself from responsibility for the murder, and that, had he lived, he would have taken the matter up with the other Christian rulers. Leaving aside the intrinsic improbability that the Assassins would have abandoned Islam in favour of Christianity, William's story is of interest as an illustration of his view of all that was wrong with the Templars: their greed and self-interest had impeded the spread of the Christian faith, jeopardized the security of the Latin possessions in the East and harmed the reputation of the king. Reluctant to risk losing their tribute – not a huge sum – they had murdered an envoy who was travelling with the king's safe-conduct and, as a result, the prospects for both a military alliance and the conversion of Muslims collapsed. Their arrogant reliance on papal privileges had, on this occasion at least, availed them nothing – maybe it was an example that other rulers should follow.[4]

There are no accounts of this episode that might reflect a Templar perspective. According to Walter Map, whose version of these events could have been written as early as the early 1180s and almost certainly before William's work had become known in the West, the Assassin envoy approached the patriarch of Jerusalem and not the king; the Templars murdered him on his journey home, apparently fearing that if peace were to prevail they would lose their *raison d'être*. Walter seems to have been more concerned with promoting the idea that the venality of the papal court prevented any action being taken against the Order and concluded by expressing his uncertainty about the truth of the story: 'What they [the Templars] do in Jerusalem, I know not; with us they live innocently enough' ('Quid agant Ierosolimis, nescio; nobiscum satis innocenter habitant'). He then goes on to criticize the Hospitallers, mentioning the attack on their privileges at the Third Lateran Council in 1179. Like William, Walter had attended this council, and it may be wondered whether his version of the story of the murdered envoy reflects a tale that was in circulation there.[5] Later writers add nothing of any real interest. James of Vitry clearly drew on William's account, but although he noted that the Assassins paid 2,000 dinars annually to the Templars, he deliberately excised any mention of the Templars' role in the killing; in his account the villain was simply 'quidam ex nostris, vir Belial et iniquus'.[6] Other writers followed William and Walter in pointing the finger of blame at the Templars, but without going into detail: thus Guy of Bazoches had a

---

4 WT, 20.29–30 (pp. 953–5).

5 Walter Map, *De Nugis Curialium: Courtiers' Trifles*, ed. and trans. M.R. James, revised by C.N.L. Brooke and R.A.B. Mynors (Oxford, 1983), pp. 67–9, cf. pp. 69–73. For Walter's presence at the Lateran Council and the date of composition, see pp. xvii, xxiv–xxx, li–liv.

6 James of Vitry, 'Historia Hierosolimitana', ed. J. Bongars, *Gesta Dei per Francos* (Hanau, 1611), 1, pp. 1047–145 at p. 1063.

brief notice which could be thought to have been derived from William's, except that he identified the king of Jerusalem as Baldwin IV,[7] and Matthew Paris similarly spoke of a King Baldwin, although, as he appended the story to an account of the Assassins' murder of Count Raymond II of Tripoli in 1152, it could be that Baldwin III was intended.[8]

William gives by far the fullest account of the story. He was well placed to know what had happened, but how he chose to construct his narrative to put across his own particular message is another matter. Clearly he had seized on the episode as a chance to cast the Templars in a poor light, but we can never know the extent to which he embellished his tale in order to achieve that purpose. What we can do, however, is see how later generations chose to modify his narrative to suit their own perspectives, and it is here that a comparison with the Old French translation of William's work comes into play. William had written his account of this incident by 1184, within ten years of its occurrence. Later, at some point between the end of the Third Crusade and the early 1230s, someone working in Western Europe translated his history into French, and it is worth considering what light the translation sheds here on the perceptions and mentality of the translator.[9] Unlike William, whose intended readership comprised literate Latin clergy, the translator's audience was likely to have been made up of members of the lay nobility, and, unlike William, the translator would have been well aware that in 1187 Jerusalem and much of the rest of the Latin East had been conquered by Saladin and, despite the best efforts of the Christian West, had remained under Muslim control. With these circumstances in mind, there are two distinct questions that can be asked: in what ways did the translator adapt William's account? and did later copyists make further changes, and, if so, how?

Although, thanks to the labours of Professor R.B.C. Huygens, we are fortunate to have an excellent edition of William's Latin text, there is no reliable modern version of the French translation.[10] A total of 51 complete or substantially complete manuscripts of the French version copied before ca. 1500 survive in public collections, and I have recently been engaged on a research project designed to lay

7 Guy of Bazoches in Alberic of Trois-Fontaines, 'Chronica a monacho novi monasterii Hoiensis interpolata', *Monumenta Germaniae Historica, Scriptores*, 23:859.

8 Matthew Paris, *Chronica Majora*, ed. H.R. Luard, RS 57 (London, 1872–83), 2, pp. 185–86. For other references, see H. Nicholson, *Templars, Hospitallers and Teutonic Knights: Images of the Military Orders, 1128–1291* (Leicester, 1993), p. 83 n. 21 (p. 160).

9 J.H. Pryor, 'The *Eracles* and William of Tyre: an Interim Report', in *The Horns of Hattin*, ed. B.Z. Kedar (Jerusalem and London, 1992), pp. 276, 288–9. See also B. Hamilton, 'The Old French translation of William of Tyre as an historical source', in *The Experience of Crusading*, vol. 2, *Defining the Crusader Kingdom*, ed. P.W. Edbury and J. Phillips (Cambridge, 2003), pp. 93–112.

10 There are two nineteenth-century editions: *L'Estoire de Eracles Empereur et la Conqueste de la Terre d'Outremer*, *Recueil des Historiens des Croisades, Historiens Occidentaux*, hereafter cited as *RHC Occid.*, 1 (1844); *Guillaume de Tyr et ses continuateurs: text français du XIIIe-siècle*, ed. Paulin Paris (Paris, 1879–80).

the groundwork for establishing a stemma.[11] One result of this work has been the identification of those manuscripts which preserve a text that is close to the original form of the translation and, on the basis of these findings, I can now present my own critical edition of the French translation of William of Tyre's book 20 chapter 30, which contains the greater part of the story of the murder. In an article published in 1973, Professor Jaroslav Folda provided the essential, up-to-date guide to the manuscripts,[12] and, for the sake of simplicity, I am following his numbering: thus for example, the fifth manuscript in his list will be referred to as F[olda]05. I should add that the preparation of this edition and the material for the discussion that follows has allowed me to test my hypotheses about the stemma and the nature of the manuscript tradition, and this paper consciously parallels another, similar paper in which I have edited and discussed the French text of William of Tyre's book 12 chapter 7, the account of the founding of the Templar Order.[13]

I have used as my base a text found in the Paris, BN, ms. fr. 9081, fols. 279r–280r (F05). This manuscript could well be the earliest extant copy with illuminations, and these have been dated to 1245–48 and ascribed to a Paris workshop.[14] To establish the text I have collated it with six other manuscripts which appear to preserve an early form of the translation. These are:

F02 Paris, BN, ms. fr. 2627 (N. France: 15th century)
F03 Paris, BN, ms. fr. 2632 (Latin East or France: 1st half of 13th century)
F04 Paris, BN, ms. fr. 2826 (Latin East or France: 1st half of 13th century)
F38 London, BL, Henry Yates Thompson ms. 12 (England: mid-13th century)
F41 Paris, BN, ms. fr. 67 (N. France: 2nd half of 13th century)
F52 Baltimore, Walters Art Gallery, ms. 142 (Paris: ca. 1300 with additions ca. 1340)

Of the other 44 manuscripts, there is one (F66) that I have not been able to consult and four others (F01, F30, F63 and F71) that are damaged and lack the chapter in question. I have not thought it helpful to publish an apparatus detailing the variants to be found in the remaining manuscripts – such an undertaking would be extremely bulky and would not add significantly to our understanding, although attention will be drawn to particular instances where later redactors have emended the text. All the manuscripts are listed in an appendix to this paper together with the foliation for this chapter.

In William's Latin text, what follows is book 20 chapter 30; in the French text, thanks to the merging of two earlier chapters in this book, it is numbered chapter 29. None of the seven manuscripts I have used to establish the text has a rubric; the

11 P.W. Edbury, 'The French Translation of William of Tyre's *Historia*: the manuscript tradition', *Crusades* 6 (2007), 69–105.

12 J. Folda, 'Manuscripts of the *History of Outremer* by William of Tyre: a Handlist', *Scriptorium* 27 (1973), 90–5.

13 P.W. Edbury, 'The Old French William of Tyre and the Origins of the Templars', in N. Housley (ed.), *Knighthoods of Christ: Essays on the History of the Crusades and the Knights Templar presented to Malcolm Barber* (Ashgate, 2007), pp. 151–64.

14 J. Folda, *Crusader Art in the Holy Land, From the Third Crusade to the Fall of Acre, 1187–1291* (Cambridge, 2005), pp. 217, 235–6.

rubrics printed in the nineteenth-century editions are not translated from William's Latin text, but represent accretions that belong to a later stage in the manuscript tradition.

William of Tyre 20:30 (29)

1 Li rois ot molt grant joie quant il oi ce message parler, et, si com il estoit bons crestiens et sages hom, il respondi mout debonerement que ja si grant chose et si haute emprise ne remanroit por la rente de .ii.m. besanz; car il estoit prez que il de ses propres rentes les asseist as Templiers en tel leu dont il se devroient bien tenir apaié. 2 Apres ce retint le message une piece del tens avec lui por acomplir les couvenances qu'il demandoit; mout li fesoit bele chiere et grant heneur. 3 Apres, quant tot fu acordé entre le roi et lui, il demanda congié et s'en parti por amener le Vieill et ses genz a fere de bon cuer ce qu'il avoient promis. 4 Li rois li bailla conduit. 5 Quant il orent passé Triple et cil estoit ja pres de son pais, ne sai quant Templier saillirent d'un guet et leur coururent sus les espees tretes. 6 Ce preudome, qui ja estoit ausint comme crestiens et mout se fioit en la leauté de nostre gent et avoit le conduit le roi, ocistrent et decopperent tot.
7 Quant li rois oi ceste novele, si grant duel ot et si grant courouz qu'il sembloit qu'il fust hors del sen. *8* Tantost envoia querre ses barons et les conjura que li donassent conseill; la chose leur conta si com il l'avoit menee. *9* Il respondirent tuit a une voiz que ce ne devoit il mie lessier qu'il ne fust bien amendé, car trop estoit li outrages lez et vilains, et grant honte avoit l'en fete a Damedieu et a tote crestienté et nomeement au roi. *10* Par acort de toz furent envoie dui haut home: li uns avoit non Sehers de Mamedunc;[15] li autres Godechauz de Torhout.[16] *11* Cil vindrent au mestre del Temple, qui avoit non frere Odes de Saint Amant,[17] et li requistrent de part le roi et de part les barons que cele traison et ce vilain forfet que si frere avoient fet feist amender sanz delai au roi et au regne. *12* L'en disoit certeinement que uns Templiers qui avoit non Gautiers del Mesnil, orgueilleus et fel, jangleus et meslis, et n'avoit qu'un oeill, avoit fete cele desleauté par le consentement des autres Templiers. *13* Dom il avint que li mestres l'en deporta ce qu'il pot, et respondi as messages le roi que il en avoit sa penitanence enjointe au frere qui ce avoit fet et l'en envoieroit a Rome o toutes ses letres por fere le comandement l'apostole; por ce deffendoit il bien au roi et as autres de par Dieu et de part l'apostole, que ne meissent main ou frere ne en leur choses. *14* Autres paroles meismes dist il assez de qu'il n'est pas mestiers a reconter, car eles mouvoient plus d'orgueill que de religion.
15 Li rois vint por ceste besoingne meismes a Saiete et trouva iluecques le mestre del Temple et des freres assez, celui meismes maufeteur qui estoit avec els. *16* Lors se conseilla li rois a ses homes qu'il avoit menez avec lui, et par le los de toz envoia genz a armes en la meison del Temple et prist par force ce Templier qui la cruiauté avoit fete; si l'envoia tot lié a Sur et le fist metre en la chartre. *17* Chascuns se douta ou reaume de Surie que li mestres des Harsaxis ne le feist ocirre par achoison de son message qu'il avoit ainsinc

15 Seher de Mamedunc witnessed as a vassal of the lords of Outrejourdain in 1168 and 1177 and attested one charter of Baldwin IV in 1179. *Regesta Regni Hierosolymitani* and *Additamentum*, ed. R. Röhricht (Innsbruck, 1893–1904) (hereafter *RRH*), nos. 454, 551, 587.

16 William noted Godechauz de Torhout's death in 1179. WT, p. 999. He is not otherwise known. Although he and his fellow envoy are described by William as 'nobiles' and here as 'haut home', the paucity of other references to them suggests that this was no high-level delegation.

17 Odo of St Amand, Templar master ca. 1171–79.

perdu; nequedant li rois s'en escusa bien et leur fist asavoir que ce avoit esté sor son pois tant qu'il l'en crurent bien. *[18]* Del templier qu'il tenoit en prison ne volt plus fere, por ce qu'il ne corroçast le Temple plus qu'il avoit fet, mes l'en cuide bien se il eust plus vescu que il eust envoié letres et bons messages par tot les princes de crestienté por mostrer le grant domage que li Templier avoient fet a la foi crestiene et nomeement au reaume de Surie; si les cuidoit bien si esmouvoir contr'els que chascuns les chaçast de son pooir. *[19]* Quant li noviaus tens fu revenuz en cel an meismes, Raoul l'evesques de Bethleem qui estoit chanceliers le roi, vaillainz hom larges et deboneres, mourut et fu enterrez ou chapitre de s'eglise. *[20]* Li chenoine s'asamblerent por eslire evesque apres lui, mes ne se porent acorder; ainçois sordie entr'els uns si granz contenz qui mout dura longuement par que l'eglise fu trop domagiee.[18]

1 ce message] F03: les messages
sages] F03: boens
deboneremement] F03: doucement
asseist] F04: asserroit
dont il se devroient] F03: que il se porroient
2 le message] F03: les messages
acomplir] F03: acointier
demandoit] F03: avoit fait
3 tot fu] F05: il fu
et s'en parti] F52 *lacks*
ses gens a] F03: sa gent et
avoient] F03: avoit
5 guet] F02: aguet; F05: guiet
6 decopperent tot] F03: decouperent
7 duel ot] F04: duel en ot
fust hors] F05: fust touz fors
8 que li] F02: qu'ilz lui; F38: qu'il li
9 ne fust bien amendé] F02: n'en preist amende
tote crestienté] F52: toute la crestienté
10 acort de toz] F02: leur conseil
furent] F52: i furent
Sehers] F38 F52: Sehiers
Mamedunc] F02: Mamedune; F03: Mamedonc
Godechauz de Torhout] F02: Godeschaulz de Torholt; F03: Godeschauz de Torhot; F04: Godeschauz de Torholz; F38: Godeschauz de Torholt; F41 F52: Godechauz de Torholt
11 Odes] F03: Othes; F04 F38: Oedes; F52: Huedes
si frere] F03: li frere
amender] F41: amendez
sanz delai au roi et au regne] F02 *lacks*; F03: sanz delai au roi
regne] F38: reaume

18 Ralph, bishop of Bethlehem (1156–74) and chancellor of the kingdom (1146–74). He is last known from a royal charter of 18 April 1174: *RRH*, no. 514. Note that the translator omits the detail that the dispute was not resolved until the second year of Baldwin IV.

12 avoit non] F03: avoit a nom
Gautiers] F02 F52: Gautier
Mesnil] F38 F41: Mesnill
fel] F03 F52: faus
et meslis] F02: et mesdisans; F03 *lacks*
avoit fete cele desleauté] F52: avoit cele desloiauté fete
cele desleauté] F02: ceste desleauté
13 sa penitanence enjointe] F04: enjointe sa penitance
Rome] F02 F52: Romme
letres] F03: penitances
l'apostole] F52: l'apostoire (x2)
au roi et as autres] F03: le roi
que ne] F03 F04 F38 F52: qu'il ne
ou frere ne en leur choses] F03: aus freres ne a lor chouse
14 assez de qu'il n'est mie mestiers a reconter] F03: que riens n'en si abeut a racorder
de qu'il n'est pas] F02 F52: que il n'est pas; F04: dont il n'est pas; F05: de qu'il n'est mie; F38: de coi il n'est pas
a reconter] F02: de racompter; F52: de reconter
15 ceste besoingne] F52: ceste reson
Saiete] F02: Saiecte; F03: Soiete; F38: Saatte
des freres] F04: des autres freres
16 qu'il avoit menez avec lui] F03 *lacks*
menez] F04 F52: amenez
a armes] F03: armees
ce Templier qui la cruiauté avoit fete si l'envoia tot lié] F03: templiers qui estoient en Temple et celui qui ce avoit fait et l'en envoia loié
17 Harsaxis] F03: Harsazins; F04: Harsasis; F52: Harsasys
18 por ce qu'il] F02: pour ce que; F03: por ce qui
corroçast] F03: retast
eust plus vescu] F52: i eust plus vescu
que il eust] F02: l'en eust
contr'els] F03: sor auz
19 revenuz] F02: venus; F52: venuz
Raoul] F05: Raous; F38: Raouls; F52: Raols
Bethleem] F03: Bellerm
chanceliers] F03: chevalier
larges] F03: cortois
s'eglise] F02: l'eglize
20 apres lui] F03 *lacks*
par que] F02: par quoy; F03 F52: par quoi
trop] F03: molt

The previous chapter records the beginning of this story. William starts by decrying the baleful effects of the episode he is about to describe before launching into an account of the Assassins; according to William they had resolved to renounce Islam and embrace the Christian faith, and, with this in mind, an envoy came to King Amaury with the proposal that, in return for remitting the 2,000 dinar tribute they were paying the Templars, the Assassins would accept baptism. Coming now to the chapter edited here, we find that the translator made no attempt to soften the allegations made against the Templars. Indeed, the opposite is true. In the first sentence, where William described the king as 'discretissimus' the translator has 'bons crestiens et sages hom', thereby introducing a comment on Amaury's piety: the king is pious as well as wise, and that explains his enthusiasm for the envoy's proposition. (By contrast, Templars will be seen to be lacking in piety.) According to William, Amaury, 'so it is said' ('ut dicitur') was prepared to refund the Order from his own revenues; the translator, however, is categorical: the king would recompense them, and to underline the point he adds the phrase 'en tel leu dont il se devroient bien tenir apaié' – words for which there are no equivalents in the Latin. The enormity of the offence is emphasized. In sentence 5 we are told that the Templars 'sallied forth from an ambush', whereas William's original had them 'fall on them unexpectedly' – perhaps the translator wants to make sure that his readers conceive the attack as cowardly and premeditated – and while William simply reports that they killed the envoy, the translator has 'killed and completely beheaded'. Curiously, the translator omits to translate William's phrase 'lese maiestatis crimen incurrentes'. Thereafter the translation stays fairly close to the Latin text until we reach sentence 17. Here the idea that everyone feared lest the master of the Assassins would avenge himself for his envoy by staging the murder of the king is the translator's invention; William instead speaks of the event bringing 'irreparable ruin' on the kingdom. The translator's chief addition, however, comes at the end: William simply said that, had Amaury recovered from his final illness, he would have taken the matter up with 'the kings and princes of the lands of the world', but in the translation the whole of the second part of sentence 18 is new:

> por mostrer le grant domage que li Templier avoient fet a la foi crestiene et nomeement au reaume de Surie; si les cuidoit bien si esmouvoir contr'els que chascuns les chaçast de son pooir ('to expose the great damage the Templars had done to the Christian faith and especially to the kingdom of Syria; thus it was reckoned that they would be so incensed against them that each would drive them from his dominion.')

So the translator, far from sparing the blushes of the Templars, goes beyond William in seeking to blacken their reputation, and by the sound of it he would have approved of their being expelled from their considerable holdings in the West. This tendency to heighten William's hostility is also discernable in the chapter (12:7) describing the foundation of the Order.[19] Evidently the climate of opinion in at least some circles in early thirteenth-century France was sufficiently sceptical about the Templar activities for such tales to find a ready audience.

Most of the manuscripts not utilized in establishing the text edited above fall into one of two groups. On the one hand there are eight extant manuscripts copied in Acre in the second half of the thirteenth century (F49, F50, F69, F70, F71, F72, F73, F78);[20] with them should be associated three rather later manuscripts which show a close textual relationship to them (F57, F74, F77), plus two fifteenth-century manuscripts (F67, F68) that can be proved to have been derived directly or indirectly from one of the Acre manuscripts (F69). Taken together these manuscripts may be thought of as representing an Acre tradition. On the other hand there is a much

19 Edbury, 'The Old French William of Tyre', pp. 157–8.

20 F71 lacks WT 20.30.

larger group of manuscripts which represent a Western tradition, and which both in the chapter discussed here and elsewhere in the text have a substantial number of features in common.[21] These manuscripts are listed in the Appendix, but it should be noted that, at least so far as their version of this chapter is concerned, within this group F60, F61, F62 and F65 form a recognizable sub-group, as do F53, F58 and F64; and F37 and F42. Of this second group, only F06 was produced in the Latin East – not in Acre but apparently in Antioch.[22] There are only two manuscripts containing William of Tyre book 20 chapter 30 that do not belong in either of these two principal categories: F31 and F35 are very similar to each other and show a marked textual affinity with F03.

In seeing how the readings in these various manuscripts differ from the original translation, it is important to avoid the trap of assigning significance to what may after all be no more than copyists' mistakes. Any additional information must indicate a deliberate decision on the part of a copyist or redactor to alter what was in the text in front of him, and any other alterations to the wording of the text may do so, but omissions are quite possibly the result of scribal error. So if a line, phrase or word has dropped out of the text, there can be no assumption that someone has intended to alter the meaning. In this chapter a number of copyists were unclear about the number of envoys, with the result that they are inconsistent as to whether to the verbs in sentences 3–6 should be singular or plural. Some changes are self-evidently erroneous: F03 describes Bishop Ralph of Bethlehem as the king's 'chevalier' rather than his 'chancelier' (sentence 19); F31 and F35 have the Templars attacking from a 'gué' (ford or ditch) rather than from a 'guet' or 'agait' (ambush), and there is similarly no significance in the fact that the fifteenth-century F37 and F42 both use the word 'embuchement' here (sentence 5); F60, F61, F62, and F65 have the king calling together his barons and requiring them to give him a 'gift' ('un don') instead of 'counsel' ('conseill') (sentence 8). In sentence 12 Gautier del Mesnil, the Templar held responsible for the murder, is described, among other things, as 'jangleus' ('deceitful'), but one fifteenth-century manuscript of French provenance (F65) turns him into 'ung anglois', and we are left to ponder whether this was a simple slip or whether a scribe had his own agenda.

Other alterations introduced into the manuscript do not change the meaning significantly but may well have been introduced for a purpose. The Acre manuscripts and those associated with them at this point in the text divide into two distinct groups: F50, F57, F73, F74, F77 and F49, F67, F58, F69, F70, F72, F78.[23] The first of these groups all read 'roiaume (or a variant spelling) de Jerusalem' for 'reaume

21 For example, in 20.30 they read 'chose ne' for 'chose et' (sentence 1), 'en ot' for 'ot' (sentence 7), 'enjointe lor penitances' (or similar) (sentence 13), 'dont il' for 'de qu'il' (sentence 14), 'autres for 'freres' (sentence 15); and omit 'leur' (sentence 8), 'meismes' (sentence 14), 'tot lié' (sentence 16), and 'trop' (sentence 20).

22 Folda, *Crusader Art*, pp. 218, 347–50.

23 There appears to have been considerable hybridization in the transmission of the Acre manuscripts with the result that the patterns of shared characteristics may last only for a short stretch. The second of these groups all merge WT 21 chapters 2 and 3. At 12:7 F57, F70, F72, F73 and F77 form a discrete group. See Edbury, 'The Old French William of Tyre'pp. 159–60.

de Surie' in sentences 17 and 18. Presumably a scribe working in the Latin East wanted to keep the correct title of the kingdom alive. The second group, on the other hand, retains 'Surie' but has the king arrest the Templar culprit at Caesarea instead of Sidon (sentence 15). It is possible that an Acre scribe would have had access to a separate tradition that associated the arrest with Caesarea, but on balance unlikely. Some of the manuscripts in this same group (F49, F67, F68, F69, F78) make another alteration which again might possibly indicate some additional knowledge. At sentence 12, where all the other manuscripts, following William's Latin text, inform us that Gautier del Mesnil had only one eye, these report instead that he 'en avoit .iii. aveuc lui qui avoit ceste deleauté faite'.[24] The manuscripts disagree as to whether the numeral should be '.iii.' (F49, F69) or '.iiii.' (F67, F68, F78), and it is only the two fifteenth-century copies (F67, F68) that, as the sense now demands, change the second 'avoit' to 'avoient'. In view of the earlier statement at sentence 5, that the author did not know how many Templars took part, this piece of information should probably be rejected, but this alteration and the others mentioned in this paragraph do illustrate the point that copyists did embellish what they found, and their changes may shed light on the intellectual climate in which they worked.

None of these manuscripts makes any attempt to tone down the hostility towards the Templars that this chapter demonstrates. It has already been observed that the translator, if anything, heightened William's denigration of the Order, and some redactors seem to have taken an even more strident line. The translator wrote that Walter and his associates killed the envoy 'par le consentement des autres Templiers', a close rendering of William's 'de conscientia tamen fratrum'.[25] Some of the manuscripts, however, change this to imply a more proactive complicity in the deed: thus for both F57 and the closely related group, F60, F61, F62 and F65, they had acted 'par le conseil' of the other Templars; while F34, F36, F43, F45, F51 have 'par le commandement' of the others. One fifteenth-century manuscript (F44) goes further: Walter acted 'par le commandement du maistre du Temple son seigneur et des autres Templiers'. Two closely related manuscripts which have been ascribed to a Parisian *atelier* and dated to the late 1290s, F31 and F35,[26] appear to make Odo of St Amand's rejoinder to the envoys even more peremptory: where most of the others say that he forbad 'au roi et as autres de par Dieu et de part l'apostoile que ne meissent main ou frere ne en leur choses' these manuscripts read: 'le roi ... qu'il ne mesfait ne meist main as freres ne a lor choses' (sentence 13). These same two manuscripts also record that the royal officers arrested more Templars at Sidon than just Gautier del Mesnil (sentence 16), but what is particularly striking about them is the rubric that they alone of all the copies share. The chapter is headed: 'La grant desloiauté que li templier fisent dont Diex les doit hair et touz li siecles'.

Whereas it is impossible to know when this particular rubric was composed, its presence in two manuscripts copied in Paris some ten years before the arrest of the Templars in 1307 is suggestive. The Order had always had its detractors, but the

24 Following the orthography to be found in F49.

25 WT, p. 953 lines 29–30.

26 J. Folda, *Crusader Manuscript Illumination at Saint-Jean d'Acre, 1275–1291* (Princeton, 1976), pp. 205, 208, cf pp. 146–51.

hardening of the hostile attitudes that such words would seem to imply, coupled with the more general tendency in the textual tradition to heighten rather than lessen the criticism of the Templars, must have had some influence in shaping the body of opinion that was prepared to believe the charges against the Order. Of the extant manuscripts of the French translation of William of Tyre, around a third can be ascribed to northern France and dated to somewhere between the 1260s and 1307, and although there is no way of knowing how widely read these stories of Templar skulduggery would have been, the wealthy and therefore, presumably, influential owners of these manuscripts could well have had a part, directly or indirectly, in hounding the Order out of existence.

Appendix: The Manuscripts

In his handlist, Folda, following the lead of the nineeenth-century scholar Paul Riant, listed the manuscripts according to whether they had a continuation and, if so, where it ended.[27] In his list F01–F06 have no continuation; F30–F51 end in or before 1232; F52–F66 contain the so-called 'Rothelin' continuation ending in 1261; and F67–78 contain the 'Acre' or 'Noailles' continuation for the period beyond 1232.[28]

I Manuscripts Used here to Establish the Text of 20.30

F02 Paris, BN, ms. fr. 2627, fol. 152v (N. France: 15th century)
F03 Paris, BN, ms. fr. 2632, fols 168v–169r (Latin East or France: first half of 13th century)
F04 Paris, BN, ms. fr. 2826, fol. 114v (Latin East or France: first half of 13th century)
F05 Paris, BN, ms. fr. 9081 fols 279r–280r (Paris: ca. 1245–48)
F38 London, BL, Henry Yates Thompson ms. 12, fol. 152r–v (England: mid 13th century)
F41 Paris, BN, ms. fr. 67, fols 258v–259r (N. France: second half of 13th century)
F52 Baltimore, Walters Art Gallery, ms. 142, fols 209v–210r (Paris: ca. 1300 and ca. 1340)

II The Acre Manuscripts and those Associated with them

F49 Paris, BN, ms. fr. 9085, fols 278v–279v (Acre: ca. 1277–80)
F50 Paris, BN, ms. fr. 9086, fols 317v–318v (Acre: ca. 1255–60) (= RHC Occid., 2, ms. C)
F57 Paris, BN, ms. fr. 2634, fol. 274r–v (Ile de France: first quarter of 14th century)

27 Folda, 'Manuscripts of the *History of Outremer*'; P. Riant, 'Inventaire sommaire des manuscripts de *l'Eracles*', *Archives de l'Orient latin* 1 (1881), 247–52.

28 F7–F15 are manuscript fragments; F16–F29 are not manuscripts of William of Tyre but of the *Chronique d'Ernoul et de Bernard le Trésorier* or of the text known as the *Estoires d'Outremer et de la naissance Saladin*. Four other items in Folda's list have been disregarded: F56 is an abbreviated version of the French William of Tyre; F59 is an eighteenth-century copy of F60; F75 is an eighteenth-century copy of F77, and F76 is an eighteenth-century copy of the continuation as published by the Maurists in 1729.

(= RHC Occid., 2, ms. A)

F67 Amiens, Bibliothèque Municipale, ms. 483, fol. 179v (Flanders: mid 15th century)

F68 Bern, Bürgerbibliothek, ms. 25, fols 359r–360r (N. France: first half of 15th century)

F69 Boulogne-sur-Mer, Bibliothèque Municipale, ms. 142, fols 248r–249r (Acre: ca. 1287)

F70 Florence, Biblioteca Medicea-Laurenziana, ms. Plu. LXI. 10, fol. 245r–v (Acre: ca. 1290, and Italy: first half of 14th century)

F72 Lyon, Bibliothèque de la Ville, ms. 828, fol. 253r–v (Acre: ca.1280) (= RHC Occid., 2, ms. D)

F73 Paris, BN, ms. fr. 2628, fols 217v–218v (Acre: late 1250s/early 1260s and late 1270s) (= RHC Occid., 2, ms B)

F74 Paris, BN, ms. fr. 2631, fols 323v–324r (Lombardy: ca. 1291–95)

F77 Paris, BN, ms. fr. 9082, fols 240r–241r (Rome: 1295) (= RHC Occid., 2, ms. G)

F78 Paris, BN, ms. fr. 9084, fols 289r–290r (Acre: ca. 1286)

III The Western Tradition

F06 Rome, Biblioteca Apostolica Vaticana, ms. Pal. lat. 1963m fol. 231r–v (Antioch: ca. 1260–68)

F32 Bern, Bürgerbibliothek, ms. 112, fol. 180r–v (N. France: ca. 1270)

F33 Bern, Bürgerbibliothek, ms. 163, fol. 208v–9r (N. France: third quarter of 13th century)

F34 Besançon, Bibliothèque Municipale, ms. 856, fols 187v–188r (N. France: ca. 1300)

F36 Geneva, Bibliothèque Publique et Universitaire, ms. 85, (Artois: third quarter of 15th century)

F37 London, BL, Royal ms. 15. E. I, fols 259v–260r (Flanders: late 15th century)

F39 Paris, Bibliothèque de l'Arsenal, ms. 5220, pages 495–6 (N. France: 3rd quarter of 13th century)

F40 Paris, Bibliothèque du Ministère des Affaires Etrangères, Memoires et Documents 230*bis*, fol. 156v (S. France: third quarter of 13th century)

F42 Paris, BN, ms. fr. 68, fols 338v–339r (Flanders: ca. 1450)

F43 Paris, BN, ms. fr. 779, fols 215v–216r (N. France: ca. 1275)

F44 Paris, BN, ms. fr. 2629, fol. 268r–v (Flanders: ca. 1460)

F45 Paris, BN, ms. fr. 2630, fol. 197v–198r (N. France: ca. 1250–75)

F46 Paris, BN, ms. fr. 2754, fols 114v–115v (N. France: ca. 1300)

F47 Paris, BN, ms. fr. 2824, fols 144v–145r (N. France: ca. 1300)

F48 Paris, BN, ms. fr. 2827, fol. 189r–v (N. France: ca. 1250–75)

F51 Paris, BN, ms. fr. 24208, fol. 185r–v (N. France: ca. 1250–75)

F53 Brussels, Bibliothèque Royale, ms. 9045, fols 248v–249v (Flanders, ca. 1460)

F54 Brussels, Bibliothèque Royale, ms. 9492–3, fol. 289r–v (Paris: ca. 1291–95)

F55 Lyon, Bibliothèque de la Ville, ms. Palais des Arts 29, fol. 202r–v (Paris: ca. 1295–96) (= RHC Occid., 2, ms. E)

F58 Paris, BN, ms. fr. 2825, fols 226v–227r (Paris: early 14th century) (= RHC Occid., 2, ms. F)

F60 Paris, BN, ms. fr. 9083, fols 222v–223r (Ile de France: second quarter of 14th century) (= RHC Occid., 2, ms. H)

F61 Paris, BN, ms. fr. 22495, fols 200v–201r (Paris: 1337) (= RHC Occid., 2, ms. I)

F62 Paris, BN, ms. fr. 22496–7, vol. 2, fol. 76r–v (Paris: ca. 1350)

F64 Rome, Biblioteca Apostolica Vaticana, ms. Reg. Suec. lat. 737, fol. 256r–v

(Paris: early 14th century)
F65 Turin, Biblioteca Nazionale, ms. L I. 5, fols 358r–359r (N. France: 15th century)

IV Manuscripts that Preserve a Textual Affinity with F03

F31 Baltimore, Walters Art Gallery, ms. 137, fols 250v–251r (Paris: ca. 1295–1300)
F35 Epinal, Bibliothèque Municipale, ms. 45, fols 190v–191r (Paris: ca. 1295–1300)

Four manuscripts lack 20.30: Cambridge, Sidney Sussex College, ms. 93 (England, late 13th century) (F01); Arras, Bibliothèque Municipale, ms. 651 (N. France: early 14th century) (F30); Paris, BN, ms. fr. 24209 (Ile de France: third quarter of 14th century) (= *RHC Occid.*, 2, ms K) (F63); St Petersburg, National Library of Russia / Российская Национальная Библиотека (formerly M.E. Saltykov–Schchedrin State Public Library), ms. fr. fol. v. IV.5, (Acre: ca. 1280) (F71). I have not seen the Turin, Biblioteca Nazionale, ms. L. II. 17 (Ile de France: first quarter of 14th century) (F66).

Chapter 4

Caring for the Sick or Dying for the Cross? The Granting of Crusade Indulgences to the Hospitallers

Judith Bronstein

In February 1217, following requests from the Order, Pope Honorius III granted crusade indulgences to Hospitaller brothers and their servants who devoted their lives to defend and serve the Holy Land.[1] This is a surprising privilege and one of the few pieces of evidence I have found of the Order making a request to have their service considered equal to the taking of the Cross. As Anthony Luttrell has already explained in his important article on the definitions of the military orders, Hospitaller brothers were not crusaders: 'the cross on the brethren's mantle was worn in the case of the Hospital in memory of Christ's crucifixion and it was not the crusading cross of the *crucesignatus* ... their role was one of perpetual, continuous resistance to the infidel and it did not depend upon occasional and limited papal declarations of a crusade'.[2] What then induced the Hospitallers, as members of a religious order, to ask for a crusade indulgence? How did they perceive their aims and their spiritual reward? Could requests for crusade indulgences imply a change in their perception?

The Hospital of St John was established some time before 1071 as a hospice for pilgrims coming to Jerusalem. Because the hospice was located near the Benedictine monastery of St Mary of the Latins, its members adopted an almost religious life as Benedictine lay brothers and *conversi*. After 1099 the Benedictine attachment

1 *Cartulaire général de l'Ordre des Hospitaliers de Saint-Jean de Jérusalem, 1100-1310*, ed. J. Delaville le Roulx, 4 vols (Paris, 1894–1906), vol. 2 (hereafter *Cart. Hosp.*), no. 1550: *vestris piis postulationibus inclinati, auctoritate vobis presentium indulgemus ut fratres et servientes domus vestre, in defensione ac servitio Terre Sancte fideliter in vera penitentia commorantes, illam peccatorum suorum veniam consequantur que crucesignatis a sede apostolica est indulta*. This topic has been dealt with briefly by A. Forey, 'Recruitment to the Military Orders, Twelfth to mid-Fourteenth Centuries', *Viator: Medieval and Renaissance Studies*, 17 (1986), 168; A. Luttrell, 'Templari e Ospitalieri in Italia', in Luttrell, *The Hospitallers of Rhodes and their Mediterranean World* (Aldershot, 1992), article I, pp. 2–3; 'Gli Ospitalieri e l'eredità dei Templari: 1305–1378', ibid., article III, p. 68.

2 A. Luttrell, 'The Military Orders. Some Definitions', in *Militia Sancti Sepulcri. Idea e Instituzioni*, ed. K. Elm and C. Damiano Fonseca (Città del Vaticano, 1998), p. 86.

was dissolved and the Hospital, now under the influence of the canons of the Holy Sepulchre, adopted some aspects of the Augustinian rule, which was more suitable for its charitable activities.[3] The aim of the Order, as stated in *Pie postulatio voluntatis* of Pope Paschal II, of 1113, was the support of pilgrims and care for the poor.[4] Those who wished to fulfil these aims joined a community bound together by a religious way of life. This combination of service to the poor and a religious life was the key to their salvation. This was clearly expressed in the first clause of the rule of Raymond du Puy: 'all the brethren, engaging in the service of the poor, should keep the three things with the aid of God, which they had promised to God: that is to say, chastity and obedience ... and to live without property of their own: because God will require these three things of them at the Last Judgment'.[5] The spiritual benefits of serving the poor were reiterated in the statutes of the master, Roger des Moulins. The statutes call upon the commanders of the Order's houses to serve the sick, saying that 'by these good deeds they may deserve to have their rewards in the glories of heaven'.[6] These ideals were not alien to twelfth-century spirituality; they were influenced by the canonical movement which saw its vocation in service to the poor.[7]

Charters of affiliation give the impression that to contemporaries it was clear that joining a military order meant adopting a religious way of life. Counts William and Bertrand of Forcalquier, who committed themselves as *confratres* to the Hospital of Manosque in 1168, promised that if they decided in the future to take up a religious life they would do so only in the Hospital.[8] Peter Garsin, who entered the priory of St Gilles as a *confrater* in 1146, made an agreement whereby, should he decide to relinquish the secular life, the brothers would be obliged to accept him into the Order. Peter of Aguda, who became a *confrater* of the Templar house of Barbera in Catalonia in 1192, made a similar agreement with this house.[9] Peter of Huesca's

---

3 A. Luttrell, 'The Earliest Hospitallers', in B. Kedar, J. Riley-Smith and R. Hiestand (eds), *Montjoie: Studies in Crusade History in Honour of Hans Eberhard Mayer* (Aldershot, 1997), pp. 38–40; J. Riley-Smith, *The Knights of St John in Jerusalem and Cyprus, c. 1050–1310* (London, 1967), pp. 32–52. On the legal problem of definition of the military orders by canon lawyers see J. Brundage, 'Crusades, Clerics and Violence: Reflections on a Canonical Theme', in M. Bull and N. Housley (eds), *The Experience of Crusading*. vol. 1. *Western Approaches* (Cambridge, 2003), p. 153.

4 *Cart. Hosp.*, no. 30: *ad sustentandas peregrinorum et pauperum necessitates.*

5 *Cart. Hosp.*, no. 70. Rule of Raymond of Puy. English translation from *The Rule, Statutes and Customs of the Hospitallers, 1099–1310*, ed. E.J. King (London, 1934), p. 20.

6 *Cart. Hosp.*, no. 627.

7 J.W. Brodman, *Charity and Welfare. Hospitals and the Poor in Medieval Catalonia* (Philadelphia, 1998), pp. 2–5; J.W. Brodman, 'Rule and Identity: the Case of the Military Orders', *The Catholic Historical Review* 88 (2001), pp. 395–6; G. Constable, *The Reformation of the Twelfth Century* (Cambridge, 1996), pp. 148–50, 236–40.

8 *Cartulaire du Prieuré de Saint Gilles de l'Hôpital de Saint Jean de Jérusalem (1129–1210)*, ed. D. Le Blevec and A. Venturini (Paris, 1997), no. 335. For the depiction of the military orders' monastic roles in medieval literature see H. Nicholson, *Love, War and the Grail* (Leiden, Boston and Cologne, 2001), pp. 35–75.

9 *Cartulaire du Prieuré de Saint Gilles*, no. 266; *Collecció diplomàtica de la casa del Temple de Barberà (945–1212)*, ed. J.M. Sans i Travé (Barcelona, 1997), no. 164: *in tali vero pacto ut qualicumque hora in domum vestra intrare voluero et secularem vitam relinquere,*

charter of affiliation to the Templar commandery of Huesca in Aragon, of July 1192, states that Peter 'has relinquished this world and all its pomposity, for the sake of heaven'.[10]

Alan Forey has shown the difficulties arising in the attempt to identify the real motives that caused men to join military orders. Motives such as family pressure or economic reasons are not stated in the affiliation charters.[11] In most cases these charters only note spiritual concerns, but it is on them that I would like to focus. The main spiritual reason for entering military orders is the salvation of the soul. In some cases the formula *pro salute anime* is combined with other formulas, such as fear of the torments of hell and the wish to enjoy the pleasures of paradise.[12] Charters of affiliation to the Hospital show the link between care for the poor and the redemption of the soul. Count Peter of Asturias expressed his hope that by entering the Order, which was established for the service of Christ's poor, and granting a generous entry fee, he would save his soul and would come to heavenly Jerusalem.[13] Peter Garsin, who entered St Gilles in 1146, gave his body and soul and all he owned in the village of Scieure-Basse, to the Order and the poor of the Hospital.[14]

It is significant that the militarization of the Order did not break this link between service to the poor and spiritual reward. The Order's additional role of fighting the infidels and defending the crusader states is hardly ever mentioned in charters of affiliation.[15] If the Peter of Mirmanda mentioned in the sources is the same man, he joined the commandery of Alleyras (part of Le Puy en Velay) in 1163 and was sent to the East, where he most probably served and fought as a brother-knight. After Hattin he held commanding posts, which could be occupied only by brothers with military experience: he was the castellan of Crac des Chevaliers in 1193 and the grand commander of the Order, the master's second-in-command, in 1202. Peter's expected career in the Order would have been military – defence of the Christians in

me in societate sua benigne recipient. The ideal of entrance into a religious community is common to all military orders – the approval of Calatrava by the General Chapter of Citeaux of 1186 refers to the brothers who were *a militia mundi ad Christi militiam conversi.* See *Bullarium Ordinis Militiae de Calatrava*, ed. I.J. Ortega y Cotes (Madrid, 1761, reprint Barcelona, 1981), no. XXII, pp. 20–1. The Templars chose Holy Orders. See *The Rule of the Templars*, ed. J. Upton-Ward (Woodbridge, 1992), clause 2.

10 *Cartulario del Temple de Huesca*, eds A. Gargallo Moya, T. Iranzo Muñio and J. Sánchez Usón (Zaragoza, 1985), no. 123: *abrenuncians huic mundo et omnibus pompis eius et ob terrenis cupiens adipisci celestia.*

11 Forey, 'Recruitment to the Military Orders', pp. 162–71.

12 *Cartulario del Temple de Huesca*, nos. 87, 170.

13 *Libro de privilegios de la Orden de San Juan de Jerusalén en Castilla y León*, ed. C. de Ayala Martínez (Madrid, 1995), no. 111.

14 *Cartulaire du Prieuré de Saint-Gilles*, no. 266.

15 It is important to emphasize, however, that many of the brothers who joined European commanderies never went to the East, and for those who did it is extremely difficult to track down their affiliation charter. See J. Bronstein, 'The Mobilization of Hospitaller Manpower from Europe to the Holy Land in the Thirteenth Century', in J. Burgtorf and H. Nicholson (eds), *International Mobility in the Military Orders (Twelfth to Fifteenth Centuries): Travelling on Christ's Business* (Cardiff, 2006), pp. 25–7.

the East – but this is not expressed in his charter of affiliation, which only states his commitment to the poor of the Hospital of Jerusalem.[16]

For the Order of the Hospital in the twelfth and thirteenth centuries, charters of affiliation are the only surviving evidence in which the brothers' motivations are expressed. Yet these charters have their flaws: they state the official line of the Order and are usually written according to a repetitive formula. These charters of affiliation express a perception and acceptance by members of the Order of a doctrine by which salvation can only be achieved by taking permanent vows within a religious community devoted to the service of the poor. This ideal of salvation due to service in a religious community seems to have encompassed other activities in which the Order was involved, mainly military activity for the defence of Christendom.[17] But were these ideals indeed fully understood by all the members of the Order? A number of papal privileges granting crusader indulgences may hint otherwise.

Crusader indulgences were first given by Pope Lucius III in December 1184. In recognition of the Order's great efforts in preserving the Holy Land and its charitable work, he granted the Hospitallers and their *familia* a general indulgence similar to the one given to the faithful who came to assist the Holy Land.[18] This privilege symbolizes the conclusion of the internal dispute over the nature of the Order and the changing attitude of the papacy to its militarization.[19] By the 1180s the Order's

---

16 On Peter of Mirmanda see J. Bronstein, *The Hospitallers and the Holy Land. Financing the Latin East, 1187–1274* (Woodbridge, 2005), pp. 138, 151. Damien Carraz has shown that the military character of the order of the Temple was expressed in a number of charters of affiliation to the Order from Provence; see D. Carraz, *L'Órdre du Temple dans la Basse Vallée du Rhône (1124–1312). Ordres militaires, croisades et sociétés méridionales* (Lyon, 2005), pp. 180–1. This link can also be seen in some charters of donation: in July 1156, for example, William of Ponts and his wife Stephany, who were in their way to Jerusalem, gave, for the remission of their sins, all they had in the town of Balaguer to Peter of Rovira, master of the Temple in Provence and Spain, and to the knights Templars *qui pro redemptione et salute Ecclesie laborare et mori proposuerunt*. See *Collecció diplomàtica de la Casa del Temple de Gardeny (1070–1200)*, ed. R. Sarobe I Huesca (Barcelona, 1998), vol. 12, no. 69.

17 In the order of the Temple, which had been established from the outset as a military order, the spiritual reward was clearly linked with fighting for the Cross. This was expressed in 1139 by Innocent II in *Omne datum optimum*: 'as you are known by name to be knights of the Temple, you have been established by the Lord as defenders of Christ … we enjoin both you and those serving you for the remission of sins, by the authority of God and Blessed Peter the Prince of the Apostles, to labor intrepidly, calling upon the name of Christ, to protect the Catholic Church and, by fighting the enemies of the cross, to rid those pagans from their faith': R. Hiestand, *Papsturkunden für Templer und Johanniter*, Vorarbeiten zum Oriens Pontificius, vol. 1, *Abhandlungen der Akademie der Wissenschaften in Göttingen*, 77, (Göttingen, 1972), pp. 205–6; English translation from J. and L. Riley-Smith, *The Crusades. Idea and Reality, 1095–1274* (London, 1981), p. 93. On *Omne datum optimum* see M. Barber, *The New Knighthood. A History of the Order of the Temple* (Cambridge, 1994), pp. 54–60.

18 *Cart. Hosp.*, no. 712. The indulgence was given to the Order which *ad conservationem terre Hierosolimitane, tam operibus pietatis, que incessabiliter exercetis, quam etiam in laboribus aliis, quos eundo et redeundo suscipitis, majora noscimini gravamina sustinere.*

19 On the Order's militarization see Riley-Smith, *The Knights of St John*, pp. 52–4; R. Hiestand, 'Die Anfänge der Johanniter', in J. Fleckenstein and M. Hellmann (eds), *Die*

dual role of caring for the sick and defending the Holy Land was recognized and supported by the papacy. This is clearly expressed in Lucius III's *Cum bona fratribus* of 1182–3, which exempts the Hospitallers from the taxation raised to help subsidize the fortification of castles and villages, in recognition of the Order's devotion to the defence of the Holy Land as well as to charitable activity.[20] The timing of the bull is not accidental. The Order's military power was necessary to contain onslaughts by Saladin, who at this time was ravaging Christian territories on all fronts.[21] The deteriorating situation of the Holy Land resulted in an embassy to the West, headed by the patriarch of Jerusalem and the masters of the Hospitallers and the Templars, to seek the assistance of European leaders and to promote a new crusade.[22] By September 1184 they met the pope in Verona and, probably as a result of his meeting with the Hospitaller master Roger of Moulins, Lucius III issued a great number of bulls aimed at protecting the Order's men, property and privileges.[23] In August 1185 he reconfirmed Raymond de Puy's rule of 1153: the pope recognized the Hospital as an Augustinian order dedicated to the care of the sick, for the sake of which it should maintain four physicians and four surgeons, as well as provide the sick with food and all other necessities. This bull follows the traditional line of the papacy and was given to the Hospitallers in recognition of their everyday labour for the comfort of the poor and the sick.[24] And yet the pressing situation of the Holy Land reported by the embassy, and also by King Baldwin IV of Jerusalem in a letter that reached

---

geistlichen Ritterorden (Sigmaringen, 1980), pp. 64–78; A. Forey, 'The Militarisation of the Hospital of St John', in Forey, *Military Orders and the Crusades* (Aldershot, 1994), article 9, pp. 75–89; L. García-Guijarro Ramos, 'La militarización de la Orden del Hospital: líneas para un debate', *Ordens Militares: guerra, religião, poder e cultura-Actas do III Encontro sobre Ordens Militares*, ed. I.C. Ferreira Fernandes (Palmela, 1999), vol. 2, pp. 293–302. On the attitude of the papacy to the Order's militarization see Bronstein, *The Hospitallers and the Holy Land*, pp. 103–4; Riley-Smith, *The Knights of St John*, pp. 76–7.

20 *Cart. Hosp.*, no. 628. In the previous year, in April 1183, Lucius confirmed the privileges of the Templars and renewed *Omne datum optimum*, which, as shown above (note 17), specified that the remission of their sins would result from the performance of their military duties: Patrologia Latina, 201, cols. 1195–1196.

21 J. Richard, *The Crusades, c.1071–c.1291*, trans. J. Birrell (Cambridge, 1999), pp. 195–8.

22 On the embassy see J. Phillips, *Defenders of the Holy Land. Relations between the Latin East and the West, 1119–1187* (Oxford, 1996), pp. 251–66.

23 *Cart. Hosp.*, nos. 609, 612, 629, 630–42, 654–9, 666–75, 679–82, 686–9, 691–4, 697–702, 705–11, 713, 715, 724–5, 727–9, 731–40, 743–53, 756, 759, 761. Among these many bulls were *Quam amabilis Dei*, which urged the clergy to preach in favour of the Order, and *Querelam gravem recepimus*, which granted the Order the right to preach in parochial churches. This also shows the curia's active support for the Order's preaching. Rudolf Hiestand estimated that between December 1184 and January 1185 the papal chancery issued more than 100 bulls in response to the master's requests: see R. Hiestand, 'Some Reflections on the Impact of the Papacy on the Crusader States and the Military Orders in the Twelfth and Thirteenth Centuries', in Z. Hunyadi and J. Laszlovzky (eds), *The Crusades and the Military Orders. Expanding the Frontiers of Medieval Latin Christianity* (Budapest, 2001), p. 15.

24 *Cart. Hosp.*, no. 690, 723, 726, 741, 762; Patrologia Latina, 201, no. 240. On this bull see also Riley-Smith, *The Knights of St John*, pp. 48, 50.

the curia at the time of the embassy's presence there –describing, among other things, the devastation by Saladin's forces of the surroundings of the Hospitaller castle of Belvoir[25] – also demanded Lucius's support for the Order's military roles. In recognition of the dangers to which the Hospitaller brothers and their associates were exposed, the pope granted them a crusade indulgence, similar to the one given to those going to the aid of the Holy Land.[26]

Honorius III was the next pope to grant a crusade indulgence to the Hospitallers. It was granted, following the Order's requests, to brothers and servants who defend and serve the Holy Land and lead a life of real penitence.[27] In February 1217, the date this grant was given, the Christian world was about to set out on a new crusade. This was to conclude years of preparation, organization and preaching, through which the papacy, especially since the pontificate of Innocent III, strove to create a highly emotional crusader atmosphere. At the heart of the intensive preaching stood the taking of the Cross as the only way to salvation.[28] The Hospitallers made an important contribution to the Fifth Crusade, supplying men, money and war machines, and suffering grave losses, while at the same time playing an important role in the defence of the Latin Kingdom.[29] The charged atmosphere on the eve of the crusade seems to have had an effect on the Hospitallers, who specifically asked the pope for a crusade indulgence. Honorius complied, praising their charitable activities and also their determination in defending the Christian name in Outremer. With this service to God, wrote Honorius, the Hospitallers' hearts were fervently motivated.[30]

While Lucius' and Honorius' indulgences were granted both to Hospitaller brothers and to their associates, Gregory IX's indulgence of December 1229 did not mention the brothers. It refers in general terms to those who devote themselves to the service of the Order, fight the Saracens in Outremer, and live as true penitents.[31] It is possible that this privilege, in response to persistent requests from the Hospitallers,

25 Ralph of Diceto, 'Ymagines Historiarum', *Opera*, ed. W. Stubbs, (London, 1876) Rolls Series (hereafter RS) 68, pp. 25–6.

26 *Cart. Hosp.*, no. 712: *Ea propter, dilecti in Domino filii, labores et pericula vestra benignius intuentes, vobis et familie vestre, ea qua fungimur auctoritate, concedimus ut illius indulgentie generalis, qua ceteris fidelibus pro subventione illius terre providimus, speciali participatione gaudentes, sicut estis laborum participes, ita etiam sitis in ipsius indulgentie perceptione consortes.*

27 *Cart. Hosp.*, no. 1550 : *vestris piis postulationibus inclinati, auctoritate vobis presentium indulgemus ut fratres et servientes domus vestre, in defensione ac servitio Terre Sancte fideliter in vera penitentia commorantes, illam peccatorum suorum veniam consequantur que crucesignatis a sede apostolica est indulta.*

28 J.M. Powell, *Anatomy of a Crusade, 1213–1221* (Philadelphia, 1986), pp. 20, 51–6; J. Riley-Smith, *The Crusades. A Short History* (London and New Haven, 1987), pp. 142–3; P. Cole, *The Preaching of the Crusades to the Holy Land, 1095–1270* (Cambridge, Mass., 1991), pp. 98–145.

29 Bronstein, *The Hospitallers and the Holy Land*, pp. 19–20.

30 *Cart. Hosp.*, no. 1550.

31 To those who *se domus vestre servitio devoverunt, nos…ut tales, in ultramarines partibus contra Sarracenos fideliter in vera penitentia existentes, illam consequantur suorum veniam peccatorum que crucesignatis a sede apostolica est indulta*: *Cart. Hosp.*, no. 1950.

was given to their secular knights, the *milites ad terminum*, who served in the Order for a fixed term.[32] The circumstances that led to the granting of this privilege were probably connected with the return of Frederick II to Europe in May 1229. Although the Emperor had previously signed a ten-year truce with Egypt, this was not recognized by the papacy or the Frankish leaders in the East. They feared the truce would not hold and that the massive departure of crusaders would result in a severe shortage of manpower. To prepare for renewed hostilities they hired mercenaries, and probably tried to persuade crusaders to remain by rewarding them with extraordinary privileges, such as plenary indulgences to those who would serve with the Hospitallers for a period of time.[33]

Granting of crusade indulgences to those who assisted the orders in their military activities was not exceptional and was probably a common way to attract men to this service. Crusade indulgences were granted to those who would help defend the castles of the Spanish military orders. In 1221, for example, an indulgence was granted by Honorius III to those who would help defend the castles of Calatrava. This privilege was extended by Gregory IX in 1240 to include those who would fight under the standard of that order.[34] In 1245 Innocent IV granted those taking the Cross to help the Teutonic Knights in Prussia a plenary indulgence, like that given to those going to the Holy Land.[35] In 1248 Innocent IV promised crusade indulgence to those associated with the Hospital in Hungary and who would assist in the defence of the kingdom against the Mongols.[36]

Nevertheless, granting crusade indulgences to members of the Hospital is surprising, considering, as we have seen, that the brothers were committed to the

32 On *milites ad terminum* see J. Riley-Smith, *The First Crusaders, 1095–1131* (Cambridge, 1997), pp. 158–60; G. Ligato, 'Fra Ordini Cavallereschi e crociata: "milites ad terminum" e "confraternitates" armate', *'Militia Christi' e Crociata nei secoli XI–XIII. Atti della undecima Settimana internazionale di studio Mendola*, 28 agosto–1 settembre 1989 (Milan, 1992), pp. 645–97.

33 For a letter sent by the patriarch of Jerusalem to the pope describing the events which preceded Frederick's departure see Matthew Paris, *Chronica Maiora*, ed. H.R. Luard, RS 57 (London, 1877–82), vol. 3, pp. 179–84. See also J. Prawer, *A History of the Latin Kingdom of Jerusalem* (Jerusalem, 1963), vol. 2, pp. 186–97 (in Hebrew); Bronstein, *The Hospitallers and the Holy Land*, p. 111. On mercenaries serving in the Latin East see R.C. Smail, *Crusading Warfare, 1097–1193* (Cambridge, 1956, repr. 1995), pp. 93–4.

34 *Bullarium Ordinis Militiae de Calatrava*, nos. XI, XIV, XXII, pp. 55, 57, 73. See also H. Prutz, *Die Geistlichen Ritterorden* (Berlin, 1908), p. 82; Riley-Smith, *The Crusades. A Short History*, p. 140–1; J.F. O'Callaghan, *Reconquest and Crusade in Medieval Spain* (Philadelphia, 2003), pp. 97–8; C. de Ayala Martínez, *Las órdenes militares hispánicas en la Edad Media (siglos XII–XV)* (Madrid, 2003), pp. 425, 548.

35 *Regesta Pontificum Romanorum*, ed. A. Potthast (Graz, 1875), vol. 2, nos. 11657, 11803. See also A. Ehlers, 'The Crusade of the Teutonic Knights against Lithuania Reconsidered', in A.V. Murray (ed.), *Crusade and Conversion on the Baltic Frontier, 1150–1500* (Aldershot, 2001), pp. 27–30.

36 *Cart. Hosp.*, nos. 2445, 2477; *Les Registres d'Innocent IV*, ed. É. Berger, 4 vols (Paris, 1884–1921), no. 4000. On fears of the Mongols' invasion of Hungary in the 1240s see N. Berend, *At the Gate of Christendom: Jews, Muslims and 'Pagans' in Medieval Hungary, c.1000–c.1300* (Cambridge, 2001), pp. 163–5.

Order for life and their salvation was assured by the fulfilment of their monastic vows and the performance of their duties: care for the sick and the poor. The request and granting of crusade indulgences could hint, however, that with the Hospital's militarization this traditional doctrine was not satisfactory to all the brothers. Those who risked their lives in the defence of the Holy Land and Christendom may have identified more with crusade ideology and its benefits than with a doctrine of salvation through monastic service and care for the poor. It seems that the Hospital was not the only religious order undergoing this change. The Mendicants, who risked their lives preaching the Cross in different crusade theatres, as well as the Teutonic Knights fighting for the Cross in the Holy Land and Prussia, were also granted plenary indulgences during the course of the thirteenth century.[37] The issue of granting crusade indulgences to monastic orders is interesting and intriguing. It remains to be investigated in a broader context, as crusade indulgences seem to have become a major incentive in religious orders involved in crusading activities that carried the possibility of martyrdom, hence raising expectations of the appropriate reward.

37 This issue is far beyond the scope of this paper. For further details on crusade indulgences granted by Gregory IX to Franciscans and Dominicans preaching the Cross see J. Brundage, *Medieval Canon Law and the Crusader* (Madison, 1969), pp. 154–5; M. Purcell, *Papal Crusading Policy: the Chief Instruments of Papal Crusading Policy and Crusade to the Holy Land from the Final Loss of Jerusalem to the Fall of Acre, 1244* (Leiden, 1975), pp. 60–1, 75; C.T. Maier, *Preaching the Crusades. Mendicants Friars and the Cross in the Thirteenth Century* (Cambridge, 1994), pp. 43, 101–2. For granting of crusader indulgences to members of the Teutonic order see, for example, *Tabulae Ordinis Theutonici*, ed. E. Strehlke (Berlin, 1846), no. 539; Riley-Smith, *The Crusades*, pp. 163–5.

Chapter 5

The Dispute between the Hospitallers and the Bishop of Worcester about the Church of Down Ampney An Unpublished Letter of Justice of Pope John XXI (1276)

Peter Herde

The Archive of the Order of St John of Jerusalem in the National Library of Malta at Valletta preserves an original letter of justice (*littera de iustitia*)[1] of Pope John XXI dated Viterbo, 30 September 1276, instructing the bishop of Exeter, the abbot of St Albans and the archdeacon of Wells to provide for the strict observance of the sentences of suspension, interdict and excommunication issued by the prior of Royston against the bishop of Worcester in a dispute with the prior of Provence (Saint-Gilles) and the brethren of the Order of St John of Jerusalem about the church of Down Ampney, south-east of Cirencester in the county of Gloucester. The original is considerably damaged by water, and the right margin has been partially torn off, so that part of the text has to be reconstructed. It was probably this bad state of preservation that prevented Joseph Delaville le Roulx from publishing the letter in his *Cartulaire*. The question how this papal letter came into the central archives of the Order of St John of Jerusalem cannot be answered with certainty; we would expect to find it in the archives of the recipients, that is, the bishop of Exeter, the abbot of St Albans and the archdeacon of Wells, where apparently no traces of it have been discovered.[2] A possible explanation could be that, according to a chancery mark,[3] two originals of the letter were to be made. Thus one original letter may have

1 On papal *littere de iustitia* and *littere de gratia* see Harry Bresslau, *Handbuch der Urkundenlehre für Deutschland und Italien*, vol. 1, 2nd edn (Leipzig, 1912; repr. Berlin, 1958), pp. 80ff.; Italian edition: *Manuale di diplomatica per la Germania e l'Italia,* traduzione di Anna Maria Voci-Roth (Rome, 1998), pp. 78ff.; Peter Herde, *Beiträge zum päpstlichen Kanzlei- und Urkundenwesen im 13. Jahrhundert*, 2nd edn (Kallmünz, 1967), pp. 59ff. and passim; Thomas Frenz, *Papsturkunden des Mittelalters und der Neuzeit,* 2nd edn (Stuttgart, 2000), p. 13 and passim; Italian edition: *I documenti pontifici nel Medioevo e nell'Età Moderna,* (Città del Vaticano, 1989), p. 14 and passim.

2 Professor Jane Sayers informed me that she does not know of any original or copy of the papal letters mentioned below, including the one edited here.

3 See remarks at the end of the edition, below p. 54.

been sent to England and later been lost, like so many other papal letters, and a second one may have been kept by William de Villaret for the record and may have later found its way to Malta, possibly via Provence.

The *narratio* of John XXI's letter states that Pope Clement IV (1265–68), hearing of the great damages that the prior of Provence and the brethren had suffered in persons and property by the enemies of the Cross, the faithless Saracens, wished to support them by granting them the church of Down Ampney in the diocese of Worcester with all its rights and appurtenances, on condition that the Hospitallers held the *ius patronatus*, the advowson,[4] to this church. Should the *rector* (parson) leave or die, or should the church become otherwise vacant, the Hospitallers were allowed to take possession of it with all its rights and appurtenances without seeking the permission of the diocesan bishop or any other person, provided that they appointed a stipendiary vicar for perpetual service in the church, assigning him an appropriate portion (*congrua portio*) of its revenues for his own subsistence and for to support the burdens of the church.[5] This letter of grace has apparently been preserved neither as an original nor as a copy.[6] At the same time, Clement IV, in a letter of justice, had appointed the Augustinian prior of Royston[7] executor of this grant, ordering him, should a vacancy occur, to introduce the prior and brethren or their proctor into the corporeal possession of the church with its rights and appurtenances, according to Clement's letter and defend them, proceeding against contradictors with ecclesiastical censures without the right of appeal. When afterwards, so the *narratio* continues, parson Hugh died and the church thus became vacant, the prior and the brethren holding the advowson to the church had legally taken possession of it with the help of the executor, after first appointing a chaplain and assigning him the *congrua portio* of the revenues. But the bishop of Worcester (Godfrey Giffard) dared to molest the prior and the brethren in their peaceful possession of the church and, after admonishing him to desist from his obstructions (for which the bishop did not adduce any rational reasons), the executor, because of the notoriety of this action, suspended the bishop – without any formal legal action[8] but by virtue of Clement's letter – from executing the pontifical rites and later forbade him to enter the church, and when the bishop's contumacy increased, placed his chapel under the interdict and finally excommunicated him.[9] But Bishop Godfrey Giffard disregarded all these sanctions, continuing to hold services and even bestowing holy orders

4 See Frederick Pollock and Frederick William Maitland, *The History of English Law before the Time of Edward I*, vol. 2, 2nd edn (Cambridge, 1968), pp. 136ff., and R.H. Helmholz, *The Oxford History of the Laws of England*, vol. 1: *The Canon Law and Ecclesiastical Jurisdiction from 597 to the 1640s* (Oxford, 2004), pp. 477ff.

5 On the canonistic background of the *congrua portio* see Herde, *Audientia* (see below, n. 44 of the edition), vol. 1, p. 341, and Helmholz, p. 166.

6 See below, n. 31.

7 See below, n. 38.

8 On proof by notoriety in canon law see Helmholz p. 328. On the standard wording in papal letters of justice concerning notoriety see e.g. Herde, *Audientia*, vol. 2 (see below, n. 44) no. K 235, p. 390.

9 On the sanctions of suspension, excommunication and interdict see Helmholz, pp. 619ff.

and exercising other episcopal functions in prejudice of the prior and the brethren. They therefore asked the pope to confirm the sentences of suspension, interdict and excommuncation issued by the prior of Royston against the bishop of Worcester. John XXI decided to delegate the case, instructing the addressees of the letter, that is, the bishop of Exeter, the abbot of St Albans and the archdeacon of Wells, to provide, at a meeting at Wells, for the strict observance of these sanctions until the bishop of Worcester gave adequate satisfaction. However, should he stubbornly disobey the sentences, provided that they had been correctly issued, the addressees were ordered by the pope to pronounce these sentences publicly and solemnly – with bells ringing and candles alight – on all Sundays and holidays in whatever places they considered appropriate, until the bishop gave adequate satisfaction, or to entrust others to do so, and to make sure that he was shunned by all people, regardless of papal indulgences that might have been granted to him prohibiting his punishment by suspension, interdict or excommunication, or similar indulgences. If all of them were not able to execute this mandate, two of them would be sufficient to do so.[10]

The question why this papal grant was made to the prior of Provence, not to the prior of England, cannot be satisfactorily answered on the basis of the available source material. Probably it was due to the fact that Ferrand de Barras, who was prior of Provence and possibly also Grand Commander of Outremer during the pontificate of Clement IV,[11] and therefore the recipient of the first papal letter of grace, was held in high regard by the pope because of his abilities, receiving, for example, the rare exemption from fulfilling the obligation to visit the Convent of the East.[12] His successor William de Villaret, the addressee of the renewal of the donation by Innocent V,[13] was also close to the popes of his time as well as to Charles I and Charles II of Anjou, kings of Sicily.[14] Furthermore, the grant of the church of Down Ampney was made, as the *narratio* of the papal letters states, in recompense for great damages the prior of Provence had suffered in Outremer.

But it was disputed from the very beginning. Bishop Godfrey Giffard of Worcester considered Clement IV's letter suspect and defective, and various disputes had therefore been raised before various judges.[15] Clearly these defects in Clement's

---

10 See below, n. 44.

11 Delaville le Roulx, *Les hospitaliers* (see below, n. 30), pp. 416f.; Riley-Smith, *The Knights of St John* (below, n. 30), pp. 281ff.

12 Riley-Smith, p. 281. Dr Luttrell also thinks that this may have been the reason for granting him the church of Down Ampney.

13 See below, n. 31.

14 See below, n. 30; Pierre Santoni,'Les deux premiers siècles du prieuré de l'Hôpital de Saint-Jean de Jérusalem', *Des Hospitaliers de Saint-Jean de Jérusalem de Chypre et de Rhodes hier aux Chevaliers de Malte aujourd'hui: Guillaume de Villaret, 1er Recteur du Comtat Venaissin, Grand Maître de l'ordre des Hospitaliers de Saint-Jean de Jérusalem, Chypre 1296*, ed. Centre d'Ètudes Historiques et Archéologiques du Château du Barroux (Paris 1985), p. 162; Andreas Kiesewetter, *Die Anfänge der Regierung Karls II. von Anjou (1278–1295): Das Königreich Neapel, die Grafschaft Provence und der Mittelmeerraum zu Ausgang des 13. Jahrhunderts* (Husum, 1999), pp. 223, 368f., 491, 553.

15 *The Register of Walter Bronescombe* (see below, n. 34), no. 1227, p. 110. I am grateful to Professor Jane Sayers and Drs Helen Nicholson and Anthony Luttrell for valuable

letter were the reason why the Hospitallers had the letter renewed by Innocent V, who expressly states in his new letter of grace that two phrases concerning the *congrua portio* to be assigned to the vicar had been omitted from Clement's letter.[16] Innocent confirmed the letter of his predecessor, notwithstanding the omissions.

But Clement IV's defective letter was obviously not the only cause of the dispute. As we have seen, the grant was made on condition that the Hospitallers were in possession of the advowson to the church of Down Ampney. But in reality this patronage was claimed by King Edward I. In a petition[17] addressed to the king, which does not bear a date but has to be dated 1276/77, Bishop Godfrey Giffard of Worcester stated that Edward, holding the patronage of the church of Down Ampney, was suing the prior and brethren of the Hospital of St John of Jerusalem because they had occupied the church, asserting that they were its true patrons.[18] They and the parishioners, the bishop continues, are nonetheless suing him before the official of Canterbury and his commissary, and he requests a writ to the justices ordering them not to allow the prior and the brethren to harass him while the suit before the king's court is pending; similar writs should be directed to the prior and the brethren and to the parishioners.[19]

Since the prior of Provence had obviously asserted in his petition to Clement IV that the Hospitallers were in possession of the *ius patronatus* concerning the church of Down Ampney, which was apparently not the case, he could have been

---

information about English publications not available to me.

16 Delaville le Roulx, *Cartulaire* (see below, n. 31), vol. 3, no. 3600, p. 339: *Verum quia due dictiones, videlicet competens portio, que immediate ante prefatam dictionem assignetur, scribi debuerunt, fuerunt omisse in indulgentia memorata ...*

17 The National Archives, Kew, SC 8/197/9802. I am grateful to The National Archives for providing me a copy via the Internet. Since it is stated in this petition that the Hospitallers had already taken possession of the church, which must have taken place some time between the unknown date of Clement IV's (died 29 November 1269) letter and Innocent V's confirmation of it (4 May 1276; here it is also mentioned that they had meanwhile occupied the church), and also that the king was still suing them, i.e. before he ordered the judges of the King's Bench to discontinue the investigation into the matter (28 April 1277, see n. 22), the petition has to be dated 1276/77.

18 Ibid.: *Significat regie maiestati Godefridus dei gratia Wygorniensis episcopus, quod, licet dominus noster rex Anglie ecclesie de Dounameneye dicte diocesis verus existat patronus et super declaracione et conservacione iuris sui in premissis litem moverit [...] contra priorem et fratres hospitalis Ierosolimitani [...], tamen prior et fratres se predicte ecclesie falso confingentes patronos in ipsam se temere intruserunt et eandem adhuc detinentes occupatam[...].* On the competence of secular courts, especially the king's courts, to try disputes about the advowson see Pollock and Maitland, *The History of English Law*, vol. 2, pp. 136f.; Helmholz, *The Oxford History of the Laws of England*, vol. 1, p. 478.

19 Continuation of the text of the preceding note: *[...] ipsum super dicta ecclesia et iuribus parrochialibus et aliis pertinentibus ad eandem ecclesiam coram .. officiali Cantuariensi et eius commissario per se et parrochianos fatigant minus iuste [...]. Unde petiit episcopus memoratus breve regium dictis iudicibus demandari, ne per dictos priorem et fratres et parrochianos memoratos super dicta ecclesia seu pertinentibus ad eandem lite pen[dente in]decisa aliquatenus in posterum fatigetur. Item breve consimilis tenoris priori et fratribus dirigatur et aliis parrochianis.*

accused of giving false information. The validity of the papal letter depended on the *veritas precum* of the petitioner, and the canon law, reverting to the *praescriptio mendaciorum* of the Roman law, declared any papal or other document granted on the basis of wrong or incomplete information given by the petitioner a forgery, and the petitioner subject to punishment.[20] It is not known whether the bishop of Worcester used this as an argument against the validity of Clement IV's letter. However, on 28 April 1277 King Edward I ordered the judges of the king's court to discontinue the investigation in his dispute with the prior and the brethren of the Knights of St John of Jerusalem concerning the church of Down Ampney.[21] Finally, on 11 February 1284 Edward I announced that he had stopped all litigation in the court of the King's Bench and, for the salvation of his soul and the souls of his predecessors and heirs, quitclaimed the advowson to the church of Down Ampney in favour of William de Henley, prior of England of the Hospitallers, and his successors.[22]

It needs to be emphasized that King Edward's opponent in this dispute about the advowson was the prior of England, not the prior of Provence, the recipient of the papal grant. Prior of England up to 1281, when he went to the Holy Land, was the king's treasurer Joseph Chauncy, whom Edward may already have met in Acre during his crusade and who, as treasurer, played an important role in the government of England.[23] His close relationship with the king may have caused Edward's renunciation of the Down Ampney patronage. Nothing is known so far[24] about the further history of the church, especially whether it was the prior of Provence who took possession of it. But the Hospitallers did receive the church, since it is listed in their report to Rhodes in 1338.[25] It belonged to the commandery of Quenington (north-east of Down Ampney) until the dissolution in 1540.

---

20 See Peter Herde, 'Römisches und kanonisches Recht bei der Verfolgung des Fälschungsdelikts im Mittelalter', *Traditio* 21 (1965), 326f.; Peter Herde, 'Die Bestrafung von Fälschern nach weltlichen und kirchlichen Rechtsquellen', in *Fälschungen im Mittelalter. Internationaler Kongreß der Monumenta Germaniae Historica, München 16.–19. September 1986. Teil II: Gefälschte Rechtstexte. Der bestrafte Fälscher* (Monumenta Germaniae Historica, Schriften, vol. 33/II; Hanover 1988), pp. 594f.

21 *Calendar of the Close Rolls preserved in the Public Record Office, prepared under the Superintendence of the Deputy Keeper of the Records, Edward I, A.D. 1272–1279* (London, 1900), p. 378.; Delaville le Roulx, *Cartulaire*, vol. 3, no. 3621*bis*, p. 354.

22 Delaville le Roulx, *Cartulaire*, vol. 3, no. 3850, p. 457. See John Stillingflete's record of the Hospitallers' properties in England (early 15th century), in *Monasticon Anglicanum*, ed. William Dugdale, new edn revised by John Caley, Henry Ellis and Bulkeley Bandinel, vol. 6, part 2 (London, 1846), p. 836.

23 T.F. Tout, *Chapters in the Administrative History of Medieval England: The Wardrobe, the Chamber and the Small Seals,* vol. 2 (Manchester, 1920, repr. 1967), pp. 12f.; Riley-Smith, *The Knights of St John*, p. 312; Michael Prestwich, *Edward I* (London, 1988, repr. 1990), p. 324.

24 Further unpublished documents concerning this litigation may be found in English archives, especially in those of the bishops of Worcester and Exeter, which I have so far been unable to consult. Dr Nicholson kindly informed me that the section of the Hospitallers' English cartulary that contained the records of the Quenington commandery has not survived.

25 *The Knights Hospitallers in England, being the Report of Prior Philip de Thame to the Grand Master Elyan de Villanova for A.D. 1338*, ed. Lambert B.Larking with an historical

Edition

Pope John XXI instructs the bishop of Exeter, the abbot of St Albans and the archdeacon of Wells to provide for the strict observance of the sentences of suspension, interdict and excommunication issued by the prior of Royston against the bishop of Worcester in his dispute with the prior of Provence of the Order of St John of Jerusalem about the church of Down Ampney.

Viterbo, 1276 September 30

Original letter of justice damaged by water, the right margin partially torn off. Archive of the Order of St John of Jerusalem in the National Library of Malta, Valletta, Arch. 13 no. 7; see Records of the Order of St John of Jerusalem in the Royal Malta Library, vol. 1 (Malta, 1964), p. 70 (with wrong incipit: Quia a nobis dilecti*). Reconstruction of the text in square brackets. The bull is missing.*

Iohannes episcopus servus servorum dei. Venerabili fratri .. episcopo Exonien.[26] et dilectis filiis .. abbati monasterii de sancto Albano[27] Lincolnien.[28] diocesis et .. archidiacono Wellen.[29] Sa[lutem et apostolicam benedictionem]. Sua nobis dilecti filii .. prior et fratres hospitalis Ierosolimitan. in Provincia[30] petitione monstrarunt, quod felicis recordationis Clemens papa,[31] predecessor noster, audito, [quod] priori

introduction by John Mitchell Kemble (Camden Society 1st series, 65, 1857), p. 28: *Bajulia de Quenyngton [...] Et ecclesia de Dounamaneye per annum XXVI li.*

26 Walter Bronescombe, bishop of Exeter (Devon) (1258–1280), see Conradus Eubel, *Hierarchia catholica medii aevi*, vol. 1, 2nd edn (Münster, 1913), p. 253; *Fasti Ecclesiae Anglicanae 1066–1300*, comp. Diana E. Greenway, vol. 10: Exeter (London, 2005), pp. 5f.

27 Abbot Roger of Norton(e) of St Albans (1263–1290), see *The Heads of Religious Houses: England and Wales*, vol. 2, 1216–1377, ed. David M. Smith and Vera C.M. London (Cambridge, 2001), p. 63.

28 Lincoln (Lincs.).

29 Wells (Som.) Master Thomas of Bitton, see *Fasti Ecclesiae Anglicanae, vol. 7. Bath and Wells* (London, 2001), p. 35.

30 William de Villaret, prior of Provence (Saint-Gilles) (1271–1296), see J(oseph) Delaville le Roulx, *Les hospitaliers en Terre Sainte et à Chypre (1100–1310)* (Paris, 1904), pp. 416f.; Jonathan Riley-Smith, *The Knights of St John in Jerusalem and Cyprus c.1050–1310* (London, 1967), pp. 206ff. and passim.

31 Pope Clement IV (1265–1268). No pertinent letter of grace by Clement IV is known; it is missing in *Cartulaire général de l'ordre des hospitaliers de S. Jean de Jérusalem (1100–1310)* par J(oseph) Delaville le Roulx, vol. 3 (1261–1300) (Paris, 1899), and in the papal registers, see *Les registres de Clément IV (1265–1268)*, ed. Édouard Jordan (Paris, 1893–1904), *Tables* (Paris, 1945); *Calendar of Entries in the Papal Registers relating to Great Britain and Ireland, Papal Letters vol. 1, A.D.1198–1304* (London, 1893, repr. Nendeln, 1971), pp. 419ff., and no original has been preserved, see Jane E. Sayers, *Original Papal Documents in England and Wales from the Accession of Pope Innocent III to the Death of Pope Benedict XI (1198–1304)* (Oxford, 1999), pp. 316ff. But there exists a confirmation of Clement IV's letter by Pope Innocent V of 4 May 1276, ed. Delaville le Roulx, *Cartulaire*, vol. 3, no. 3600, p. 339, which is not mentioned in the above letter of John XXI.

et fratribus[32] personarum et rerum[33] quam plurima dampna gravia per inimicos crucis, perfidos Sarracenos dicebantur illata, super eis universitati eorundem prioris et [fratrum affectu pa]terno compatiens eisque subventionis solamento de suo dono gratie volens favorabiliter provenire ecclesiam de Mihamenel[34] Wigornien.[35] diocesis, si in ea hospitale predictum ius patronatus hab[eret, cum] iuribus et pe[r]tinentiis[36] sive[37] omnibus eis et per eos eidem hospitali apostolica auctoritate concessit, ita quod ipsi cedente vel decedente rectore ipsius ecclesie seu alio quovis modo ecclesia predicta vacant[e] possessionem illius ac iurium et pertinentiarum eorundem predictis applicandarum usibus libere possent ingredi diocesani episcopi aut cuiusvis alterius assensu minime requisito, proviso tamen, quod vicario in eadem ecclesia perpetuo servituro assignaretur de ipsius proventibus congrua portio pro sustentatione sua et supportandis oneribus ecclesie memorate. Idem quoque predecessor dilecto filio .. priori de Cruce Roys[38] Londonien.[39] diocesis per litteras suas iniunxit,[40] ut cedente vel decedente memorato rectore sive alio quovis modo ecclesia predicta vacante dictos priorem et fratres seu procuratorem eorum pro ipsis in possessionem corporalem ecclesie ac iurium et pertinentiarum predictarum iuxta huiusmodi concessionis sue tenorem per se vel per alium aut alios induceret et defensaret inductos, contradictores per censuram ecclesiasticam appellatione postposita compescendo. Cumque postmodum predicta ecclesia per mortem quondam Hugonis rectoris ipsius ecclesie vacuisset, dicti prior et fratres ius patronatus obtinentes in illa possessionem[41] eiusdem ecclesie ac iurium et pertinentiarum ipsorum iuxta concessionis apostolice predicte tenorem per executorem eundem ingredi legitime curaverunt capellano

32 There follows a gap of about five letters, filled by a line.

33 The same gap filled as before.

34 Reading of the first two letters uncertain. In Innocent's letter (see above, n. 31) the village is called *Dunhamekel*, which Delaville le Roulx corrects to *Dunameneye* (*Cartulaire* vol. 3, p. 339 n. 1). *Dunam(m)eneye* is used by Edward I in his charters of 1277 and 1284 renouncing the advowson (*advocacia*) to the church in favour of the prior of the Hospitallers of England, William de Henley, see *Cartulaire,* vol. 3, no. 3850, p. 457 and vol. 4, no. 3621*bis*, p. 354. In Walter Bronescombe's register it is called *Dounhameneye*: *The Register of Walter Bronescombe, Bishop of Exeter 1258–1280*, vol. 2, ed. Olivia F. Robinson, Canterbury and York Society 87 (Woodbridge, 1999), p. 110. In the report to Rhodes of 1338 (see above, text n. 25) it is called *Dounamaneye.* It is Down Ampney, Gloucestershire, south-east of Cirencester; see David Verey, *Gloucestershire, vol. 1: The Cotswolds*, 2nd edn (London 1970), pp. 219ff.

35 Worcester.

36 Erroneously *petinentiis.*

37 Erroneously for *suis.*

38 Royston (Herts.; *de Cruce Roisia*), Augustinian canons. A prior *Laurencius* is documented 13 October 1278, see *The Heads of Religious Houses*, vol. 2, p. 454; his predecessor Osbert is documented 1247–1262, his successor Richard de Leccinton 1279 (?)-1294, ibid. On Royston see also David Knowles and R. Neville Hadcock, *Medieval Religious Houses: England and Wales* (London–New York–Toronto, 1953), p. 151, and *The Religious Houses: England and Wales*, vol. 1 946–1216, 2nd edn, ed. David Knowles, C.N.L. Brooke and Vera C.M. London, with new material by C.N.L. Brooke (Cambridge, 2001), p. 182.

39 London.

40 Letter of Clement IV not identified.

41 There follows a gap of about six letters, filled by a line.

ibidem perpetuo servituro congrua de illis proventibus portione servata, et demum [qui]a G. Wigornien. episcopus[42] dictos priorem et fratres, quominus prefatam ecclesiam possent pacifice possidere, presumebat multipliciter impedire et diligenter per executorem ipsum monitus ab impedimento huiusmodi desistere contumaciter recusavit nullam ostendens causam rationabilem, quare id facere non deberet, dictus executor, cum ea essent ita notoria, quod nulla possent tergiversatione celare, eundem episcopum primo ab executione pontificalium et deinde ab ingressu ecclesie auctoritate litterarum ipsarum iustitia exigente suspendere ac eius excres[cente] contumacia capellam suam episcopalem ecclesiastico interdicto supponere nec non demum in ipsum excommunicationis sententiam promulgare curavit. Sed dictus episcopus huiusmodi suspensionis, interdicti et excommunicationis sententias pro sue voluntatis libito vilipendens divina officia et etiam ordines celebrare, immo verius, quantum in eo est, prophanare, et alia, que ad officium episcopale pertinent, exercere presumit in anime sue periculum, dictorum prioris et fratrum preiudicium et scandalum plurimorum. Quare dicti prior et fratres humiliter petierunt a nobis, ut predictas suspensionis, interdicti et excommunicationis sententias ro[borari] face[remus et] firmitatis debitum obtinere. Quocirca discretioni vestre per apostolica scripta mandamus, quatinus apud Wellias[43] sententias ipsas, sicut rationabiliter sunt prolate, [faciatis pro par]te nostra usque ad satisfactionem condignam appellatione remota inviolabiliter observari. Si vero dictus episcopus sententias ipsas, postquam eas constiterit rite f[uisse] latas, [per] unum mensem animo sustinuerit pertinaci, vos eas extunc singulis diebus dominicis et festivis pulsatis campanis et candelis accensis per omnia loca, in quibus expedire videritis, usque ad satisfactionem premissam sollempniter publicetis et per alios publicari faciatis ac dictum episcopum ab omnibus artius evitare, non obstante, si [ei] a sede apostolica sit indultum, quod suspendi vel interdici et excommunicari non possit sive qualibet alia indulgentia sedis eiusdem, per quam effectus iustitie in hac pa[rte] impediri valeat vel differri et de qua in nostris litteris fieri debeat mentio specialis. Quod si non omnes hiis exequendis potueritis interesse, duo vestrum [ea nichilominus exequantur].[44]
Dat. Viterbii II kal. octobris, pontificatus nostri anno [p]rimo.

Chancery marks: The scribe's mark is missing since the right margin of the plica is torn off. – Taxation mark below the plica left: X. *– Underneath the taxation mark:* R[ecipe] Iac *(..., hole)* .[45] [R]ecipe f. d... *(both marks crossed out). – Under the plica*

42 Godfrey Giffard, bishop of Worcester (1268–1302), see Eubel, *Hierarchia catholica medii aevi*, p. 560; *English Episcopal Acta 13: Worcester 1218–1268*, ed. Philippa M. Hoskin (Oxford, 1993), p. XXXVII; *Fasti Ecclesiae Anglicanae, vol. 2: Monastic Cathedrals* (London, 1970), pp. 101f.

43 See edition n. 29.

44 On the canonistic importance of this clause see Peter Herde, *Audientia litterarum contradictarum. Untersuchungen über die päpstlichen Justizbriefe und die päpstliche Delegationsgerichtsbarkeit vom 13. bis zum Beginn des 16. Jahrhunderts*, vol. 1(Tübingen, 1970), pp. 199ff.

45 Most likely *Iac. Bocl.* (*Iacobus Boclus*), a scribe, see Gerd Nüske, *Untersuchungen über das Personal der päpstlichen Kanzlei 1254–1302, Zweiter Teil*, Archiv für Diplomatik 21 (1975), pp. 250ff. no. 122; Sayers, *Original Papal Documents*, p. 510, no. 150.

right: m. – *Recto above left:* ex. R[ecipe] f.[46] fiant duo. – *Recto above, centre, mark of the corrector:* cor. *(crossed out).* – *No proctor's mark verso.*

Figure B Hospitaller Church (All Saints' Church) of Down Ampney (Photo: Peter Herde, June 2007).

46 On this scribe see Nüske, *Erster Teil*, Archiv für Diplomatik 20 (1974), pp. 198f. no. 71; Sayers, p. 502 no. 91.

Chapter 6

Hospitaller Ships and Transportation across the Mediterranean

David Jacoby

The main functions of the Order of St John, after its militarization, were the maintenance of Christian rule in the Holy Land and caring for the pilgrims and the poor. The priories in the West, especially in present-day France and in the Kingdom of Sicily, supported the Convent in the Levant with resources of cash, manpower, military equipment, horses, mules, fodder, grain, other foodstuffs, and some additional commodities. Maritime transportation was vital for the operation of the Order, since it ensured the eastward flow of reinforcements and supplies, as well as communication between its houses across the Mediterranean. Surprisingly, the Order's involvement in maritime transportation has so far been addressed in passing only, and not always accurately.[1] Several issues regarding that involvement warrant a thorough investigation. Three of them are examined here: since when did the Hospitallers own ships, the functions of these vessels, and the development of the Order's fleet until the fall of the Frankish states in 1291. In view of space limitations, the focus of this study is on the role of Marseilles in relation to these issues, a role that is fairly well documented.

The earliest extant record of a Hospitaller ship appears in the business account of a Genoese merchant who returned home in 1156.[2] Considering the oriental

---

1 In the last four decades: J. Riley-Smith, *The Knights of St John in Jerusalem and Cyprus, c. 1050–1310* (London, 1967), (Woodbridge, 2005) p. 539, Index, s.v. 'Fleet of the Order'; H.E. Mayer, *Marseilles Levantehandel und ein akkonensisches Fälscheratelier des 13. Jahrhunderts*, Bibliothek des Deutschen historischen Instituts in Rom, Band XXXVIII (Tübingen, 1972), pp. 80–9; J.H. Pryor, '*In subsidium Terrae Sanctae*: Exports of Foodstuffs and War Materials from the Kingdom of Sicily to the Kingdom of Jerusalem, 1265–1284', *Asian and African Studies* 22 (1988) [= B.Z. Kedar and A.L. Udovitch (eds), *The Medieval Levant. Studies in Memory of Eliyahu Ashtor (1914–1984)*], 133–6, 145–6; M.-L. Favreau-Lilie, 'The Military Orders and the Escape of the Christian Population from the Holy Land in 1291', *Journal of Medieval History*, 19 (1993), 205–11; J. Bronstein, *The Hospitallers and the Holy Land. Financing the Latin East, 1187–1274* (London 1967), (Woodbridge, 2005) p. 189, Index, s.v. 'Shipping'. On Templar maritime transportation, see M. Barber, 'Supplying the Crusader States: The Role of the Templars', in B.Z. Kedar, (ed.), *The Horns of Hattin* (Jerusalem–London, 1992), pp. 322–6, and references in M. Barber, *The New Knighthood* (Cambridge, 1994), p. 438, s.v. 'shipping'. Here I deal only with some issues of Templar transportation coinciding with those of the Hospitallers.

2 J. Delaville le Roulx, *Les Hospitaliers en Terre Sainte et à Chypre (1110–1310)* (Paris, 1904), p. 343, contends that the Order had no ships in the twelfth century and, therefore,

commodities he handled, among them spices, it is likely that the ship had visited Acre. Marseilles was presumably its final destination, rather than Genoa, which never served as a base for Hospitaller vessels. In 1161 another Genoese merchant was due to sail, on a large vessel that had formerly belonged to the Order.[3] The reason for its sale cannot be established. Interestingly, Hospitaller and Templar ships were carrying pilgrims from Narbonne around that time, as is revealed by that city's treaty of 1166 with Genoa.[4] In 1178 the Hospitallers obtained from Bertrand of Marseilles and his nephews William le Gros and Raymond Barral, joint viscounts of Marseilles, tax exemption for the transit, sale or purchase of their vessels and marketable goods in the harbour adjoining the sector of the city and other territories under their rule.[5] In 1190 King Richard I of England transferred a ship to the Hospitallers.[6] It is likely that it transported men and provisions of the Order to the vicinity of Acre, which was then besieged by Christian forces participating in the Third Crusade. Shortly after the death of Emperor Henry VI of Hohenstaufen on 28 September 1197 his widow, Empress Constance, granted the Hospitallers in the Kingdom of Sicily the right to export goods to support the Convent in the Holy Land without paying taxes. In addition, they were allowed to carry *peregrini* on their ships without having to transfer a portion of the fare collected from them to the royal court.[7] The term *peregrini* covered both pilgrims and crusaders, as is evidenced, for instance, with respect to the passengers of the ship *St Victor* in 1250.[8] Occasionally, though, the former were distinguished from the latter, called *milites peregrini* or *peregrini*

relied on Catalan and Provençal carriers, while Riley-Smith, *The Knights of St John*, p. 329, states that the Order possessed ships, citing one instance (see below, n. 6), yet 'for most of the transport relied on the vessels of Provençal and Catalonian sailors'. Neither author provides evidence regarding these services.

3 M. Chiaudano and M. Moresco (eds), *Il cartolare di Giovanni Scriba* (Turin, 1935), 2: 248–50, no. I; pp. 32–3, no. 871.

4 C. Devic and J. Vaissète, *Histoire générale du Languedoc* (Toulouse, 1872–1905), 8, pp. 263–4: *exceptis peregrinis quos possemus portare in navi una per annum, quae tamen non sit Hospitalis vel Templi.*

5 *Cartulaire général de l'Ordre des Hospitaliers de Saint-Jean de Jérusalem, 1100-1310*, ed. J. Delaville le Roulx, 4 vols (Paris, 1894–1906) (hereafter *Cart.*), vol. 1, p. 369, no. 542: *concedimus [...] quicquid juris et consuetudinis de transitu et reditu et venditione et emptione, tam navium quam aliarum rerum venalium de rebus propriis Hospitalis*. At that time Marseilles was divided between the viscounts and the bishop. There was a second harbour, used by residents of the bishop's sector of the city: see R. Pernoud, *Les statuts municipaux de Marseille* (Monaco–Paris, 1949), pp. xxxvi–xxxvii.

6 *The Great Roll of the Pipe for the Second Year of the Reign of* King *Richard I*, ed. D. M. Stenton Publications of the Pipe Roll Society 39 (London, 1925), p. 9.

7 E.A. Winkelmann, *Acta imperii inedita, saeculi XIII et XIV: Urkunden und Briefe zur Geschichte des Kaiserreichs und des Konigreichs Sizilien* (Innsbruck, 1880–85), 1: 66–7, no. 71.

8 On the passengers of that ship, see B.Z. Kedar, 'The Passenger List of a Crusader Ship, 1250', *Studi medievali* 3a serie, 13 (1972), 268, 270–72, 274–8, repr. in B.Z. Kedar, *The Franks in the Levant, 11th to 14th Centuries* (Aldershot, 1993), no. XVI.

crucesignati.[9] *Peregrini* sailing with their horses were obviously crusaders.[10] The Hospitallers' request from Empress Constance was apparently related to their wish to participate in the transportation of German crusaders from southern Italy to Acre, which had been proceeding since March 1197.[11] It is doubtful, however, that the Order was regularly carrying pilgrims or crusaders from the Kingdom of Sicily to the Levant by that time. Significantly, in 1211 Otto IV confirmed the Order's taxation privileges in the Kingdom of Sicily without referring to ships, and Frederick II acted likewise in 1209, 1215, 1216 and 1224.[12]

The evidence regarding Hospitaller vessels becomes more abundant from the early thirteenth century onwards. In 1210 King Hugh I of Cyprus granted tax exemption throughout the island for the Order's trade in its own goods, the purchase of commodities for its own needs, and free anchorage in Cypriot ports for its ships carrying them.[13] However, the Order could not fully ensure the transportation of its men and provisions. Two years later, in 1212, Guy, lord of Gibelet (Jubail in present-day Lebanon) granted the Hospitallers tax exemption for trade in the city and the territory of his lordship, as well as for any ship visiting Gibelet for provisioning.[14] He did not directly refer to the Order's own ships and clearly alluded to chartered vessels.

In March 1216 Hugh I of Baux and his wife Baralle granted the Hospitallers the right to build or anchor in the port and territory of Marseilles any type or number of ships that would sail to the Frankish Levant, Spain, or any other region to defend Christendom. The transport of their own goods, pilgrims, crusaders, merchants and the latter's money on these ships, whether for fare and freight or without payment, was to be tax exempt. The concession also covered the operation of ships chartered by the Order for its own needs.[15] This grant of shipping privileges to the Order in Marseilles was not the first of its kind, but rather the confirmation of an earlier concession. A shorter version of the privileges enjoyed by the Hospitallers and the Templars appears in a charter of 1233, which reveals that they had been jointly bestowed by the five viscounts of Marseilles holding portions of the seigniorial rights in the city, namely, Hugh I of Baux, Raymond of Baux and Giraud Adhémar and their respective wives, in addition to Roncelin and Raymond-Geoffrey of Trets.[16] It

9 J.L.A. de Huillard-Bréholles (ed.), *Historia diplomatica Frederici secundi* (Parisiis, 1852–61), 5.2: 773, in 1240; Pernoud, *Les statuts*, p. 150 (IV, chap. 12): *exceptis peregrinis crucesignatis aut aliis Sanctorum limina visitantibus.*

10 Pernoud, *Les statuts*, pp. 49 (I, chap. 35), 158 (IV, chap. 24).

11 E.N. Johnson, 'The Crusades of Frederick Barbarossa and Henry VI', in K.M. Setton, *History of the Crusades* (Madison, Wis., 1969–89), 2: 120–1.

12 Winkelmann, *Acta*, 1: 60–1, 107–9, 112–14, and 244–5, respectively nos. 63, 127, 134 and 268.

13 *Cart.*, 2: 121–2, no. 1354: *cum omnibus vassellis propriis.*

14 Ibid., 2: 134–6, no. 1372: *cum [...] pro suis negotiis vassellum aliquod conduxerint.*

15 Ibid., 2: 186, no. 1464: *possitis facere et habere navem vel naves et alia navigia propria vel aliena quecumque volueritis.* On shipyards in the harbour, see Pernoud, *Les statuts*, p. xxxvi.

16 *Cart.*, 2: 462, no. 2067. On the split ownership of seigniorial rights in 1213, see H. de Gérin-Ricard and É. Isnard, *Actes concernant les vicomtes de Marseille et leurs descendants*

is likely that the concession to the two Orders was made while the five viscounts held all the seigniorial rights in their sector of Marseilles. Raymond-Geoffrey of Trets and his sister Alasacie, married to Raymond of Baux, inherited portions of the viscounts' rights from their father, Hugh Geoffrey, at some unknown date before the last days of March 1213. The former sold some of his rights to the commune of Marseilles on the 28th of that month, Roncelin acted likewise two days later, and a third sale, by Raymond of Baux, took place on 2 April.[17] It follows that the Hospitallers and the Templars obtained their shipping privileges before late March 1213.

The sales of seigniorial rights to the commune of Marseilles in March and April 1213 and a further sale negotiated by Raymond-Geoffrey of Trets in March 1216 must have seriously worried the Hospitallers.[18] In addition, after the death of viscount Roncelin on 21 December 1215 the abbey of St Victor of Marseilles claimed his entire portion of seigniorial rights.[19] The Hospitallers obviously feared that the commune and the abbey would refuse to uphold their shipping privileges. In March 1216, therefore, they requested confirmation of the original concession from Hugh I of Baux, who had retained his portion of the viscounts' rights. The charter he jointly issued with his wife, Baralle, mentioned above, appears to reflect faithfully the wording of that concession. In addition, the Order turned to Pope Honorius III, who on 20 December 1216 confirmed the original shipping privileges obtained from the five viscounts of Marseilles.[20]

The pope also ordered, again in response to the Hospitallers' request, that the archbishop of Arles and his suffragans should prevent churchmen and laymen from taxing the Order for the transit of timber assigned for shipbuilding, as well as for goods intended for the assistance of the Holy Land.[21] The wording of Honorius III implies that the timber did not necessarily originate from the Order's estates, yet was clearly intended for ships it commissioned. The request was motivated by

(Monaco–Paris, 1926), pp. xlviii–xlix.

17 Charters of 28 March and 2 April 1213 in V.-L. Bourrilly, *Essai sur l'histoire politique de la commune de Marseille des origines à la victoire de Charles d'Anjou (1264)* (Aix-en-Provence, 1925), pp. 273–82, nos. XIII–XIV. Summary of the three sales in Gérin-Ricard and Isnard, *Actes*, pp. xlviii–xlix and 112–13, nos. 365–7. On the confraternity of the Holy Spirit representing the commune of Marseilles, see Bourrilly, *Essai*, pp. 46–80.

18 This sale took place on 1 April 1216: Bourrilly, *Essai*, pp. 288–94, no. XVII; Gérin-Ricard and Isnard, *Actes*, pp. xlix and 119–20, no. 391.

19 For the date of Roncelin's death, see ibid., pp. xlviii and 118, no. 390. On the controversy surrounding the transfer of his rights, see the letter of Pope Innocent III in Patrologia Latina, CCVI, cols. 457–8, and Gérin-Ricard and Isnard, *Actes*, pp. xlvi–xlviii and 108–9, no. 352.

20 *Cart.*, 2: 203–4, no. 1519: *in [...] Hugonis de Baucio et predictorum dominorum Massilie instrumento publico*. Delaville's heading of the document mistakenly refers to the privilege of March 1216 granted by Hugh I and his wife, mentioned above.

21 *Cart.*, 2: 203, no. 1518: *de diversis mundi partibus ligna pro navibus fabricandis, helemosina et alia bona subsidio Terre Sancte super aquas et terras deferunt*. Favreau-Lilie, 'The Military Orders', p. 207 and n. 15, also refers to a charter issued by Frederick II in 1209. However, that charter fails to mention naval timber, while allowing the Hospitallers to take wood from royal forests in the Kingdom of Sicily for the repair of their houses and for heating: *Cart.*, 2: 110–11, no. 1335.

the location of Arles and several cities within the bishopric along waterways that enabled the floating of timber to shipyards in Marseilles. It has been suggested that the timber was to be sent to Acre for shipbuilding in the Hospitaller's *darsana* or shipyard, presumably located in the *Cale dou Marquis* just north of the suburb of Montmusard.[22] This construct is not plausible for several reasons. First, the transfer of timber to Acre would have been costly and contrary to economic rationale, since ships could be built in Marseilles. Secondly, the *darsana* of the Hospitallers attested in 1250 was clearly situated in the Old City of Acre, because it was contiguous to a Genoese garden and close to other houses of the Order. The presence of houses of the Order north of the city walls is excluded. Finally, the *darsana* was located at some distance from the shore. Therefore, it must have been a workshop for an undisclosed activity rather than a shipyard.[23] In any event, the recently excavated shipyard in Acre, which on fourteenth-century maps appears as *arsenal* to the east of the Venetian quarter, was only suitable for the building and repair of small and medium-sized vessels, whereas the Order was using large vessels by 1250.[24]

It is noteworthy that the Templars obtained from the five viscounts of Marseilles the same shipping concessions as the Hospitallers, presumably at the same date as the latter, and faced the same problems. They, too, appear to have been troubled by the viscounts' sales of seigniorial rights to the commune of Marseilles and by the death of Roncelin. However, instead of turning, like the Hospitallers, to Pope Honorius III to strengthen their privileges, they asked Frederick II to confirm them. In September 1216 he issued a charter to that effect, mentioning the five viscounts.[25] It is noteworthy that a vessel of the Templars was about to leave Constantinople for

22 M.-L. Favreau-Lilie, *Die Italiener im Heiligen Land vom ersten Kreuzzug bis zum Tode Heinrichs von Champagne (1098–1197)* (Amsterdam, 1989), pp. 17, 23, and Favreau-Lilie, 'The Military Orders', pp. 207–8. The supposed dispatch of timber to Acre rests on a misreading of the passage cited above, n. 21. It is clear that only the money and goods were to be sent to the Levant, for reasons explained below. On the location of the *Cale dou Marquis*, see D. Jacoby, 'Conrad, Marquis of Montferrat, and the Kingdom of Jerusalem (1187–1192),' in L. Balletto (ed.), *Atti del Congresso Internazionale 'Dai feudi monferrini e dal Piemonte ai nuovi mondi oltre gli Oceani'*, Alessandria, 2–6 April 1990, Biblioteca della Società di Storia, Arte e Archeologia per le province di Alessandria e Asti, N. 27 (Alessandria, 1993), p. 223, repr. in D. Jacoby, *Trade, Commodities and Shipping in the Medieval Mediterranean* (Aldershot, 1997), no. IV.

23 C. Desimoni, 'Quatre titres des propriétés des Génois à Acre et à Tyr', *Archives de l'Orient latin* 2/2 (1884), 224: a Genoese garden adjoining on one side *deversus mare* (i.e. in the direction of the sea) *retro murum darsana facta per hospitale Beati Iohannis.* See also another *darsana* surrounded by buildings in the Genoese quarter, ibid., p. 217. The Arabic term *dar al-sina'a*, from which *darsana* derived, had the broad meaning of 'workshop' and 'building' for any type of activity: see C. Picard, 'Les arsenaux musulmans dela Méditerranée et de l'océan Atlantique (VIIIe–XVe siècle)', in D. Coulon, C. Otten-Froux, P. Pagès and D. Valérian (eds), *Chemins d'outre-mer. Études sur la Méditerranée médiévale offertes à Michel Balard*, Byzantina Sorbonensia 20 (Paris, 2004), 2: 692.

24 See D. Jacoby, 'Aspects of Everyday Life in Frankish Acre', *Crusades* 4 (2005), 93.

25 Winkelmann, *Acta*, 1: 117–18, no. 139. It is not impossible that the Templars had obtained a confirmation of their privileges from Hugh I of Baux in March 1216, like the Hospitallers.

Acre in April 1207.[26] Apparently the same or another ship of that Order, the name of which is garbled, sailed from Constantinople to Venice in the spring of 1210.[27]

The evidence surveyed so far warrants several observations. The Hospitallers already owned one or several transport ships crossing the Mediterranean around the mid-twelfth century. However, the Order also relied on private carriers or chartered whole ships. The loss of numerous estates in the Levant in 1187 substantially reduced its self-supply and revenues in that region, as well as the income from the sale of its produce, such as sugar, despite the temporary recovery of some lands until the mid-thirteenth century.[28] As a result, the Hospitallers in the Levant were compelled to rely, far more than before 1187, on supplies from the West. The papacy assisted them by prohibiting the imposition of taxes on the movement of their goods.[29] The frequent transfer of reinforcements, and especially of supplies, across the Mediterranean after 1191 induced the Hospitallers to purchase ships or commission their construction on a much larger scale than before, as implied by the shipping privileges they obtained in Marseilles before late March 1213. As noted above, these included a sweeping tax exemption both on the operation and on the building of vessels. All these considerations also applied to the Templars.

The acquisition and operation of ships by the two Orders was primarily aimed at cutting transportation costs. As noted above, they also enabled profit-generating maritime activities consisting in the transportation of merchants, private cargo, crusaders and pilgrims on ships not filled to capacity with the Orders' own men and goods. Some of these services are already attested by 1156, possibly also by 1197 in the Kingdom of Sicily, if we may rely on the charter issued by Empress Constance, and in any event by the second decade of the thirteenth century. The Hospitallers and the Templars offered these services until the fall of the Frankish states in 1291. Three factors account for the intrusion of the two Orders into the highly competitive business of pilgrim transportation. There was a large demand for that service after 1191, closely related to greater geographic mobility in the West. Ships of increasing carrying capacity were being built from the second half of the twelfth century. And the sailing across the high seas from the late twelfth century onwards shortened trans-Mediterranean voyages, reduced their cost, and further enhanced the profitability of pilgrim transportation.[30] It is likely that the two Orders expected and encouraged

26 R. Morozzo della Rocca and A. Lombardo (eds), *Documenti del commercio veneziano nei secoli XI–XIII* (Turin, 1940), 2: 27–8, no. 487.

27 A. Lombardo and R. Morozzo della Rocca (eds), *Nuovi documenti del commercio veneto dei sec. XI–XIII* (Venice, 1953), pp. 82–3, no. 75: *cum nave que vocatur Teplera.*

28 On the loss of Hospitaller estates, see M. Balard, 'I possedimenti degli Ospedalieri nella Terrasanta (secoli XII–XIII), in J. Costa Restagno (ed.), *Cavalieri di San Giovanni e territorio. La Liguria tra Provenza e Lombardia nei secoli XIII–XVII*, Atti del Convegno Genova – Imperia – Cervo, 11–14 settembre 1997 (Genoa–Bordighera, 1999), pp. 473–505, especially the maps; Bronstein, *The Hospitallers*, pp. 11–63.

29 Bulls of Celestine III in 1194 and Innocent III in 1199: *Cart.*, 1: 612, no. 964, and p. 668, no. 1071.

30 On this last factor, see D. Jacoby, 'Byzantine Crete in the Navigation and Trade Networks of Venice and Genoa', in L. Balletto (ed.), *Oriente e Occidente tra medioevo ed età moderna. Studi in onore di Geo Pistarino*, Università degli Studi di Genova, Sede di Acqui

the pilgrims sailing to Acre on their ships to be particularly generous towards their respective houses in that city, both of which owned a number of relics.[31]

The two Orders faced some tough competitors in Marseilles. One of them was Count Hugh of Ampurias who, like them, enjoyed shipping and fiscal privileges in the city's harbour. Returning from Acre, where he is attested on the ship *St Maurice* on 1 May 1219,[32] he concluded an agreement with the commune in Marseilles on 24 July. It stipulated that he or any of his subjects permanently residing in the territory under his rule were entitled to anchor one ship per year in the port of Marseilles, whether their own vessel or one jointly held with a resident of the viscounts' sector of the city. The ship was allowed to sail from Marseilles to the Levant with pilgrims on board or to Alexandria, Bougie, Ceuta (the latter two cities in the Maghreb) and other ports, with or without cargo. All these operations were tax free. The ship's operator was also entitled to establish a counter in the harbour for the recruitment of passengers and the collection of cargo, like the Marseillais. However, he would pay the customary old tax and the duty levied by the Sea Table at varying rates, as imposed upon local residents for their ships.[33] The count of Ampurias may have contemplated the transport of crusaders to Egypt, where Christian forces were besieging Damietta.

There were also tour operators, who attracted pilgrims by offering package trips at attractive fares.[34] Andrea of Ventimiglia, who had booked a large number of places on board the *St Francis*, concluded an agreement on 25 March 1248 with two agents who were to speed up the recruitment of passengers before the expected sailing around the end of the month. For a specific sum per pilgrim he promised to assume all expenses for fare, food and beverage for servants attending to the pilgrims, at the rate of four per 100 pilgrims, in accordance with the municipal legislation,[35] and fifteen for more than 400 of them, as well as the payment of taxes to the commune of Marseilles and the deposit of a warranty for the agents. He also undertook to

---

Terme, Collana di Fonti e Studi, 1.1, (Acqui Terme, 1997), pp. 536–7, 540, repr. in D. Jacoby, *Byzantium, Latin Romania and the Mediterranean* (Aldershot, 2001), no. II.

31 On pilgrim donations in Acre, see D. Jacoby, 'Society, Culture and the Arts in Crusader Acre', in D.H. Weiss and L. Mahoney (eds), *France and the Holy Land: Frankish Culture at the End of the Crusades* (Baltimore, 2004), pp. 100–1. On the relics of the two Orders, see D. Jacoby, 'Pilgrimage in Crusader Acre: The *Pardouns d'Acre*', in Y. Hen (ed.), De Sion exibit lex et verbum domini de Hierusalem. *Essays on Medieval Law, Liturgy and Literature in Honour of Amnon* Lindner, Cultural Encounters in Late Antiquity and the Middle Ages, vol. 1 (Turnhout, 2001), pp. 114–15.

32 D. Puncuh (ed.), *I Libri Iurium della Repubblica di Genova*, I/2, Fonti per la storia della Liguria, IV; Pubblicazioni degli Archivi di Stato, Fonti XXIII (Genova, 1996), pp. 265–7, no. 369. This may have been the count's own ship.

33 Bourrilly, *Essai*, pp. 310–14, esp. 310–11, no. XXXI*bis*: *excepto usatico antiquo et excepta dacita tabule Massilie de mari.* On these taxes, see R. Pernoud, 'Le Moyen Age jusqu'en 1291', in R. Busquet [et] R. Pernoud, *Histoire du commerce de Marseille* (Paris, 1949), pp. 336–9.

34 For what follows: L. Blancard (ed.), *Documents inédits sur le commerce de Marseille au moyen-âge* (Marseille, 1884–85), 1: 333–4, no. 165, and 2: 248–9, no. 914.

35 Pernoud, *Les statuts*, p. 157 (IV, chap. 24).

accompany the pilgrims on their maritime voyage at his own expense. On 19 June 1248 the three owners or operators of the *St Leonard* granted 200 places for pilgrims on board their ship to master Garnier de Marignino and promised to abstain from similar contracts with other individuals. In return Garnier undertook to pay the remainder of the sum he owed by the sailing date of mid-August, while recruiting pilgrims for the voyage. The activity of the tour operators, called *cargatores*, was closely supervised by the commune of Marseilles, as illustrated by its statutes – compiled in 1253 but reflecting earlier legislation.[36]

Still, the Hospitallers enjoyed a clear edge over their competitors. The shipping privileges granted by the viscounts of Marseilles before the last days of March 1213 were particularly important in that respect. They freed the Hospitallers from all taxes, including the *terciaria*, a third of the fare collected from pilgrims embarking in Marseilles, which the owners and operators of foreign ships were compelled to transfer to the commune.[37] As noted earlier, the count of Ampurias had obtained the same exemption in 1219. The full tax exemption also established an advantage over subjects of the viscounts' city engaged in pilgrim transportation, who paid harbour taxes.[38] Furthermore, from 1216 the Hospitallers apparently benefited from tax exemption on the supply of naval timber from their own lands and on the transit of timber in the region of Arles, regardless of its origin, all of which lowered the cost of the ships they commissioned. From 1178 they enjoyed tax exemption for the transit, purchase or sale of their own goods in the port and territory of Marseilles ruled by the viscounts.[39] In March 1209 or March 1210 Hugh I of Baux and his wife, Baralle, had granted them a similar concession for the transit of their goods through the ports of Trinquetaille, Petit Rhône, Bourg, Saint-Gilles and others, all situated along waterways leading to the Mediterranean.[40] These privileges enabled the Hospitallers to supply food and wine on board their ships at a cost below the market price, especially when these commodities originated in their own estates.

The growing intrusion of the Hospitallers and Templars into the field of maritime transportation between Marseilles and Acre was clearly successful by 1230, in particular with respect to pilgrims. It generated a strong reaction from the leaders of the commune of Marseilles, who were merchants and ship operators. They taxed the shipping services provided by the Orders, in complete disregard of the latter's privileges. This measure, which also had the advantage of providing substantial revenue, was presumably introduced shortly after the commune completed the

---

36 Ibid., pp. 49–50 (I, chap. 35), 157–62 (IV, chaps. 24–9), 206–7 (VI, chap. 25). On the dating of the compilation, see ibid., pp. xxiv–xxxi.

37 L. Méry and F. Guindon, *Histoire analytique et chronologique des actes et des délibérations du corps et du conseil de la municipalité de Marseille depuis le Xe siècle jusqu'à nos jours* (Marseille et Aix-en-Provence, 1841–73), 1: 331: *de terciaria peregrinorum*, in the commune's statutes of 1229.

38 On these taxes see above, n. 33.

39 See above, n. 5.

40 *Cart.*, 2: 106–7, no. 1327.

acquisition of all the viscounts' seigniorial rights in Marseilles on 16 January 1230.[41]

In the spring of 1233 at the latest the Hospitallers and the Templars in Acre complained that the Marseillais had infringed their privileges and inflicted them with losses estimated at 2,000 silver marks, as well as further damage.[42] The sum they mentioned was presumably the amount of *terciaria* that they had been compelled to transfer to the commune. The additional damage may have been caused by the forced cancellation of contracts and delays in sailing, due to pressure exerted by the commune. The two Orders submitted their grievances to the constable of the Kingdom of Jerusalem, Eudes of Montbéliard, and expressed their willingness to present both written and oral evidence to support their claims. They requested the immediate seizure of Marseillais vessels and goods to compensate them for their losses. They presumably also sought to recover their shipping privileges. The consul of Marseilles in Acre, John of Saint-Hilaire, refused to answer the charges. He argued that neither he nor any Marseillais in Acre, all of them merchants, had a mandate to deal with the case from either Count Raymond VII of Toulouse, whom the commune of Marseilles had recognized as lord in 1230, or from the commune itself.

The seizure of Marseillais assets in Acre that was demanded by the Orders apparently took place, as is implied by the dispatch to Acre of two representatives of the commune of Marseilles entrusted with the settlement of the dispute, in the summer or autumn of 1233. Arbitration by Eudes of Montbéliard, assisted by John of Ibelin of Beirut and other Frankish lords, produced a compromise that was confirmed by all parties on 3 October. It stipulated that each of the Orders retained full tax exemptions in the port of Marseilles for two of their own ships, one during the sailing season of August and the other during that of March or Easter. They were entitled to embark or disembark their own goods and to take on board each ship up to 1,500 pilgrims and an unlimited number of merchants, but only in Marseilles. The Orders were exempt from the obligation imposed upon all owners or operators of vessels returning from the Levant to deliver to the commune a crossbow purchased at their expense, but the merchants on board were required to do so.[43] Moreover, the commune maintained its right to tax merchants or other passengers in its territory. The Orders were allowed, if necessary, to operate additional ships to carry their own goods, but without embarking pilgrims or merchants in Marseilles. This was also strictly prohibited along a stretch of coast extending from Monaco to Collioure, to the south-east of Perpignan. Still, the Orders' vessels were permitted to transport their respective goods between that region's ports and Marseilles.[44] The two representatives of the commune promised to

41 On this acquisition, see Bourrilly, *Essai*, pp.356–64, no. XXXI; Gérin-Ricard and Isnard, *Actes*, pp. xlviii–xl and 146–7, nos. 465–6.

42 *Cart.*, 2: 462–4, no. 2067, for what follows.

43 This clause is not explicitly stated in the document, yet appears in the commune's statutes of 1253, which reflect earlier legislation: Pernoud, *Les statuts*, p. 58 (I, chap. 47, par. 3). The compulsory delivery of a crossbow may have been introduced after the commune had acquired all seigniorial rights from the viscounts in 1230 and decided to gather military equipment to protect itself.

44 The restriction regarding pilgrims and merchants outside Marseilles applied to all foreign ships equipped in the port of Marseilles: Pernoud, *Les statuts*, p. 148 (IV, chap. 6). It

obtain confirmation of the agreement from Count Raymond VII of Toulouse and the commune of Marseilles. The latter sanctioned it on 17 April 1234.[45]

The Hospitallers and Templars had been compelled to make substantial concessions. The sweeping rights and tax exemptions they had enjoyed in the past on the building and operation of ships, which had generated substantial profit, had been severely limited. In 1246 the commune of Marseilles went one step further: it cancelled unilaterally the agreement of 1233 and prevented the two Orders from anchoring their ships in the port of Marseilles. This action occurred while it was conducting talks with representatives of Louis IX of France for the hiring of ships required for the king's projected crusade. It was most likely aimed at preventing the Orders from participating in the transport of crusaders, equipment and horses. The agreement between the commune of Marseilles and the king was reached on 19 August 1246.[46] The Hospitallers and the Templars appealed to Pope Innocent IV, who, on 21 April and again on 7 December 1246, intervened on their behalf in letters addressed to the bishop of Marseilles to prevent the infringement of their privileges.[47]

The agreement of 1233 was reinstated at some unknown date and was still in force by 1253, as suggested by the exemption of the two Orders from the delivery of crossbows, by ships returning from the Levant, mentioned in the commune's statutes.[48] It was still maintained by December 1270, when King Charles I ordered his representative in Marseilles, then under his rule, to allow the Hospitaller ship *Angel*, carrying his brother Count Alphonse of Poitiers, to anchor in the port. The count had hired the ship in Marseilles. The king acknowledged that the ship's arrival in the port would be contrary to the city's custom, yet the latter would nevertheless remain valid.[49] The wording implies that two ships of the Hospitallers involved in commercial transportation had already visited the port earlier that year and that the *Angel* was in excess of the agreed number.

Official and private documents offer convincing evidence about the capacity of ships embarking pilgrims in Marseilles in the thirteenth century.[50] In 1248 Andrea of

may have been extended to them around April 1234, when the commune of Marseilles ratified its agreement with the Hospitallers and the Templars; for that date, see below.

45 *Cart.*, 2: 469, no. 2079.

46 J.J. Champollion-Figeac (ed.), *Documents historiques inédits sur l'histoire de France. Mélanges historiques*, (Paris, 1841), 1: 605–9.

47 Bourrilly, *Essai*, p. 173. É. Berger (ed.), *Les registres d'Innocent IV*, Les registres des papes du XIIIe siècle. Bibliothèque des Ecoles françaises d'Athènes et de Rome, Série II (Paris, 1884–1921), 1, no. 2417. The pope's two letters refer to the ships of the Templars, yet the Hospitallers undoubtedly faced the same problems and obtained similar papal support.

48 See above, n. 43.

49 R. Filangieri et al. (eds), *I registri della cancelleria angioina* (Naples, 1950–) (hereafter: Filangieri), VI, p. 266, no. 1441: *non obstante consuetudine Marsilie, quam propter hoc infringi non vult.* The count died in Italy during the return voyage: L.T. Belgrano and C. Imperiale di Sant'Angelo (eds), *Annali genovesi di Caffaro e de' suoi continuatori dal MXCIX al MCCXCIII* (Rome, 1890–1929), 4: 144 and n. 4.

50 Literary sources reflect estimates and, therefore, are not reliable to the same extent: see D. Jacoby, 'Il ruolo di Acri nel pellegrinaggio a Gerusalemme', in M.S. Calò Mariani (ed.), *Il*

Ventimiglia offered space for more than 400 pilgrims on the *St Francis*.[51] In 1250 the *St Victor*, which most likely sailed from Marseilles, carried 453 passengers, whose names were recorded in Messina.[52] It is unclear whether these ships also carried cargo. The agreement of 1246 between Marseilles and King Louis IX regarding the hiring of ships refers to the *Countess*, belonging to the Hospitallers (*Comitissa del Hospital*), as standard, the price to be paid for the vessels being determined according to whether they would have larger or smaller dimensions and carrying capacity than the *Countess*. Each party to the contract had the specifications of that ship in writing, yet unfortunately these are not recorded.[53] Still, a comparison with a proposal made in 1268 for the hiring of ships in Marseilles for the second crusade of King Louis IX offers useful information in this respect. It refers to the relative cost of their service in terms similar to those of 1246, taking as standard a vessel capable of carrying 1,000 pilgrims, for which measurements are provided.[54] We may thus safely assume that this figure also applied to the *Countess*.[55] It was by no means exceptional, as is attested by one of Marseilles' statutes recorded in 1253.[56] Incidentally, in 1248 the Genoese ship *Oliva* was capable of carrying 1,100 passengers.[57] The large figures, from 1,000 to 1,500 *peregrini*, the latter mentioned in 1233, clearly refer to pilgrims and exclude crusaders with their military equipment and horses. It is likely that the Templar ship *Falcon*, apparently the largest vessel sailing in the Mediterranean in 1291, also carried pilgrims before evacuating people from Acre in that year.[58] The reference to a maximum number of *peregrini* in the agreement of 1233 between Marseilles and the Hospitallers and Templars implies that the ships of the two Orders transporting pilgrims and crusaders were regularly inspected by the commune's officers, like any other vessels. These officers ensured that passengers enjoyed proper

---

cammino di Gerusalemme, Atti del II Convegno Internazionale di Studio, Bari-Brindisi-Trani, 18–22 maggio 1999 (Bari, 2002), p. 28.

51 See above, n. 35.

52 Kedar, 'The Passenger List', pp. 267–72. Kedar already assumed that the vessel had sailed from a Provençal port. Note that it carried the same name as the abbey of St Victor in Marseilles.

53 Champollion-Figeac, *Documents*, pp.605–9, esp. 608.

54 Ibid., pp. 609–14.

55 As convincingly argued ibid., p. 608, n. 2, and p. 611, n. 1.

56 Pernoud, *Les statuts*, p. 49 (I, chap. 35).

57 Contract edited by E.H. Byrne, *Genoese Shipping in the Twelfth and Thirteenth Century* (Cambridge, Mass. 1930), p. 81, no. XV. J.H. Pryor, 'The Naval Architecture of Crusader Transport Ships: A Reconstruction of some Archetypes for Round-Hulled Sailing Ships', *The Mariner's Mirror* 70 (1984), 374–5, repr. in Pryor, *Commerce, Shipping and Naval Warfare in the Medieval Mediterranean* (London 1987), no. VII, estimates at some 580 the maximum number of passengers carried by a thirteenth-century three-decker. Recently Pryor expressed amazement at the number mentioned for the *Oliva*: J. Pryor, 'The Venetian Fleet for the Fourth Crusade and the Diversion of the Crusade to Constantinople', in M. Bull and N. Housley (eds), *The Experience of Crusading*, vol. 1 (Cambridge, 2003), p. 116, n. 69. His reconstruction and calculations are obviously incorrect.

58 The ship had been bought from the Genoese: Ramon Muntaner, *Crònica*, chap. 194, in F. Soldevilla (ed.), *Les quatre grans cròniques* (Barcelone, 1971), pp. 841–2.

space and conditions, in accordance with the commune's legislation, and prevented the embarkation of passengers in excess of the ship's capacity.[59]

Some Hospitaller ships sailing from Marseilles carried private cargo to Acre, namely, the *Falcon* in 1238 and 1248,[60] an unnamed vessel in 1242 and 1243,[61] and the *Griffon* in 1244 and 1248.[62] The *Countess*, mentioned in the agreement of 1246 between Marseilles and King Louis IX, was being equipped for sailing in the harbour of Marseilles between April and August 1248.[63] There is good reason to believe that, like the *Countess*, all the other *naves* or round-hulled sailing ships just mentioned had been built in Marseilles and that this was their home port. Three of them were sailing simultaneously in 1248, namely, the *Griffon*, the *Falcon* and the *Countess*, the latter capable of carrying a large number of pilgrims. Still, between 1244 and 1249 part of a large grain consignment sent by the Order from Marseilles to Acre was carried by private vessels, and Hospitallers occasionally travelled on such ships, as in 1250.[64]

The *Angel* and the *Bonaventura*, attested respectively in 1270 and 1278, were also *naves* based in Marseilles that occasionally carried private passengers and cargo, as revealed by letters of King Charles I of Sicily.[65] One letter, to the master of the royal vessels and shipyard in Brindisi, states that the Hospitaller prior of Saint-Gilles, who had authority over his brethren in Marseilles, had offered the service of the *Bonaventura* to the king. The latter ordered that the vessel be repaired and equipped at royal expense.[66] Together with the royal sailing ships *St Mark*, *St Nicolas* and *St Paul* it was to proceed to Acre with provisions for Roger of San Severino, the king's representative in the Kingdom of Jerusalem.[67]

Marseilles clearly fulfilled a major function in the Hospitaller shipping system. The city was the outlet for the largest supply network of the Order in the West.[68] The abundant supply of timber in Provence and the tax exemptions enjoyed by the Hospitallers on its transit to shipyards, mentioned above, undoubtedly promoted the commissioning of vessels in Marseilles, although it is likely that the Hospitallers also bought some ships that were already in service. In 1273 James I of Aragon granted the Hospitallers tax exemption in Montpellier for cordage, caulking materials and

59 On that legislation, see above, n. 36.

60 Blancard, *Documents*, 1: 120–2, no. 80; 1: 405, no. 345, and 2: 295–6, no. 1003.

61 Ibid., 1: 153–6, nos. 94, 96.

62 Ibid., 1: 162–3 and 338–9, respectively nos. 101 and 178; 2: 19–21, no. 396: note the reference to revenue from fare or freight.

63 Ibid., 1: 403–4, no. 344.

64 *Cart.*, 2: 615–16, no. 2322; Kedar, 'The Passenger List', p. 270: a knight Templar.

65 On the *Angel*, see above, n. 49.

66 Filangieri, 19: 170, no. 249.

67 Ibid., 18: 106–8, no. 208; 19: 181–2, no. 272; 21: 103–5, no. 109. In all the documents cited in this and the previous note the *Bonaventura* is called *navis*. The term 'galley' only appears in the summary of another document by C. Minieri-Riccio (reproduced in Filangieri, 19: 50–1, no. 181), which is clearly faulty. It has misled Pryor, '*In subsidium Terrae Sancta*', pp. 132, 135, 146, to consider that the *Bonaventura* was a galley.

68 Bronstein, *The Hospitallers*, pp. 64–97.

other commodities required for the fitting of their ships.[69] In 1248 the two Hospitaller brothers acting as shipmasters of the *Griffon*, the *Falcon* and the *Countess* obtained loans in Marseilles for equipping their vessels and were responsible for the repayment.[70] A Hospitaller officer stationed in Marseilles appears as first witness in each of the three loan contracts, concluded in the Order's house, namely Berengarius, cited on 7 April 1248 as treasurer and on the following 23 July as prior of that house, with W. of Garda, whose function is not stated, as second witness.[71] These officers were under the authority of the prior of St Gilles.[72] In 1278 the latter intervened directly to offer the service of the *Bonaventura* to King Charles I, as noted earlier. It follows that he was in charge of the ships operating from Marseilles.[73] The city also served as a transit and trans-shipment station for the Order. The privileges it obtained from the viscounts before late March 1213 refer to ships sailing to Spain. While this suggests the conveyance of supplies to that region, it also enabled the transfer of goods for shipping to the Levant on the return voyage.[74] In 1290 King Charles II of Sicily allowed the brethren and horses coming from the kingdoms of France and Majorca to leave Marseilles on a Hospitaller ship or another vessel.[75]

A contract concluded in Ayas or Laiazzo, Armenian Cilicia, on 24 March 1279 documents a particular aspect of the Hospitallers' financial dealings involving their ships.[76] The *St Andrew* had been chartered by Genoese partners,[77] who agreed to carry three merchants and their cargo to Genoa or to the latter's *Riviera* extending from Porto Venere to Nola, in accordance with the decision of the majority of merchants on board. The same fare and freight would apply should any of the three merchants wish to reach Marseilles. The Genoese partners further declared that they had cancelled the clause of their contract with Boniface of Calamandrana, Grand Commander of the Order, concerning the date of the vessel's departure, and promised that the ship would sail on 19 April at the latest. Their unilateral decision to change the departure date suggests that they had hired the entire ship from the Hospitallers and were operating it on their own without interference from the Order's members. This also explains why the ship anchored in Ayas to take passengers and cargo on board. The reference to Marseilles as the ultimate destination suggests that this port was the vessel's base and that the partners were to deliver it there to the Order's officers.

69 *Cart.*, 3: 285, no. 3491. On the production of sails and cordage in Marseilles, see Pernoud, 'Le Moyen Age', p. 308.

70 For references, see above, nn. 60, 62 and 63.

71 Blancard, *Documents*, 2: 21, no. 396 and p. 296, no.1003; 1: 404, no. 344.

72 They are missing in the list of brethren serving in the priory of St Gilles compiled by Bronstein, *The Hospitallers*, pp. 156–65.

73 Contrary to Bronstein, *The Hospitallers*, p. 10.

74 See above, n. 16.

75 Filangieri, 35: 125–6, no. 322.

76 L. Balletto (ed.), *Notai genovesi in Oltremare. Atti rogati a Laiazzo da Federico di Piazzalunga (1274) e Pietro di Bargone (1277, 1279)* Collana storica di fonti e studi, diretta da G. Pistarino, 53 (Genoa, 1989), pp. 324–6 and 341–3, Pietro di Bargone, no. 92, for what follows.

77 On this type of partnership, usually divided into six portions, see Pernoud, 'Le Moyen Age', pp. 254–5.

Few, if any, Hospitaller men and likewise little cargo for the ship's westward sailing had induced the Grand Commander residing in Acre to entrust the vessel to the Genoese charterers. As counterpart of the prior of St Gilles, he was responsible for the operation of the Hospitaller vessels in the Levant.[78]

The evidence examined above provides some insight into the development of the Hospitallers' fleet. The Order operated barks and small vessels for short-distance transportation, as in the Dead Sea and between Acre and its sugar-cane plantations along the river Na'aman flowing into the Bay of Acre.[79] It used small or medium-sized craft, not exclusively its own, to concentrate goods in specific ports from where they were shipped on larger vessels to the Levant. This practice is attested, for instance, in 1273 for the port of Bari, to where products were brought from the Order's estates in the region,[80] and was most likely the rule with respect to Marseilles, as suggested by the various tax exemptions the Hospitallers obtained for river navigation to the Mediterranean.[81] Sound economic considerations induced them to acquire large ships capable of ensuring long-distance transportation, a costly service when using private vessels, especially since the Order had to maintain regular shipping to the Levant. Clearly, its transport vessels were based in Western ports from where reinforcements and supplies were sent. However, since the Order could not always fill them to capacity, it occasionally embarked merchants, goods and pilgrims to reduce sailing expenses. The problem was particularly acute on return voyages, when the Order's reduced requirements left ample space on the ships. Instead of searching for passengers and cargo for a one-way voyage, it was sometimes more profitable to lease the entire ship to merchants who operated it on their own behalf, as in 1279.[82]

The Hospitallers' exclusive transportation of pilgrims on specific vessels practically ensured that the ships were filled to capacity on both the outward and the return journeys, although some pilgrims may have died on the way to or in the Holy Land, and others may have decided to stay there. This was a purely financial operation. While it prevented the loading of cargo, it must have yielded substantial revenue that could be spent on the purchase of ships, goods or services. Hospitaller ships carrying only pilgrims are attested in Marseilles until 1253, but we do not

78 Boniface of Calamandrana appears as Grand Commander of Acre in 1261 and as Grand Commander of the Hospital in 1268, 1269, 1271 and 1279, in Acre in all these instances: see respectively, *Cart.*, 3: 60–1, no. 3047; p. 175, no. 3292; p. 146, no. 3236; pp. 253–4, no. 3422, and the contract mentioned above, n. 76. He was also in Acre in 1288: L. Minervini (ed.), *Cronaca del Templare di Tiro (1243–1314). La caduta degli Stati Crociati nel racconto di un testimone oculare* (Napoli, 2000), p. 192, par. 236. Riley-Smith, *The Knights of St John*, pp. 205–6, 298–300, 366–7, 370–1, considers him Grand Commander of Outremer, yet without referring to his authority over the Order's ships in the Levant.

79 Respectively H.E. Mayer, *Die Kreuzfahrerherrschaft Montreal (Sobak). Jordanien im 12. Jahrhundert*, Abhandlungen des Deutschen Palästinavereins, 14 (Wiesbaden, 1990), pp. 133, 276–7, and *Cart.*, 2: 486–7, no. 2117. On the sugar plantations, see Bronstein, *The Hospitallers*, p. 53.

80 Filangieri, 10: 39, no. 134.

81 See above, p. 64.

82 See above, n. 79.

know how long this type of operation continued beyond that year. In view of the strong competition from Italian carriers, it is excluded that such ships sailed from Apulia and Sicily.[83] On the other hand, it is likely that some of the Order's vessels carried pilgrims together with merchants and cargo to Acre, although evidence of this is lacking.

The growth of the Hospitaller fleet in the thirteenth century appears to have been rather slow. There is no evidence of Hospitaller vessels transporting crusaders at the time of the Fifth Crusade, which lasted from 1218 to 1221, presumably because they only carried the Order's own forces and supplies.[84] Despite their having several ships in 1248, none appears to have transported pilgrims or crusaders during the crusade of Louis IX, which began in that year. The *Falcon*, first attested in 1238, had been sailing for at least ten years by 1248.[85] The ships hired by King Louis IX in 1246 were to be less than six years old.[86] A Venetian maritime statute of 1233 refers to the loading of ships of that age. Another Venetian statute, dated 1255, deals with the maximum cargo a ship of 94 metric tons or more, travelling outside the Adriatic, was allowed to carry, and imposes a reduction after five years of sailing and a further one after two additional years.[87] In 1248 the priory of St Gilles had ready cash, which it invested in the enlargement of its property.[88] However, it appears to have been reluctant to finance the replacement of the *Falcon* at that time. It has been noted that the Hospitallers failed to participate in the evacuation of Acre's population in the last months before the city's fall to the Muslims, although the Templars' *Falcon* did participate in the operation.[89] This was clearly not owing to a lack of Hospitaller ships. Rather, it is likely that the Order's vessels carrying pilgrims and supplies stopped on the way to Acre when news of that city's siege reached them.

The Hospitallers resorted to four options for conveying their men, provisions and messages across the Mediterranean. They took advantage of private ships engaging in commercial sailings, hired whole vessels, purchased them, or commissioned their construction.[90] The simultaneous resorting to these options, which apparently continued until 1291, implies that the Order was never capable of ensuring on its own

83 This competition will be discussed elsewhere.

84 The same applies to Templar ships. Some of these were involved in the fighting: *Historia Damiatina*, chaps. 12 and 21, in H. Hoogeweg (ed.), *Die Schriften des kölner Domscholasters, späteren Bischofs von Paderborn un Kardinal-Bischofs von S. Sabina Oliverus*, Bibliothek des litterarischen Vereins in Stuttgart, 202 (Tübingen, 1894), pp. 181, 194. Similar evidence for Hospitaller ships is missing.

85 See above, n. 60.

86 Champollion-Figeac, *Documents*, p. 605.

87 R. Predelli and A. Sacerdoti (eds), *Gli statuti marittimi veneziani fino al 1255* (Venice, 1903), pp. 73–4, par. 2, and pp. 129–30, par. LXI.

88 Bronstein, *The Hospitallers*, pp. 82–3.

89 Favreau-Lilie, 'The Military Orders', pp. 209–11, and see above, n. 58.

90 For the hiring of ships in Marseilles, see above, p. 62. Shipping from southern Italy on board a private *panzonus* is attested in 1272: Filangieri 9: 293, no. 22. This type of vessel was capable of carrying a heavy cargo, often of grain: see U. Tucci, 'L'impresa marittima: uomini e mezzi,' in G. Cracco and G. Ortalli (eds), *Storia di Venezia dalle origini alla caduta della Serenissima*, II, *L'età del Comune* (Rome, 1995), pp. 636–7.

the volume of maritime transportation that it needed, despite increasing investment in ocean-going ships after 1191. It also contradicts the common belief, expressed again recently, yet never documented, that the Order owned a considerable number of vessels in the thirteenth century.[91] All the ships mentioned above were *naves*. In 1288 the Hospitallers in Acre equipped a *saitie*, an elongated oared vessel capable of swift sailing, yet no galleys of the Order are attested until 1291.[92] This distinguishes the Hospitaller fleet before that year from the one operating later from Cyprus, which included a naval force of galleys.

91 Bronstein, *The Hospitallers*, p. 75: 'their fleet was already significant at the beginning of the thirteenth century'.

92 Minervini, *Cronaca del Templare di Tiro*, p. 192, par. 236. The Templars equipped thirteen galleys in 1279: ibid., p. 150, par. 163. On the *saitie*, see Tucci, 'L'impresa marittima', p. 641.

Chapter 7

A Mediterranean Career in the Late Thirteenth Century: The Hospitaller Grand Commander Boniface of Calamandrana

Jochen Burgtorf

According to Anthony Luttrell, the Hospitaller Boniface of Calamandrana (d. 1298) was 'one of the most important brethren of his time',[1] yet scholars have not paid particular attention to him thus far. While evidence survives only for the last three decades of his life, the documentation is sufficient to show that Boniface played a key role during the final years of the Latin kingdom of Jerusalem as well as the decade after the relocation of the Hospitallers' headquarters to Cyprus (1291). He was a high-level diplomat, operating in the crusader states, Mamluk territory, Cilician Armenia, Italy, the Iberian peninsula and the papal *curia*. Why was he so successful? Were his talents and connections used to capacity? And what kind of personality emerges from the 'facts' of his career? To answer these questions, which have noteworthy implications for the history of the Hospitallers, I will address five aspects of Boniface's life, in chronological order: his origins; his debut as a Hospitaller; his term as Grand Commander in the East; his diplomatic activities in northern Syria until 1288; and his role as Grand Commander of the West.

Origins

Boniface's date of birth is unknown. Considering that he functioned as grand commander in the Hospitallers' central convent by the late 1260s and died in 1298, he was probably born by 1240.[2] Calamandrana is a location in Piedmont (north-western Italy). Does this mean that Boniface was Piemontese?[3] In 1288, King Alfonso III

1 A. Luttrell, 'The Hospitallers' Interventions in Cilician Armenia: 1291–1375', in T.S.R. Boase (ed.), *The Cilician Kingdom of Armenia* (Edinburgh, 1978), p. 121.

2 J. Burgtorf, 'Führungsstrukturen und Funktionsträger in der Zentrale der Templer und Johanniter von den Anfängen bis zum frühen 14. Jahrhundert', Ph.D. Dissertation, Heinrich-Heine-Universität Düsseldorf, 2001, pp. 424–32.

3 Cf. A. Barbero, 'I signori di Canelli fra la corte di re Manfredi e gli ordini monastico-cavallereschi', in R. Bordone (ed.), *Bianca Lancia d'Agliano: Fra il Piemonte e il Regno di Sicilia* (Alessandria, 1992), p. 232, note; E. Bellomo, 'Mobility of Templar Brothers and Dignitaries: The Case of North-Western Italy', in J. Burgtorf and H. Nicholson (eds),

of Aragon referred to Boniface as his most beloved blood-relative (*consanguineus noster carissimus*).[4] Does this imply that he was Aragonese?[5] Alfonso III (b. 1265) was a son of Peter of Aragon (the future King Peter III) and Constance of Sicily; Constance was the granddaughter of Bianca Lancia, who, apart from probably being married to the Emperor Frederick II, was related to the Piemontese family of Canelli; Calamandrana was owned and, as a name, used by that noble house.[6] The Canelli family had ties to the military orders throughout Italy,[7] and it is possible that Boniface was a kinsman of Hubert of Calamandrana, the Templar commander of Lombardy in 1271.[8] At any rate, it appears that Boniface belonged to the extended family of Constance of Sicily and may have come to Aragon when she did, namely around the time of her marriage to Peter (1262). Thus, the question whether Boniface was Aragonese or Piemontese is anachronistic. To Alfonso, Boniface was a blood-relative – a fact that in medieval Europe superseded regional considerations. If Boniface joined the Hospitallers in or after 1262, his membership may have been intended to serve as a connection between the Aragonese court and the Order.

Hospitaller debut

It has been stated that Boniface assumed the office of Grand Commander in or by November 1266.[9] Chronologically, this would make sense because Stephen of Meses, the previous holder of the office, had been killed in October 1266.[10] However, the document cited for Boniface's above-mentioned status, while headed '1266' in Joseph Delaville Le Roulx's *Cartulaire*, is dated *l'an de l'incarnacion ... mil et deus*

International Mobility in the Military Orders (Twelfth to Fifteenth Centuries) (Cardiff, 2006), p. 112, note.

4 *Acta Aragonensia: Quellen zur deutschen, italienischen, französischen, spanischen, zur Kirchen- und Kulturgeschichte aus der diplomatischen Korrespondenz Jaymes II., 1291–1327*, ed. H. Finke, 3 vols (Berlin, 1908–22), 3, pp. 3–4 n. 2; *Cartulaire général de l'Ordre des Hospitaliers de Saint-Jean de Jérusalem, 1100–1310*, ed. J. Delaville le Roulx, 4 vols (Paris, 1894–1906) (hereafter *CH*), 3, pp. 518–519 no. 4007; cf. Luttrell, 'The Hospitallers' Interventions in Cilician Armenia', p. 121, note.

5 Cf. H. Rohde, *Der Kampf um Sizilien in den Jahren 1291–1302* (Berlin, 1913), p. 43; A. Luttrell, 'The Aragonese Crown and the Knights Hospitallers of Rhodes: 1291–1350', *English Historical Review* 76 (1961), 11; M.-L. Bulst-Thiele, *Sacrae domus militiae Templi Hierosolymitani magistri: Untersuchungen zur Geschichte des Templerordens, 1118/19–1314* (Göttingen, 1974), p. 275, note.

6 Barbero, pp. 219–33.

7 Barbero, pp. 229–33; Bellomo, pp. 103, 106–7, 109, 111–12.

8 F. Bramato, *Storia dell'ordine dei templari in Italia*, 2 vols (Rome, 1994), 2, p. 143, n. 297.

9 J. Delaville Le Roulx, *Les Hospitaliers en Terre Sainte et à Chypre: 1100–1310* (Paris, 1904), p. 410; J. Bronstein, *The Hospitallers and the Holy Land: Financing the Latin East, 1187–1274* (Woodbridge, 2005), p. 148.

10 *Annales de Terre Sainte*, ed. R. Röhricht and G. Raynaud, in *Archives de l'Orient latin*, 2 vols (Paris, 1881–84) (hereafter *AOL*), 2, p. 453 (documents).

cens et sissante et noef,[11] thus, it unequivocally belongs to 1269 and is not the first trace of Boniface's career.

While 'Stephen', 'Gerard' and 'William' were common names for Hospitallers at that time, 'Boniface' was not. Thus, since Boniface of Calamandrana took over as Grand Commander by 1269, it is likely that the *Bonifacius* who appears without cognomen as the last Hospitaller witness to an agreement concluded on 29 October 1267 between the Hospitaller Master Hugh Revel and the abbot of St Mary of the Latins was Boniface of Calamandrana.[12] At first glance, the subordinate position of his name in the witness list might suggest that he was not an important Hospitaller. However, this 1267 transaction brought together a powerful military order and a prestigious ecclesiastical institution, two bishops as witnesses and, among the Hospitallers, the Order's marshal and former marshal; thus, Boniface was in prominent company. Hugh Revel's mastership (1258–77/8) facilitated a considerable number of careers of non-French brothers,[13] and it may be that Boniface, who brought Italian as well as Aragonese connections to the table, was one of his protégés.

Grand Commander in the East

Boniface's tenure as Grand Commander reflects some of the diverse responsibilities of this office. On 10 February 1268/69, he confirmed an inventory of 'things' that were in the safekeeping of Brother John, the prior of the Order's church in Acre (*recognovit frater Boniffacius de Calamandrana magnus preceptor domus Hospitalis sancti Johannis de Accon se invenisse res infrascriptas in custodia fratris Johannis prioris ecclesie domus predicte*).[14] The inventory as such has not survived, but according to another summary of the same document the 'things' were liturgical instruments (*vases sacrés et ornements*).[15] Unlike most of the other functionaries of the central convent, the prior did not have to render an account during the Order's general chapter.[16] Since the only other mention of a prior's inventory before 1310 dates from 1285,[17] it is possible that it was first introduced under Hugh Revel, in which case Boniface may have been one of the first grand commanders to oversee it.

Sometime between the spring and the fall of 1269, *frere Boniface de Calamandrane, grant comandor d'Acre*, appeared as a witness in the later invalidated

11 *CH* 3, p. 146, n. 3236 (wrongly dated '1266'); *Regesta Regni Hierosolymitani and Additamentum*, ed. R. Röhricht (Innsbruck, 1893–1904) (hereafter *RRH*), n. 1367 (correctly dated '1269').

12 *CH* 3, p. 166, n. 3283.

13 J. Burgtorf, 'The Templars' and Hospitallers' High Dignitaries: Aspects of International Mobility', in *International Mobility* (cf. note 3 above), p. 14.

14 Marseilles, Archives départementales (Bouches-du-Rhône), Ordre de Malte, 56 H 68, Inventaire de Manosque, a. 1531 (ms. s. XVI), fol. 178 (19 H). I am grateful to Professor Rudolf Hiestand, Düsseldorf, for allowing me to use his transcription of the Inventaire.

15 *CH* 3, p. 175, n. 3292.

16 *CH* 2, pp. 536–61, n. 2213 (usance 109).

17 Inventaire de Manosque, fol. 467' (51 B).

draft of a charter by which Hugh Revel acknowledged that the Hospitallers had rented the lordship of Arsuf from Balian of Ibelin.[18] The Hospitallers had taken over Arsuf by 1262, and the Mamluk Sultan Baybars had conquered it in 1265; thus, the documents issued in 1269 merely served to sort out the legal obligations between the two parties.[19] My above-mentioned dating (spring–autumn 1269) is based on prosopographical information: one of the document's witnesses, Roger of Vere, Hospitaller prior of England, came to the East during the spring of 1269;[20] another witness, the Draper William of Villaret, left the Holy Land in the autumn of 1269 to become lieutenant-prior and eventually prior of St Gilles.[21] William of Villaret and Boniface of Calamandrana would see each other again many years later.

According to the fourteenth-century Arab chronicler Ibn al-Furāt, a Frankish delegation came to Baybars while he was in Syria during 667 AH (10 September 1268–29 August 1269) in order to negotiate a truce. Baybars had the envoys incarcerated, 'although he did free one of them, the vizier of the Hospitallers, who had been of service to him'.[22] Jonathan Riley-Smith has speculated that this 'vizier of the Hospitallers' may have been the Grand Commander, 'at this time perhaps Boniface of Calamandracen'.[23] Indeed, if one had to find an equivalent for the oriental *vizier* in the order of the Hospital, the Grand Commander would be a good match: both ran the 'nucleus' of their respective institutions. Thus, Boniface, who served as Grand Commander during 667 AH is a likely candidate. The Mamluk sultans maintained good relations with several members of the military orders;[24] regrettably, there is no further information on how Boniface might have been of service to Baybars.

Boniface retained the office of Grand Commander for another two years beyond these events, namely until 1271.[25] After that, he his nowhere to be found – until 1279, when some Genoese individuals leased the *St Andrew*, a Hospitaller ship, to several other Genoese individuals and rescinded an agreement they had entered into with the Hospitaller Grand Commander Boniface of Calamandrana concerning the return of the said ship (*insuper cassamus ... pactum ... inter nos et dictum fratrem Bonifacium de Calamandrana, preceptorem magnum dicti Hospitalis de recessione dicte navis*).[26] The lease was documented in the coastal city of Ayas in Cilician

18 *CH* 3, pp. 60–1, n. 3047.

19 J. Riley-Smith, *The Knights of St John in Jerusalem and Cyprus, c. 1050–1310* (London, 1967), pp. 133–4; Bronstein, pp. 35, 37–8.

20 *CH* 3, pp. 197–8, nos 3337–9.

21 *CH* 3, p. 215, n. 3376.

22 Ibn al-Furāt, *Tārīkh al-Duwal wa'l-Mulūk (Ayyubids, Mamlukes and Crusaders)*, ed. U. and M.C. Lyons, notes by J. Riley-Smith, 2 vols (Cambridge, 1971). 2, pp. 132–3.

23 Ibn al-Furāt, *Tārīkh al-Duwal wa'l-Mulūk*, 2, p. 234, note.

24 J. Burgtorf, 'Die Ritterorden als Instanzen zur Friedenssicherung?', in D. Bauer, K. Herbers and N. Jaspert (eds), *Jerusalem im Hoch- und Spätmittelalter* (Frankfurt, 2001), pp. 191–8.

25 1269: *CH* 3, p. 146 n. 3236 (wrongly dated '1266'); *RRH*, n. 1367 (correctly dated '1269'). 1271: *CH* 3, pp. 253–4, n. 3422.

26 'Actes passés en 1271, 1274 et 1279 à l'Aïas (Petite Arménie) et à Beyrouth par devant des notaires génois', ed. C. Desimoni, in *AOL*, 1, pp. 511–2, no. 32; *CH* 3, p. 382, n. 3694.

Armenia. Does this mean that Boniface was there at the time?[27] Possibly, since there is no evidence for any other Hospitaller Grand Commander in that year. However, if Boniface had been present in Ayas in 1279, would the Genoese simply have voided their agreement with him? Moreover, in the Order's first two centuries the Grand Commander very seldom travelled beyond the borders of the kingdom of Jerusalem. According to Delaville le Roulx, it is more likely that the charter in question refers to a contract between the Genoese and the Grand Commander drawn up at an earlier date[28] – and that would mean that there is no trace of Boniface during the mastership of Nicholas Lorgne (1277/8–85). Maybe Boniface had been a candidate for the mastership as well, and Nicholas, once elected, decided to leave him without an office? Maybe his 'absence' has to do with the fact that the records are incomplete? At any rate, the document of 1279 is an early example of the Grand Commander's involvement with his Order's maritime activities. That Boniface did pay a visit to Armenia, albeit at a later date, will be seen below.

Diplomatic activities

Following the death of Prince Bohemond VII of Antioch–Tripoli in October 1287, his territories passed to his sister Lucy, who was then living in Apulia. But the Frankish nobles of northern Syria turned to Bohemond's mother, Sibylla of Armenia, and asked her to appoint someone to rule over Tripoli. Discontented with her choice, the inhabitants of Tripoli founded their own commune (with Bartholomew Embriaco taking the lead) and enlisted the support of the Genoese, who dispatched five galleys under the command of Benedict Zaccaria to Tripoli. Meanwhile, Lucy's husband, Narjot of Toucy, encouraged his wife to claim her inheritance and to ask the Hospitallers for their support. The commune of Tripoli declared its willingness to receive Lucy on condition that she would accept their rights as well as those of the Genoese, whose leader, Benedict Zaccaria, had just travelled to Armenia (maybe because Bohemond's mother was an Armenian princess). When Benedict heard of the negotiations between Lucy and the commune, he invited her to come to Tyre and consult with him.[29] At Tyre, the Hospitaller Boniface of Calamandrana, 'a great lord' (*j. grant seignor*), met her, they both negotiated with Benedict[30] and an agreement was reached. Thus, in 1288 Boniface played a prominent role in his order, which was now governed by Master John of Villiers (1285–1293/4). Bartholomew Embriaco, however, was not pleased with the outcome of the negotiations and turned to the Mamluk Sultan Qalāwūn who, convinced that the alliance between Tripoli and Genoa was not in his best interests, conquered the city in 1289.[31]

---

27 Cf. Luttrell, 'The Hospitallers' Interventions in Cilician Armenia', p. 121.

28 Delaville Le Roulx, p. 410, note.

29 *Les gestes des Chiprois: Recueil des chroniques françaises écrites en Orient au XIIIe & XIVe siècles*, ed. G. Raynaud (Geneva, 1887), pp. 231–4, §§ 464–72.

30 *Les gestes des Chiprois*, p. 234, § 472.

31 P.M. Holt, *Early Mamluk Diplomacy (1260–1290): Treaties of Baybars and Qalawun with Christian Rulers* (Leiden, 1995), p. 22.

The impact of Boniface's involvement in these affairs can be gathered from a letter that Alfonso III of Aragon wrote to the Hospitallers in June 1288. The king claimed that the Order's master had sent away two brothers, namely Boniface of Calamandrana, the king's most beloved blood-relative, and Raymond of Ribells, the king's faithful friend – 'both men of great nobility, wisdom and piety, whose understanding, laudable conduct and good reputation had contributed much to the order' (*viros utique magne nobilitatis, magne discrecionis ac magne religionis, per quorum discrecionem, laudabilem conversacionem ac fame serenitatem ordini vestro multum accrevisse credimus*). Where had the master sent them? 'One to Armenia, where he would be destined to die due to that kingdom's bad aerial quality, the other one back to Alfonso himself with a presumptuous message' (*ipsorum alterum in Armeniam cito moriturum propter illius regni infeccionem aëris destinavit, alium vero ad nos cum ambaxiata seu legacione frivola duxit*).[32] What was going on?

According to Anthony Luttrell, both Boniface and Raymond had 'supported the [Aragonese] crown against the Angevins in 1285'.[33] After the Sicilian Vespers of 1282 the Anjou had been expelled from the island, and King Peter III of Aragon, based on his wife Constance's hereditary claims, had established Aragonese rule over Sicily. Given his own familial connections to Aragon through the same Constance, Boniface must have been content with these developments. Jonathan Riley-Smith has speculated that, 'because of his advocacy of the cause of Aragon at a time when the ... [Hospitallers were] supporting France and the papacy against it', Boniface may have been left without office in the 1280s and sent off to Armenia, yet was back as 'chief negotiator for the Hospital' the same year the Aragonese king protested Boniface's treatment.[34] But where is the evidence that he was actively working on behalf of Aragon in the 1280s? Boniface was a Hospitaller and had taken a vow of obedience, his order's interests had to come first and he lacked the authority to set the tone of the Hospitallers' 'foreign' policy. Would he have advocated Aragonese interests during chapter meetings? Surely. Would that have been reason enough for the Order to ignore his many years of expertise and cast him aside? Surely not. Would he, after two decades in the East and at a time when the Hospitallers were exposed to all sorts of dangers, have complained to his Aragonese relatives about the climate in Armenia? Unlikely.

Is it not possible that there is a connection between Boniface's travel to Armenia and his role in the negotiations of 1288, which may, in fact, have started as early as October 1287 – a connection already suspected by Marie-Luise Bulst-Thiele (in a footnote) in 1974?[35] Considering the dynastic ties between Antioch–Tripoli and Armenia, the trip that Benedict Zaccaria took to Armenia, and the Hospitallers' own interests there, it seems that Boniface's stay in Cilician Armenia was not intended as a death sentence. He was acting on behalf of his order and Princess Lucy. Yet, Lucy's Angevin ties – her husband, Narjot of Toucy, was the admiral of Charles II of Anjou – cannot have pleased Alfonso of Aragon. Maybe the king's rant concerning

32 *Acta Aragonensia*, 3, pp. 3–4, no. 2; *CH* 3, pp. 518–19, no. 4007

33 Luttrell, 'The Aragonese Crown and the Knights Hospitallers of Rhodes', p. 11.

34 Riley-Smith, p. 371.

35 Bulst-Thiele, p. 282, note.

Boniface's alleged exposure to the bad aerial quality of Armenia had more to do with Boniface's activities than with his health. As an aside: Anthony Luttrell has pointed out that Boniface owned a translated copy of the *Libellus de Alchimia* (for centuries erroneously ascribed to Albertus Magnus) which had been given to him by an Armenian king;[36] thus, his 'Armenian connection' seems to have left Boniface not only with sufficiently good health for yet another busy decade in his life, but also with an interesting souvenir.

Grand Commander of the West

It is unknown whether Boniface was present during the fall of Acre in May 1291; however, later that year, he resurfaced as his order's Grand Commander of the West – an ad hoc office that had been filled as needed (usually when the master was very busy in the East), but not continuously, since the second half of the twelfth century.[37] Brother Ferrand of Barras had functioned as Grand Commander of the West until 1262.[38] In 1291, at a time when the Order had to reconstitute itself, it was a wise move to revive this office and to select someone of Boniface's calibre to hold it. His appointment probably took place in Cyprus, and since there is no evidence that he ever returned to the East, it may have been one of his first acts as 'grand commander of the west' to ask Master John of Villiers to free a certain Theodore of Kolossi, a layman from the diocese of Limassol, who subsequently became Boniface's chamberlain (*camerarius*).[39] Boniface must have been fond of him or impressed with his abilities, or both, to petition for his release. At any rate, the incident seems to reveal a rather pleasant side of Boniface's personality.

In his new office, Boniface was involved in rebuilding the forces of Latin Christianity in the East. On 13 December 1291, Pope Nicholas IV informed Charles of Anjou that he had ordered Boniface of Calamandrana, the Hospitallers' 'general commander of the west' (*generalis [preceptor] Hospitalis sancti Johannis Jerosolimitani in partibus cismarinis*), to send several galleys of arms and troops to the East.[40] In the following year, the Genoese brothers Manuel and Benedict Zaccaria chartered armed galleys for the fight against the Muslims; they were acting on behalf of 'Master' Boniface of Calamandrana (*fratris Boniffatii de Calamandrana magistri*) who was to receive the galleys for the (actual) Hospitaller master.[41] The creative titles given to Boniface at this time are indicative of the high regard in which he was held.

36 Luttrell, 'The Hospitallers' Interventions in Cilician Armenia', p. 121; cf. A. Forey, 'Literacy and Learning in the Military Orders during the Twelfth and Thirteenth Centuries', in *The Military Orders*, vol. 2, ed. H. Nicholson (Aldershot, 1998), p. 196.

37 Delaville Le Roulx, pp. 358–61, 414–15.

38 *CH* 3, pp. 36–42, no. 3035.

39 *CH* 3, pp. 797–8, no. 4488; cf. N. Coureas, *The Latin Church in Cyprus, 1195–1312* (Aldershot, 1997), p. 168.

40 *CH* 3, p. 602, no. 4177; cf. A. Luttrell, 'The Hospitallers in Cyprus after 1291', *Acts of the First International Congress of Cypriot Studies, II* (Nicosia, 1972), p. 163, note.

41 P. Accame, *Notizie e documenti inediti sui Templari e Gerosolimitani in Liguria* (Finalborgo, 1902), pp. 124–36, no. 4.

Moreover, one can see here that Boniface was able to rely on an old acquaintance, Benedict Zaccaria, to assist him in some of his responsibilities.

Once Boniface had returned to the West, it was only a matter of time before the affairs of Aragon required his attention. In 1291, Alfonso III had passed away and his younger brother, James II, had succeeded him as king of Aragon. On 26 December 1292, James announced that – because of the insistence and entreaties of Brother Boniface of Calamandrana (*ad instanciam et preces venerabilis et religiosi viri fratris Bonifacii de Calamandrana*) – he had decided to improve the conditions of those who were being held as hostages together with the sons of Charles II of Anjou, by removing their shackles whenever feasible.[42] Charles himself had been a hostage in Aragon between 1284 and 1288; upon his release, he had to leave three of his sons and many nobles from Provence in his place. Kings were expected to show grace, particularly around Christian feast days; thus, Boniface had timed his request well. Was he, however, really acting on behalf of Charles of Anjou here?[43] One should consider that a peace between Aragon and the house of Anjou was, of course, in the interests of the Hospitallers, who were trying to refocus everybody's attention on the urgent needs of the East. Boniface enjoyed trust from all sides and used it to his order's benefit.

In January 1293, James of Aragon met with his father-in-law, King Sancho IV of Castile, at Guadalajara.[44] Afterwards, James informed the emir of Granada that Boniface, 'grand master of the order of the Hospital' (*Don Fray Bonifacio, maestro mayor de la horden del Espital*), had been present as well.[45] Considering that the letter's addressee was a high-ranking Muslim, the use of the title 'grand master' may have been an attempt on James's part to make Boniface appear particularly distinguished. One may wonder how the Hospitaller master would have reacted to the liberal use of the title. Yet, within his own order Boniface was clearly held in the highest esteem as well: in 1293, Pedro Miguel of Iriverri, the Hospitaller commander of Calchetas, referred to Boniface as the 'grand and general commander' in the West (*Grant et General Comendador en las partidas denant mar*);[46] since Pedro Miguel functioned as Boniface's lieutenant in Navarre[47] this may, of course, have been an attempt at self-aggrandizement by inflating the respective diplomatic *formula*.[48]

A letter written by James of Aragon in 1293 indicates the scope of Boniface's involvement with regard to the above-mentioned peace negotiations. James reports

---

42 *Acta Aragonensia*, 3, pp. 27–8, note.

43 Cf. Rohde, p. 48.

44 L. Vones, 'Guadalajara, Zusammenkunft', in *Lexikon des Mittelalters*, 9 vols (Munich and Zurich, 1977–99), 4, col. 1757.

45 G. Digard, *Philippe le Bel et le Saint-Siège de 1285 à 1304*, 2 vols (Paris, 1936), 2, pp. 284–5, n. 14.

46 S.A. García Larragueta, *El gran priorado de Navarra de la orden de San Juan de Jerusalén (siglos XII–XIII)*, 2 vols (Pamplona, 1957), 2, pp. 606–7, no. 533.

47 García Larragueta, 2, pp. 610–614, no. 537.

48 J. Burgtorf, 'Das Selbstverständnis der Templer und Johanniter im Spiegel von Briefen und Urkunden', in *Selbstbild und Selbstverständnis der geistlichen Ritterorden (Ordines militares, Colloquia Torunensia Historica, XIII)*, ed. R. Czaja and J. Sarnowsky (Toruń, 2005), pp. 26–9.

that the king of Castile, his father-in-law, and 'the venerable Brother Boniface of Calamandrana, the envoy of the said king of Castile to the king of France and to King Charles of Jerusalem [i.e. Charles II of Anjou]' (*ven[erabilis] fr[ater] Boniffacius de Calamandrana missus per dictum regem Castelle ad ... regem Francie et Karolum regem Jherusalem*), had written to him about the peace treaty.[49] The reference to Charles of Anjou as 'king of Jerusalem' illustrates the intricacy of diplomatic relations in the late thirteenth century: the title was claimed by the Lusignans of Cyprus, where the Hospitallers had their headquarters, but, since 1277, also by the Angevins. During his negotiations with Aragon, Charles put the crown of Jerusalem on the table, which – since the offer was actually met with interest by the Aragonese[50] – must have made things even more delicate for the Hospitallers, whose focus remained on the East.

In the midst of all this, Boniface found the time to renew his acquaintance with William of Villaret. William had taken over the prestigious priory of St Gilles and was thus, after Boniface, the highest-ranking Hospitaller in the West. In 1293, both Hospitallers sent a complaint concerning their Order's affairs in Aquitaine to King Edward I of England, and Edward issued orders to have the case investigated.[51] Boniface and William may even have met somewhere in southern France, because the documentation for 1293 suggests that Boniface was travelling outside of Aragon. In August, James of Aragon issued an order to his officials to ensure Boniface's unobstructed return into the kingdom,[52] but he also expressly forbade Boniface to send non-Aragonese visitors or other officials into his kingdom;[53] in these politically sensitive times, James did consider Boniface 'Aragonese' and trustworthy, but was not willing to extend this sentiment to all Hospitallers. In the same month, Boniface was back in Aragon,[54] and the peace negotiations between James and Charles began to pick up speed.[55] On 12 December 1293, a first formal agreement was reached at La Junquera.[56]

The year 1294 turned into another busy one. When a question arose regarding the election of the prioress of the convent of the Hospitaller sisters of Sigena, James of Aragon sent Boniface to Sigena to obtain copies of the respective privileges – only to realize later that the sisters had held on to two papal documents that the king then had to acquire through a second envoy.[57] It is curious that the sisters had not complied with the request when it was presented to them by one of the highest

49 *Acta Aragonensia*, 3, p. 4, note; *CH* 3, pp. 618–19, no. 4213.

50 P.W. Edbury, *The Kingdom of Cyprus and the Crusades, 1191–1374* (Cambridge, 1991), pp. 107–8.

51 *CH* 3, pp. 622–3, no. 4222.

52 *CH* 3, p. 623, no. 4224.

53 *CH* 3, p. 623, no. 4225; cf. H. Prutz, *Die geistlichen Ritterorden: Ihre Stellung zur kirchlichen, politischen, gesellschaftlichen und wirtschaftlichen Entwicklung des Mittelalters* (Berlin, 1908), p. 304.

54 *Acta Aragonensia*, 3, pp. 4–5, note.

55 S. Schein, *Fideles Crucis: The Papacy, the West, and the Recovery of the Holy Land, 1274–1314* (Oxford, 1991), p. 189.

56 Vones, 'Guadalajara, Zusammenkunft', 1757.

57 *CH* 3, p. 646, no. 4249.

officials of their Order. Later in the year, Boniface travelled to Italy – copies of some of Sigena's papal privileges obviously had to be procured in Rome[58] – and reported back to James periodically.[59]

James, for his part, took up Boniface's views in his own letters, for example one sent to the veteran crusader John of Grailly, the former seneschal of the Latin kingdom of Jerusalem.[60] In order to help the Latin Christians in the East, James intended to equip a fleet under the command of Boniface and the Catalan admiral Roger of Lauria.[61] Yet, Pope Celestine V seems to have been 'less enthusiastic'[62] and ordered Boniface to transfer to papal bankers 15,000 gold florins of the sum that he had received to outfit the fleet.[63] By October 1294, Boniface was travelling back to Aragon with messages from the pope[64] and Charles of Anjou.[65] In December, he was at James's court, where he interceded on behalf of Florentine merchants who intended to do business with Aragon.[66] Boniface had connections on many levels, and his position at the Aragonese court made him an ideal intercessor (or 'lobbyist').

Meanwhile, things had changed at the Hospitallers' headquarters: the new master, Odo of Pins (1293/4–1296) had somehow managed to irritate both Boniface and William of Villaret. In March 1295, James of Aragon instructed his envoys to bring to the attention of the new pope, Boniface VIII, how Odo had treated Boniface of Calamandrana (*qel maestre del Espital ha fet contra frare Bonifaci*).[67] It is conceivable that Odo had summoned Boniface to Cyprus – maybe regarding the *responsiones* that the Western Hospitaller priories were expected to send to the East[68] – and that Boniface had refused to go, owing to his involvement in the ongoing peace negotiations between Aragon and Angevin Naples, which, in June 1295, culminated in the treaty of Anagni.[69] Yet, the pope backed his namesake. On 11 August 1295, he sent him on a new mission, this time to receive, as the pope's representative, liege homage from Roger of Lauria for two islands off the coast of Tunisia,[70] and on the following day he dispatched a stern letter to Odo of Pins, ordering the master to amend his conduct which, based on what the pope had heard from trustworthy people (*persones dignes de foy*), left much to be desired.[71] Boniface

58 *CH* 3, p. 648, no. 4254.

59 *Acta Aragonensia*, 1, pp. 14–15, no. 10 and 19–20, no. 14.

60 *Acta Aragonensia*, 3, p. 10, note.

61 *Acta Aragonensia*, 1, p. 15, note; cf. Schein, p. 189, note.

62 Luttrell, 'The Hospitallers in Cyprus after 1291', p. 163, note.

63 *CH* 3, pp. 652–653, no. 4260; cf. Schein, p. 142; *Acta Aragonensia*, 1, pp. 91–3, no. 64 (it is possible that this last document is connected to the 15,000 gold florins mentioned above).

64 *Acta Aragonensia*, 3, pp. 28–31, no. 17.

65 *Acta Aragonensia*, 3, pp. 25–8, no. 15.

66 *CH* 3, p. 654, no. 4265 and 660, no. 4273.

67 *Acta Aragonensia*, 3, pp. 33–42, no. 20.

68 Cf. *CH* 3, p. 662, no. 4276.

69 L. Vones, *Geschichte der Iberischen Halbinsel im Mittelalter (711–1480): Reiche – Kronen – Regionen* (Sigmaringen, 1993), p. 140.

70 *CH* 3, pp. 670–2, no. 4290.

71 *CH* 3, pp. 672–3, no. 4293.

of Calamandrana and William of Villaret had taken the offensive against their own master and may have even had his deposition in mind.

According to the famous collection of statutes compiled by *Guill[aume] de Saint Estenne* (Paris, BN, fr. 6049), several Hospitallers launched a complaint against Odo of Pins at the papal *curia*, and among these Hospitallers was 'one who was grand commander of all the land of the west and whose name was Brother Boniface of Calamandrana, a man with a great reputation in both the "world" and the order' (*estoit I d'eaus, celuy qui avoit esté e fu grant comandor de tote la terre d'outre mer. Et avoit nom frere Bonaface de Calamandraine, home de grant renomée au siecle et en la religion*), and the other was William of Villaret, 'a man known and loved by kings and barons and princes, then prior of St Gilles'. They submitted to the pope a catalogue of reforms that, if implemented, would have changed the Order's monarchial leadership to a system of collective governance reminiscent of the Cistercian *definitorium*. The project died when William of Villaret left the *curia* 'for other business' (*por autres besoignes*)[72] – probably because of his own election as master of the Order (1296). Why did the brothers elect William and not Boniface? There had not been a non-French master since the days of the highly controversial Alfonso of Portugal (1202/3–1206). Boniface had a more interesting résumé than William who, between 1269 and 1299, hardly ever left southern France, yet, the brothers may not have been 'ready' for a leader of Piemontese–Aragonese extraction.

Meanwhile, Boniface continued his activities on Italian soil. According to the treaty of Anagni, James of Aragon had renounced his claim to Sicily, which returned to being a papal fief, yet his younger brother Frederick had not accepted these terms. On 15 January 1296, Frederick was proclaimed king by the Sicilian *parlamentum*.[73] The pope saw this as an affront and, in February, sent Boniface of Calamandrana (*generalis preceptor hospitalis s[ancti] Johannis Jerosolimitani in partibus cismarinis*) and the bishop of Urgell to negotiate.[74] However, the envoys either failed or came too late: on 25 March, Frederick was crowned in Palermo (as 'Frederick III'), whereupon the pope excommunicated him.[75]

In 1297, Boniface of Calamandrana attended the general chapter that Master William of Villaret had summoned to Marseille.[76] Unlike the brothers of the central convent in Cyprus, who later held the practice of convening general chapters in the West against William, Boniface does not appear to have been troubled by the invitation; one gets the impression that the two understood each other. It is noteworthy that William retained Boniface as 'grand commander of the west' even though he himself stayed in the West as well (and there actually seems to have been no Grand Commander in the East between 1291 and 1299). Was William trying to move the Order's headquarters to the West permanently?

---

72 *CH* 3, pp. 655–8, no. 4267.

73 S. Fodale, 'Sizilien. (B) II. Herrschaft der Anjou und Aragón', in *Lexikon des Mittelalters* (cf. note 46 above), 7, col. 1961.

74 *Acta Aragonensia*, 3, pp. 48–53, no. 25, note; *CH* 3, p. 677, no. 4299.

75 Fodale, 1961.

76 Cf. *CH* 3, pp. 766–8, no. 4461.

In 1298, Boniface returned to the kingdom of Naples to claim the monastery of St Trinity of Venosa for the Hospitallers, since the pope had granted it to them, and on 23 February, Robert of Anjou, who was Charles of Anjou's general vicar of the still (or again) disputed kingdom of Sicily, ordered the royal justiciar to act accordingly.[77] On the same day, Pope Boniface VIII wrote to Boniface of Calamandrana regarding his quarrels with the influential Roman house of Colonna, which supported Frederick III; the pope demanded that Boniface procure 12,000 gold florins from his Order to aid the papal cause,[78] yet it is doubtful that Boniface had time to comply with the papal wishes. In a letter dated 25 October 1298, and addressed to the Hospitaller Master William of Villaret, the pope refers to Boniface with the adverb *quondam*,[79] thus indicating that Boniface had passed away. According to a document issued by the Order's central convent in the spring of 1299, the news of Boniface's death reached Cyprus during the 'passage of the cross' (*passage de la sainte Crois*) which is presumably named after the feast of *exaltatio crucis* (celebrated on 14 September). This suggests that Boniface had died before mid-September 1298.[80]

The story does not end here. In December 1298, the pope confiscated 5,565 gold florins that Boniface had deposited with a Florentine bank[81] – a nice contribution to the papal war chest. This seems to have set off the alarm bells at the Hospitallers' headquarters on Cyprus. William of Villaret had summoned another general chapter to the West, to be held in Avignon on 1 August 1300, but the central convent now demanded that this event be relocated to Cyprus. The brothers reminded William that the pope had confiscated Boniface's (and thereby the Order's) possessions and asked: 'How damaging would it be to the order should the pope decide to confiscate the possessions of the master if the latter should die in the West?[82] With the death of Boniface of Calamandrana, William of Villaret had lost his staunchest Hospitaller ally in the West, and maybe even a close friend. Thus, he bowed to the will of the central convent and returned to the East,[83] where – curiously enough according to an Aragonese source – he was soon troubled by the bad aerial quality.[84]

In conclusion: Much of Boniface of Calamandrana's success was based on the Piemontese–Aragonese extent and the 'royal' quality of his family ties. Without these (and without Hugh Revel's protection), his brilliant Hospitaller career and his far-reaching diplomatic service probably would not have happened. Yet, these non-French family ties may have ultimately limited his success as well: despite all his achievements, the Order did not elevate him to the mastership. The other source

77 *CH* 3, pp. 733–4, no. 4406.

78 *CH* 3, p. 735, no. 4408; cf. N. Housley, *The Italian Crusades: The Papal-Angevin Alliance and the Crusades against Christian Lay Powers, 1254–1343* (Oxford, 1982), p. 182.

79 *CH* 3, pp. 750–1, no. 4433; *Les registres de Boniface VIII*, ed. Bibliothèque des Écoles Françaises d'Athènes et de Rome (Paris, 1907–39), no. 2825.

80 *CH* 3, pp. 766–8, no. 4461.

81 *Registres de Boniface VIII*, no. 2827.

82 *CH* 3, pp. 766–8, no. 4461; cf. ibid., 769–76, no. 4462 and 782–4, no. 4468.

83 *CH* 3, pp. 810–6, no. 4515.

84 *CH* 4, pp. 35–6, no. 4573; *Acta Aragonensia*, 3, p. 11, note.

of his success was his ability to hold his ground in potentially charged situations. Baybars was presumably impressed by him, Benedict Zaccaria became one of his allies, the pope believed his accusations against his own master, and the Aragonese kings listened when he interceded – be it on behalf of incarcerated enemies or of foreign merchants (only the Hospitaller sisters of Sigena were not so easily swayed). Were his talents and connections used to capacity? It appears, at first glance, that his extensive experience in the crusader states was not really utilized in the East after 1291. Yet, both the administrative and the diplomatic skills that he had first honed as his Order's Grand Commander were easily transferable to the West. Moreover, who could be a more convincing advocate for the needs of the Latin Christians in the East than someone who had lived among them? Finally, and with all due caution, a few words should be said about the personality of Boniface of Calamandrana as it emerges from the historical record. His attention to the emancipation of the *homo Hospitalis* Theodore of Kolossi certainly endears him to the modern reader, even though the act itself was neither that unusual nor spectacular. Yet, the bond between him and William of Villaret, which spanned three decades, does impress. It surpassed the obedience that they were willing to exhibit toward their Order's master, and it obviously survived when one was promoted over the other. History may have relegated Boniface of Calamandrana to the background. That is, however, not where he belongs.

Chapter 8

Judicial Processes in the Military Orders: The Use of Imprisonment and Chaining

Alan Forey

Chaining and imprisonment were used for a variety of purposes in the Middle Ages. In the secular world detention was frequently employed in the earlier part of the period as a coercive measure for the payment of a ransom or debt, and in the thirteenth century it often had a custodial function. Imprisonment as a form of punishment was more common in the ecclesiastical sphere, although in time the practice of church tribunals was increasingly imitated by lay courts.[1] The intention of this paper is to examine the purposes for which military orders, which were religious institutions but composed mainly of laymen, employed chaining and imprisonment up to the early fourteenth century, and the extent to which they use made of them. It will be concerned only with the detention of brothers and of those who were employed in a paid or unpaid capacity in their houses; vassals and captives will not be discussed.

Although in some circumstances brothers and employees might be both imprisoned and chained, these measures could, of course, be employed separately. Some regulations allude to chaining *or* imprisonment,[2] and the Templar Customs state that a brother who was sentenced to lose his habit and to be put in irons was to reside and eat in the almoner's house, and work with the slaves: he was not kept in prison.[3] Imprisonment and irons were the two normal methods of restricting movement, but references also occur to house arrest, which did not allow an individual to go beyond the door of his residence. The pillory is mentioned in regulations only with reference to slaves.[4]

In the military orders, chaining and imprisonment were not used primarily for custodial purposes. Brothers were expected to confess their faults in chapter – or, if they failed to do so, accusations could be made against them there – and sentence was

1 J. Dunbabin, *Captivity and Imprisonment in Medieval Europe, 1000–1300* (Basingstoke, 2002), pp. 2–3; E.M. Peters, 'Prison before the Prison: The Ancient and Medieval Worlds', *The Oxford History of the Prison. The Practice of Punishment in Western Society*, ed. N. Morris and D.J. Rothman (New York, Oxford, 1995), pp. 27–9, 34, 37–43.

2 *La Règle du Temple*, ed. H. de Curzon (Paris, 1886) (hereafter *RT*), p. 166 (art. 271). In the Catalan version 'or' is replaced by 'and': *The Catalan Rule of the Templars. A Critical Edition and English Translation from Barcelona, Archivo de la Corona de Aragón, Cartas Reales, MS 3344*, ed. J. Upton-Ward (Woodbridge, 2003), p. 26 (49).

3 *RT*, p. 163 (266); *Catalan Rule*, p. 48 (119). For a distinction between chaining and imprisonment in monastic regulations, see Patrologia Latina, 149, col. 736; 150, col. 1047.

4 *RT*, p. 193 (336).

usually imposed in the same assembly.[5] It was not therefore the norm for brethren to be held in custody before judgment. Yet in some cases judgment was deferred to a higher authority,[6] and there were certainly occasions when brothers were held in prison, chains or house arrest for the purposes of security before judgment was passed. Detention was, for example, employed in some cases involving violence. The Hospitaller general chapter in 1288 decreed that a brother who killed another could not be received back into the community without the permission of the master and chapter: in the meantime, he was to be put in prison if he could be taken.[7] Dietrich of Altenburg, master of the Teutonic order, ruled in the fourteenth century that if a brother attacked another, the brethren were to seize him and he was to be held in irons until he appeared for judgment.[8] In the Teutonic order it was further decreed that those who engaged in conspiracy within the order were to be detained in prison until the general chapter.[9] When in 1313 the delegate of the abbot of Morimond – to which Calatrava was affiliated – investigated claims of a conspiracy hatched against the master of Calatrava, García López de Padilla, some of the accused were brought before the hearing in chains.[10] A less rigorous detention is mentioned in the Catalan version of the Templar Customs: in a case in Catalonia involving the forging of papal bulls, sentence was deferred to the master and convent in the East, and in the meantime those accused were dispersed to various houses and commanded not to go outside the gate.[11]

Imprisonment for security purposes after a judgment had been made, but before it was implemented, is mentioned in a letter of the Templar seneschal Gerard of Ridefort in the later twelfth century. Robert of Sourdeval, who had been deprived of his habit and was to be sent back to the West, was detained in custody in Acre until a ship sailed.[12]

Brothers who had absconded were apparently also at times subjected to chaining or imprisonment, apparently as a custodial measure. Henry of Livonia reports that in the early thirteenth century Wickbert of Soest, a member of the Swordbrethren, was pursued to Idumea and taken back to Wenden, where he was put in chains, and in 1251 the chapter of the order of Santiago decreed that if any brother left the

---

5 See, for example, *RT*, pp. 217 (389), 218 (392), 221–3 (399–405).

6 Ibid., pp. 164 (267), 277–8 (528–30), 289–90 (554); *Cartulaire général de l'Ordre des Hospitaliers de Saint-Jean de Jérusalem, 1100–1310*, ed. J. Delaville le Roulx, 4 vols (Paris, 1894–1906) (hereafter *CH*), 3, pp. 118–21, doc. 3180 (10).

7 *CH*, 3, pp. 525–9, doc. 4022 (14).

8 *Die Statuten des Deutschen Ordens nach den ältesten Handschriften*, ed. M. Perlbach (Halle, 1890) (hereafter *SDO*), p. 151 (24); G. Schmidt, *Die Handhabung der Strafgewalt gegen Angehörige des Deutschen Ritterordens* (Kitzingen-Main, 1954), pp. 138–9.

9 *SDO*, p. 153 (II, 1); Schmidt, p. 139.

10 C. de Ayala Martínez, 'Un cuestionario sobre una conspiración. La crisis del maestrazgo de Calatrava en 1311–1313', *Aragón en la edad media* 14–15 (1999), 88–9.

11 *Catalan Rule*, p. 76 (174). The translation, ibid., p. 77, is not altogether accurate.

12 F.-M. Abel, 'Lettre d'un Templier trouvée récemment à Jérusalem', *Revue biblique*, 35 (1926), 289–90; M.L. Bulst-Thiele, *Sacrae domus militiae Templi Hierosolymitani magistri. Untersuchungen zur Geschichte des Templerordens, 1118/19–1314* (Göttingen, 1974), p. 360, doc. 1.

order because he did not like the work he was given, he should be seized and put in chains and obliged to carry out his duties.[13] The evidence is not altogether free from ambiguity: Henry of Livonia's comment does not indicate whether there was a judicial process when Wickbert was back at Wenden, but the circumstances would suggest that there was a custodial element to his being placed in irons; and although in some monasteries imprisonment was imposed on apostates as a punishment,[14] regulations of military orders do not specify either imprisonment or chaining among the penalties to be imposed on deserters.[15]

More commonly, however, imprisonment and chaining in the military orders had the function of punishment, as they did in other religious institutions, which could not impose sentences of death or mutilation as were passed in secular courts.[16] It might, of course be argued that the military orders were different from other religious foundations in that their officials were usually laymen: in 1283 a Hospitaller statute excluded only brother chaplains from appointment to bailiwicks where the Order had the power to pass death sentences.[17] Yet some earlier Hospitaller statutes had forbidden all brothers to impose death sentences on those under their lordship:[18] military orders apparently sought to put themselves on a par with other religious. Imprisonment involved being cut off from the community, probably often living in isolation. Irons, apart from impeding movement, were, as a punishment, also regarded as a sign of shame. The Templar Customs state at one point that *l'on le devroit metre en fers et faire li de la honte asses.*[19] To live within the community in chains was a more visible sign of disgrace than being shut away in prison, just as the punishment of eating off the floor was performed in the sight of other brethren, from whom the delinquents were nevertheless separated.[20] Some clauses in the Templar

---

13 *Heinrici Chronicon Livoniae*, cap. 13, ed. L. Arbusow and A. Bauer, Monumenta Germaniae Historica, Scriptores rerum germanicarum (Hanover, 1955), p. 67; Madrid, Biblioteca Nacional, MS 8582 fol. 56. During the Templar trial, Stephen of Troyes asserted that he had apostasized but had been seized and held captive by his colleagues: H. Finke, *Papsttum und Untergang des Templerordens*, 2 vols (Münster, 1907), 2, p. 336, doc. 155; but his evidence is of doubtful validity.

14 F.D. Logan, *Runaway Religious in Medieval England, c.1240–1540* (Cambridge, 1996), p. 152.

15 During their trial some Templars asserted that they had been told, or feared, that they would be imprisoned if they deserted and were caught, but these were probably seeking to explain why, despite admitting some of the main charges against their order, they had not left the Temple: see, for example, J. Michelet, *Procès des Templiers*, 2 vols (Paris, 1841–51), 1, p. 218; 2, pp. 194, 251–2. In a non-judicial context, detention was employed by the Templars as a means of ensuring that the insane could not harm themselves or others: *Catalan Rule*, p. 22 (42). No comparable regulation is found in the decrees of other orders, but presumably similar action would have been taken.

16 Dunbabin, pp. 144–6; R.B. Pugh, *Imprisonment in Medieval England* (Cambridge, 1968), pp. 375–7.

17 *CH*, 3, pp. 450–5 doc. 3844 (22).

18 Ibid., 3, pp. 118–21, 225–9, docs. 3180 (7), 3396 (10).

19 *RT*, pp. 234–5 (432); cf. ibid., pp. 233–4 (430), 235–6 (434), 241–2 (449).

20 Cf. V.I.J. Flint, 'Space and Discipline in Early Medieval Europe', in *Medieval Practices of Space*, ed. B.A. Hanawalt and M. Kobialka (Minneapolis, 2000), pp. 151–5.

Customs imply that chaining was also a cause of certain disqualifications in the future: article 612 ruled that from the time that a brother was put in irons, he could never carry a banner, be a commander in battle or participate in the election of a master.[21] But the situation is not altogether clear, as another clause states that these disqualifications applied to all who had been sentenced to loss of habit and penance for a year.[22]

Yet imprisonment and chaining were not among the most common penalties inflicted for offences committed by brothers or those in an order's employ. Regulations of military orders focus more on expulsion, loss of habit, fasting and beating.[23] In the surviving regulations of some orders there is little reference to imprisonment or chaining in the twelfth and thirteenth centuries: Hospitaller decrees for this period make only one allusion to the imprisonment of a brother in a punitive context.[24]

The normal penalty for the most serious offences committed in a military order was expulsion, which meant that an offender was obliged to transfer to a stricter order or, in the case of those who had lied about their status at admission ceremonies, return to a spouse, lord or creditor. Yet expulsion was sometimes accompanied, or replaced, by chaining or imprisonment. Article 267 of the French version of the Templar Customs, which lists the types of punishment which could be inflicted, begins: *La premiere est de la maison perdre; et si y a choses dont l'en le puet metre en fers et en prison perpetuel.*[25] Those who lied about their qualifications on entering the Temple, unless they were priests,[26] were put in irons for a period, before being expelled; and although in one clause it was stated merely that such recruits might be put in irons,[27] the wording of other sections implies that a period of chaining was the norm.[28] These Customs also mention instances in which those guilty of sodomy, deserting to the Muslims and killing Christian merchants – offences for which the penalty was expulsion – were held perpetually in chains and prison.[29] Imprisonment or chaining of Templars for offences which were normally punished by expulsion are also mentioned in other kinds of sources. Roger of Howden records that Gilbert

21 *RT*, p. 316 (612); cf. ibid., pp. 243 (452), 306 (589), 315 (611).

22 Ibid., p. 254 (478). These disqualifications could also be incurred in other ways: ibid., pp. 323 (627), 325 (631).

23 For summaries of punishments in the leading orders, see M. Barber, *The New Knighthood: A History of the Order of the Temple* (Cambridge, 1994), pp. 219–21; J. Riley-Smith, *The Knights of St John in Jerusalem and Cyprus, c.1050–1310* (London, 1967), pp. 267–71; I. Sterns, 'Crime and Punishment among the Teutonic Knights', *Speculum* 57 (1982), 89–92; for the Spanish orders, see C. de Ayala Martínez, *Las órdenes militares hispánicas en la edad media (siglos XII–XV)* (Madrid, 2003), pp. 399–400.

24 *CH*, 2, pp. 536–61, doc. 2213 (3). This clause could also be interpreted as having a coercive element.

25 *RT*, p. 164 (267); cf. *Catalan Rule*, p. 48 (120).

26 *RT*, pp. 235–6 (434), 241–2 (449).

27 Ibid., pp. 237–8 (438).

28 Ibid., pp. 233–4 (430), 234–5 (432), 241 (446), 342 (669); *Catalan Rule*, pp. 30–2 (62).

29 *RT*, pp. 289–90 (554), 297–8 (573), 312 (603); *Catalan Rule*, pp. 54 (129), 70 (164), 96 (198).

of Orgestan, who had been appointed to collect the Saladin Tithe in England in 1188, was put in irons for stealing a large sum,[30] and the records of the Templar trial similarly mention that Walter le Bachelor, Templar master in Ireland, was put in prison for appropriating some of his order's possessions.[31] Templars interrogated in the early fourteenth century also quoted examples of perpetual imprisonment for theft and sodomy, and some seem to have thought that it was the normal punishment for the latter offence.[32] Yet, according to the Templar Customs, sentences of to expulsion, other than for lying on admission, were not necessarily accompanied by imprisonment or chaining. In a fourteenth-century decree of the Teutonic order, however, it was ruled that those guilty of sodomy should suffer perpetual imprisonment: this may have been a new ruling, for earlier *Gesetze* apparently refer only to expulsion.[33] In orders linked to the Cistercians there seems similarly to have been a trend for expulsion to be replaced by imprisonment for some offences. Calatravan statutes from the turn of the twelfth and thirteenth centuries decree that a brother who struck another and caused bleeding should be expelled from the order and should not be received back without the permission of the visitor; *definiciones* for the order of Montesa in 1331, on the other hand, rule that if a brother gravely wounded another, he was to be held in a house in irons and chains, until the master showed mercy to him.[34]

Those who committed lesser offences, for which the penalty was the loss of habit for a period, might also be put in irons or imprisoned. When a list of punishments was drawn up in the Temple in the second half of the twelfth century, it was stated that those who were guilty of such faults might be put in irons, especially if the offence was of a serious nature or caused considerable harm. A brother who struck a colleague might be put in irons *se la bateure est laide*, and a Templar carrying a

30 *Chronica*, ed. W. Stubbs, 2 vols, Rolls Series 51 (London, 1868–9), 2, p. 354; *Gesta Regis Henrici Secundi Benedicti Abbatis*, ed. W. Stubbs, 2 vols, Rolls Series 49 (London, 1867), 2, pp. 47–8.

31 D. Wilkins, *Concilia magnae Britanniae et Hiberniae*, 4 vols (London, 1737), 2, pp. 337, 346.

32 Finke, 2, pp. 325, 327–8 doc. 154; L. Ménard, *Histoire civile, ecclésiastique et littéraire de la ville de Nismes*, 7 vols (Paris, 1750–8), 1, Preuves, p. 188; Michelet, 1, pp. 382, 386–7; 2, pp. 7, 223. When interrogated, many French Templars claimed that they had been threatened with imprisonment, or feared that they would be incarcerated, if they revealed what had allegedly happened at admission ceremonies: see, for example, Michelet, 1, pp. 191, 219, 226, 295; R. Sève and A.-M. Chagny-Sève, *Le procès des Templiers d'Auvergne, 1309–1311* (Paris, 1986), pp. 123, 126, 140; but they may have been influenced by the wording of the articles of accusation and by a desire to explain away their supposed failure to publicize the alleged happenings. Templar regulations refer only to expulsion as a penalty for revealing chapter proceedings: *RT*, pp. 153 (225), 228 (418), 288 (550); *Catalan Rule*, p. 38 (74). The further claims that imprisonment was threatened to those who refused to deny Christ and spit on the Cross during the Templar admission ceremony require comment only if the validity of the accusations is accepted.

33 *SDO,* pp. 86–7 (39), 135 (III, 2); cf. Schmidt, p. 137.

34 D.W. Lomax, 'Algunos estatutos primitivos de la orden de Calatrava', *Hispania* 21 (1961), 492–4 (26); J.F. O'Callaghan, 'Las definiciones medievales de la orden de Montesa, 1326–1468', *Miscelánea de textos medievales* 1 (1972), 237 (1331: 16).

banner who charged without permission could similarly be chained *se grant damaige en avenist.*[35] The *Gesetze* of the Teutonic order similarly state that graver – as distinct from the gravest – offences might be punished by chaining and imprisonment as well as a year's penance, if the circumstances demanded:

> Etsi excessus enormitas vel diuturnitas aut iteracio aut penitentis impaciencia penam exaggerari per vincula et carcerem aut anno penitenciali secundum annum vel minus superaddi vel eciam penam carceris perpetuari exegerit, superiorum et fratrum iudicio decernatur.[36]

As in the Temple, the matter was left to the discretion of those in authority. In later additions to the Templar Customs, however, which give further information about punishments, the statement that a brother could be put in irons was sometimes replaced by the ruling that in some circumstances he ought (*doit*) to be chained. Both in the section on the holding of chapters, which possibly dates from the later twelfth century, and in another section, which has been ascribed to the years 1257–67, it was said of a brother who was found to have slept with a woman that he ought to be put in irons.[37] Yet there was no consistent change in wording: article 612 in the later Customs still stated that if a brother charged with a banner without permission and great harm was done, *li porroit l'on regarder a metre en fers*; and in other clauses chaining was similarly still left to the discretion of the chapter.[38] Nevertheless, the increasing use of the word 'ought' suggests that there was a trend towards the imposition of chaining, rather than leaving the matter to the discretion of the chapter. That chaining was becoming more common in the Temple is also implied by a case in the mid thirteenth century when a Templar who had struck another was put in irons, even though the blow had not been serious. Some questioned the decision, but the marshal, who was presiding over the chapter, ruled with the majority that it was in accord with Templar Customs.[39]

In regulations drawn up in the early decades of the fourteenth century for orders with Cistercian ties, obligatory imprisonment was part of the statutory penalty for some offences that did not incur expulsion, and in some instances this punishment is not found for comparable offences in earlier rulings. *Definiciones* for Calatrava issued in 1304 state that rebellious brothers were not only to undergo a penance but were also to be imprisoned.[40] Imprisonment was similarly stipulated in

---

35 *RT*, pp. 155 (234), 157 (242); *Catalan Rule*, pp. 40 (86), 42 (94); see also *RT*, pp. 154–5 (233), 156 (236), 157 (241), 159–60 (249–50), 162 (260); *Catalan Rule*, pp. 38–40 (84), 42 (93–4), 44 (101–2), 46 (112).

36 *SDO*, pp. 85–6 (38).

37 *RT*, pp. 243 (452), 309 (594).

38 Ibid., p. 316; cf. ibid., pp. 245 (457), 306–7 (589), 311–12 (600), 315–16 (611), 321 (620); *Catalan Rule*, pp. 40 (85), 74 (170).

39 *RT*, pp. 308–9 (592–3). At the end of the thirteenth century, it was decreed in the Teutonic order that turcopoles and *knechte* guilty of assault should be put in irons for a year: *SDO*, p. 142 (II, 5).

40 J. F. O'Callaghan, 'The Earliest "Difiniciones" of the Order of Calatrava, 1304–1383', *Traditio* 17 (1961), 264–5 (1304: 10, 11).

comparable decrees for Alcántara and Montesa in the same period.[41] Yet Calatravan statutes enacted at the turn of the twelfth and thirteenth centuries had only ruled that a disobedient brother *prima die disciplinam accipiat, tribus diebus panem et aquam sine mantili in terra comedat, equum et arma anno dimidio perdat.*[42] And whereas these earlier Calatravan statutes had merely forbidden brothers to apply to the king without the master's permission, in 1304 the penalties imposed for this offence included obligatory imprisonment.[43] At the turn of the twelfth and thirteenth centuries the penalty for fornication in Calatrava consisted of eating sitting on the ground for a year, being allowed only bread and water for three days a week and being beaten on Fridays, besides being deprived for a year of horse and arms; however, in the fourteenth century, brothers of Montesa who committed this offence were to be imprisoned.[44] These rulings are to be seen against the background of thirteenth-century decrees issued by the general chapter of Cîteaux which specify imprisonment as the penalty for a growing number of offences.[45]

The adoption of detention as a punishment might in certain instances be linked with particular circumstances. Its use in cases of sodomy might be linked to hardening attitudes towards homosexuality,[46] and it could be argued that early-fourteenth-century rulings in Calatrava were prompted by conflicts within that order at that time,[47] Yet it would seem that there was also a more general trend towards the use of imprisonment and chaining as a punishment in religious orders, and this was perhaps a consequence of harsher sentencing in secular courts and the perceived inadequacies of other ecclesiastical penalties.[48]

No doubt it was hoped that the hardships of imprisonment and chaining would dissuade brothers from repeating their crimes, and persuade others not to offend. But there are no more than hints that these punishments were also expected to produce repentance and to be reformative. As has been seen, imprisonment was in some instances to be perpetual. Some early-fourteenth-century decrees for Calatrava and Montesa do state that the master or convent could show mercy to an offender, but these do not explicitly declare that this was to be done because of a prisoner's

41 *Colección diplomática medieval de la orden de Alcántara (1157?–1494)*, ed. B. Palacios Martín, 2 vols (Madrid, 2000–3), 1, pp. 284–8 doc. 434 (1306: 12, 33); P. Josserand, 'Pour une étude systématique de la documentation statutaire des ordres militaires: Deux manuscrits des "definiciones" inédites d'Alcántara de 1306', *En la España medieval* 20 (1997), 333–4; O'Callaghan, 'Definiciones de Montesa', p. 233 (1326: 25).

42 Lomax, pp. 492–4 (24).

43 Ibid., pp. 492–4 (33); O'Callaghan, 'Earliest "Difiniciones"', p. 264 (1304: 9); cf. ibid., p. 275 (1336: 8).

44 Lomax, pp. 492–4 (30); O'Callaghan, 'Definiciones de Montesa', p. 231 (1326: 5).

45 J.-M. Canivez, *Statuta capitulorum generalium ordinis Cisterciensis ab anno 1116 ad annum 1786*, 8 vols (Louvain, 1933–41), 2, pp. 53 (1226: 25, 26), 76 (1229: 6), 87–8 (1230: 20).

46 R.I. Moore, *The Formation of a Persecuting Society* (Oxford, 1987), pp. 91–4.

47 Ayala Martínez, 'Cuestionario', pp. 73–4; J.F. O'Callaghan, 'The Affiliation of the Order of Calatrava with the Order of Cîteaux', *Analecta sacri ordinis Cisterciensis* 16 (1960), 256–8.

48 Dunbabin, p. 144.

repentance; and while in some cases an indefinite period of detention was decreed, which would last until mercy was shown, the reasons for showing mercy were not explained.[49]

Chaining and imprisonment were, on occasion, further employed as means of coercion, as they were not only in the secular world but also in some circumstances by ecclesiastical authorities. Imprisonment was used by the Inquisition as an interrogation technique, with the purpose of securing confessions.[50] In 1225 the Cistercian chapter ruled that a monk who stole property was to be held in chains until he restored the goods in question; and this regulation would have applied to some military orders.[51] In the Temple, a brother who refused to go to a stricter order when he was sentenced to be expelled was to be put in irons *tant que il ait pense, ou autre por lui, de son ordenement*, while Dietrich of Altenburg decreed that detention was to used as a means of dissuading a brother of the Teutonic order from leaving it: he was to be kept in prison or irons until he abandoned his intention.[52] The Catalan version of the Templar Customs also states that if a brother was reported by an outsider to have committed an offence, and refused to admit it, he might not only be put on bread and water but also placed in a room and forbidden to leave it until he confessed, although house arrest is also mentioned as a possible measure in these circumstances.[53] According to an early-fourteenth-century version of the Hospitaller *esgarts*, irons might also be used to coerce a sergeant in the employ of the Hospital who left a house and did not fulfil his obligations. On the fourth refusal to return to his house and perform his work, he was to be put in irons until he gave a pledge to complete his year's contract of service.[54]

Most information about chaining and imprisonment in military orders, for whatever purpose, is contained in surviving rules and regulations. Yet not all cases of confinement were in accordance with an order's decrees. In *definiciones* drawn up for Calatrava in 1325, Juan Palazuelos, the abbot of Morimond, referred to the *muy gran escandalo en la casa de Calatrava por prissiones e penitencias, sin Dio, e sin orden*, and he forbade the master to incarcerate brothers without counsel.[55] As has been noted, this ruling was made in a period of dissension within Calatrava, and the master had clearly been seeking to silence opponents by locking them up.[56] Earlier, in 1311, the master had himself been threatened with incarceration, for his opponents had informed him, when he was in Aragon, that if he entered the Campo de Calatrava, they would imprison him.[57]

49 O'Callaghan, 'Earliest "Difiniciones"', pp. 264 (1304: 10), 275 (1336: 8); O'Callaghan, 'Definiciones de Montesa', pp. 231 (1326: 5), 237 (1331: 16).

50 J.B. Given, *Inquisition and Medieval Society. Power, Discipline, and Resistance in Languedoc* (Ithaca, 1997), pp. 52–65.

51 Canivez, 2, p. 42 (1225: 36).

52 *RT*, p. 237 (437); *SDO*, p. 149 (5); Schmidt, pp. 139–40.

53 *Catalan Rule*, p. 16 (32–3).

54 *CH*, 2, pp. 536–61 doc. 2213 (16).

55 O'Callaghan, 'Earliest "Difiniciones"', p. 270 (1325: 6).

56 See Ayala Martínez, 'Cuestionario', p. 85.

57 Ibid., pp. 77, 80, 87–9. Claims of arbitrary imprisonment were also made during the Templar trial: Finke, 2, p. 331; but such evidence is suspect.

Regulations of military orders include few rulings about the establishment of prisons or the nature of irons. The general chapter of the Cistercians, to whom some Spanish military orders were affiliated, in 1206 allowed monasteries to establish prisons, and in 1229 it decreed that strong and secure prisons were, if possible, to be built in all abbeys;[58] but the only comparable ruling in regulations of military orders themselves was that of Conrad of Feuchtwangen, master of the Teutonic order, who ordered in 1292 that each *Landkomtur* should have one or two prisons in his district[59]: the ruling does not suggest that prisons were then common in houses of that order, although the issuing of such a decree reinforces the suggestion that imprisonment was becoming a more common penalty.

It is usually difficult to discover information about the nature of the prisons that did exist for the incarceration of brothers or employees, or about the methods of chaining delinquents. During the Templar trial several witnesses referred to the severity of that order's prisons. Those detained were said to have been treated inhumanely and usually did not long survive: a brother who claimed to have been *custos* of a Templar prison said that in his time nine brothers had died because of harsh conditions.[60] Yet these claims are to be explained partly by the context in which they were made; and, although Templars in prison would also be subject to fasting and other punishments, there is no reason to believe that these gaols were of exceptional harshness: cold, disease, and a lack of food and of clothing were common features of prison life, and deaths were frequent.[61] When chaining was mentioned, reference was usually made merely to 'irons' (*fers*), although when a more precise word was used it was normally *compedes*, which in the context presumably signifies leg irons.[62] Ramón of Guardia, the Templar commander of Mas-Déu, when interrogated in 1310, admittedly claimed that according to the order's statutes those convicted of sodomy were detained not only in leg irons but also *in collo catenis appositis et in manibus manicis ferreis*[63]; but this is not stated in surviving Templar regulations, and Ramón was probably merely seeking to counter as forcibly as possible the accusation that the order encouraged homosexuality.

Inventories of Templar houses and castles compiled after the arrest of brethren in the early fourteenth century do not refer to prisons or chains although, as they are primarily lists of movables, and as these are not always comprehensive, the omission is not necessarily significant.[64] Castles no doubt had underground chambers or other

---

58 Canivez, 1, p. 320 (1206: 4); 2, p. 76 (1229: 6); cf. *Les statuts de Prémontré réformés sur les ordres de Grégoire IX et d'Innocent IV au XIIIe siècle*, ed. P.F. Lefèvre (Louvain, 1946), pp. 120–1.

59 *SDO*, p. 141 (7).

60 Michelet, 2, p. 176; Finke, 2, pp. 337–8, doc. 155.

61 Dunbabin, pp. 121–3.

62 Ayala Martínez, 'Cuestionario', pp. 88–9; *The Rule of the Spanish Military Order of St James, 1170–1493*, ed. E. Gallego Blanco (Leiden, 1971), p. 130 (52); Michelet, 1, pp. 383, 473, 588; 2, p. 228; Wilkins, 2, p. 337; on *compedes*, see Pugh, p. 371.

63 Michelet, 2, p. 460.

64 Among published inventories, see J. Rubió, R. d'Alós and F. Martorell, 'Inventaris inèdits de l'orde del Temple a Catalunya', *Anuari de l'Institut d'Estudis Catalans* 1 (1907), 385–407; A. Higounet-Nadal, 'L'inventaire des biens de la commanderie du Temple de Sainte-

places that could be used for the purposes of detention – in 1313, for example, reference was made to the prison of the castle of Calatrava[65] – even if it is usually no longer possible to locate where defaulters were held.

Although the Templar Customs mention brothers who were imprisoned at Atlit, archaeological surveys have not revealed a location.[66] A prison has been identified at the Hospitaller compound in Acre, but this may have been for captives.[67] This appears to have been the case at Beit Gibrin, which came under Hospitaller lordship in 1136. Usamah describes a dungeon there, to which access was by means of a trapdoor in the roof. But his information derived from a Muslim captive who had been held in chains there for a year.[68] Templar regulations allude to a *frere de prison*, but the reference was made in a clause relating to the treatment of slaves.[69] That some Templars, who were not based at Atlit, were sent to be imprisoned there, suggests that not all Templar castles in the Holy Land had prisons that housed brothers. In the later twelfth century an erring brother was guarded in a *camera privatorum* at Acre, but the term is not explained.[70]

Nor could it be expected that in convents away from frontier districts, which housed only a handful of brothers and were not necessarily located in fortified buildings, there would normally be a specially constructed prison for delinquent brothers. It is true that Templars entering the order in various French houses, including Laigneville, Payns, Lagny-le-Sec, Soisy and Ferté-Gaucher, argued that they had been imprisoned on the day of their admission for refusing to deny Christ or spit on the Cross,[71] and such statements could be interpreted – even if the brothers were not in fact incarcerated – to suggest that many French houses had prisons. But these brothers were probably just trying to distance themselves from the alleged practices about which they had confessed, and the prisons may not have existed. Two Templars interrogated at Poitiers in 1308 did, however, refer to a prison at Merlan, in the diocese of Reims.[72] This was not a major Templar house,[73] but one brother stated that he had been *custos* there, and there seems to have been no reason for him to give false evidence on this point. The Templars certainly had a prison in

---

Eulalie du Larzac en 1308', *Annales du Midi*, 68 (1956), 255–62; G. Lizerand, *Le dossier de l'affaire des Templiers* (Paris, 1964), pp. 46–54.

65 Ayala Martínez, 'Cuestionario', p. 89.

66 *RT*, pp. 289–90 (554), 297–8 (573), 312 (603); *Catalan Rule*, pp. 70 (164), 96 (198); C.N. Johns, *Guide to 'Atlit: The Crusader Castle, Town and Surroundings* (Jerusalem, 1947), reprinted in C.N. Johns, *Pilgrims' Castle ('Atlit), David's Tower (Jerusalem) and Qal'at ar-Rabad ('Ajlun)* (Aldershot, 1997).

67 Y. Friedman, *Encounter between Enemies. Captivity and Ransom in the Latin Kingdom of Jerusalem* (Leiden, 2002), pp. 112–13.

68 P.K. Hitti, *Memoirs of an Arab-Syrian Gentleman or an Arab Knight in the Crusades* (repr. Beirut, 1964), pp. 109–10.

69 *RT*, p. 193 (336).

70 Abel, pp. 289–90; Bulst-Thiele, p. 360, doc. 1.

71 Michelet, 2, pp. 284, 338, 343, 354, 390.

72 Finke, 2, pp. 331, 337–8 doc. 155.

73 E.G. Léonard, *Introduction au cartulaire manuscrit du Temple du Marquis d'Albon* (Paris, 1930), p. 140.

Paris, but in 1289 a non-Templar murderer was being held there[74]: some Templar prisons in the West may have been mainly for outsiders. During the proceedings of the Templar trial brother Walter the Bachelor was, however, reported to have been held in prison and in irons at the New Temple in London,[75] and it is possible that a special place of confinement, which was used for offending Templars, did exist at the order's English headquarters, although attempts that have been made to identify a penitential cell in the Templar church there are unconvincing.[76] Yet the number of specially built Templar prisons in Western Europe was probably small. The Catalan version of the Templar Customs reports that a runaway brother in Provence was seized and merely put in a room;[77] and the use of house arrest in Catalonia would also suggest a lack of prisons.

That orders sometimes lacked secure places in which to detain brothers is further suggested by reports of escapes. The Templar placed in a room in a Provençal house quickly absconded when he found the door was not locked.[78] On the other hand an attempted escape from Atlit apparently ended in death: to escape from prison there seems to have been a perilous undertaking.[79] But in some instances reliance was placed merely on the inadvisability of escaping. A Templar who was put in a room or under house arrest for not admitting a charge made by an outsider was instructed not to leave the room or the house, but the Templar Customs add that if he did so he would then be considered to have committed a serious fault: security depended not on locks or guards but merely on the threat of further punishment.[80] Although imprisonment, as well as chaining, appears to have been coming into more common use in military orders, it is questionable whether, by the early fourteenth century, the orders' facilities for incarcerating brethren and those in their employ were altogether adequate.

74 A. Beugnot, *Les Olim ou registres des arrêts rendus par la cour du roi*, 3 vols (Paris, 1839–48), 2, p. 296; G. Etienne, 'La Villeneuve du Temple à Paris aux XIIIe et XIVe siècles', in *Etudes sur l'histoire de Paris et de l'Ile-de-France* (Actes du 100e Congrès National des Sociétés Savantes, 2, Paris, 1978), p. 99, n. 46.

75 Wilkins, 2, pp. 337, 346.

76 C.G. Addison, *The History of the Knights Templars* (London, 1842), pp. 301–2; see also H. Wood, 'The Templars in Ireland', *Proceedings of the Royal Irish Academy* 26 (C) (1906–7), 333; for comment, see E. Lord, *The Knights Templar in Britain* (Harlow, 2002), p. 140.

77 *Catalan Rule,* p. 86 (181).

78 One of the brothers under house arrest in Catalonia similarly disappeared.

79 *RT*, p. 298 (573); *Catalan Rule*, p. 70 (164); Michelet, 2, p. 223.

80 *Catalan Rule*, p. 16 (33).

PART 2
Rhodes and the Latin East

Chapter 9

The Migration of Syrians and Cypriots to Hospitaller Rhodes in the Fourteenth and Fifteenth Centuries

Nicholas Coureas

During the fourteenth and fifteenth centuries Hospitaller Rhodes attracted settlers from various regions, including Cyprus, Latin Syria and Egypt. The Hospitallers themselves actively encouraged such settlement, given that Rhodes at the time of the Hospitaller conquest of circa 1310 had been depopulated on account of Turkish and even Latin raids.[1] The Syrians settling on Rhodes for whom evidence survives fall mostly into two categories: sergeants serving in the Hospitaller forces and merchants, although they also include one doctor and one servant of the Latin Church of Rhodes. The Cypriots are socially more diverse, including a sergeant, Cypriots performing the *servitudo marina*, which was a form of galley service, a merchant and serfs, although the latter are recorded in a document of the early sixteenth century. Except in the case of Cypriots with recognizably Greek names, it is probable that the 'Cypriots' mentioned in Hospitaller documents were Syrians who had moved to Cyprus after or even shortly before the fall of Acre and Tyre in 1291, when the Hospitallers established their headquarters at Limassol, and had then migrated to Rhodes following the Order's conquest of this island in 1309–10.

The Hospitallers had employed local Syrian Christians in its forces in Latin Syria prior to the loss of the last Latin territories there in 1291, and the office of lay master sergeant existed.[2] Some of them followed the Hospitallers to Rhodes. In 1384 a certain Antonius Machami succeeded his father, Nikita, as *magister sergentie* and he was perhaps Syrian, while a text of 1395 refers to the *officium magisterie sergentarie surianorum*.[3] The above-mentioned Nikita is probably the Nikita de Assiza mentioned in a famous case of 1400. This person, the son of Manoli Thomas and Eirene, a Greek woman from the island of Kos, claimed that his ancestors had been Syrians who had participated in the Hospitallers' conquest of Rhodes from the

---

1 A. Luttrell, 'Settlement on Rhodes, 1306–1366', in P. Edbury (ed.), *Crusade and Settlement* (Cardiff, 1985), p. 273; A. Luttrell, *The Town of Rhodes: 1306–1356* (Rhodes, 2003), pp. 63–8, 77–8.

2 J. Riley-Smith, *The Knights of St John in Jerusalem and Cyprus 1050–1310* (London, 1967), pp. 324–7.

3 A. Luttrell, 'The Military and Naval Organization of the Hospitallers at Rhodes, 1310–1444', in A. Luttrell, *The Hospitallers of Rhodes and their Mediterranean World*, XIX (Aldershot, 1992), 137 and note 25.

Byzantines and that several uncles of his had perished fighting for the Hospitallers at various times and places. He also claimed to have been long and honourably resident in Rhodes, stating that he, his father, his mother, Eirene, and all his lineage had been exempt from the *servitudo marina*, the service on board Hospitaller galleys to which native Greeks of Rhodes were conscripted, and under the terms of which they rowed the galleys for part of the year, by way of a *corvée*. Nikita asked to prove his exempt status by summoning trustworthy witnesses, Latin and Greek. A number of such witnesses were duly summoned to give testimony, and on the basis of their depositions both Nikita and his mother, Eirene, were declared exempt of the obligation of *servitudo marina* on 17 September 1400.[4]

Another Syrian sergeant serving the Hospital was George Saliba, recorded in 1347 as stationed at the Hospitaller castle of Pharaklon, a fortification on Rhodes dating from Byzantine times and located on the eastern coastline.[5] The one extant reference to a sergeant who may have been Cypriot concerns a certain Libity de Zipro, who was stationed at the castle of Lindos on the south-east coast of the island in 1348. In January of the same year the Hospitaller grand master, Dieudonné de Gozon, granted him a garden of three *cafisa*, a measure for the volume of grain. The name Libity, however, does not sound Greek, and this sergeant was probably a Syrian who had simply sojourned on Cyprus during the period 1291–1310 – that is, after the fall of Acre and prior to the Hospitaller conquest of Rhodes.[6] At the beginning of the fifteenth century, however, Cypriots on Rhodes are recorded as entering the *servitudo marina* voluntarily as replacements for persons exempted from this service. In January 1422 the Hospitaller grand master Antoni di Fluvià, in declaring George Beltrami, a servant of the Order, his wife Arfaradena and his three daughters and their descendants exempt from this service, states that three replacements had been found for them. One was a Rhodian named Bartholomew and the other two were the Cypriots Thomas of Famagusta and his wife Maria, all of whom Beltrami had presented to the Hospitallers to fulfil the obligation of *servitudo marina* in the place of Beltrami and his family. The document specifies that the descendants of the three replacements would likewise be liable to perform this service. It also confirms an earlier document whereby Lucius de Vallinis, the marshal of Rhodes and lieutenant of the late Philibert de Naillac, had exempted George Beltrami and his son Nicholas from this obligation.[7]

Five years later, in November 1427, Antoni di Fluvià and the Hospitaller convent of Rhodes emancipated from the *servitudo marina* John the son of the vintner George Zalapi, as well as the children born to John and his wife. In their place

4 A. Luttrell, 'The *Servitudo Marina* at Rhodes: 1306–1462', in A. Luttrell, *The Hospitallers in Cyprus, Rhodes, Greece and the West, 1291–1440*, IV (Variorum, 1979), 52–3 and 57–8.

5 Luttrell, 'Settlement on Rhodes', p. 276 and note 43.

6 A. Luttrell (in collaboration with V. von Falkenhausen), 'Lindos and the Defence of Rhodes, 1306–1522', in A. Luttrell, *The Hospitallers of Rhodes and their Mediterranean World*, VII (Aldershot, 1992), 325.

7 *Anekdota engrapha gia ten Rhodo kai tes Noties Sporades apo to arkheio ton Ioanniton Hippoton, 1421–1423*, ed. Z. Tsirpanlis (Rhodes, 1995), no. 4; Luttrell, '*Servitudo marina*', p. 62.

John had presented the Cypriots John Trigonari of Famagusta and his wife Xene Aracliane, who would henceforth be liable for the *servitudo marina* along with those descendants born to them from that time onwards. The document carefully stipulates, however, that those children of theirs born prior to the date on which they undertook to perform the service, namely Theodore, Peter, Orphane and Eirene, were wholly exempt from performing the *servitudo marina*. Nonetheless, Theodore would substitute John Trigonari if the latter ever took it into his head to flee from Rhodes and not return there, and his children would also be obliged to perform the service. The document also records that John Trigonari and his family were personally summoned into the presence of the Hospitaller grand master and other high officers of the Order, including the marshal, the admiral and the preceptor of Naples, and agreed there, without any coercion or deception having taken place, to replace George Zalapi and his dependants as regarded performing the *servitudo marina*.[8] It is noteworthy that both Cypriot families summoned as replacements for this marine service originated from Famagusta, the main port of the Lusignan kingdom of Cyprus, which, however, was under Genoese occupation from 1373 to 1464. Perhaps these Cypriots, originating from a harbour town, were better suited to marine service than others from inland would have been, while the good relations the Hospitallers had with the Genoese may have facilitated the migration to Rhodes of Cypriots from Famagusta.[9]

Merchants from Syria and Cyprus were present on Rhodes, as well as sergeants and mariners. In September 1439 the Hospitaller grand master, John de Lastic, addressed an appeal in writing to various officers and governors of islands in the Aegean, and in particular to those in the island of Crete, a Venetian possession since the early thirteenth century, and to the Venetian Andrea Corner, asking them to assist the Cypriot merchant Stephen of Nicosia when he came to visit the islands for the purposes of recovering debts owed to him.[10] The merchant in question maintained a depot in the city of Rhodes, having been established there for some time, selling textiles and other merchandise. On occasion he sold such goods on credit, and consequentially there were now various persons in a number of places owing him sums of money. He was clearly having difficulty in recovering his debts, for he had written to the grand master imploring his assistance. The latter, who clearly held Stephen in high regard, now wrote to the various officers of islands where Stephen's creditors resided, telling them that this Cypriot merchant, whose request he had approved, had led a reputable existence in the city of Rhodes as a buyer and seller of cloths and other goods, and asking them to assist him in recovering his debts. The fact that the grand master's appeal was directed to the officers in Crete and to Andrea Corner, an official on the island of Karpathos, between Rhodes and Crete, which likewise belonged to Venice, indicates that Stephen's creditors were resident in Venetian territories outside the legal jurisdiction of the Hospitallers, hence the dispatch of this appeal to them.

---

8 Tsirpanlis, *Engrapha*, no. 17; Luttrell, '*Servitudo marina*', p. 62.

9 E. Ashtor, *Levant Trade in the Later Middle Ages* (Princeton, 1983), p. 333.

10 Tsirpanlis, *Engrapha*, no. 116.

Several documents of the mid fourteenth century attest to the existence of Syrian merchants on Rhodes who, at times but not invariably, were citizens of the island. The first document, dated 22 April 1440, was a certificate of citizenship issued to the Syrian Anthony Masota, declaring him to be a Rhodian citizen and recommending him to all, and in particular to navigators, so that they might receive him and his goods kindly. It thereby makes it clear that he was a merchant by profession regularly travelling back and forth from Rhodes.[11] The second document, dated 12 April 1450, is a safe conduct for the Syrian merchant Mark Salvatore. John de Lastic requested those setting eyes on the letter, with special reference to the captains and patrons of galleys, to welcome this merchant and protect him from harm.[12] The document states that Mark travelled on a regular basis between Rhodes, Syria and Egypt with a number of boats and a variety of merchandise, not only on his own account but also behalf of persons of the Order, for whom he clearly acted as a factor. It specifies that Mark Salvatore was not a Rhodian citizen, describing him as a native of Syria, but asks those coming into contact with him to treat him as if he were a native of Rhodes and a subject and servant of the Order because he had always served the Order faithfully and well. The document concludes by stating that the Order will consider itself obliged to all those assisting Salvatore in his affairs. One notes that this document, unlike most documents of the Order, which were written in Latin, was written in Italian, the nautical *lingua franca* of the Mediterranean, and so more comprehensible to the mariners likely to set eyes on it.

A more unusual instance of a Syrian settling in Rhodes concerned that of the doctor George Suriano of Cairo. His surname indicates a Syrian origin even though he and his family lived in Egypt; other residents of Rhodes with the surname Suriano, such as Prospero and his brothers Angelo and Benedetto, merchants trading regularly with Egypt and Damietta in particular, are specifically designated as Venetians. All of them probably fell into the legal category known as White Venetians, encompassing people originating from the Eastern Mediterranean and elsewhere who were Venetian subjects and so enjoyed Venetian protection as well as certain economic and legal advantages.[13] In May 1453 John de Lastic addressed a written appeal to Sir Bernard de Villamarin, the captain-general of the fleet of King Alfonso V of Aragon, in particular and to the captains or patrons of galleys and other ships in general, requesting them to assist George Suriano and refrain from harming him so that he could implement his wish to come and settle in Rhodes with his family and become a subject of the Hospitallers. The document makes reference to the slaves, textiles and other goods he might be bringing with him and asks those setting eyes on it to treat George Suriano and his dependants as though they were already subjects of the Order.[14] A subsequent document, of July 1453, records how John de Lastic had Rhodian citizenship bestowed on George Suriano, thereby granting him burgess status along with the privileges and immunities attendant on this and placing him,

11 Tsirpanlis, *Engrapha*, no. 118.

12 Tsirpanlis, *Engrapha*, no. 203

13 D. Jacoby, 'Citoyens, sujets et protégés de Venise et de Gênes en Chypre', *Byzantinische Forschungen*, 5 (1977), 160–1 and 166–8.

14 Tsirpanlis, *Engrapha*, no. 306.

his family and his goods under the protection of the Order. For his part, George Suriano had first taken an oath to serve the Order, its officers and their successors in whatever part of the world he might happen to be in and to inform the Order and its officers should he happen to discover any overt or covert plots being hatched against them.[15]

The merchant Prospero Suriano mentioned above petitioned the Order for assistance some time before March 1440, explaining that although he had rendered thorough and effective services and large amounts of money to various merchants he had suffered damages on account of the perils of the sea and had difficulty in paying off his creditors. John de Lastic, moved by his rightful requests, had now conferred a grace period of one year upon him, during which his fixed and movable goods were protected from his creditors' demands, so as to enable him to restore his finances, and this protection was publicized in writing to all brothers and officers of the Order, secular officials and creditors.[16] The Hospitallers' assistance was also extended to Prospero's brothers, Angelo and Benedetto. In October 1453 John de Lastic issued a written appeal to all captains or patrons of galleys and other sailing ships requesting them to afford them assistance and refrain from harming them in the course of a journey the brothers were about to undertake, along with their goods and textiles, to Damietta in Egypt and other destinations for the purpose of obtaining victuals, goods and others things necessary for human sustenance, which they would bring back with them to Rhodes.[17] The references to victuals suggest that Rhodes was undergoing a grain shortage and that Angelo and Benedetto, described as residents (but not citizens) of Rhodes, were journeying as factors of the Order to procure supplies of grain.

More indirect evidence for the settlement of Cypriots and Syrians on Rhodes derives from deeds concerning the donation of property. In November 1347 the Hospitaller grand master, Dieudonné de Gozon, allowed Margarita de Negroponte to grant her daughter Simona a windmill with a bathhouse adjoining it, located on a hill in the main town or *borgo* of Rhodes. This property was bounded on three sides by public thoroughfares and on the fourth by some hospices, including one belonging to a certain George of Cyprus.[18] Nearly one century later, in March 1440, the Hospitaller grand master John de Lastic mentioned above granted the request submitted to him by Judge John Rocundo for remission of an annual payment of five florins owed to the Order from one of its properties called de Dyamanti (tou Diamanti), located in the citadel of Rhodes and currently in John's possession.[19] This property, consisting of vines, houses, a garden and other lands, had been brought to near ruin on account of the excessive payments exacted from it, which, other than the sum paid annually to the Order, included 12 florins annually to the Augustinian convent in Rhodes and an additional six to the church of St George of the Syrians. Both these foundations had likewise remitted a portion of the payments normally due to them in order to

15 Tsirpanlis, *Engrapha*, no. 307.
16 Tsirpanlis, *Engrapha*, no. 115.
17 Tsirpanlis, *Engrapha*, no. 327.
18 Luttrell, *Town of Rhodes*, pp. 241–2.
19 Tsirpanlis, *Engrapha*, no. 114.

restore the property's finances. The Hospitaller grand master now decided to do the same, not only so as to ameliorate the property but also in view of John's services to the Order. The location of this Syrian church is not known, nor whether it belonged to the Catholic or the Greek rite, or even to one of the Eastern Christian confessions, such as the Jacobites, the Maronites or the Nestorians, but its existence indicates that the Syrians in Rhodes were numerous enough to have their own church and, in consequence, their own communal organization.

A donation of property dated February 1446, in which John de Lastic granted the church or chapel of the Virgin Mary of Blachernae to the priest Stephen Koquero on a lifetime basis, also affords information on Syrian settlement. This Greek-rite church was situated in the main town of Rhodes in the neighbourhood of Blacherniotissa, which clearly derived its name from the church, and was bounded on the north side by buildings belonging to Khalili the Syrian.[20] A subsequent donation, dated July 1451, in which John de Lastic granted a vine to the Hospitaller preceptor William Ponz, who administered the Order's house at Leselles in the priory of Auvergne, in recognition of the latter's services towards the Order states that the vine, formerly a possession of the late Vitali Gratiani, a Jewish physician of the Order, was located in the citadel of Rhodes and bounded on the west side by a number of properties, including those of a Syrian named Nargela.[21] The fact that this Syrian owned property within the citadel is worthy of note, for in general Syrian properties were located in the *borgo*, the part of the town of Rhodes located south of the citadel area, although Greeks and other groups, such as Latins not belonging to the Hospitallers, did also live there. Perhaps Nargela, the owner of the property, was descended from those Syrians who had initially accompanied the Hospitallers to Rhodes at the time of their conquest of the island around 1310.

The only recorded instance on Rhodes of a Syrian serving the secular Latin Church concerns a certain Constantine Habibi. This resident of Rhodes, born into the Greek Church, was a servant of the Latin archbishopric on Rhodes. In 1431 the Dominican Andreas Chrysoberges, himself a Greek convert to the Catholic faith, became archbishop of Rhodes, a post he held until 1447, and as a convert himself who was fluent in both Latin and Greek he energetically set about trying to win over to Catholicism Greeks and Eastern Rite Christians resident in Rhodes. With the consent of Pope Eugenius IV he preached numerous sermons in Greek, and Greek replaced Latin in the celebration of the divine offices in the Latin churches of the town of Rhodes, presumably so as to facilitate conversion.[22] One successful case of conversion was Constantine Habibi, whom Pope Eugenius IV praised for having attended various sermons conducted by Andreas Chrysoberges, which caused him to renounce the errors of the Greeks in which he had been born and brought up and embrace the Catholic faith. 'And you serve it now and live and intend to live for evermore according to the rite of the Roman Church', states the pope's letter. Habibi had also accepted confirmation by Archbishop Andreas. In September 1438 this pope confirmed his emancipation by the same archbishop and his new status as

20 Tsirpanlis, *Engrapha*, no. 159.
21 Tsirpanlis, *Engrapha*, no. 241.
22 Tsirpanlis, *Engrapha*, pp. 211–213.

a free man and a Roman citizen (*liber et cives Romanus*). Constantine's acquisition of this new status following conversion in itself suggests that ulterior motives may have impelled him to embrace Catholicism.[23] Some years later, in August 1445, Constantine Habibi was released from all obligations and expenses incurred towards the Catholic Church, on account of having continuously served Archbishop Andreas for over 12 years and having accompanied him by land and sea to various parts of the world.[24]

Hospitaller Rhodes continued to attract settlers up to the end of the fifteenth century and beyond. A letter of February 1504 from the Venetian *luogotenente* of Cyprus, a Venetian possession from 1473 onwards, addressed to the Council of Ten in Venice, informed them that Cypriot serfs escaping from the island long before had settled in Rhodes and in other places, where they had married free women and had children by them.[25] Their return to Cyprus could no longer be expected, but some were prepared to pay sums in Venetians ducats so as to secure their legal as well as practical emancipation from servitude, so that they would be able to come and go freely from Rhodes to Cyprus and trade commodities there. Both socially and numerically the Cypriots in Rhodes appear to have been at a disadvantage with respect to the Syrians. Only one merchant and one owner of a hostel are recorded, and perhaps one sergeant, the remainder being serfs or belonging to the social class liable for the seasonal galley service known as *servitudo marina*. The Syrians, in contrast, were mostly merchants or sergeants, included a doctor in their ranks, had their own church dedicated to St George, and secured various letters from the grand master and officers of the Hospitaller Order indicating that he held them in high regard.

23 *Acta Eugenii IV*, ed. G. Fedalto, Pontificia Commissio Recogniscendo Codici Iuris Canonici Orientalis, ser. 3, 15 (Rome, 1965), no. 730.

24 *Acta Eugenii IV*, no. 1323.

25 *Anekdota engrapha tes kypriakes historias apo to arkheio tes Venetias*, vol. 1 (1474–1508), ed. A. Aristeidou (Nicosia, 1990), no. 64.

Chapter 10

Hospitaller Rhodes: The Epigraphic Evidence

Anna-Maria Kasdagli

A considerable amount of information about the inscriptions of Hospitaller Rhodes (1309–1522) lies scattered in various publications, although it seldom forms their main theme.[1] What follows is an attempt to gather together and examine in context what is known to have survived. To begin with, the material can be divided into three main groups:

'Western' inscriptions Inspired by the culture imported into Rhodes by the Knights of the Hospital and other Latins. Most of them are in stone. Several are still *in situ* on lay buildings and the fortifications of the town. Most are actually funerary inscriptions, or fragments thereof.

Greek inscriptions Generally in the Byzantine style, although a few were the result of Western influence and are cut in stone; the rest are on frescoes, in churches. It seems that survivals reflect a cultural difference in burial customs: the Greeks lagged behind in the commemoration of the individual, although class may also have played a role. In any case, most of the Greek inscriptions are associated with

1 A. Gabriel, *La cité de Rhodes*, vol. 1 (Paris, 1921), esp. pp. 93–104; ibid., vol. 2 (Paris, 1923); G. Gerola, 'I monumenti medioevali delle tredici Sporadi', *Annuario della Regia Scuola Archeologia di Atene* I (1914), 169–365 and ibid. II (1916), 1–101; G. Gerola, 'Gli stemmi supestiti nei monumenti delle Sporadi appartenute ai cavalieri di Rodi', *Rivista del Collegio Araldico* (1913); B.E.A. Rottiers, *Description des monuments de Rhodes* (Brussels, 1830); G. Sommi Picenardi, *Itinéraire d'un Chevalier de Saint-Jean de Jérusalem dans l'île de Rhodes* (Lille, 1900); J.-B. de Vaivre, 'Les tombeaux des Grands Maîtres des Hospitaliers de Saint-Jean de Jérusalem à Rhodes', *Fondation Eugène Piot, Monuments et Mémoires publiés par l'Académie des Inscriptions et Belles-Lettres*, 76 (1998), 35–88; P. Lojacono, 'La chiesa conventuale di San Giovanni dei Cavalieri in Rodi', *Clara Rhodos*, 8 (1936), 247–74; S. Düll, 'Drei Johanniter in Istanbul. Neue Untersuchungen zu den rhodischen Grabsteinen im Archäologischen Museum', *Istanbuler Mitteilungen*, 39 (1989), 107–14; A. Luttrell, *The Town of Rhodes: 1306–1356* (Rhodes 2003), pp. 39–47; A. Luttrell, 'A Hospitaller *soror* at Rhodes, 1347', in *Dei Gesta per Francos: Crusader Studies in Honour of Jean Richard*, ed. M. Balard et al. (Aldershot, 2001), pp. 129–43; G. Konstantinopoulos, *Rhodes Museum, I, Archaeological Museum* (Athens, 1977), pp. 13–44; A.-M. Kasdagli, 'Τρεις ταφόπλακες της Ιπποτοκρατίας στη Ρόδο', *Αρχαιολογικόν Δελτίον*, 44–6 (1989–91), Μελέτες, pp. 191–6; A.-M. Kasdagli, 'Τα ταφικά μνημεία της Ιπποτοκρατίας στη Ρόδο', *Δελτίον Εραλδικής και Γενεαλογικής Εταιρείας της Ελλάδος*, 11 (Athens, 2001), pp. 121–43; etc.

the decoration of churches and ought to be examined within the wider context of late Byzantine art and epigraphics rather than that of Hospitaller Rhodes, except where visibly affected by Western influence.

Heraldry[2] This specialized kind of inscription is very important in Rhodes, owing to the number of survivals and the amount of information they can yield when handled in context. It is mostly associated with Westerners, and members of the Order in particular, with certain masters of the Hospital dominating. It is often encountered together with script and most frequently a date, although this is by no means the rule. When heraldry and text are combined, they supplement and clarify each other. In a very limited number of cases heraldry is also encountered with inscriptions in Greek: these date from the later period, and generally signify cultural integration and Renaissance tastes. Here heraldry will be discussed only as an adjunct to textual inscriptions.

Survivals of Latin inscriptions on murals are meagre: a few names of saints in the Latin cathedral and in the chapel of St George within the south-east corner tower of the Collachio, and a few almost completely effaced – and illegible – captions on the murals of a hall – perhaps the meeting place for some guild – on the ground floor of a building in the eastern part of the town.[3] In comparison, evidence in stone abounds, with the added advantage of its often being dated with precision. On the fortifications of Rhodes[4] 18 inscriptions of varying length are still *in situ*; another 20 survive on lay buildings,[5] and 13 more are preserved out of context.[6] There are also three inscriptions associated with churches from the countryside. About ten further small fragments found in excavations cannot be classified, but by far the greatest number of textual inscriptions we have from Rhodes are funerary in character: including pieces kept at Cluny and Istanbul,[7] about one hundred epitaphs survive entirely or in part. A few inscriptions on portable items, such as two cannon cast in Rhodes and an icon apparently painted on the island shortly before the Ottoman conquest, are also of epigraphic interest.[8]

2 A.M. Kasdagli, 'Κατάλογος των θυρεών της Ρόδου', *Αρχαιολογικόν Δελτίον* 48–9 (1994–95), Μελέτες, pp. 212–46; A.M. Kasdagli, 'Εισαγωγή στην εραλδική της Ρόδου,' *Δελτίον Εραλδικής και Γενεαλογικής Εταιρείας της Ελλάδος*, 7 (1988), pp. 18–48; A.M. Kasdagli, 'Τα ροδίτικα οικόσημα- μερικές παρατηρήσεις για τη σημασία τους', *Ιστορία και Προβλήματα Συντήρησης της Μεσαιωνικής Πόλης της Ρόδου* (Athens, 1992), pp. 115–22.

3 *Αρχαιολογικόν Δελτίον*, 44 (1989), Χρονικά, pp. 518–19.

4 Gabriel, *La cité de Rhodes*, vol. 1, pp. 93–104.

5 Gabriel, vol. 2; Gerola, *Annuario della Regia Scuola Archeologia di Atene*, 1, pp. 278–81, 284, 291, 295–6, 299, 313.

6 Rhodes Museum inventory nos F3, F29, F52, F62, F69, F73, F74, F80, F112, F124, F130, F214.

7 E. du Sommerard, *Musée des Thermes et de l'Hôtel de Cluny. Catalogue et description des objets d'art de l'Antiquité, du Moyen Age et de la Renaissance exposés au Musée* (Paris, 1883), pp. 39–41; S. Düll; E. Rossi, 'Memorie dei Cavalieri di Rodi a Costantinopoli', *Annuario della Regia Scuola Archeologia di Atene*, 8–9 (1920), 331–40.

8 R. Bishop-Smith, *Five 16th Century Cannons in the Turkish Military Museum and an Unknown Naval Gun in the Babur Nama* (Lisbon, 2002), pp. 6–8; E. Kollias, *The Medieval City of Rhodes and the Palace of the Grand Master* (Athens, 1998), p. 53; K. Kefala, 'Η

In the examination of this material the inscriptions of Hospitaller Cos and the castle of St Peter at Bodrum[9] have to be taken into account because they complement and highlight features of the Rhodian evidence – not least because they come from narrower contexts. Thirteen Latin inscriptions survive on Cos; seven can still be seen *in situ* on the walls of the castle of Nerangia within the town; of the rest one may also be from the castle; three others, identifying Hospitaller governors of the island, are probably from secular buildings and just one is funerary. This should, perhaps, be expected from an urban centre of only minor importance compared to Rhodes – historically, Cos has always been more prosperous in its countryside, being more fertile than the larger island.

The material at Bodrum is more unequivocal: there are 42 surviving inscriptions, all of them associated with heraldry and commemorating building work by masters of the Hospital and captains of the castle. They are often embellished with carvings such as fleurs-de-lis and roses and combinations of different types of script, and must have reflected, to a considerable extent, the individual tastes of those who commissioned them. To these may be added a large number of graffiti identifying members of the garrison; but in any case these inscriptions – and the relatively enormous number of coats of arms (about three hundred) – appear to be a response to the nature of the establishment: an isolated outpost at the extreme limits of Latin Christendom. In comparison, the walls of Rhodes itself are rather sober: various saints may identify gates and towers, but there are no invocations to them or to the Christian faith, as at Bodrum (cf. *In Domino Confido*, *Spes Mea Est In Deo*, *Cum Christo Vigilamus et In Pace Requiescamus*, *Propter Catholicam Fidem Tenetur Locum Istum* etc.) Some of the invocations at Bodrum may be mottoes (cf. Jacques Gâtineau's *In Deo Confido*), but the masters of the Hospital who, at least in the later period, regarded the mounting of heraldry on the walls of Rhodes as their exclusive prerogative, did not see fit to advertise their faith in a like manner. And from secular buildings within Rhodes only five examples include mottoes and invocations of a religious character (the *Firma Fe* of Diomede de Villaragut,[10] the *Voluntas Dei Est*, *St Denis* and *Dieu Conduit le Pèlerin* with the arms of France,[11] and a psalm verse in Greek[12]).

On Rhodes, as has already been observed, the inscriptional material is more complex. The town was a commercial and administrative centre of some importance, with a mixed urban population in which the Latin element was strongly represented

---

εικόνα του αγίου Ιωάννη του Προδρόμου στην ομώνυμη εκκλησία της Ρόδου', *15 χρόνια έργων αποκατάστασης στη μεσαιωνική πόλη της Ρόδου*I (Athens, 2007), I, pp. 445–53 (text), II. pls. 385–9 (plates).

9 G. Gerola, *Annuario della Regia Scuola Archeologia di Atene* II, pp. 28–54; G. Gerola, 'Il castello di S. Pietro in Anatolia ed i suoi stemmi dei Cavalieri di Rodi', *Rivista del Collegio Araldico* (1915), pp. 67–78, 216–27; A. Maiuri, 'I castelli dei Cavalieri di Rodi a Cos e a Budrum (Alicarnasso)', *Annuario della Regia Scuola Archeologia di Atene*,4–5 (1921–1922), 275–343.

10 Mansion of Villaragut, Street of the Knights.

11 'Inn of France', Street of the Knights.

12 A.-M. Kasdagli, 'Ο ροδιακός μεσαιωνικός Ελληνισμός στο μεταίχμιο της αλλοτρίωσης; Μία επιγραφική μαρτυρία', *Δωδεκανησιακά Χρονικά* 21 (Rhodes, 2007), pp. 450–72. But see also the reference in Rottiers, p. 314 and Pl. LXXIII.

and politically dominant. The widespread use of heraldry (about eight hundred shields survive, most of them in the town)[13] may partly be explained by rivalry between individuals from different nations or by the eagerness of officials to highlight their importance – but may also be due to the emotional forces that declared themselves most strongly in the more extreme conditions of Bodrum. Most of the heraldry on the fortifications, and all the inscriptions, commemorate the works of various masters of the Hospital;[14] of those, Pierre d'Aubusson (1476–1503) seems to have been particularly anxious to advertise his efforts through inscriptions, with Fabrizio del Carretto (1513–21) coming a rather more restrained second. In the earliest inscription on the fortifications, dating from the times of Antoni de Fluvià (1421–37), the Lombard and Greek Byzantine script were used together (Pl. 1); but Gothic characters also appeared during his mastership, replacing the Lombard script under Lastic, Milly and Zacosta.[15] These inscriptions also included dates, in Latin numerals. The Gothic script, at some time early under Pierre d'Aubusson, gave way to Renaissance capitals which sometimes consciously imitate ancient Roman script. The first dates in Arabic numerals on the fortifications appeared late, under Carretto, although they could be seen with heraldry on buildings within the town by 1483 at the latest.[16]

Public buildings generally bore the arms of the master in power at the time when they were built – whether because his goodwill was essential for such enterprises, or because he was directly involved in the work – and of the officers in charge of the task or of the function served by the new edifice. Inscriptions accompany the heraldry in a number of cases, although usually they are very brief and limited to identification, date and/or name and office. There are, of course, variations, and sometimes the inscriptions, as well as the heraldry, seem to have fulfilled a basically decorative function, as at the 'Inn of France' in the Street of the Knights: the name of Emery d'Amboise, *de france le grant prior*, appears no less than three times on the façade of the building, and his arms ten times.[17]

Many of the knights maintained their own houses in the Collachio (upper town). Such houses may preserve the arms of the owner, sometimes accompanied by the name, offices held and the date (or just one of the three), as well as other brief elements – such as *Feso Estes Keses* (brother L. Soldero),[18] or *Tot Per Lomilor* (brother H. de Canel).[19] With stray finds it is sometimes difficult to say whether the inscription and accompanying arms were mounted on a building or incorporated into the masonry of a church, thus marking a nearby grave. The inscriptions still to be seen on secular

13 Kasdagli, 'Κατάλογος...'

14 Supra, n. 4.

15 Gabriel, *La cité de Rhodes*, vol. 1, pp. 93–104, nos. 38, 44, 57.

16 Gabriel, *La cité de Rhodes*, vol. 2, p. 89.

17 Gabriel, *La cité de Rhodes*, vol. 2, p. 39 ff.

18 *Rhodes from the 4th century AD to its Capture by the Ottoman Turks (1522), Palace of the Grand Master* (Athens, 2005), pp. 70–1, ill. 91, 7.

19 Gabriel, vol. 2, p. 91.

Plate 1: Fortifications of Rhodes; relief bust of St. Athanasius

buildings date from after 1481, when a series of violent earthquakes devastated Rhodes and caused a wave of rebuilding that lasted until the eve of the Ottoman conquest.[20] Most are in Renaissance capitals, although some of the inscriptions on the façade of the 'Inn of France', and the plaque mounted on the façade of the 'Inn of Auvergne' by Guy de Blanchefort some 15 years later, were in elegant Gothic.[21]

A few survivals are more unusual. A small, marble double basin bearing miniature spouts in the form of lions' heads and the arms and name of a private individual of the later Hospitaller period must surely have belonged to the fountain of a domestic

20 Kollias, *Palace,* p. 93.

21 Gabriel, vol. 2, pp. 63ff.

garden in the town.[22] More remarkably, a round marble pillar preserves a collection of ancient wise sayings in Latin, signed by Christoforo Buondelmonti, the travelling cleric who left us the earliest surviving maps of the islands composing the Hospitaller state in the Aegean.[23] The top of the inscription has been effaced by the column's reuse as an Ottoman tomb marker, and the purpose of the work is elusive – perhaps Buondelmonti set up the column at his residence in order to advertise his erudition; this would make more sense, if he ever taught on Rhodes. More earnest appears to be the invocation from Psalm 70 (the Greek version of *Make haste, O God, to deliver me; make haste to help me, O Lord*), coupled with a shield bearing a composition rich in symbolism; this, taking into account the use of the invocation in Catholic services, might be a declaration of faith by an apostasizing Greek.[24] Also remarkable is the apparent adoption of a Greek motto, *Pali Tharo* ('I regain courage'), combined with a hourglass, symbol of time and its reversals (as a badge?), by brother Jacques de Bourbon, a relative of Louis, bishop–prince of Liège (d. 1482).[25] An imposing mansion in the eastern part of the town, possibly the residence of the Orthodox bishop, displays the sentence 'May peace reign in this house and among all those who live within', in Greek and Latin.[26] The signature of the Greek founder on a cannon cast in the early sixteenth century is curious in a different way: the inscription *Georgios Lambadis de Rodo* is in Greek characters, and the ending of the Latin dative is spelled with a subscript omega – a remarkably erudite combination![27]

Although a number of heraldic emblems have been preserved in the Rhodian hinterland, only three inscriptions have survived, all associated with churches: at the villages of Yennadi (porch of the cemetery church of St Anastasia), Soroni (country chapel of St Luke) (Pl. 2), and the fortress of Asklipio (depicting seven canons kneeling before the Virgin and Child, with names and date)[28] (Pl. 3). The activity of Latin churchmen amid the Greek Orthodox population of the countryside may be evidence of endeavours to impose the articles of the Council of Florence in the second half of the fifteenth century – they apparently led to riots in the town at the close of Orsini's mastership (1467–76).[29] To the material connected with church building must be added the dedicatory inscription of St Sebastian's church in the town, which somehow found its way to Cos, probably as ship's ballast in Ottoman times.[30]

---

22 Rhodes Museum inventory, no. F112.

23 F214; *Rhodes from the 4th century*, ill. 105. C. Barsanti, 'Costantinopoli e l'Egeo nei primi decenni del XV secolo: la testimonianza di Cristoforo Buondelmonti', *Rivista dell'Istituto Nazionale d'Archeologia e Storia dell'Arte*, 56 (III Serie, XXIV), 2001, pp. 109–10.

24 Supra, n. 12.

25 Kefala.

26 Gabriel, vol. 2, pp. 110ff.

27 *Crusades, Myth and Realities* (vol. eds Toumazis, A. Pace, M.R. Belgiorno, S. Antoniadou) (Pierides Foundation 2005), p. 140.

28 *Rhodes from the 4th century*, ill. 92.

29 Z. Tsirpanlis, *Η Ρόδος και οι Νότιες Σποράδες στα χρόνια των Ιωαννιτών Ιπποτών (14ος–16ος αι.)* (Rhodes, 1991), pp. 298–300.

30 E. Brouskari, 'Η κτητορική επιγραφή του Αγίου Σεβαστιανού στη Ρόδο', *Άνθη Χαρίτων* (Venice, 1998), pp. 439–47.

Plate 2: Chapel of St. Luke, Soroni; lintel

Plate 3: F118, inscribed relief from Asklipio; detail

The style of script used in private commissions generally accords with the chronology traced on the fortifications of the town. The Asklipio inscription, dated to 1473, has the date in Gothic script and the text in Renaissance capitals. The employment of the 'Lombard' script on the Buondelmonti pillar appears to be a conscious choice, as the dated inscriptions we have from this period (ca. 1414–22)[31] use the Gothic script.[32] Latin is the dominant language in the inscriptions, followed by French, and the occasional Italian or Spanish dialect.

By far the greater number of extant inscriptions or fragments are epitaphs. Most are in Latin, although some use French, and a handful of other vernaculars. They usually conform to a general formula which begins with *+Hic iacet* followed by a general designation such as *nobilis* (for laymen) or *venerabilis / reverendus dominus frater* (for clerics or brethren of the Hospital) and then by the personal and family name, with the nationality sometimes added; then the offices held by the deceased (*prior*, *preceptor*, *hospitalerius* etc.), or his status (e.g. *burgensis*, if a layman or *miles*, if a knight) and the date of his death – *qui obiit anno domini* (sometimes with month and day); and, finally, the standard *cujus anima requiescat in pace amen*. Sometimes there are slight rearrangements in the word order, but only towards the close of the fifteenth century, or for masters of the Hospital, do the epitaphs occasionally expand into eulogy. There is little emotion in the vast majority of the epitaphs, penitence is not expressed, and only in one or two cases is the injunction to pray for the dead included. Some, nevertheless, betray erudition: in the Greek slab of 1508, for instance, the composer of the text included spelling which had disappeared from the language with the ending of the classical era.[33]

Those funerary inscriptions preserving the date – 37 out of 97 – are not evenly spread over time. One actually dates from 1306,[34] slightly earlier than the establishment of the Hospital on Rhodes, and is in Byzantine Greek, although it also betrays Western influence: we thus know that the knights did not introduce the inscribed heraldic gravestone to the island. The earliest find of Hospitaller times comes from the site of the conventual church of the Hospital, St John of the Collachio, and commemorates a woman.[35] It consists of the left end of two lines of text incised in Lombard characters and bears the date 1318. The next dated epitaph is a fragment containing part of the date (MCCCXX...) from an inscription which ran round the edge of a rectangular gravestone.[36] More firmly dated (to 1330 and 1334 respectively) are the next two survivals, preserving the entire texts of two epitaphs incised in consecutive lines for a Florentine, Gregoire Girardini, and a married Frenchwoman, Marguerite LaVadiere: remarkably, they are both in French and came from the Latin cathedral.[37] The incised effigial slab of Bernard, Latin

31 Barsanti, pp. 97, 106.

32 But see the SANCT(us) (Ath)ANASIUS on the saint's relief, Gabriel I, p. 97, no 44.

33 F202. Grand Masters' Palace. *Αρχαιολογικόν Δελτίον*, 39 (1984), B, Χρονικά, p. 340.

34 F101; Luttrell, *The Town*, pp. 42–3.

35 F120; ibid., p. 43.

36 F128/140.

37 F201 and F197; Luttrell, *The Town*, pp. 43–4.

archbishop of Rhodes (d. 1335), preserves the epitaph round its edge quite well.[38] Then comes a small fragment, the lower left corner of another incised effigial slab with the epitaph running round the edge (Pl. 4), dated to 1342.[39] The earliest dated heraldic gravestone of Hospitaller times follows (1348).[40] Another fragment, also the lower left corner of an incised effigial slab, preserves part of the date of death (August MCCCL...).[41] Roughly contemporary is the fragment from the sarcophagus of grand master Déodat de Gozon (d. 1353), preserved in the Musée des Thèrmes de Cluny in France;[42] he is the only master of the Hospital known to have had an epitaph in his native French. The sarcophagus of master Pierre de Corneillan (d. 1355) survives virtually intact and is on display in the Archaeological Museum of Rhodes.[43] Another heraldic slab, belonging to a burgess of Rhodes,[44] is dated by the partly effaced inscription to MCCCLX... (Pl. 5), and is followed by the armoured effigial slab of a Cypriot nobleman who died at Rhodes some time between 1356 and 1359 (MCCCLXV...).[45] He probably belonged to the retinue of King Peter I of Cyprus and must have been a young man, since the epitaph concentrates on his father ('...re] de Morf, fils du puissant baron messire Jean du Morf, comte de Rohas et maréchal du royaume de Chypre ...') The next dated items are a heraldic slab of 1358[46] and a fragment preserving the ends of four lines of text from another slab of 1370[47] – they are both worn by treading feet. The well-known relief effigy of Gulielmus Becharius, burgess of Rhodes who died in 1373, is kept in Istanbul[48] and the epitaph running round the edge of the slab is in elegant characters raised from the field in two-dimensional relief. The sarcophagus of grand master Robert de Juillac (d. 1377),[49] kept at Cluny, has an incised epitaph much like that of Corneillan; this and a fragment from the gravestone of another burgess of Rhodes who had died two months before the master,[50] are the latest epitaphs dated to the fourteenth century.

All the survivals listed so far use the Lombard script, with minor variants in certain letters (A, D, M, U) – at times a single inscription may contain different variants of the same character. The next gravestone to have survived bears the date

38 F37; ibid., p. 44; Gerola, 'I monumenti', p. 272.

39 F125.

40 F121; *Αρχαιολογικόν Δελτίον* 53 (1998), B', Χρονικά, p. 986; Luttrell, *The Town*, p. 45.

41 F175.

42 Inv. no. 422; De Vaivre, pp. 42–6.

43 F17; ibid., pp. 45, 48–9.

44 F119; *Αρχαιολογικόν Δελτίον*, *loc. cit.*; Luttrell, *The Town*, p. 46.

45 F44; Kasdagli, 'Τρεις ταφόπλακες'

46 F18; Konstantinopoulos, p. 27, 12.

47 F145.

48 Inv. no. 944; Rossi, p. 331, fig. 2; A.-M. Kasdagli, 'Funerary Monuments of Hospitaller Rhodes – an Overview', in *The Military Orders, History and Heritage* (forthcoming); A.-M. Kasdagli, 'Heraldry in Medieval Rhodes: Hospitallers and Others', in *The Military Orders On Land and By Sea* (forthcoming).

49 Inv. no. 424; De Vaivre, pp. 51, 53–6.

50 F183. *Αρχαιολογικόν Δελτίον*, 52 (1997), Χρονικά, p. 1152.

Plate 4: F125, fragment of incised effigial slab

Plate 5: F119, fragment of heraldic slab

Plate 6: F45, effigial slab of turcopolier Peter Holt; detail

1402 and belongs to a Frenchman, Pierre de la Pymoraye;[51] it introduces a new style of effigial slab cut in very shallow, two-plane relief with the epitaph round the edge raised from the ground and using the boldest form of the Gothic script – the so-called black letter. Judging from the presence of the arms of the Hospital, Pymoraye must have been an associate of the Order, if not a full member. The earliest dated gravestone of a confirmed Hospitaller brother belongs to turcopolier Peter Holt (d. 1414)[52] and, although worn, resembles the Pymoraye slab – most notably, its very shallow relief and the use of raised black letters in the epitaph (Pl. 6). Another slab showing similar features dates to 1415,[53] but the work is much more refined – the inscription delicately carved and the moulding of the effigy more competent; unfortunately, it is worn and only the end of the inscription is legible (Pl. 7). The last two dated funerary inscriptions from Rhodes to use the Gothic script – incised this time, and beautifully finished – are both on the lid of the sarcophagus of grand master Jacques de Milly (d. 1461),[54] kept at Cluny. The first commemorates the

51 F20; Konstantinopoulos, p. 28, 17; Kollias, *Palace*, pp. 132, 134.

52 F45; Konstantinopoulos, p. 32, 34, 22; Kasdagli, 'Funerary Monuments'.

53 F42; Konstantinopoulos, p. 32, 20.

54 Inv. no. 425; ibid., pp. 63, 65.

Plate 7: F42, effigial slab; detail

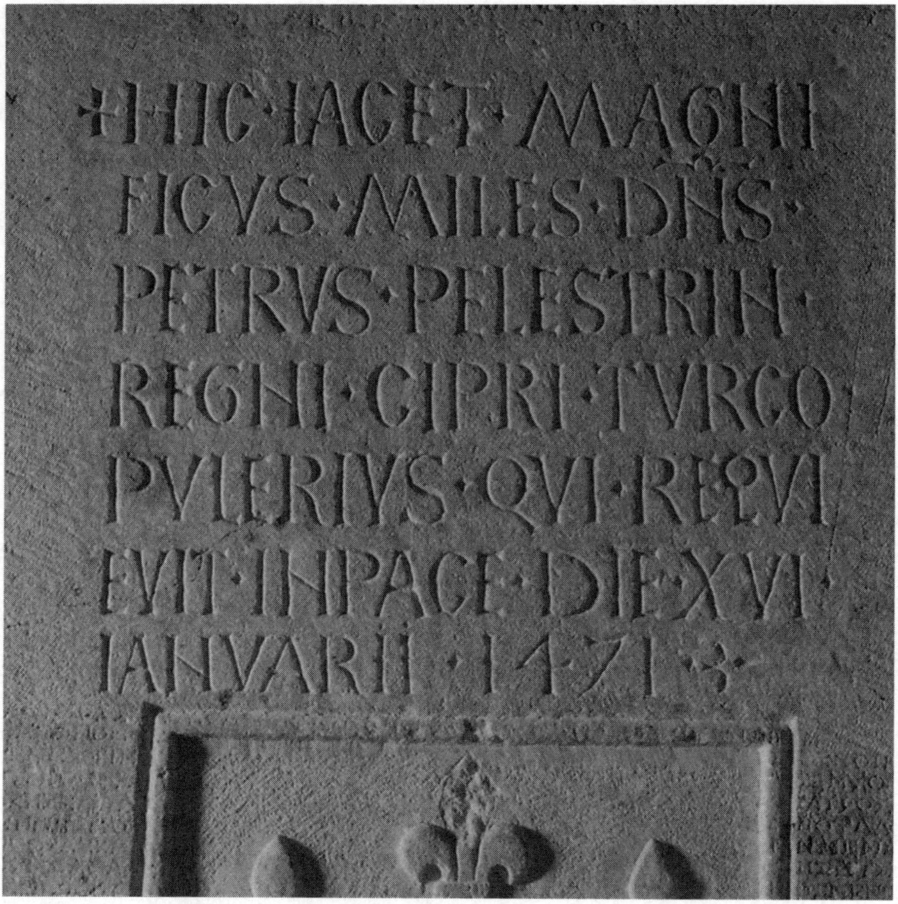

Plate 8: F14, heraldic slab of Pierre Pelestrin; detail

master, and the second the infant son of queen Carlotta of Cyprus, who was buried in the master's sarcophagus (*super magistri pectus*) in 1464. The dated epitaphs using the Gothic script also employ Latin, rather than the vernacular, and Latin remained most popular in funerary inscriptions after other features on the gravestones had changed.

The next change in style is introduced by the gravestone of Peter Pelestrin, turcopolier of Carlotta, who died on the island in 1471.[55] This is a heraldic slab, without effigy, and the epitaph is arranged in seven lines above the arms (Pl. 8). Here the Gothic script has been replaced by capitals. They are narrower and less crisp than 'Roman' capitals and the date is in Arabic numerals for the first time. All the dated slabs from now on have epitaphs in capitals – they are, usually, well-designed capitals and pairs of letters may occasionally be joined together or one letter may

55 F14; Kasdagli, 'Funerary Monuments'.

Plate 9: F212, heraldic slab of Martinus de Rossca

enclose another to save space (cf. Pl. 10). The single exception is an effigial slab reused in 1481,[56] a time of stress, when the devastation of the great siege of 1480 was followed by a series of earthquakes that damaged or levelled most of the buildings. The epitaph is scratched, rather than cut, round the edge of the underside of the earlier effigy, and its clumsy Gothic characters are not fully legible.

The finest and best preserved gravestones still to be seen on Rhodes date from the later Hospitaller period, from the 1470s to the 1510s. They are all dominated by heraldry, the arms of the deceased often framed by a laurel wreath. The first such slab belonged to a Venetian of the Prioli family,[57] buried at Rhodes in 1474. The epitaph is arranged in seven lines on a scroll opened lengthwise, with the coat of arms set within a laurel wreath below. The execution of the design lags behind the concept of the slab, something which cannot be said for later examples of this type – namely the gravestones of Thomas Provana (1499)[58] and Thomas Newport (1502),[59] both brethren of the Hospital, and of Martinus de Rossca (Pl. 9), a privateer who died in 1505,[60] and also the fragments of a Greek slab dated to 1508.[61] The execution of the epitaphs on these – incised or inlaid – is on a par with the competence of the relief decoration: the heraldry and its setting. It is worth noting that the style of the lettering is not identical, betraying both adaptability and the availability of designers.

Analysis of the lettering can trace the work of particular craftsmen in gravestones of different styles. For example, the lettering on the gravestone of Renier Pot (d. 1498) (Pl. 10), the most elaborate heraldic slab without a wreath,[62] is closely related to the Provana epitaph. As regards context, however, the Pot epitaph recalls the lengthy laudatory inscription on the sarcophagus of grand master Giovanni Battista degli Orsini (d. 1476), now at Cluny.[63] Very similar to each other in style – and content – are two epitaphs of 1493, belonging to Pedro Fernández de Heredia,[64] castellan of Amposta (Pl. 11), and Jeanne de Perier, a Breton noblewoman who died at Rhodes on her way back from the Holy Land[65] (Pl. 12). The same hand behind the design of the lettering is obvious on both, although the Heredia slab had lettering inlaid with lead. It is less easy to compare the lettering of the Heredia epitaph with that of Besso von Lichtenberg,[66] grand bailiff of the Order who died in the siege of 1480,

---

56 F16; *Rhodes from the 4th century*, ill. 82.

57 F207; *Αρχαιολογικόν Δελτίον*, 52 (1997), Χρονικά, p. 1150, pl. 432.

58 F12; Konstantinopoulos, p. 20, 5; A.-M. Kasdagli and Y. Katsou, 'Η κοινωνική διάσταση στα επιτύμβια. Δύο προσωπογραφίες', *Γλυπτική και λιθοξοϊκή στη λατινοκρατύμενη Ανατολή 13ος-17ος αιώνς* (Heraklion, 2007), pp. 90–101; English version: 'The Social Context of Gravestones: Two Portraits', *Crusades* 6 (2007), [forthcoming].

59 F10; Kollias, *Palace*, pp. 134, 137; Kasdagli and Katsou.

60 F212; Kasdagli and Katsou.

61 E. Kollias, *Η μνημειακή εκλεκτική ζωγραφική στη Ρόδο στα τέλη του 15ου και στις αρχές του 16ου αιώνα* (Athens, 2000), pp. 12–13, fig. 1.

62 F22; Konstantinopoulos, pp. 29–30, 18; Kollias, *Palace*, pp. 135, 137.

63 Inv. no. 426; De Vaivre, pp. 66–8.

64 F13; Konstantinopoulos, pp. 20–1, 6; Kasdagli and Katsou.

65 F213; Kasdagli and Katsou.

66 F15; Kasdagli, 'Τρεις ταφόπλακες'.

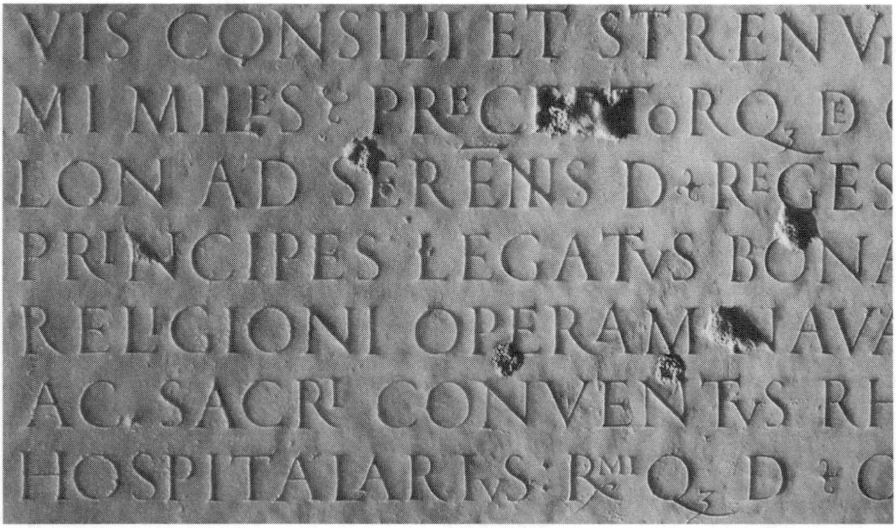

Plate 10: F22, heraldic slab of Renier Pot; detail

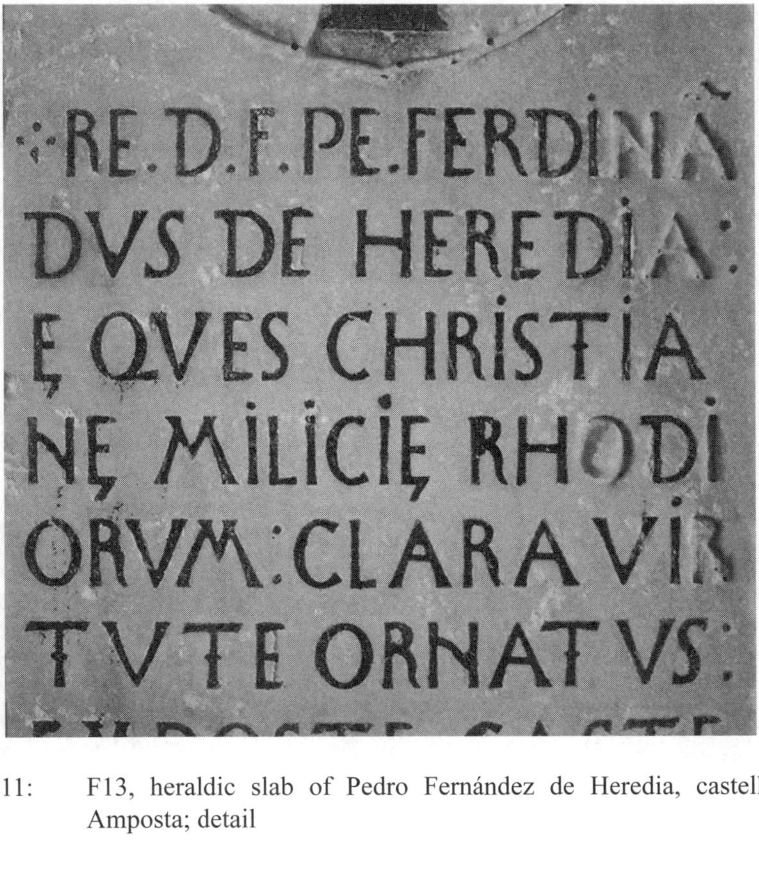

Plate 11: F13, heraldic slab of Pedro Fernández de Heredia, castellan of Amposta; detail

Plate 12: F213, heraldic slab of Joanna de Perier; detail

which appears quite similar. This is another slab with inlaid arms and epitaph, but the lead was prised off its setting when the gravestone was cut to pieces in Ottoman times to serve as building material. The gap of 13 years separating the death of the two personages is not necessarily great, if the unusual circumstances reported about the burial of Lichtenberg are taken into account: he was originally buried in the cemetery of St Anthony outside the walls, but the body would not decompose, even after a reburial; finally, it was translated to a tomb near the place where he had fallen in battle inside the walls, and there it finally went the way of all flesh. The fanciful story, recounted by German visitors to Rhodes who venerated his grave in the early sixteenth century, is supported by the fact that the pieces of his gravestone were recovered from buildings about the area penetrated by the janissaries in their memorable assault of 28 July 1480. If the peregrinations of the restless dead took a few years to accomplish, then the execution of his tombstone may have post-dated his death by a number of years, narrowing the gap from the Heredia work.

The gravestone of another official, grand hospitaller Nicholas de Montmirel (d. 1511),[67] presents other features of interest. The epitaph includes the standard information – name, office, date of death – but is headed by the invocation *Domine in Te Confido* (a motto?) and concludes with the English phrase *As God Will* – perhaps expressing the resignation of those who commissioned the slab for the loss of a friend. The inventory of dated funerary inscriptions from Rhodes is concluded by the epitaph of grand master Fabrizio del Carretto (d. 1521),[68] a specimen of republican austerity with an irregularity in the date: in the text the year reads MDXX, perhaps to be explained by reckoning the start of the new year from the feast of the Annunciation.

This survey has omitted some sixty undated gravestones and fragments of funerary inscriptions, most of them containing a few words and which, to assist scholarship, should be assigned an approximate date. Although Gothic epitaphs with dates are limited in number, it is still striking that they are contained between the years 1402 and 1464 – and that we have no dated epitaph in the Lombard script later than the 1370s or in Renaissance capitals earlier than 1471. This suggests that local choices in funerary monuments were rather limited, something not too surprising in a small town. It is true that the local Latins were far from homogeneous as a group; but this feature may have been offset by a rather limited choice in tomb craftsmanship for most of the period under examination. The Gothic script was introduced on Rhodes rather late;[69] and then, as far as we can tell, it displaced the Lombard script. Our evidence is, perhaps, less than adequate to support a complete shift: there is, after all, the Buondelmonti pillar, but this was probably the conscious choice of a cultured

67 F11; *Rhodes from the 4th century*, ill. 84.

68 F36; Gerola, *Annuario della Regia Scuola Archeologica di Atene* I, p. 254, n. 5; De Vaivre, p. 70. The slab is actually on display in the Archaeological Museum of Rhodes, in the Great Ward.

69 Cf. A.F. Greenhill, *Incised Efigial Slabs: A Study of Engraved Stone Memorials in Latin Christendom, c. 1100 to 1700* (London, 1976), pls. 61a (1340, France), 114a (1349, France), 58a (1352, France), 18a (1364, E. Germany), 140b (1351, Belgium), 64a (1384, England).

Italian. Indeed, it seems that traditional styles in the choice of a particular script were more closely followed when solemnity was of greater importance – as in epitaphs – whereas personal taste carried more weight in other contexts, with individuals being less constrained in their choices. In funerary monuments, the earthquake of 1481 was the point of no return for the Gothic script: the influx of artisans from the West who came to assist the rebuilding of the town disseminated a new Renaissance aesthetic, at the same time providing the means to indulge it. It is probably no accident that on the fortifications, where the masters of the Hospital took most trouble to mark as their own, the last Gothic inscriptions were carved for Fort St Nicholas under grand master Pere Ramon Zacosta (d. 1467); the legend *D. paul'* on the saint's relief decorating the tower of St Paul is also in the Gothic script – but d'Aubusson's inscription underneath is in Renaissance capitals, while the whole work most likely dates from the 1470s.[70] Actually, the latest Gothic inscription on Rhodes comes from the countryside and dates from the period of Orsini (1467–76). It is associated with the cemetery church of Yennadi, some 70 km distant from the town, which could have been a Latin church at that time.

Thus, it is probably safe to assume that fragments of epitaphs in the Lombard script are likely to belong to the fourteenth century, and assign those in the Gothic style to the first 70 years of the fifteenth century. This, although true for the single inscription surviving on the small island of Symi,[71] does not apply to the Hospitaller strongholds at Cos and Bodrum. They apparently often enjoyed the services of different craftsmen and, at Bodrum, elaborated their own decorative code. For example, the earliest known inscription in Renaissance capitals is found on Cos, dated 1454[72] – the next one, on Rhodes, does not appear until 1471. Also, those responsible for the design of the Gothic Carmadino[73] inscriptions at Nerangia (ca. 1472–78)[74] took unusual pains to avoid contractions; and the reversed N on inscriptions of Cos dated to the governorship of Francisco Sans (1513–14)[75] appears nowhere else (although Sans was also active on Rhodes). At Bodrum, too, the only inscription in the Lombard script,[76] a delicately rendered invocation, is unexpectedly late and the date itself, 1509, is in the Gothic script: M·V^{C} / ·ix· The obviously decorative mood is reflected in the heraldry.

Of the epitaphs assigned to the fourteenth century by the use of the Lombard script there are some worth mentioning:

F19.[77] ... IACE[T HONO]RABILIS / ...US FRATER BERNARDUS B[AI... U]S BASCO DE MAL… If the dating is correct, this might be the earliest surviving effigial slab of

70 Gabriel, vol. 1, p. 70.

71 Gerola, *Annuario della Regia Scuola Archeologia di Atene*, II, p. 4.

72 Maiuri, p. 287, no. 26.

73 Edoardo di Carmadino, governor of Cos (1471–95). Gerola, *Annuario della Regia Scuola Archeologia di Atene*, II, p. 28–9.

74 Gerola, *Annuario*, II, pp. 28–9, nos. 27–31.

75 Gerola, *Annuario*, II, p. 46.

76 Gerola, 'Il castello', p. 71, no. XLI; Maiuri, p. 324.

77 Konstantinopoulos, p. 27, 14.

a member of the Order on Rhodes.

F90. ...ONIS HOSPITALIS·SA(n)CT(i) IOH(an)/ NIS IH(e)R(usa)L(e)M...

F167. ...(prec)EPTORI(s) DE ...

F168. ...PRIO[R...

These three fragments, recovered from the site of the conventual church, indicate that brethren were being buried there in the fourteenth century. The quality of F167, whose lettering is raised from the field, recalls the Becharius effigy now in Istanbul and may be roughly contemporary with it. Another example of this technique is encountered in the damaged top of a gravestone dedicated to three noble children (+HIC IACENT NOBILES ET... (requi)ESC]ANT IN [PACE AMEN]) of the same family buried under the care of the Hospital.[78]

F129. ...COLOSS(ensis) [QU... Perhaps a fragment from the gravestone of another fourteenth-century Latin archbishop of Rhodes.

F133. +HIC IACET IOHANES / GAUALLA CIVIS RO / DI. Reverse of a slab originally used for two ladies of the same family earlier in the century.[79] It shows that some upper-class Greeks were being assimilated by the Latin community. This Gavallas also displayed arms with a lion rampant on his tomb.

F138. ...GIRA(ldo) G[U]ELFI / D(e) VIG(no)LO ET SUO(rum) QUI OBII[T... Fragment of an incised effigial slab which, perhaps, sealed the family tomb of the Vignolo who assisted the Knights in their conquest of Rhodes, or some relative.[80]

Of the Gothic funerary inscriptions with date missing, worth remarking is F48. + ... *capella nobillis qu'dam / Joh... suoru*(m) *qui obiit anno d*(omi)*ni / mcc... cui]us a*(n)*i*(m)*a requiescat in pace*. The reference to a chapel, alongside a shield with a bend chequy, may imply that this came from the chapel of the Cibo in the church of the Augustinian monks.[81]

78 Actually the back of the Aubusson arms on the Tower of the Windmills in the harbour of Rhodes, as the slab was cut to pieces and reused in Hospitaller times.

79 Luttrell, 'A Hospitaller *soror*', p. 136–7; Luttrell, *The Town*, p. 46.

80 *Αρχαιολογικόν Δελτίον*, 53 (1998), Β', Χρονικά, p. 986; Luttrell, *The Town*, p. 47.

81 G. Dellas, 'Νέα στοιχεία για ένα μοναστήρι στη μεσαιωνική πόλη της Ρόδου', *Δελτίον Χριστιανικής Αρχαιολογικής Εταιρείας*, 21 (2000), pp. 52–3.

Chapter 11

Historical Memory in an Aegean Monastery: St John of Patmos and the Emirate of Menteshe

Elizabeth A. Zachariadou

The emirate of Menteshe, situated in the fertile plain of the river Meandros (Menderes), was one of the vigorous Turkish emirates which emerged after the break-up of the Seljuk state of Anatolia. It seems to have been the earliest emirate that developed naval activity in the Aegean Sea. In the very early years of the fourteenth century (c. 1302–3) the Lords of Menteshe possessed a number of light vessels and began to raid their neighbouring islands. In 1306 a new Christian state, that of the Knights Hospitallers, was established on Rhodes and the surrounding islands,[1] which struggled to check the maritime expansion of the Menteshe Turks. However, the Menteshe Turks went on with their raids and in the 1330s, if not earlier, they obliged several islands, as well as certain territories on the littoral, to pay them an annual tribute in order to be left in peace.

The Venetian administration of Crete maintained commercial relations, regulated by treaties, with the lords of Menteshe. It is from the text of these treaties that we are informed about the annual tributes, as the duke of Candia was involved in their collection. More precisely, one clause of the treaty concluded in 1337, which was repeated in a later treaty in 1375, stated that if those paying tribute to the lord of Menteshe did not fulfil their obligation, the latter was obliged to notify the duke of Candia, who, in turn, was obliged to send notice to those who did not pay; if two months elapsed and the tribute was still not paid, the lord of Menteshe was entitled to send his fleet to collect it, which actually meant to pillage the disobedient territory and capture its inhabitants to sell them as slaves. We know those who were paying tribute thanks to another clause in which certain territories and islands, belonging to Venice (e.g. Korone and Methone) or ruled by a Venetian lord (e.g. Santorini, Kythera) were named and declared to have been included in the treaty so that they would benefit from it. It is also reported by other sources that other islands and territories, not included in the treaties because they did not belong or

1 A.T. Luttrell, 'The Genoese at Rhodes: 1306–1312', in L. Balletto (ed.), *Oriente e Occidente tra medioevo ed età moderna. Studi in onore di Geo Pistarino*, Università degli Studi di Genova, Sede di Acqui Terme, Collana di Fonti e Studi 11 (Acqui Terme, 1997), pp. 737–61. On the beginnings of the state of Menteshe see Elizabeth A. Zachariadou, *Trade and Crusade, Venetian Crete and the emirates of Menteshe and Aydin (1300-1415)* (Venice, 1983), pp. 4–6, 11–12, 18–20.

were not attached to Venice, also paid an annual tribute to the lords of Menteshe as, for example, the duchy of Naxos.[2] The small island of Patmos, which constituted a monastic city-state, possibly paid also, as we are going soon to see.

The annual tribute was by no means the only revenue of the lords of Menteshe. They were prosperous because trade was fairly developed in their state, which attracted merchants from many countries. Cereals, which constituted the main local produce, horses and other domestic animals, slaves, alum and some other items were exported in considerable quantities and important custom fees were accumulated. In the 1370s the lord of Menteshe Ahmed appears with the title *gazi* – that is, warrior of Islam – in one inscription as well as in Latin texts. This title was borne by his contemporary, Ottoman Sultan Murad I, and it reflects prestige deriving from exploits against the Christians and also ambition for further expansion.[3] However, the emirate of Menteshe shared the same fate as the other Turkish emirates of Anatolia; it was annexed to the unstoppably growing emirate of the Ottomans. The first time the emirate was annexed was in the days of the Sultan Yildirim Bayezid (1389–1402) and after the latter's defeat by the Mongol Khan Timur it was re-established, but only for a short time. After that, in 1425 it was annexed again, by Sultan Murad II, and this time it finally became an Ottoman province, retaining the name of the emirate.[4] After that not much was heard about the province and its past. It is hardly mentioned in the early Ottoman chronicles or in their contemporary Byzantine sources. In the Western European accounts of the fifteenth century concerning the Ottoman military administrative system, Menteshe is mentioned fairly laconically. The Veneto-Cretan scholar Lauro Quirini, who wrote around 1430, simply states that the province of Menteshe produced 7,000 horsemen; the Genoese Iacopo de Promontorio, writing approximately 45 years later, in 1475, mentions Menteshe together with two other Aegean provinces, those of Sarukhan and Aydin, but he seems confused about its exact location because he places it near Lesbos.[5] Thus, Iacopo de Promontorio's text reveals that the glorious past of the province of Menteshe was almost forgotten.

Given that Menteshe had faded from memory, it is highly surprising that in a petition composed by the abbot of the monastery of Saint John the Theologian of Patmos and submitted to the Sultan, the former recalls that his monastery possessed Stylos, a village in Crete, in the province of Chania, from the time of Menteshe and that his monastery had been paying tribute to the Muslim monarch, also from the

---

2 Zachariadou, *Trade and Crusade*, pp. 35–6, 73, 90–1, 101.

3 Zachariadou, *Trade and Crusade*, pp. 73, 111–12.

4 Zachariadou, *Trade and Crusade*, pp. 81–9.

5 A. Pertusi, 'Le epistole storiche di Lauro Quirini sulla caduta di Costantinopoli e la potenza dei Turchi', *Lauro Quirini Umanista,* ed. V. Branca (Florence, 1977), pp. 237, 251; on this text cf. E.A. Zachariadou, 'Lauro Quirini and the Turkish sandjaks (ca. 1430)', *Raiyyet Rüsûmu, Essays presented to Halil Inalcik on his seventieth birthday by his colleagues and students, Journal of Turkish Studies*, 11 (1987), pp. 239–42, 246–7. F. Babinger, 'Die Aufzeichnungen des Genuesen Iacopo de Promontorio-de Campis über die Osmanen um 1475', *Bayerische Akademie der Wissenschaften, Philosophisch-Historische Klasse, Sitzungsberichte*, 1956, Heft 8 (Munich, 1957), p. 58.

time of the country, or the state, of Menteshe (*Menteshe-ili*).[6] The purpose of the petition was to implore the Ottoman sultan to recognize the Patmos monastery's ownership of a monastic establishment (*metochion*) that was situated in Stylos. The petition has no date; but as I shall soon explain, it must be dated around the mid seventeenth century, before the complete conquest of the island of Crete, which was accomplished with the surrender of the town of Candia in September 1669. This means that this unexpected mention of Menteshe occurs more than two centuries after its disappearance as an independent state.

The monastic establishment of Stylos, which prompted the abbot's petition to the sultan, was an old possession of the monastery of Patmos. It is mentioned for the first time in a document of 1219, when the island of Crete was under Venetian domination.[7] Nevertheless, we can assume that it was granted to the monastery of Patmos when Crete was still a Byzantine territory, that is, before 1204, the year of the Fourth Crusade, when the Venetians founded their mercantile establishment in the Aegean, with Crete as their principal colony. It is hard to imagine that only 15 years after the capture of Constantinople by the Latins, the Venetians would grant a piece of land, situated in a territory newly conquered by them, to a Greek Orthodox monastery. On the contrary, it seems quite likely that they recognized an already existing monastic establishment belonging to the most venerated Monastery of Patmos, the island on which Saint John had written the Apocalypse. It is not known when exactly theVenetian administration of Crete officially recognized the property of the monastery of Patmos on their island; it is only known that it was recognized in 1267 by the doge of Venice. Several documents issued after this year – some of them kept in the archive of Patmos and some others in that of Venice – testify to the relations between Venetian Crete and Patmos, which were good on the whole. One of those documents, dated 1321, includes an account of the borders of the monastic establishment of Stylos, which were fixed for the use of the chancery of the department of Chania.[8]

In 1645 a war broke out between Venice and the Ottoman empire which began with the arrival of a huge fleet near Crete and the disembarkation of sultanic troops near Chania. They conquered Chania rather easily and by the end of the year 1646 they also conquered Rethymnon.[9] The monastic establishment of Stylos, situated to the east of Chania, passed under the rule of the Ottomans, although the war was still going on and would last for approximately another 24 years, albeit confined to the area around the well-fortified harbour-city of Candia, which resisted fiercely and successfully.

---

6 Archive of the Monastery of Saint John the Theologian, Patmos, file 20, doc. 103. On the Turkish section of the archive of the monastery see N. Vatin, 'Note préliminaire au catalogage du fonds ottoman des archives du monastère de Saint-Jean à Patmos', *Turcica*, 33 (2001), 333–8.

7 Era L. Vranoussi, *Βυζαντινά Έγγραφα Μονής Πάτμου, 1. Αυτοκρατορικά* (Athens, 1980), pp. *89–*90, 215–16.

8 On these documents see C.A. Maltezou, 'Τα λατινικά έγγραφα του πατμιακού αρχείου', *Symmeikta*, 2 (1970), pp. 361–2.

9 On these events see K.M. Setton, *Venice, Austria, and the Turks in the Seventeenth Century* (Philadelphia, 1991), pp. 122–42.

Historical research has clearly shown that the Greek Orthodox monks were fairly eager to place their monasteries under the protection of the Ottoman sultans, as this would involve recognition of their properties and, often, favourable taxation. Their attitude can be explained if we recall the enmity prevailing between the Greek Orthodox and the Roman Catholic worlds at that time. On the other hand, the sultans listened to the monks' appeals because they wanted to win the Greek Orthodox population over to their side, which would make their state's expansion easier. The approach between sultans and monks was more noticeable after the conquest of a territory by the Ottomans, and even before it, when its conquest seemed imminent. The monasteries of Mount Athos as well as the monastery of Saint John Prodromos of Serres appealed to the sultan for protection during the second half of the fourteenth century, before the conquest of Macedonia. It is worth mentioning a case from the Aegean region that also concerns the monastery of Saint John the Theologos of Patmos. When Rhodes and the other islands of the Hospitallers surrendered to the Sultan, that is, in the very first days of January 1523, the monks acted quickly to preserve their monastic establishments on the islands of Leros and Kalymnos. At the end of the same year they obtained an order (*firman*) from Sultan Süleyman the Magnificent commanding an investigation into their claims; if the claims were sound, the monks would be entitled to keep their possessions.[10] As it turned out, their claims were confirmed and the monastery of Patmos kept its possessions on Leros and Kalymnos.

From the above we can infer that the monks acted in this way in order to keep their monastic establishment of Crete. Another document found in the archive of Patmos helps us to clarify the situation. This document was dated and issued by the Ottoman great admiral (*Kapudan Pasha*) in the beginning of the year 1650,[11] that is, approximately four years after the territory of Stylos passed under the Ottoman rule. The great admiral acknowledged that the monks of Patmos had a document dating from before the Ottoman conquest and showing that they possessed the land of Stylos in full property; that they also had documents of pacts which had been given to them by the grand viziers after the conquest; and that the monks of Stylos cultivated their property and paid the tithe and some customary taxes.

The documents mentioned in this text require some comment. The document certifying the full property (*mülkname* in the Turkish text) was possibly Byzantine, but more probably Venetian, while the documents of pacts (*ahdnames*[12] in the Turkish text) given by the grand viziers were presumably issued during a visit of the abbot (or of a representative of his) of Patmos to the Sultan's court in Constantinople and, certainly, in response to a petition (*arz-u hal*).

10 E.A. Zachariadou, 'Ottoman documents from the Archives of Dionysiou (Mount Athos) 1495–1520', *Südost-Forschungen*, 30 (1971), p. 14; E.A. Zachariadou, 'Η Κως και η μονή της Πάτμου με την έναρξη της Τουρκοκρατίας', *Ιστορία – Τέχνη – Αρχαιολογία της Κω, First International Conference, Cos 2–4 May 1997* (Athens, 2001), pp. 465–8.

11 Archive of the Monastery of Saint John the Theologian, Patmos, file 16, doc.5; it is a *temessük*; i.e., a document acknowledging a claim.

12 On the term *ahdname* see D. Kolodziejczyk, *Ottoman-Polish diplomatic relations (15th–18th century)* (Leiden, 2000), pp. 3–7.

This petition may well have been the document mentioned above which refers to Menteshe and which prompted me to write this short article. Its contents can be summarized as follows. The abbot, appealing to the sultan, informed him about a village in Crete, Stylos, which had been donated to the monastery of Patmos and had been administered by the monastery since the time of Menteshe; also that the monks had been paying tribute to the Muslim monarch since the time of the country of Menteshe. The monks of Patmos, who were tribute-paying subjects of the Muslim monarch, were humbly demanding a written order from him which would forbid all others to interfere in the affairs of Stylos. Furthermore, the abbot gave an account of the borders of Stylos, which was based on a document of the 'infidels'. The petition ended with some additional pleas but without date and without the name of the abbot, who simply signed himself as 'the sultan's humble slave.'[13]

Some short comments on the contents of the document would not be out of place here. The tribute paid since the time of Menteshe (*Menteshe-ili*, i.e. the 'country of Menteshe' and by 'country' we understand 'emirate') to the monarch (*hünkâr* in the Turkish text, which is a synonym of 'sultan') is called in the document kharadj, which could mean either the land tax or the poll tax paid by the non-Muslims to their Muslim Lord;[14] but as the payers are called *kharadj-güzar* it is clear that the document is referring to the poll tax that the monastery had been paying for a long time. The first piece of written evidence that Patmos was paying tribute to the Ottoman sultan dates from the year 1453. However, we may guess that the tribute was imposed considerably earlier, probably in 1425, when the littoral of Asia Minor became an Ottoman territory, if not before.[15] The document of the 'infidels' used by the abbot to describe the fixed borders of Stylos in detail is fairly certainly the Latin document of 1321, composed to be used by the chancery of the department of Chania, as has already been mentioned. This document, together with its Greek translation of a later date, is found in the archive of the monastery of Patmos[16] and a quick comparison shows the close resemblance with the Turkish text. It is obvious that the abbot consulted his monastic archive before departing for the Ottoman capital to apply for confirmation of his monastery's property rights. The document that he obtained in response has not been located in the archive of Patmos. However, it is certain that there was a document issued then in response to the abbot's petition, and this is mentioned in the document of the Ottoman admiral who saw it. Apparently the abbot, having his rights confirmed by the sultanic service, visited or sent a representative to the Ottoman admiral, who was present in the Aegean as the war for the conquest of Crete was going on and Venetian ships were continuously sailing between the Dardanelles and the harbour of Candia. His purpose was to inform the Ottoman admiral about the arrangements concerning the property of Stylos and, in addition to

13 He could have been Iakovos Mantalakes or Savvas Kalogeras: Chr. Florentes, *Βραβείον της Ιεράς Μονής Αγ. Ιωάννου του Θεολόγου Πάτμου* (Athens, 1980), pp. 37–8.

14 F. Lokkegaard, *Islamic taxation in the classic period with special reference to circumstances in Irak* (Copenhagen, 1950), pp. 81–7.

15 E.A. Zachariadou, *Romania and the Turks (c. 1300–c. 1500)* (London, 1985), XVII, pp. 195–8, 208–10.

16 Maltezou, pp. 361–3.

this, to get a second confirmation from a figure with authority in the vicinity of both Patmos and Crete.

The whole story of the monastic establishment of Stylos can be used as an example of historical continuity in the face of political change – in this case, the continuity in the history of the monastery of Patmos and its dependencies, despite the change from Venetian to Ottoman domination. This kind of historical continuity is typical of several Greek Orthodox institutions of that time, and many examples of this kind have been known and studied. More interesting is the mention of Menteshe, which the abbot invoked to demonstrate how old were the relations between his monastery and the Turks. It is obvious that the abbot was conscious of the continuity in the monastery's history from the time of Menteshe to that of the Ottoman state, and this is why he used the title of *hünkâr* for both rulers, that of Menteshe and the Ottoman one, to whom the inhabitants of Patmos paid their poll tax. The evolution of the Turkish emirates of Anatolia into the Ottoman empire has been well established by current historical research. Nevertheless, it seems strange when noticed and reported by an abbot in the middle of the seventeenth century, more than two centuries after the end of the emirate of Menteshe.

Menteshe was certainly well known to the monastery of Patmos. Since Byzantine times the monastery had had a monastic establishment in the region of the Meandros river, in the centre of the territory of Menteshe, which was known as the *metochion* of Meandros. This establishment was later recognized as a property of the monastery of Patmos by the Ottomans but absolutely nothing is known about it when it was under the lords of Menteshe. We may guess that the island of Patmos, as all the islands of the eastern Aegean, paid an annual tribute to Menteshe, when this state was in its prime; after all, this is stated in the abbot's petition that I have examined. However, no contemporary documents have been preserved to confirm whether this was indeed the case. The only, but substantial, evidence known to me that concerns contact between the emirate and the monastery is that after the battle of Ankara (1402) some monks of Patmos served as envoys sent by the lord of Menteshe to the duke Candia;[17] but one piece of information is an insufficient basis for general conclusions.

If, as we are allowed to imagine, there had been documents issued by the lords of Menteshe in the archive of the monastery of Patmos, they would probably have been shown and submitted to the Ottoman chancery when the Ottoman state annexed the emirate of Menteshe and reached the vicinity of Patmos; as a result the monastery would have had to negotiate its position under the sultan and earlier documents could have been useful. On the other hand, once the emirate ceased to exist as a political entity, the documents of its chancery must have lost their importance compared to the new ones granted by the new masters. This would provide some explanation of their total absence from the archive of Patmos.

Still, a difficult question remains unanswered, namely how, in the mid seventeenth century, the abbot knew about the past relations of his monastery with Menteshe. The only possible answer is that a vivid oral tradition of the island's history must

17 E.A. Zachariadou, 'Monks and sailors under the Ottoman Sultans', in K. Fleet (ed.), *The Ottomans and the Sea*, *Oriente Moderno*, 20 (2001), p. 143.

have been repeated from one generation of monks to the next within the monastery. If this is so, the historian must not discard any suspected evidence of oral tradition that may have become embedded in written sources.

P.S. In the meantime an important article confirming the commercial relations of Patmos with the emirate of Menteshe in the middle of the fourteenth century has been published; see Guillaume Saint-Guillain, 'L'Acpocalypse et le sens des affaires. Les moines de Saint-Jean de Patmos, leurs activités économiques et leurs relations avec les Latins (XIIIe et XIVe siècles)', *Chemins d'outre-mer, Ètudes sur la Méditerranée médiévale offertes à Michel Balard*, Publications de la Sorbonne, 2004 (Byzantia Sorbonensia 20), pp. 765–90; my view about the monks' historical memory has not changed.

E.A.Z.

Chapter 12

Emmanuele Piloti and Crusading in the Latin East

Norman Housley

Although Anthony Luttrell has specialized in the history of the Order of St John, he has also written a good deal about the development of crusading in the fourteenth and early fifteenth centuries. His 1965 essay on 'The crusade in the fourteenth century' remains the most satisfying account of the awkward and problematic process by which crusading in the Eastern Mediterranean changed its character from that of a war to recover the Holy Land to a mechanism for defending lands under the control of Catholic Europeans from the advance of the Anatolian Turks, initially the coastal emirates but by 1400 increasingly the Ottoman sultan.[1] One of the most intriguing and revealing pieces of evidence for this overall process of change is Emmanuele Piloti's treatise (*tractatus)* on the recovery of the Holy Land. Piloti began writing his text in 1420 but finished it only in 1438 or shortly thereafter.[2] The end result was a lengthy document, almost 240 pages in the edition that Pierre-Herman Dopp published in 1958. Dopp used the French text of the sole surviving manuscript, MS 15701 in Belgium's Bibliothèque Royale; the Latin text from which this translation was made has almost certainly been lost, as has the original text, which Piloti probably composed in his own vernacular. Although this issue of translations, and the errors that they may have introduced, is just one of several question marks that still hang over Piloti's text,[3] it has attracted little attention since 1958.[4] The neglect

1 A. Luttrell, 'The Crusade in the Fourteenth Century', in J. Hale et al. (eds), *Europe in the late Middle Ages* (London, 1965), pp. 122–54.

2 *Traité d'Emmanuel Piloti sur le Passage en Terre Sainte (1420)*, ed. P.-H. Dopp, Publications de l'Université Lovanium de Léopoldville (Louvain, 1958) (hereafter cited as *EP*). It will be noted that the title of Dopp's edition gives only the starting date of 1420; this has misled the unwary, e.g. N. Housley, *The Later Crusades, 1274–1580: From Lyons to Alcazar* (Oxford, 1992), p. 45. The *terminus ante quem* for the completion of the original text is Sultan Barsbay's death on 7 June 1438. The French translation was made in 1441.

3 There is, for example, the question of whether the text featured in the sizeable collection of crusade-related manuscripts held by the library of the dukes of Burgundy. Contrast Dopp in *EP*, pp. v–x, who does not question it ('infiniment probable', p. x), and most recently J. Paviot, *Les Ducs de Bourgogne, la croisade et l'Orient (fin XIVe siècle–XVe siècle)*, Cultures et civilisations médiévales (Paris, 2003), pp. 205, 247–8, 262, who is sceptical in the absence of direct evidence.

4 The only recent treatment of which I am aware of is A. Leopold, *How to Recover the Holy Land: The Crusade Proposals of the Late Thirteenth and Early Fourteenth Centuries* (Aldershot, 2000), pp. 198–200. There is a description of the content based on an earlier

is unfortunately typical for this period of crusading, and it is regrettable because, provided due allowance is made for his idiosyncrasy, Piloti's opinions and advice can function as windows into contemporary views about crusading in the decades just before the Ottoman capture of Constantinople directed the attention of all but a few commentators northwards, away from Egypt, Palestine and Syria towards Anatolia and the Balkans.

Like so many medieval texts, Piloti's *tractatus* resists ready categorization. Most obviously it is a late entry to the genre of 'recovery treatises' that had enjoyed its heyday a full century previously. In this respect its clearest predecessor was Marino Sanudo Torsello's *Liber secretorum fidelium crucis* of 1306–21. Piloti may have read Sanudo's text, though he nowhere refers explicitly to it.[5] Although his family had settled in Crete, Piloti shared Sanudo's Venetian patriotism and he saw the republic as the only practicable source of shipping for his crusade. His basic military plan of action had much in common with Sanudo's for many of the same reasons, in terms of their commercial expertise and knowledge of the region's geography and trade routes. Like Sanudo,[6] Piloti believed in personal lobbying as the best way to get his ideas across, and the offhand way in which he was treated at the *curia* of Pope Eugenius IV surely contributed towards his negative judgement of the role that the *curia* should play in his crusade.[7] For the reason stated at the close of the previous paragraph, Piloti's text is arguably the last detailed recovery treatise;[8] but it is also more than that. In its avoidance of rhetorical flights of fancy and its reliance on information and close reasoning, Piloti's text bears a close resemblance to the reconnaissance reports of de la Broquière and de Lannoy, whose visits to the Eastern Mediterranean took place during the years when Piloti was writing up his ideas.[9] And one of the text's longest and most informative sections is that describing the provenance of the products that passed through Egypt's leading port, Alexandria. The value of these pages for our knowledge of the Mediterranean carrying trade has long been acknowledged. Anthony Luttrell has referred to Piloti's 'extremely shrewd perceptions of economic and political realities' in the territories ruled by the Mamluks.[10] Eliyahu Ashtor described Piloti's *tractatus* as 'a most original and authentic source', 'summing up the experience and knowledge of a merchant who

edition of the text in A.S. Atiya, *The Crusade in the later Middle Ages* (London, 1938), pp. 208–12.

5 See *EP*, p. 132 note, where Dopp states that Piloti 'a certainement lu cet ouvrage' [the *Liber secretorum*], although, aside from the appearance of similar themes and ideas in both texts, the evidence consists only of their shared use of two rare words, which hardly seems clinching proof. Leopold, *How to Recover the Holy Land*, p. 199, is more cautious.

6 See C.J. Tyerman, 'Marino Sanudo Torsello and the Lost Crusade: Lobbying in the Fourteenth Century', *Transactions of the Royal Historical Society*, 32 (1982), 57–73.

7 *EP*, pp. 169–70.

8 Leopold, *How to Recover the Holy Land*, p. 200, comments that 'his proposal seems to belong more to the early fourteenth century than the early fifteenth'.

9 See Housley, *The Later Crusades*, pp. 92, 471; Paviot, *Les Ducs de Bourgogne*, passim.

10 A. Luttrell, 'The Latin East', in C. Allmand (ed.), *The New Cambridge Medieval History* vol. 7 *c. 1414–c. 1500* (Cambridge, 1998), pp. 796–811, at p. 799.

had carried on trade in Egypt during a lifetime and had distinguished himself by deep insight in economic matters'.[11] It is not clear why Ashtor rates Piloti more highly than Sanudo, whose credibility he questions,[12] but his high estimation has the effect of placing Piloti alongside such well-known sources as Pegolotti's *Pratica della mercatura*.

It follows from this that the *tractatus* can be profitably approached from several directions; indeed Anthony Luttrell showed as much in his article about Piloti and the Knights of St John.[13] In relation to crusading I should like to use the text to look at a number of issues. The first of these is contextual, Piloti's overall approach towards Islam. The depth of Piloti's familiarity with the Mamluk lands, their geography, economy, the ethnic composition of their inhabitants, and political and military affairs there, is undoubtedly impressive. He had traded in Egypt from the mid-1390s, and provided a telling anecdote of seeing 200 prisoners arriving at the citadel in Cairo after the battle of Nicopolis (1396); all attractive young men, they had been despatched as a gift to the sultan, and they had all converted to Islam.[14] Piloti estimated that he spent a total of 22 years in Egypt. Syria, too, he clearly knew well, since he saw Damascus before its sack by Tamerlane in 1401, in ruins after that event, and a third time following its reconstruction.[15] He discussed religious matters with the Muslims with whom he got on best and knew a reasonable amount about their devotional practices. For example, he was well informed on Ramadan, knew that Muslims venerated the Virgin Mary, and was confident enough about the status that Jesus held within Islam to turn in a Muslim guilty of blaspheming the prophet.[16] Yet he remained content to peddle one of the most hackneyed of the traditional stories about Muhammad, and referred, like so many before him, to implausible Muslim predictions of Islam's imminent end.[17] Even though he acknowledged the role of charity in Muslim religious practices,[18] this did not prevent him from incessantly labelling Islam as a 'bestial faith', the implication being that it focused on an empty hedonism and was void of any spiritual content.[19] He even claimed that in private Muslims admitted that their religion was an unworthy one, 'foy de bufles et de chameaulx et de toutes aultres bestes'.[20] The faith thrived only because

11 E. Ashtor, *Levant Trade in the Later Middle Ages* (Princeton, 1983), pp. xix–xx.

12 Ashtor suggests, ibid., p. xix, that Sanudo 'greatly exaggerated' the volume of trade between Egypt and the West because it was in his interests to do so, but the same could be said of Piloti. Ashtor's response to this is to emphasize the greater depth of Piloti's personal experience, which hardly seems convincing.

13 A. Luttrell, 'Emmanuele Piloti and Criticism of the Knights Hospitallers of Rhodes: 1306–1444', *Annales de l'ordre souverain militaire de Malte*, 20 (1962), 11–17.

14 *EP*, p. 229.

15 *EP*, p. 240.

16 *EP*, pp. 48, 51, 85.

17 *EP*, pp. 39–42, 45, 114–15.

18 *EP*, p. 188.

19 E.g. *EP*, pp. 32, 38, 54, 112, 113, 115, 116, 131, 163, 187, 236.

20 *EP*, p. 38.

its leaders enforced it at the point of the sword and forbade any open discussion of its beliefs.[21]

In fact Piloti's two decades of experience of day-to-day life in Islamic lands were arguably less formative than his subscription to a number of tenets that could have been shared by contemporaries who never set eyes on a Muslim. The first tenet was that Christianity and Islam were locked in a combat that could only end with the annihilation of one of them. In the long term there could be no coexistence. This he illustrated with the assertion that each new Mamluk sultan had to make a vow to the caliph, before being invested with the robes of his office, that he would work constantly to destroy Christianity and expand the faith of Muhammad.[22] The second tenet was that the Christians were currently losing this combat. This was evidenced most dramatically by the Ottoman military advance in the Balkans, but it was also happening because of the Mamluks' practice of converting to Islam the boy-slaves whom they imported from the Black Sea region. Piloti placed the emphasis less on the material gain that this brought the sultanate than on the adroit propaganda use that the oligarchy made of this annual influx of converts to the faith.[23]

The third tenet was that a major reason for Christianity's poor showing was the sinfulness of Christians, their poor organization of their military affairs, and the corruption that was on display at the papal court and in the lands that it administered.[24] In this respect the key reason for Piloti to praise the Muslims, notably in terms of their charity, the keenness with which they converted to Islam, the justice to be found at the sultan's court, and the *bonhomie* that characterized relations between the major Islamic powers, was overtly or implicitly to criticize the Christians. In this he followed in the footsteps of many others, for example the author of *Mandeville's Travels*.[25] Far too often such praise and appreciation have been wrenched out of context and interpreted as proof of a *rapprochement* between the two faiths; in reality it was exactly the opposite, a means of establishing the enemy's good points so that they could be emulated by the Christians with a view to fighting them with greater hope of success. This is evident from the constant tension that runs through Piloti's treatment both of the Mamluks as a regime and of Islam as a faith: recognition of their achievements and strengths is constantly subverted by the underlying current of contempt.[26] The last tenet was that while the Christians undoubtedly faced a hard job in winning God back to their side in this eschatological struggle for the salvation of mankind, they were assured of ultimate victory; both the shallowness of Muslim commitment to their faith, and their own prophecies of doom, were proof of this. Of course from Piloti's standpoint this would be to the benefit of all: 'que toutes créatures demeurent en la grâce du Puissant Dieu, et que tous puissons aller par une

21 *EP*, p. 51.

22 *EP*, pp. 33–4.

23 *EP*, pp. 52–3, 222–3.

24 See esp. *EP*, pp. 7, 15, 54, 161–70, 173, though there are numerous instances throughout the *tractatus*.

25 See my 'Perceptions of Crusading in the mid-fourteenth Century: the Evidence of three Texts', *Viator*, 36 (2005), pp. 415–33.

26 *EP*, p. 113.

voye en paradis'.[27] In summary, Piloti's views on Islam, like those of so many other Catholics in the late Middle Ages, fluctuated between the twin poles of anxiety and triumphalism.

Crusading, 'ceste sainte enterprise',[28] was an expression of this struggle between the two faiths, and from a purely eschatological perspective it hardly mattered where it took place. Wherever Islam was defeated, the scales would tip towards the Christian cause and the rival's end would be hastened.[29] On this Piloti was probably in agreement with St Louis's reading of the situation when he set sail for Tunis rather than the East in 1270, or with those many noblemen who, throughout the fourteenth century, had fought Muslims, and 'Saracens' generally, at any front where fighting was guaranteed to occur. So although he was under no illusions about the recent revival of Ottoman power, sensed the ambitions that lay behind it, and foretold the fall of Constantinople (not that this was a hard thing to do in the 1430s),[30] Piloti proposed a crusade to the Nile delta. The reasons as he stated them were heavily traditional: the holy places of Palestine were polluted by 'icelle gent payene ennemie de Dieu', God's honour was at stake there and Christianity's holiest shrines called out for vengeance.[31] Nor was his central strategy new: as in the case of the Fifth Crusade, Louis IX's first expedition, the proposals of many theorists in the past (above all Marino Sanudo), and Peter I of Cyprus (at least in his public statements),[32] Jerusalem was to be regained 'on the banks of the Nile'. This process of recovery would commence with the capture of one of the great delta ports, in this case Alexandria, 'laquelle conqueste seroit commencement, moyen et fin de conquester Yhérusalem'.[33] What was radically new in Piloti's approach was his view of how the military situation would develop after the seizure of Alexandria. For Sanudo the bridgehead would be secured by a *passagium particulare* that would cost over two million florins; this would have to be followed by a general passage, which would last two years and cost a further five million florins.[34] Piloti swept these huge figures away with the bold claim that no second stage would be needed: the Mamluk sultanate could be overthrown, Egypt won for Christianity, and the Holy Land regained, by 'petite quantité et puissance de seigneurs crestiens',[35] and with a total expenditure of no more than 200,000 ducats.[36]

---

27 *EP*, p. 186.

28 *EP*, p. 6.

29 Cf. Dopp's comment, *EP*, p. x, 'la cause était la même en Egypte qu'en Hongrie'.

30 *EP*, p. 223.

31 *EP*, p. 6.

32 Peter I of Cyprus's goals for his crusade of 1365 remain debatable. For summaries of the various arguments see Housley, *Later Crusades*, pp. 39–43; P. Edbury, 'Christians and Muslims in the Eastern Mediterranean', in M. Jones (ed.), *The New Cambridge Medieval History vol. 6, c. 1300–c. 1415* (Cambridge, 2000), pp. 864–84, at pp. 876–81.

33 *EP*, p. 161.

34 See N. Housley, 'Costing the Crusade: Budgeting for Crusading Activity in the Fourteenth Century', in M. Bull and N. Housley (eds), *The Experience of Crusading, Volume 1: Western Approaches* (Cambridge, 2003), pp. 45–59, at pp. 48–9.

35 *EP*, p. 116.

36 *EP*, p. 162.

The reasoning that lay behind this remarkable optimism was based on two factors: first, the inherent fragility of the Mamluk sultanate's hold on Egypt and secondly, the dependence of Egypt, especially Cairo, on imported foodstuffs. Both factors owed much to Piloti's first-hand experience. The vast majority of the native Egyptians, he asserted, felt no loyalty towards the cruel and oppressive Mamluk oligarchy, and the Bedouin Arabs were positively hostile towards it; Piloti mischievously compared the latter with the population of Bologna,[37] who looked for any opportunity to rebel against the Church's rule. Unlike the native Egyptians, who were good-natured ('purs et sans malice'),[38] but had no fighting traditions, the Bedouin were skilled combatants, allies in waiting. It was essential to capture Cairo ('eue celle, on aroit tout'),[39] but this would not be a difficult task: Piloti drew a vivid picture of the city's swarming population and depicted Alexandria as its mouth; once the mouth was stopped the body would quickly expire.[40] The Mamluks had not yet made good the heavy losses they had sustained in their war of 1429 against Kara Yuluk and the Turcoman 'White Sheep' on the Syrian frontier.[41] Repelled by the sultan's policy of periodically purging the ranks of his amirs, some high-ranking Mamluks who had been Christians would make their way to Alexandria to join the Christian cause.[42] Disunited and facing internal revolt, the sultanate would simply crumble away. The occupation of Cairo would open the door to a programme of mass conversion. When discussions were properly convened between groups of ten experts representing the rival faiths, it would soon become apparent which was superior.[43]

The focus of Piloti's *tractatus* was therefore on the pivotal role of Alexandria in commercial terms, and this was not just because it was the key to the recovery of Jerusalem, but also because the people who controlled the port held a stranglehold on the trade of the entire Mediterranean and those regions further afield that fed their products into the sea's carrying trade. Given the hostility displayed towards western merchants in recent years by Sultan Barsbay (1422–38), this meant that the continuing grip on Alexandria by the Mamluks was inherently perilous. So the recovery of the holy places was bound up with the defence of Catholic Europe's economic well-being: 'besoigneroit doncques, premièrement pour la dévotion de l'amme, et aussi pour povoir vendre et achatter, que nous allissons à Yhérusalem'.[44] For this reason a commercial embargo on Alexandria, one of the most cherished notions of previous recovery theorists, was not just impracticable but would actually be self-defeating. This was a major advance in thinking and one that the pope himself had difficulty accepting.[45]

37 *EP*, pp. 57–8.

38 *EP*, p. 187.

39 *EP*, p. 19.

40 *EP*, pp. 116–17.

41 *EP*, pp. 211–12.

42 *EP*, p. 218.

43 *EP*, pp. 185–6. Sanudo had held a similar view, but with more emphasis on coercion. See B.Z. Kedar, *Crusade and Mission: European Approaches toward the Muslims* (Princeton, 1984), p. 188 and note 106.

44 *EP*, p. 112.

45 *EP*, pp. 160–1.

Piloti's planned crusade was therefore a remarkably stripped-down version of Sanudo's: there should be no initial trade embargo and there need be no general passage, just the seizure of Alexandria by a *coup de main* and the reaping of the harvest, at once military, economic and religious, that this would create. Too often in the past the importance of Lower Egypt had been grasped, but implementing a strategy of conquering it had been bungled. The First Crusade had failed to capture the delta and Louis IX had mismanaged his invasion (curiously termed 'le second passage' by Piloti).[46] Marshal Boucicaut in 1403 had made his plan to attack Alexandria clear, giving the sultan time to take defensive measures; even if the Genoese fleet under Boucicaut's command had not been stalled by contrary winds, his attack would have failed.[47] A subsequent raid by two Genoese 'naves grandes' had achieved nothing, simply provoking the sultan.[48] Alexandria was not well-fortified or garrisoned but the element of surprise was crucial, as was a suitably equipped fleet with enough barges to land troops quickly on the beaches to storm the walls. Even if the garrison attempted to defend the city, it would be stormed within the eight days that it would take for a relief army to arrive from Cairo.[49]

Piloti gave much thought to the character of the Christian possession of Alexandria and indeed Lower Egypt generally. The spices stored in the port's rich warehouses were fair game for pillaging, but its Muslim inhabitants should be neither harmed nor dispossessed; in this way they would quickly accept Christian rule.[50] That rule must be exercised without challenge by the commander who had captured the port: on many occasions in the past, including Acre in the thirteenth century, divisions and disunity had proved disastrous for the Christian cause.[51] The surrounding plain could easily be flooded to facilitate its defence against any force that marched to recover it from the interior.[52] By a natural process of immigration Alexandria would in just two to three years be full of Christians, who would relish the opportunity to move their families to a great trading port that was now under the control of their co-religionists, 'et seront seurs comme en leur maison propre, et ne seront pas desoubz payens'.[53] This would be the point at which to reintroduce the papal embargo on trading directly with ports under Muslim control, so as to maximize Christian trade with Alexandria.[54] The Christian ruler of Alexandria would maintain a flotilla of two naves (sailing ships) and two or three war galleys; these would police the coasts of Syria and southern Anatolia.[55] Damascus would suffer the fate of Famagusta when it was bypassed by trade after its period of prosperity.[56] Alexandria alone would become 'la royne de tout marchans et de toutes marchandises de crestiens et de

46 *EP*, pp. 15–22.
47 *EP*, p. 201.
48 *EP*, pp. 199–201.
49 *EP*, p. 179.
50 *EP*, p. 187.
51 *EP*, pp. 124, 212–15.
52 *EP*, p. 227.
53 *EP*, p. 125. And cf. ibid., pp. 184–5.
54 *EP*, p. 130.
55 *EP*, p. 131.
56 *EP*, p. 125.

poyens'.[57] All of this was cogently argued on the basis of Piloti's familiarity with the city, which included a clever dodge to avoid paying duties by knocking a hole in a wall in the customs house, through which he smuggled his goods.[58]

Like Sanudo a century previously, and Boucicaut a couple of decades earlier, Piloti provided full and interesting details on the invasion force that he needed. Thirty barks would each hold four crossbowmen and two artillery pieces (bombardelles). There would be 20 galleys and 30 galioctes. The fighters would be transported on ten naves, each holding 200 crossbowmen and 100 marines. This would constitute an army of fewer than 4,000 men and a fleet of 120 sail.[59] The price tag attached, 200,000 ducats, was pitched low, as one would expect, but it was not wildly out of line with the 132,000 florins that Marshal Boucicaut had estimated in 1407 to be the cost of an expedition comprising a similar size and profile.[60] The contrast, as already noted, is with the figures that had been provided by Sanudo; these had been the stuff of nightmare, though they had not been out of line with other figures discussed at that time.[61]

For a man who placed such emphasis on the perils of disunity, Piloti spent a good deal of his time criticizing others. In particular, he was an overt and harsh critic of his contemporaries in the East. The Nicopolis expedition had been a total disaster.[62] The Knights of St John had failed to honour the commitment made when they conquered Rhodes to maintain ten galleys on a constant war footing against the Muslims; the Hospitallers started by meeting this obligation but over the course of time allowed their provision to fall to just one galley. Had they maintained the full complement they could have prevented both the rise of the Ottoman Turks and the terrible damage inflicted by the Mamluks on Cyprus. As Luttrell pointed out, Piloti's negative view of the Hospitallers constitutes another point of contact with Sanudo.[63] The track record of the Lusignan dynasty of Cyprus was no better. King Janus II's futile attacks on the Mamluks between 1400 and 1415 had provoked Sultan Barsbay's invasion of Cyprus in 1426; the Lusignans had failed in their duty as rulers of Cyprus and they should be dethroned.[64] Marshal Boucicaut and the Genoese had wasted the opportunity they had to attack Alexandria in 1403, when the marshal had commanded a sufficiently large force to take the port, but 'tout s'en alla en fumée'.[65] Only the Catalans came in for praise for grasping the fact that carefully directed violence was the best way to react to the bullying that was now central to Mamluk policy towards western traders.[66]

57 *EP*, p. 227.

58 *EP*, p. 181.

59 *EP*, pp. 176–7.

60 Housley, 'Costing the Crusade', 52–3. Boucicaut costed for a campaign of just 4 months' duration; Piloti did not mention an anticipated length of service. The values of the ducat and florin were almost equivalent by this point.

61 Ibid., 50–1.

62 *EP*, pp. 218–19.

63 *EP*, pp. 216–17; Luttrell, 'Emmanuele Piloti', pp. 13–14 and passim.

64 *EP*, pp. 174–6.

65 *EP*, p. 219.

66 *EP*, p. 236.

Venice was not criticized, and in this there was irony: for it was thanks to Venice's strong trading links with the sultanate, which it managed to sustain even during the stormy period of Barsbay's bullish interventionism, that Piloti was able to gain such expert inside knowledge of Egypt, and to use this in order to construct his crusade project.[67] Why should Venice abandon a policy of restraint that on the whole served it well, in favour of becoming the standard-bearer of the new crusade? The economic argument, as opposed to the religious one, would have been that the sultanate had become hopelessly extortionate and hostile towards Christian merchants, thereby threatening a trade that had become crucial for Christendom. Yet this was hard to square with Piloti's own assessment of the key importance of the Alexandria–Cairo axis. It might well have been asked why, if Piloti could make such an assessment, the sultan and his advisors could not. His synthesis of faith with economic interests hinged on the argument that greed had blinded the Mamluk court to the dictates of common sense and would continue to do so; given Piloti's advocacy of traditional stereotypes of Muslim carnality and hedonism it is not hard to imagine him saying this. The trouble was that the tragic recent history of Cyprus was a grave warning of the dangers of misjudging the sultanate, and it is hardly surprising that the Venetian authorities made a more cautious assessment in the expectation that the sultan's approach could be softened. There are strong grounds for arguing that Venice had planned the conquest of the Nile delta two centuries earlier,[68] but the republic had long since shied away from supporting such aggressive programmes.

In a sense the problem that faced anybody proposing crusading warfare against the Mamluks at this stage was not the difficulty of attacking and seizing Alexandria, but the deceptive ease with which this could be done. Alexandria was an incomparably tempting target for a seaborne attack. Peter I had taken the port without problems in 1365, and Boucicaut might well have managed it again in 1403 or indeed some years later, when he planned his joint Genoese-Cypriot expedition. In 1415 Janus II had imposed a virtual blockade on the port with just two vessels.[69] Peter I had shown that its capture could be hugely lucrative in terms of both booty and renown, 'trèsgrant avoir et … trèsgrant honnour' as Piloti put it,[70] and it is likely that Boucicaut was planning to repeat the king's great coup. It is less easy to see why the Genoese were willing to accommodate the Marshal's wishes; perhaps it was because, as Ashtor has suggested, they shared the Catalans' judgement that the Mamluks needed occasionally to be taught a lesson.[71] As Piloti was well aware, it was carrying the campaign inland from Alexandria that was the problem, and it was in this respect that his insider knowledge played a crucial role. On the face of it, it paid dividends, enabling him to avoid not just the ephemeral character of Peter's capture of the port in 1365, but also the fiscal implausibility of campaigning on the scale that had earlier

---

67 See Ashtor, *Levant Trade*, pp. 200–366 passim.

68 See J.H. Pryor, 'The Venetian Fleet for the Fourth Crusade and the Diversion of the Crusade to Constantinople', in Bull and Housley (eds), *The Experience of Crusading*, pp. 103–23.

69 *EP*, p. 174.

70 *EP*, p. 201.

71 Ashtor, *Levant Trade*, pp. 216–36.

been advocated by Sanudo. But it was also a remarkable gamble because it hinged to such a large extent on one trader's reading of the situation. Wishful thinking played a part in most crusade planning, and some of its elements, such as the existence of Prester John's kingdom,[72] and Muslim predictions of doom, duly cropped up in the *tractatus*. But few, if any, previous recovery theorists had expected their audience to place as much confidence in the author's judgement as Piloti did.

In Piloti's eyes, locating shipping for an assault on Alexandria posed no problem: the strength and prudence of Venice would provide. Crete alone, which enjoyed the advantage of close proximity to Egypt, could arm and crew 25 galleys and ten naves. Men and money were a different matter, and Piloti gave due consideration to both. He seems to have expected that the Cross would be preached, writing that people who could not respond with cash donations for the expedition could take up arms to accompany the army in person (a curious reversal of the time-honoured procedure).[73] Most of the funds needed must derive from the Church, and in this respect Piloti was outspoken to the point of recklessness. He wrote that over the course of the ten years that had passed since he had first spoken with the pope on the subject of the crusade, the 200,000 ducats needed for the project could have been accumulated by the simple expedient of saving 5,000 ducats a month, 'qui fust esté tant seullement une petite vacation de quelque bénéfice';[74] instead of which papal income to the sum of more than two million ducats had been thrown away ('gettés en mer').[75] He called for a 50 per cent tax on all vacant benefices.[76] This was a heavy burden, and it was surely rendered less palatable by the fact that the demand was accompanied by a sustained assault on the corruption of the papal *curia* and its policies. Moreover, the pages dedicated to this assault in the *tractatus* formed just the tip of the iceberg, for Piloti refers to letters and writings on the subject as well as to his meetings with the pope.[77]

Our evaluation of this attack is hindered by our lack of knowledge of Piloti's intended audience; the *tractatus* is formally addressed to Pope Eugenius IV, but one suspects that at times its author is addressing an unknown third party. Indeed, certain passages of criticism, such as that on the incessant and brutal fighting that the pope was funding in central Italy, are expressed in such harsh language that it is hard to believe that Piloti really expected his views to be taken seriously by the pope and cardinals.[78] The Roman church, he wrote, had been lavishly endowed by the Emperor Constantine to defend the faith against the pagans, not to wage war against Christians.[79] On the other hand, neither the duke of Burgundy nor the republic of Venice would have objected to such attacks on papal policy; the fiercest charge, that of endless sums of money being wasted on the hopeless task of restoring control

72 *EP*, pp. 130–1.
73 *EP*, p. 171.
74 This would have raised 600,000 ducats, not 200,000.
75 *EP*, p. 162.
76 *EP*, p. 171.
77 *EP*, p. 169.
78 *EP*, p. 173.
79 *EP*, pp. 162–4.

over the papal state, would have appealed strongly to the Venetians, who had reason to fear the consequences for their own lands. But such arguments are inferential, and this section of Piloti's treatise could equally well have no other basis than his personal opinions. In this respect, yet again, Piloti resembled Sanudo, who in some of his surviving letters argued that Pope John XXII's pursuit of crusades against rebel Christian rulers in Italy must not be allowed to stand in the way of a recovery *passagium.*[80] Even Sanudo, however, had not gone so far as to propose that the defeat of Islam depended on the thoroughgoing reform of the papal *curia*, in particular the establishment of an ambassadorial system by which Christendom's secular rulers would keep permanent agents lodged at Rome to make their views felt.[81]

Piloti represented the Mamluk sultan gloating over the division of Christendom by the Great Schism,[82] but it is apparent from such passages as these that he did not consider the end of the schism in 1417 to herald a fresh dawn for the Catholic Church and faith. His crusade would require deeper measures of reform in the Church. It also called for a secular commander whose authority was unquestioned, who could draw on sound advice and enjoyed the backing of his people.[83] It would be best if this commander recruited his troops from among his own subjects in order to ensure their obedience,[84] and in a passage that recalls the earlier ideas of Philippe de Mézières, Piloti called for soldiers who were well trained, disciplined and purposeful, 'qu'ilz veullent premièrement darrier mectre toute aulteresse, toute continence, tous orguel et toute aultre chose que peusent ester contraire alla somme humilité et obédience envers son chief et capitaine'. This was standard comment in treatises on military affairs, but it is possible that Piloti was making a veiled reference to the strictures that had been levelled at the divided leadership and poor discipline of the participants in the Nicopolis expedition of 1396.[85] Where such a commander and troops of such calibre could be found in the Europe of the 1430s, in the likely event that the Venetians declined the invitation, was another question. Near the start of his *tractatus* Piloti bleakly surveyed the major conflicts of his day that until recently had impeded the promotion of a crusade: Sigismund's preoccupation with Italian affairs, which had caused him to neglect his eastern borders; the emperor's conflict with Venice; and the breach, only just healed, between France and Burgundy.[86]

It is not surprising that Piloti's views on the best way to organize his crusade form the weakest part of the *tractatus*, and are unduly shaped by his *idée fixe*, the reform of a corrupt and wasteful papal *curia*. Any treatise of this type has the strengths and weaknesses of its author. Even the strengths were not absolute. Although he was unusually well informed about the trade passing between the Christian and Islamic lands, Piloti also allowed himself to draw from his experience conclusions about the

80 N. Housley, *The Italian Crusades: The Papal-Angevin Alliance and the Crusades against Christian Lay Powers, 1254–1343* (Oxford, 1982), pp. 89–91.

81 *EP*, pp. 165–9.

82 *EP*, pp. 188–90.

83 *EP*, p. 12.

84 *EP*, p. 124.

85 *EP*, pp. 12–14, with quote at p. 14.

86 *EP*, pp. 7–10.

structural weaknesses of the Mamluk sultanate that were over optimistic. And while he built up a sound knowledge of the recent history of the region in which he had travelled so much, he also had a full suite of prejudices for and against individuals, groups and nations. Piloti's passion to recover Jerusalem, which there is no reason to question,[87] was clearly not shared by sufficient people in the early fifteenth century to make his programme capable of realization, nor did he succeed in persuading contemporaries that there existed a synergy between faith and economic self-interest. This much can be deduced from the fact that the *tractatus* has survived in a single manuscript. Pope Pius II would soon find that it was difficult enough to stir Catholics into action when the Ottoman Turks threatened home and hearth; they would certainly not take up arms against the Mamluk sultanate on the grounds of the constant problems faced by Christian merchants who were trading at Alexandria, Cairo or Damascus. But while military action along the lines called for by Piloti was not forthcoming, and the vicissitudes of Mamluk commercial policy did not generate the catastrophe for the West's trade that he predicted, in one respect he did prove correct. Christianity and Islam were indeed locked in gruelling combat, and it would not end until many more generations had passed.

87 For instance, *EP*, pp. 10–11.

Chapter 13

The Convent and the West: Visitations in the Order of the Hospital of St John in the Fifteenth Century

Jürgen Sarnowsky

After Pope Clement V had abolished the Templars in 1312, only two of the greater military orders remained. The Teutonic Knights still had houses in Greece, southern Italy, France and Spain, but mainly concentrated on the Empire and the Baltic. Only the Hospitallers, who mainly operated in the Eastern Mediterranean, had a very large area from which they received support and recruited their members,[1] stretching from Spain to southern Germany and from England to southern Italy. And while the Teutonic Knights were able – at least for longer periods – to maintain their power in Prussia with the help of their regional resources, the Hospitallers depended heavily on men and money from the West.[2] It was this situation that made it necessary to organize an effective control of the houses in the West by the leading brethren in the convent. The responsions had to be paid, and the transport of men and materials had to be arranged, and both were only possible if the institutions functioned, the morale of the brothers was of a sufficient level,[3] and the single houses were efficiently administered so that they were able to produce a surplus. One means of achieving these goals was to influence the election of officials, especially priors and preceptors, in which the chapters general, master, and convent on Rhodes played an important role.[4] Another means was that of visitations, as they were conducted in many other ecclesiastical institutions.[5] The visitations had to inquire into the status of the houses in the West. This paper aims to offer some preliminary considerations on the role of visitations in the Order of the Hospital of St John in the fifteenth century.

---

1 For the differentiation between area of operation and area of recruitment cf. H. Boockmann, 'Herkunft und Einsatzgebiet. Beobachtungen am Beispiel des Deutschen Ordens', in Z.H. Nowak (ed.), *Ritterorden und Region – politische und soziale Verbindungen im Mittelalter* (Ordines militares, VIII) (Toruń, 1995), pp. 7–19.

2 For the fifteenth century see J. Sarnowsky, *Macht und Herrschaft im Johanniterorden des 15. Jahrhunderts. Verfassung und Verwaltung der Johanniter auf Rhodos (1421–1522)* (Münster, 2001), at pp. 525–52.

3 Though the aspect of personal conduct lost its importance, cf. G. O'Malley, *The Knights Hospitaller of the English* Langue*, 1460–1565* (Oxford, 2005), p. 52.

4 Cf. Sarnowsky, *Macht*, pp. 90–9, 108–12.

5 Cf. R. Puza, 'Visitation', *Lexikon des Mittelalters*, vol. 8 (Munich, 1999), cols 1740.

Taking into account the situation of the Order on Rhodes, it is no surprise that visitations were often the subject of statutes or ordinations. These distinguish between different forms of visitations: regular and general. Regulations from the second chapter general under fr. Philibert de Naillac required regular visitations in the priories, based on long tradition.[6] Every three years, the prior himself or two experienced preceptors had to visit the houses and possessions of the Order, to take action in the case of bad administration or low standards, to collect the information in writing, and to send it to the convent.[7] This was renewed in 1428 under fr. Antoni de Fluvià, with the addition that the results of the measures taken had to be reviewed within a certain period of time. Also, it was decreed that the visitation registers should include information on the administration of the preceptories, both economic and spiritual; on the incomes from the preceptories and its *membra*; on financial burdens and their cause, such as judicial quarrels of the preceptors; and on the orders of the visitors.[8] These regulations were carried over to the revised statutes of 1489–93, though with some modifications: now the interval between the visitations became four years, but the priors could also initiate visitations at any time when they were concerned about the state of the Order's houses.[9] The *stabilimenta* also renewed earlier regulations of uncertain origin which threatened with punishment those preceptors who did not follow the visitors' orders and also those priors who did not carry out the required visitations.[10]

Quite similar were the regulations concerning the regular visitations of the preceptories directly subject to the priors, and of the churches in the priories, their treasures, and possessions.[11] The brothers visiting the houses of the priors had to be nominated at the provincial chapters,[12] while the chaplains who visited the churches were delegated by the priors. Since they acted as a kind of lieutenants for the conventual prior during his stay on Rhodes, the visitors had the same powers as the conventual prior.[13] Another kind of regular visitation was related to the *melioramentum*, the 'transfer' of a brother to a preceptory with greater incomes. To be promoted, the preceptor had to meet several requirements;[14] the most important one was that he had governed well his former preceptory. This had to be confirmed

6 For the visitations by the priors before 1310 cf. J. Riley-Smith, *The Knights of St John in Jerusalem and Cyprus, c. 1050–1310* (London, 1967), pp. 348–9, 363.

7 Paris, Bibliothéque National, Ms. (henceforth: BN) franç. 17255, fol. 87r; Malta Cod. 501, fol. 168r–169r.

8 BN franç. 17255, fol. 97r–v; Malta Cod. 501, fol. 200r–201r.

9 Malta Cod. 244, fol. 85r, 86v–87r; cf. Sarnowsky, *Macht*, pp. 105–6.

10 Malta Cod. 244, fol. 86v.

11 BN franç. 17255, fol. 68v, 91v; and Malta Cod. 244, fol. 85v, 110v.

12 Statute from the time of fr. Naillac, BN franç. 17255, fol. 87v; cf. the revised statutes of 1489/93, Malta Cod. 244, fol. 85r–v.

13 Malta Cod. 244, fol. 87v–88r (and 84v–85r); the original statute in BN franc. 17255, fol. 123r.

14 Cf. Sarnowsky, *Macht*, pp. 213–16.

by the prior and the provincial chapter, based on a special, thorough visitation of the preceptory.[15]

The general visitations initiated by central institutions were also based on a long tradition,[16] but since the beginning of the fifteenth century they clearly became more important instruments for controlling the Order's houses, probably due to the Order's financial difficulties. For example, when in 1454 the first chapter general under fr. Jacques de Milly discussed how to collect the sum of 50,000 florins needed for the maintenance of the convent, it was decided to postpone the division of the financial duties for five years and to conduct a general visitation of all priories.[17] This decision was accompanied by a statute on general visitations and the financial administration of the Order. Thus, the visitors had to inquire into the value of the priories by taking oaths from all religious and secular persons concerned about the sums for which their houses and *membra* could be rented out, taking into account the customary duties. This information was to be collected with the help of three to five honourable persons, both members of the Order and men from outside. Their testimonies were to be sent to Rhodes for calculation of the value of the houses and the required payments.[18]

The statutes of 1446/7, which were initiated by Pope Eugenius IV but were never accepted in the Order, even went one step further. They created a special institution for the visitations and their documentation.[19] It is perhaps no accident that its head was to be the draper, one of the conventual bailiffs of the lesser tongues. The new institution was a group of seven 'conservators' from all tongues who would meet three times a week in their own house to debate the state of the Order and – if necessary – to apply to master and convent to take action. Their scribe would collect the reports coming in from the visitations of the Western houses, and there was to be an archive for older reports. Probably this reform would have weakened the influence both of the master and convent and of the priors over the financial administration, which would in fact have been controlled by the seven conservators, which might explain why the system was never implemented; another consequence would have been the common evaluation of regular and general visitations.

As for the earlier inquests, as in 1373,[20] the results of visitations were probably regularly compiled into lists and books, though only relatively few manuscripts

15 In general BN franc. 17255, fol. 129r, and Malta Cod. 244, fol. 112v; for the visitation of the priory see ibid., 115v.

16 For visitations ordered by the masters and for the grand preceptors in the West see Riley-Smith, pp. 365, 370; H. Nicholson, *The Knights Hospitaller* (Woodbridge, 2001), pp. 77–8; A. Luttrell, 'The Hospitaller Province of *Alamannia* to 1428' (1995), repr. in A. Luttrell, *The Hospitaller State on Rhodes and its Western Provinces, 1306–1462* (Aldershot, 1999), no. XII, p. 22.

17 Sarnowsky, *Macht*, pp. 535–6.

18 BN franc. 17255, fol. 132r–134r; Malta cod. 282, fol. 19r–v.

19 Malta Cod. 1698, fol. 43r–45v; cf. Sarnowsky, *Macht*, p. 34.

20 For 1373 see A. Luttrell, Papauté et Hôpital: l'Enquête de 1373, in J. Glénisson (ed.), *L'Enquête Pontificale de 1373 sur l'Ordre des Hospitaliers de Saint-Jean de Jérusalem*, vol. 1: *L'enquête dans le Prieuré de France*, ed. A.-M. Legras (Paris, 1987), pp. 3–42; some Italian materials in BN Lat. 5155, fol. 46r–52r, see A. Luttrell, 'Two Templar–Hospitaller

survive, both in the priories and in the central archives. For example, the acts of the visitation of 1494/5 for Germany are now in the central archives at Malta, those for St Gilles at Marseilles.[21] It seems that materials and manuscripts were sent to Rhodes, but that most of them were lost during the siege of 1522. Thus, there is a statute of 1428 describing the Order's central archives that expressly mentions *les livres des visitacions qui seront transmis des priorez par les prieurs ou visiteurs*,[22] and in 1471 excerpts were made from a register of visitations of the priory of Portugal compiled during the mission of fr. Jean Derlande, Preceptor of Avignon, in February 1460. Since these excerpts were expressly made *ex libris visitacionum*,[23] there must have been a collection of visitation registers at that point. They may have been kept in the treasury, since there is no mention of books of visitations in a (albeit very general) inventory of the chancery from 1447.[24]

It is not clear whether the regular visitations in the priories were in fact conducted every three or four years – since there are no sources from which to judge – but it is evident that in the period after 1421 there were several general visitations. The first visitations under fr. Antoni de Fluvià were ordered in 1422 or 1423 and concerned at least England and Germany.[25] Then there were visitations in Italy, France, Germany, Bohemia, Hungary, Scandinavia and other regions after the chapter general of 1428,[26] and further visitations followed in the priories of Germany, Bohemia, Hungary, Ireland and Barletta in 1433 and 1435.[27] In the time of fr. Jean de Lastic there were visitations in France, Germany, Bohemia, Hungary, Scotland, Ireland and Italy, both in 1440 and between 1446 and 1450.[28] After the chapter general of

Preceptories North of Tuscania' (1971), repr. in A. Luttrell, *The Hospitallers in Cyprus, Rhodes, Greece and the West, 1291–1440* (London, 1978), no. X, pp. 91, 122. For the inquest in the priory of Rome in 1333, in Biblioteca Apostolica Vaticana, cod. Vat. Lat. 10372, see D. Moullot, *Le* 'Liber Prioratus Urbis' *de l'Ordre de Saint-Jean-de-Jérusalem* (Melitensia, 12) (Taranto, 2004).

21 Malta cod. 45 (visitation of 1495 in the priories of Upper and Lower Germany), cf. also Haupt- und Staatsarchiv München (hereafter: HStAM), Johanniter Lit. Nr. 536; Marseille, Archives départementales Bouche-du-Rhone, 56 H 125 (visitation of 1495 in S. Gilles, incomplete), cf. *Répertoire de la série 56 H Grand Prieuré de S. Gilles (Archives départementales Bouche-du-Rhone)*, ed. E. Baratier, M. Villard (Marseille, 1966), p. 5.

22 BN franç. 17255, fol. 99v, seemingly not in the statutes of 1489/93.

23 Malta Cod. 380, fol. 92v–93r, dated 11 December 1471.

24 Edited in Sarnowsky, *Macht*, pp. 634–5. This would explain the loss of the registers, because nearly nothing from the treasury survived the second siege of Rhodes.

25 Malta Cod. 346, fol. 117r–118r, 123r–v.

26 See the bulls and letters in Malta Cod. 26, nos. 3 and 8, dated 28 May 1428 and 26 September 1430; Cod. 348, fol. 202(196)r–202(197)r, 205(199)r (incomplete), 20 May 1428 [where old and new foliation are quoted, the new foliation is in parentheses]; I. Bosio, *Dell'Istoria della Sacra Religione et Illustrissima Militia di San Giovanni Gierosolimitano*, vol. 2 (Rome, 1629, 2nd edn), p. 201.

27 Malta Cod. 16, no. 69; 350, fol. 250(243)r–251(244)r, 276(269)r–v; 351, fol. 163(159)r.

28 See Malta Cod. 354, fol. 147r, dated 20 December 1440; Cod. 358, fol. 45r–46v, 98r–99v, 109(108)r–110(109)r, dated 18, 20, 24 April 1446; Cod. 361, fol. 201r–v, 337r–v, of 23 January 1448 and 5 September 1449, cf. J.M. van Winter, *Sources Concerning the*

1459, the Catalan Prior fr. Giliberto de Loschis received orders to visit the priories of France, Aquitaine, Champagne, Auvergne, St Gilles, Toulouse and Messina,[29] and Portugal was visited by the French fr. Jean Derlande.[30] Similar instructions for the Italian and northern priories followed[31] and were renewed after the chapter general of 1462,[32] also concerning England and the Iberian Peninsula, relating to severe financial problems.[33] During the rule of fr. Pierre d'Aubusson, there were at least visitations in England, Germany (both around 1480 and in 1494/5), Bohemia, Hungary and Scandinavia,[34] and also in the priories of St Gilles, Rome and the castellany of Amposta (in 1494/5).[35] Under fr. Émery d'Amboise there were some regional visitations: one in Ireland after the chapter general of 1504[36] and probably another one in the eastern Netherlands in September 1510;[37] and there was a visitor for France in 1518 in the time of fr. Fabrizio del Carretto,[38] but it seems that general visitations were less frequent than in the middle of the fifteenth century.

Sometimes the initiative for general visitations would come from the pope, as in the fourteenth century.[39] Thus, in November 1444 Eugenius IV ordered a visitation in the priory of Capua, which had been severely damaged by the wars in

---

Hospitallers of St John in the Netherlands, 14th to 18th Centuries (Leiden, 1998), p. 45; and *The Knights of St John of Jerusalem in Scotland*, ed. I.B. Cowan, P.H.R. Mackay, A. Macquarrie (Edinburgh, 1983), p. 165; and Cod. 362, fol. 125(126)v–126(127)r, 131(132)v–132(133)r, 140(141)v–142(143)v, 143(144)r–145(146)v, and 178(179)v, dated 12 September, 3 June and 14 August 1450. For a visitation in Hungary and Bohemia cf. Cod. 366, fol. 123(124)r–v.

29 Malta Cod. 369, fol. 48(58)v–49(59)r.

30 See note 23.

31 Cf. ibid., fol. 237(271)v–238(272)v, 239(273)r.

32 Archivio Segreto Vaticano (henceforth: ASV), Reg. Vat. 508, fol. 390r–392v, 396v–397r.

33 For a visitation of the *Francia* before November 1462 see Malta Cod. 372, fol. 5r–v; for the Iberian priories and England by the prior of Portugal see Cod. 73, fol. 116(130)r, 6 March 1464; for Navarra (1470) cf. Cod. 74, fol. 29(41)v.

34 For a visitation in England and Germany in 1477 cf. Malta Cod. 385, fol. 77v–78v; 1480/1 fr. Joan de Cardona was visitor for Germany, see note 56; for 1494/95 see W. G. Rödel, *Das Großpriorat des Johanniterordens im Übergang vom Mittelalter zur Reformation* (Cologne, 1966, 2nd edn 1972), pp. 47–8; van Winter, pp. 392–6; on England in 1493/4 see Cod. 391, fol. 200(199)r–201(200)r; for Scandinavia (Eskilstuna) see ibid., fol. 231(230)r–233(232)r.

35 For the register from St Gilles see note 21; for Amposta and Rome see the instructions Malta Cod. 391, fol. 188(187)v–189(188)r, and Cod. 392, fol. 110v–111r, dated 5 August 1493 and 17 September 1495.

36 O'Malley, p. 248.

37 Malta, Cod. 400, fol. 167r–v.

38 Fr. Philippe Villiers de l'Isle-Adam, cf. Malta Cod. 406, fol. 210r–212r.

39 In 1338 by Benedict XII, cf. A. Luttrell, 'The Spiritual Life of the Hospitallers of Rhodes' (1993), repr. in A. Luttrell, *The Hospitaller State*, no. IX, pp. 89–90; similar in 1373, note 20.

southern Italy.[40] But normally, the initiative would lie with the chapters general or – in between the chapters – the master and convent. Thus the visitations after 1428, 1446, 1459 and 1462 already mentioned were decided at the chapters general. In consequence, the bulls for the visitations were mostly made out during the chapters, as for example those of May 1428 and of August 1493 for the visitations of 1428 to 1430 and 1494/5.[41] Sometimes the decision to visit the houses of a certain region was at least related to problems discussed at the chapters general. For example, when the extent of the responsions from Italy and northern Germany had been disputed at the chapter general of 1449, in 1450 a visitation was initiated for the purpose of gathering information, also from the other priories.[42]

The visitors received their powers regularly for certain priories or regions, as for example in April 1446 when the chancellor fr. Melchiore Bandini was sent out to visit the priories of France, Champagne and Aquitaine that had suffered most from the Anglo-French wars;[43] in January 1448 when fr. Michele de Castellacio was appointed visitor for Germany, Bohemia and Hungary;[44] or in the autumn of 1510 when fr. Guillaume de Quinon, preceptor of Nijmegen and Arnhem, was perhaps not only responsible for the visitation of his own preceptories, but also for some neighbouring houses and for Hainault.[45] This last case was obviously an exception – a 'mixture' of a regular and a general visitation conducted by a brother at least partly responsible for the houses in question – though in October 1459 fr. John Langstrother was empowered to visit his own priory, England.[46] Sometimes the visitors came from neighbouring priories, for example when there was a special relationship, as between the priories of England and Ireland. Thus, fr. John Langstrother was sent to Ireland in September 1450 and fr. John Rawson in May 1511;[47] and there was at least one visitation of Navarra by a brother from Catalonia or Aragón in September 1470.[48]

40 ASV Reg. Vat. 376, fol. 217r–v, 13 November 1444; visitor was the capitular bailiff of St Eufemia, fr. Sergio de Seripandis.

41 Malta Cod. 26, no. 3; and Cod. 348, fol. 202(196)r–203(197)r, bulls for the visitors, 20 and 28 May 1428; for the bull of 3 August 1493 concerning Germany, Bohemia, Hungary and Scandinavia cf. Rödel, pp. 47–8; van Winter, pp. 392–6.

42 Sarnowsky, *Macht*, pp. 65, 530–1; based on BN franc. 17255, fol. 125r–v; Malta Cod. 361, fol. 16r–17r, 21 September 1449; Cod. 362, fol. 131(132)v–132(133)r etc., 3 June 1450; cf. Bosio, p. 235. For 1454 see note 18.

43 Cf. Malta Cod. 358, fol. 45r–46v, 24 April 1446.

44 See the letter of 28 January 1448 asking for assistance by the princes, Malta Cod. 360, fol. 93(58)r.

45 Malta Cod. 400, fol. 167r–v and 168v, 24 September and 10 October 1510; concerning the standards of masses.

46 Malta Cod. 369, fol. 237(271)v–238(272)v, dated 27 October 1459; cf. O'Malley, pp. 126, 128.

47 Malta Cod. 462, fol. 125(126)v–126(127)r, 12 September 1450; Cod. 81, fol. 152(165)v–153(166)r, 5 May 1511, cf. Cod. 82, fol. 115(128)r; already in 1298, a brother of the English hospital was sent to Ireland, Riley-Smith, p. 365; fr. Hugh Middleton was even appointed visitor and prior at the same time, O'Malley, p. 240.

48 At that point, fr. Joan de Mur, perhaps from Catalonia or Aragón, received money as visitor for the priory of Navarra, Malta Cod. 74, fol. 29(41)v.

As a norm expressed by the chapter general of 1449, the visitors had to come from a foreign tongue.[49] Thus, some commissions were comprised solely of foreign visitors, as for the Order's houses in Scotland[50] and also in the case of fr. Joan de Cardona, bailiff of Mallorca, who had his own – perhaps Italian – scribes with him during his stay in Germany in the summer of 1464 and 1480, respectively.[51] But in many cases one visitor from the 'outside' was accompanied by a brother from the area under visitation.[52] Thus, in September 1420 fr. Henry de Bye, preceptor of Paris and fr. Johann von Monreall, preceptor of Cologne, were appointed visitors for Germany by Master fr. Philibert de Naillac and by the convent,[53] and in October 1459 fr. Louis de Felliens from the Auvergne was made visitor for Lombardy, Venice, Rome, Barletta, Capua, Pisa and the capitular bailiwicks of Napoli, Venosa, St Eufemia and St Stefano di Monopoli, together with fr. Ludovico di Torre from the priory of Venice.[54] Similarly, for the visitation in Germany, Scandinavia, Bohemia and Hungary in 1494/5, fr. Peter Stoltz von Bickelheim, grand bailiff and preceptor of Mainz, Frankfurt and Burg had to visit together with fr. Antonio de Actis, preceptor of Pucini, in the priory of Capua.[55] Sometimes 'single' visitors were also assisted by brethren from the regions who were not nominated in the original bull for the visitation. Thus, in the 1440s, fr. Sinibaldo de Sabelleschis, *doctor utriusque iuris*, was accompanied on his visitation throughout Germany, Bohemia and Hungary by the German fr. Matthias von Remagen, who acted as scribe and translator.[56] In all these cases, the idea was clearly to combine knowledge of the region with the necessary distance from the brethren and houses subject to the visitation.

As in the case of fr. Melchiore Bandini, who was sent out to the priories of the French tongue in April 1446,[57] the powers of the (general) visitors mostly concerned the visitation of the state of the Order's houses and properties, of their extent, the resulting incomes, and of the morale of the brethren. If there were any shortcomings or problems, the visitors were empowered to act and to amend any deficiencies.

49 Following Bosio, p. 235, it was decided that *i cavalieri d una lingua visitar doveresso i beni dell'altra.*

50 See the report of 11 August 1418, Malta Cod. 342, fol. 130r–v, Cowan et al., p. 162.

51 *Robertus Pederini secretarius dicti domini locumtenentis de eius mandato* (7 July 1464, HStAM, Ritterorden, Urkunde [hereafter: RO U] 487); *Johannes Latius de mandato prefati reverendi domini et commissarii* (29 June 1480, ibid., RO U 248). On Cardona cf. P. Bonneaud, *Le Prieuré de Catalogne, le Couvent de Rhodes et la Couronne d Aragon, 1415–1447* (Millau, 2004), p. 353.

52 For these pairs of visitors cf. O'Malley, p. 121.

53 Note in Malta Cod. 345, fol. 140r, see van Winter, pp. 37–8 ; fr. Henry de Bye was also created visitor and reformer for Scotland about the same time, Cod. 345, fol. 132v–134v, Cowan et al., p. 163.

54 Malta Cod. 369, fol. 239(273), 27 October 1459; see also the nomination of fr. Rolando de Rubeis from Venice, and fr. Konrad Scheppel, preceptor of Rottweil, for Germany, Bohemia, Scandinavia and the bailiwick of Brandenburg, ibid.

55 See van Winter, p. 393; Rödel, p. 47.

56 See the note concerning his *ancianitas*, 13 November 1447, Malta Cod. 359, fol. 135(132)r.

57 See note 43.

This would have been similar for regular visitations of any kind, though there were some special regulations, for example concerning the visitation necessary to get a *melioramentum* when – at least after 1520 – the visitors had to inquire also into the state of woods belonging to the preceptory which may have been previously cut down without the knowledge of prior and provincial chapter and not been recultivated.[58] Additionally, visitors were empowered to appoint officials and to recruit new members of the Order in the region concerned, as in March 1448, when fr. Michele de Castellacio was allowed to appoint one to three, or even more, priors in Lower Germany (and Frisia) – clearly this did not mean the German priors – and to take in up to five noblemen if they fulfilled the necessary requirements.[59]

Sometimes also the methods of collecting the information were prescribed. As mentioned above, according to the statutes for the visitations of 1454 and 1462 the measure for the value of the Order's houses and *membra* was the sum for which these could be rented out, taking into account the accustomed responsions and duties, and the visitors had to take oaths from the brothers and others involved and to gather the information with the help of three to five trustworthy men.[60] This was similar in the visitation of 1494/5, when the visitors also took oaths from the brothers, their vassals, tenants and other men, but this time the value had to be calculated from the average incomes in bad, good and average years.[61]

Some of the visitors were lieutenants of the master and convent – like the earlier grand preceptors in the West[62] – and some also had additional tasks and powers such as to collect the monies due to the treasury.[63] Thus, in 1445 (and 1446) fr. Guillaume de Lastic, seneschal to Master fr. Jean de Lastic, acted as *nostri magistralis hospicii seneschallus necnon locumtenens noster ac visitor et reformator etc. ubique generalis*, as lieutenant of the master and general visitor,[64] while in March 1518 fr. Philippe Villiers de l'Isle-Adam was appointed proctor of the Master fr. Carretto and visitor for all French priories who had the right to demand the payment of responsions due to the treasury.[65] Though these missions were also intended to control the Western priories and preceptories, they constituted a different type of general visitation because they did not produce a general survey. Rather, the visitors were empowered to visit houses only where they thought it might be necessary. A similar procedure was chosen in consequence of the Mamluk attack on Rhodes and

58 Decision of the last chapter general on Rhodes, see London, Museum and Library of the Order of St John, in H3, fol. 181v–182v.

59 Malta Cod. 361, fol. 205v, ed. van Winter, pp. 46–7.

60 For 1454 see above, note 18; for the bull from the chapter general of 1462 see the papal conformation in ASV Reg. Vat. 508, fol. 391r–v.

61 The text in van Winter, p. 394–5; cf. O'Malley, p. 77.

62 Cf. Riley-Smith, p. 370.

63 A decision in council dated 30 July 1422 mentions *visitores transmissi ad partes occidentales pro recuperatione annate, responsionum, et omnium jurium communi thesauro ... spectancium ...*, Malta Cod. 346, fol. IXv.

64 Malta Cod. 357, fol. 116(107)v, 28 August 1445, cf. also Cod. 358, fol. 50r–v, 23 April 1446, concerning the selling of rents in the West.

65 See Malta Cod. 406, fol. 210r–212r, 24 March 1518; cf. also the case of fr. Pierre Lamand, see note 77.

the first chapter general under fr. Jean de Lastic in 1440, when the receivers of the additional responsions had the right to conduct visitations to control the real incomes of the houses in the West if they did not trust the information given by the preceptors. But in this case, the visitation was solely a regional affair because the visitors had to report only to the regional assemblies.[66]

Since all priories and preceptories had their regional and local ties,[67] it was necessary to have the support of the regional rulers, kings, princes, prelates and military leaders. Thus, in January 1448, Master fr. Jean de Lastic directly turned to the authorities with an appeal to help the visitor fr. Michele de Castellacio, to allow him and his company free access and to stay wherever and how long it was necessary, and also to free him from all customs and duties.[68] Regularly, this was also followed by an appeal to the pope to confirm the powers of the visitor,[69] as in March 1463, when fr. Joan de Cardona had been elected general visitor for Germany, Bohemia, Hungary, Scandinavia and Poland. In consequence, Pius II issued a mandate directed to all ecclesiastical and secular authorities to support him, his lieutenants, company and servants in their mission.[70] When fr. Cardona returned to Germany in 1480/1, he acted not only as visitor and lieutenant of the master, but even as *commissarius* of the pope. In these capacities, he ordered the promulgation of indulgences for the dioceses of Würzburg and Bamberg by a sub-delegate, fr. Jörg von Melchingen, the preceptor of Rothenburg.[71]

Sometimes, there were also diplomatic contacts with rulers. Thus, for the visitation of the Lower German priory after the chapter general of 1449, the visitors suggested that they should begin their stay in Germany with Duke Johann I of Kleve who – on the way back from his pilgrimage to Jerusalem – had recently visited Rhodes (about 1450) and was well trusted by Master fr. Jean de Lastic. They hoped that the duke's authority would further the obedience of the brothers and thus secure the success of the visitation.[72] In England, the relationship to the kings was essential. Thus, the involvement of Prior fr. Robert Bottil for Edward IV may have helped to achieve royal support for the mission of fr. John Langstrother in 1461/2,[73] and the conventual visitor fr. Léonard de Prat was even enthusiastically greeted by Richard III in December 1484.[74] But it is clear that the royal attitude changed according to

---

66 See BN franc. 17255, fol. 116r–v.

67 Cf. J. Sarnowsky, 'Regional Problems in the History of Mendicant and Military Orders', in J. Sarnowsky (ed.), *Mendicants, Military Orders, and Regionalism in Medieval Europe* (Aldershot, 1999), pp. 1–15, at p. 5.

68 See Malta Cod. 360, fol. 93(58)r, 28 January 1448.

69 In ASV Reg. Suppl. 428, fol. 50r–v, 2 July 1448 = Reg. Vat. 407, fol. 169r–175v.

70 ASV Reg. Vat. 508, fol. 390r–392v, 396v–397r (bulls concerning the chapter), and 397r–v (papal mandate for fr. Cardona).

71 See HStAM RO U 249, 20 June 1480; cf. the bull for fr. Gabriel Hoschelmann, ASV Reg. Vat. 616, fol. 4v–5r.

72 Bosio, p. 235; for the Duke s journey see *Europäische Reiseberichte des späten Mittelalters. Eine analytische Biographie*, ed. W. Paravicini, part 1: *Deutsche Reiseberichte*, by C. Hahn (Kieler Werkstücke, D 5) (Frankfurt a. M., 2001, 2nd edn), pp. 110–13.

73 O'Malley, pp. 126, 128; fr. Langstrother received his bull in 1459, see note 46.

74 O'Malley, pp. 142–3.

the actual situation. Finally, under the anticlerical legislation of the 1530s visitations were only possible by commission from the king.[75]

It may be no accident that many of the visitors – at least from the outside – were well-known brethren with a secure standing in the Order, like the Admiral fr. Roberto de Diana or the *decretorum doctor* fr. Giovanni de Nursia who were sent out to Germany, Bohemia and Hungary in 1433 and 1440, respectively.[76] Others combined different missions and offices, such as the former proctor general at the Roman curia and newly elected Treasurer fr. Pierre Lamand who, in June 1435, was appointed both the Order's proctor at the Council of Basle and visitor for Germany.[77] Both needed their authority to put through more severe measures. Because most of them had their own incomes, it was also assumed that they would travel at their own expense, at least according to a decision of master and council in July 1430,[78] though reality may have been different. Thus, in July 1440 fr. Ramon Jou received 200 ducats for the visitation of the English priory,[79] in November 1447 fr. Sinibaldo de Sabelleschis had to be paid 150 Venetian ducats from the responsions of the Roman priory while travelling to Germany, Bohemia and Hungary,[80] and in September 1470 fr. Joan de Mur received 200 florins for his mission to the priory of Navarra.[81]

Visitations were not always conducted successfully. Thus, after the decisions of the chapter general on Rhodes in 1459, at first nothing happened, even though an assembly at Avignon was planned for August 1461 to collect the information gathered by the visitors. According to a note in a Parisian manuscript of the statutes, this assembly did not take place because the visitation was, in effect, carried out only after the election of Master fr. Pere Ramon Zacosta.[82] If the results of a visitation had come in, the registers had to be sent to Rhodes, which is explicitly mentioned, for example, in the statute of 1454.[83] Probably, the visitors were responsible for the compilation or at least for a report concerning the visitation and the measures taken, as in the case of fr. Giovanni de Nursia – sent out again after the chapter general of 1449 – who died after he had returned to Rhodes and reported what he had done in Scotland.[84] But it seems that sometimes also the priors themselves were involved. Thus, in February 1510, the Irish prior, fr. Robert Evers, was ordered to send to the convent the results of a visitation in his priory that had been initiated in 1504.[85]

The information gained by visitations was, of course, a useful basis for decisions on the Order's policies; and it was also discussed on chapters general. Thus,

75 O'Malley, p. 211.

76 Malta Cod. 350, fol. 276(269)r–v, 8 May 1433; Cod. 354, fol. 147r, 20 December 1440; this holds true also for fr. Michele de Castellacio who later became conventual prior.

77 See the bull of 26 June 1435, Malta Cod. 16, no. 69.

78 Malta Cod. 346, fol. IXv, *pro bono et utilitate communis thesauri*.

79 Malta Cod. 354, fol. 227(228)r.

80 See the letter to the prior fr. Giovanbattista Orsini, 22 November 1447, Malta Cod. 359, fol. 151(147)v.

81 Cf. Malta Cod. 74, fol. 29(41)v, 19 September 1470.

82 BN franç. 17255, fol. 140r–141r; the statute has the marginal note *nichil valet*.

83 See note 18.

84 Malta Cod. 364, fol. 117r, 26 January 1454, cf. Cowan et al., p. 167.

85 O'Malley, p. 248.

in November 1462, the results from the visitation in the priory of *Francia* led to protests, so that another, additional, visitation was ordered,[86] and in December 1466, the 16 capitulars of the second Roman chapter general reviewed the results of the visitations in England and France, and in consequence the responsions from England and the six French priories were reduced.[87]

To sum up: there were two basic types and several 'sub-types' of visitations in the Western houses (the Order's lordship in the Aegean has not been included here):[88]

1) Regular visitations in the priories, especially
   a) regular visitations of the preceptories by the priors every three or four years,
   b) regular visitations of the houses directly administered by the prior,
   c) regular visitations of the churches and their possessions, and
   d) visitations in the case of the promotion (*amelioramentum*) of brothers;
2) General (but irregular) visitations by the authority of chapter general, master and convent (and / or pope) in all or at least certain priories or regions, especially
   a) general visitations of all preceptories with the intention to produce a survey for the purposes of the central administration on Rhodes, and
   b) general visitations by lieutenants and proctors of master (and convent) with the power to interfere wherever necessary.

The results of most of the regular visitations are lost or perhaps even were not collected, either in the priories or in the convent,[89] though it was probably intended to be done by the central institutions and also by the authors of the statutes of 1446. Thus it can only be assumed that they were conducted according to the statutes and also served as a basis in general visitations. These are easier to describe because often the bulls and other related documents – though only few registers – have survived. In collecting the evidence it seems that the greatest number of general visitations was conducted between the 1440s and 1460s.

For general visitations, brothers with a certain 'standing' within the Order were chosen and received bulls from the central institutions and letters directed to the popes and to the regional authorities to secure the success of the mission. They were empowered to gather information by taking oaths from brothers and seculars and to amend deficiencies; sometimes they also collected monies or appointed officials, acting as lieutenants of masters and convent, as the earlier grand preceptors in the West. In most cases, at least one of the visitors came from a foreign tongue, receiving support from the regional brethren, who sometimes only acted as scribes and secretaries.

There were strong links between visitations and chapters general. It seems that all chapters general of the mid fifteenth century decided to conduct these surveys, though with different approaches and techniques (including the failure to collect the materials in Avignon according to the decision of 1459). In many cases, there were bulls of master and convent made out during the chapter, others followed within a short period of time; and the results were often reviewed in the next chapter. Though

86 Malta Cod. 372, fol. 5r–v, 4 November 1462.

87 Malta Cod. 283, fol. 11v.

88 For the Aegean see Sarnowsky, *Macht*, pp. 407, 425, 430.

89 This has still to be confirmed by a survey of the archives of the priories.

not much is known about the visitation registers in the central archives and their use, visitations will have been an important instrument of control for the central institutions, chapters general, master and convent, especially during the financial difficulties of the mid fifteenth century.

Chapter 14

British and Irish Visitors to and Residents in Rhodes, 1409–1522

Gregory O'Malley

In the fifteenth century Rhodes and the Dodecanese were among the more substantial and prosperous of the remaining Latin states in the Eastern Mediterranean, the government of the Order of St John over the islands providing employment, security, food, welfare and an effective administrative and judicial system under which commercial and social relations were usually conducted without unmanageable tension between Latin and Greek, or rich and poor.[1] The Order ruled over a population that was largely Greek with a capital, in Rhodes town, that was a cosmopolitan entrepôt of middling size in which Greeks rubbed shoulders with Latins of predominantly Italian, Provençal or Catalan origin, Jews, Cypriots, Syrians, and sometimes Egyptians and Turks.[2] This situation was further complicated by the presence of several hundred professed Hospitallers, of their servants, and of stipendiary and other soldiers from a variety of backgrounds.[3] Slaves acquired by the pirates and traders operating from or calling at Rhodes complete the list of

---

1 A.T. Luttrell, *The Town of Rhodes: 1306–1356* (Rhodes, 2003), pp. 77–8, 148–51, 167–70; N. Vatin, *L'Ordre de Saint-Jean-de-Jérusalem, l'Empire ottoman et la Méditerranée orientale entre les deux sièges de Rhodes (1480–1522)* (Paris, 1994), pp. 34–7, 39–47; J. Sarnowsky, *Macht und Herrschaft im Johanniterorden des 15. Jahrhunderts: Verfassung und Verwaltung der Johanniter auf Rhodos (1421–1522)* (Münster, 2001), esp. pp. 43–6, 345–468.

2 A.T. Luttrell, 'Settlement on Rhodes' in Luttrell, *The Hospitallers of Rhodes and their Mediterranean World* (Aldershot, 1992), no V, pp. 273–81; Luttrell, *Town of Rhodes*, pp. 77–9, 113–15, 134–51; K. Hattersley-Smith, 'Documentary and Archaeological Evidence for Greek Settlement in the Countryside of Rhodes in the Fourteenth and Early Fifteenth Centuries', *The Military Orders: Fighting for the Faith and Caring for the Sick*, ed. M. Barber (Aldershot, 1998), pp. 82–8; P. Bonneaud, *Le prieuré de Catalogne, le couvent de Rhodes et la couronne d'Aragon 1415–1447* (Bez-er-Esparon, 2004), 118, 146–7, 152–4; L. Butler, 'The Port of Rhodes under the Knights of St John', *Les Grandes Escales. Recueils de la société Jean Bodin* (1974), pp. 339–45; Vatin, *L'ordre*, pp. 29–33, 67; Sarnowsky, *Macht und Herrschaft*, esp. pp. 359–68, 374–5.

3 Soldiers other than turcopoles and sailors, are discussed in Luttrell, *Town of Rhodes*, pp. 79, 83; Butler, 'Port of Rhodes', 343; A.T. Luttrell, 'The Military and Naval Organisation of the Hospitallers at Rhodes: 1310–1444' in Luttrell, *Mediterranean World*, no. XIX, pp. 133–53, at pp. 136–9; Sarnowsky, *Macht und Herrschaft*, pp. 288–9, 388–90, 413–15, 417, 430–1, 434, 436–40, 500–1. For numbers of brethren in convent by *langue* see Sarnowsky, *Macht und Herrschaft*, pp. 508–9, 511.

long-term residents, and might include orthodox Christians as well as Turks and Jews.[4] Most voluntary visitors to the islands were traders, soldiers or sailors seeking employment, or pilgrims on their way to Jerusalem, but there were also crusading expeditions or enthusiasts and occasionally scholars interested in learning Greek or in other intellectual pursuits.[5]

The number of British and Irish residents in and travellers to the islands was probably very limited. The only permanent community of what might anachronistically be called Britons was made up of the Hospitallers of the English *langue* together with their servants. During the fifteenth century there were usually between one and two dozen English, Irish and Scots Hospitallers in the Aegean, although this number might rise in response to crises such as the invasion scare of 1513.[6] The sources do not allow such precision when considering how many of their countrymen – or women – the British and Irish Hospitallers brought with them to the Dodecanese. The only period during which Hospitallers other than priors were routinely required to seek royal licence to leave England, and during which such licences were enrolled with any frequency, was the mid 1530s, when preceptors were permitted to travel to Malta with up to three servants, and unbeneficed conventual brethren with one, but it would be unwise to regard these figures as more than a rough indication of what might have been usual in the Rhodian period.[7] That conventual knights were only permitted one servant was probably realistic. Their income would have been limited to the allowances provided by the common treasury,[8] together with any pensions they might manage to acquire from their families,[9] from other members of the *langue*,[10] or from the master.[11] This would have left few with the income to retain more than one or two servants, and these, of course, need not have been British or Irish. Indeed, given the expense of journeying to Rhodes, it is likely that on leaving the British Isles only brethren with family money behind them would have been accompanied by retainers. Many must, rather, have hired local servants if and when funds became available. By limiting preceptors to three servants, Henry VIII's government was probably attempting to restrict the numbers of subjects visiting an outpost of militant Romanism rather than simply reflecting what was considered

4 Luttrell, *Town of Rhodes*, pp. 78–9; Bonneaud, *Catalogne*, p. 170; Vatin, *L'ordre*, 33–4, 62, 106–13; Sarnowsky, *Macht und Herrschaft*, pp. 353, 356, 369–74, 385n, 386, 408n, 417, 497, 551.

5 V.J. Flynn, 'The Intellectual Life of Fifteenth-Century Rhodes', *Traditio* 2 (1944), pp. 239–55; A.T. Luttrell, 'The Hospitallers' Historical Activities: 1400–1530' in Lutttrell, *Latin Greece, the Hospitallers and the Crusades* (Aldershot, 1982), art. II, pp. 145–50, at p. 148.

6 G.J. O'Malley, *The Knights Hospitaller of the English Langue, 1460–1565* (Oxford, 2005), pp. 163–4, 278.

7 *Letters and Papers Foreign and Domestic of the Reign of Henry VIII*, ed. J.S. Brewer, J. Gairdner and R. H. Brodie, 22 vols in 37 parts (London, 1864–1929), 7, no. 1026 (32); 9, no. 1063 (2, 4); 10, nos 597 (37, 38), 775 (8); O'Malley, *English Langue*, p. 281.

8 Sarnowsky, *Macht und Herrschaft*, pp. 504–6; Bonneaud, *Catalogne*, p. 170; O'Malley, *English Langue*, pp. 272, 277.

9 For example, *L & P Reign Henry VIII*, 15, no. 522.

10 O'Malley, *English Langue*, pp. 48, 290.

11 Ibid., pp. 48, 51.

to be usual or appropriate, yet the restriction may also have been prompted, given the English crown's traditional concern to restrict foreign travel by its subjects, by the fact that Malta was quicker and cheaper to reach than Rhodes had been. Yet notwithstanding higher costs, some preceptors travelled with rather more than three servants in the years before 1522, at least on their return journeys. In 1436, for example, the preceptor of Templecombe, John Ellum, was granted passage for himself and up to six servants when the convent licensed him to leave Rhodes.[12] Two years earlier Brother Andrew Meldrum, preceptor of Torphichen, had been issued a safe-conduct to leave England with six companions. He too had been returning from Rhodes.[13] In September 1510 James IV of Scotland asked Henry VIII to grant safe-conduct to another preceptor of Torphichen, George Dundas, who wished to pass to Rhodes and other parts with 16 persons, although in the event Dundas did not get any further than Rome.[14] I have not found any more licences enumerating the entourages of the preceptors of British or Irish houses associated with travel to the East, but in 1436 and 1448 turcopoliers, knight-brethren who headed the English *langue* in Rhodes, were granted papal safe-conducts for themselves and parties of 12 and 15 respectively while they travelled within Latin Christendom.[15]

As might be expected, Hospitaller priors provincial, particularly priors of England, were permitted to take more substantial retinues. In 1398 the prior of Ireland and turcopolier, Peter Holt, was given safe-conduct to pass to Rhodes with up to 20 persons, while three years later the prior of England, Walter Grendon, was allowed 30.[16] In 1419 the customers of London were ordered to let prior William Hulles take to Rhodes 34 embroidered gowns for the use of his gentlemen, yeomen and grooms, a further gown for a chaplain, and 20 gowns for himself and his brethren, although some of these persons were probably already in the East.[17] The last prior of England to go to Rhodes after his election, John Weston, travelled with both Hospitaller brethren and his own servants when he visited Rome and Naples in 1481 before proceeding to the Dodecanese. Weston's party was so substantial and well equipped that observers told him that no such company had come to Italy from England in the last century, although this was doubtless an exaggeration: when he left Rome

12 Malta, Cod. 352, f. 127r.

13 *Foedera, conventiones, litterae, et cujuscunque generis, acta publica inter reges angliae, et alios quosvis imperatores, reges, pontifices, principes, vel communitates, ab ineunte saeculo duodecimo, viz. ab anno 1101 ad nostra usque tempora*, ed. T. Rymer, 3rd edn, 10 vols (London, 1739–45; repr. Farnborough, 1967), 5/1, p. 8.

14 *Registrum secreti sigilli regum Scotorum. The Register of the Privy Seal of Scotland*, ongoing (Edinburgh, 1908–), 1, ed. M. Livingstone, *A.D. 1488–1529*, no. 2128. A respite made to Dundas to leave Scotland two months before James's letter to Henry VIII permitted him 24 companions, 13 of them named. Ibid, no. 2105.

15 *Calendar of Entries in the Papal Registers relating to Great Britain and Ireland. Papal Letters 1198–1513*, 19 vols in 20 (London and Dublin, 1893–1998), 8, pp. 435–6; 10, p.25.

16 *Calendar of Patent Rolls, 1307–1563*, 56 vols (London, 1895–1939), *1396–9*, p. 249; *Foedera*, 4/1, p.19.

17 *Calendar of Close Rolls, Edward II–Henry VII*, 41 vols (London, 1892–1963), *1419–22*, p. 18.

on the return leg of his journey in 1485 he was given safe-conduct for a party of no more than 25.[18] The figures provided by the sources probably indicate *maxima* rather than actual numbers of travellers, and some members of the larger parties may only have gone as far as the Low Countries, France or Italy with their masters, who often had business in these countries as well as in convent. Nor do the sources indicate the relative proportions among the travellers of professed Hospitallers and of servants or associates. Even so it still seems likely that companies of servants usually accompanied priors of England and preceptors of Scotland to Rhodes. In the case of priors of England, such visits took place regularly between the 1380s and 1440s, the priors typically remaining in the East for between one and three years, presumably with their servants.[19] Preceptors returning to convent after a period running houses in the West might stay for much longer while awaiting promotion to another preceptory or pursuing a conventual career, giving their servants more time to find their bearings and perhaps settle in the Dodecanese. Shipping cloth and other commodities to Rhodes also required the employment of couriers and factors who might derive from the British Isles, although others were Latin citizens of Rhodes or Italians.[20]

Pinning down the identity of these servants and what they did in the East is difficult. Other than Hospitallers or those whose primary purpose in the region was pilgrimage to Jerusalem, I have only been able to identify 47 persons from the British Isles as having probably visited or resided in the Dodecanese in the period between 1438 and 1522, and some of these were crusading volunteers or are described as being in the service of the Order as a whole rather than of members of the English *langue*, the two of course not being mutually exclusive. The duties and positions of those described as servants of English Hospitallers are not always defined. In 1469, for example, after the death of the turcopolier William Dawney in England, the convent provided funds out of his *spolia* to two of his servants, his relative

---

18 *The Cely Letters 1472–1488*, ed. A. Hanham, Early English Text Society 273 (London, 1975), nos. 118, 121, 123, 129, 147, 178; O'Malley, *English Langue*, p. 140; *Cal. Papal Letters*, 14, p. 5. In 1382 the prior of England had returned home with a party of 15. C.L. Tipton, 'The English Hospitallers during the Great Schism', *Studies in Medieval and Renaissance History* 4 (1967), pp. 91–124, at pp. 102–3.

19 References to and details of prioral visits to chapters general or to convent in the fourteenth and fifteenth centuries can be found in H. Nicholson, 'The Hospitallers in England, the Kings of England and Relations with Rhodes in the Fourteenth Century', *Sacra Militia* 2 (2001), pp. 25–45, at p. 26n; Tipton, 'Great Schism', pp. 109–13, 115–17; P.J.C. Field, 'Sir Robert Malory, Prior of the Hospital of St John of Jerusalem in England (1432–1439/40)', *Journal of Ecclesiastical History* 28 (1977), pp. 249–64; A.T. Luttrell, 'English Contributions to the Hospitaller Castle of Bodrum in Turkey', *The Military Orders, vol. 2: Welfare and Warfare*, ed. H. Nicholson (Aldershot, 1998), pp. 163–72, at pp. 165, 169; J. Sarnowsky, 'Kings and Priors: The Hospitaller Priory of England in the Later Fifteenth Century', in J. Sarnowsky (ed.), *Mendicants, Military Orders and Regionalism in Medieval Europe* (Aldershot, 1999), pp. 83–102, at p. 91; J. Sarnowsky, *Macht und Herrschaft*, pp. 64n, 126, 269n, 275n; O'Malley, *English Langue*, pp. 139–41.

20 O'Malley, *English Langue*, pp. 164, 167, 188–9, 287–8.

Gilbert Green and John Mainthorpe.[21] Green and Mainthorpe were certainly in Rhodes and evidently needed the money to return home to England,[22] but I have not been able to determine whether they were long-term residents charged with looking after Dawney's interests on the island, or had been sent out as his factors with his responsions, or had come to announce the news of his death. Letters of passage were issued to other servants of Hospitallers of the English *langue* with unspecified responsibilities in 1495, 1515, 1516 and 1517. Without exception all were in the employ of senior brethren who held one of the four conventual and capitular bailiwicks in the *langue*'s gift. John Brune, or Brown, who left Rhodes in 1495, was in the service of the turcopolier Thomas Docwra. Anthony Tonge, who departed in 1515, was employed by the bailiff of Eagle, Thomas Newport. Thomas Bardsley, who returned to the West in the following year, was a servant of the prior of Ireland, John Rawson; and John Grantham, who left Rhodes in 1517, served the turcopolier William Darrell.[23] Both Brune and Grantham were stated to be long-term servants of their masters, who remained on Rhodes after their departures. Whether the same can be said of Bardsley, whose master Rawson had left Rhodes five years before, is less clear. Bardsley may have been left in charge of Rawson's property interests on the island, which included a vineyard in 1505,[24] but he may equally well have been a messenger sent to Rhodes to inform the Order of his master's difficulties in Ireland.[25] The fourth man, Anthony Tonge, was almost certainly a long-term servant, and perhaps a potential Hospitaller himself, as he was a member of a family that had produced several knight-brethren in the previous century.[26]

Other servants can be seen performing particular duties in the Dodecanese, or can be traced in the Order's records in the British Isles, so that one can gain some idea of the tasks they fulfilled or were considered suitable for. Some might represent brethren in matters of great importance, such as Henry King, an Irish priest who presented letters requesting Thomas Fitgerald's reinstatement as prior of Ireland before the Order's council in September 1450.[27] Others acted as couriers bearing messages, responsions or goods to or from the convent. Thomas West, a servant of Brother Hugh Middleton, handed over 370 Venetian ducats to the conventual common treasury on behalf of his master in January 1439, while Ralph Bringston, Bartholomew Wilton and Richard Passemer or Passmere can be found handing over money on behalf of Brother John Langstrother in January 1457.[28] Passmere

21 Malta, Cod. 377, f. 249r.

22 On 14 April 1469 the receiver of the common treasury in England, William Tornay, was instructed to reimburse brothers John Langstrother and John Weston the monies they had paid for the passage of Dawney's servants. Malta, Cod. 378, f. 149r.

23 Malta, Cod. 392, f. 170v; 404, f. 230v; 405, f. 134r; 406, ff. 156v–7r.

24 Malta, Cod. 284, f. 91v; Cod. 80, f. 122v; O'Malley, *English Langue*, p. 284. For this property, see also Sarnowsky, *Macht und Herrschaft*, p. 400 and n.

25 For these see O'Malley, *English Langue*, pp. 249–51.

26 O'Malley, *English Langue*, pp. 36, 356.

27 NLM, Cod. 362, ff. 121r, 123v–4r; Sarnowsky, 'Kings and Priors', pp. 100–1; Idem, *Macht und Herrschaft*, pp. 97, 586.

28 Malta, Cod. 353, f. 157v; Cod. 366, f. 148v. The first of these documents has been published in Z.N. Tsirpanlis, *Anekdota eggrapha gia te Rodo kai te Noties Sporades apo to*

was probably involved in the collection of the 1450 Jubilee Indulgence, which was extended in the Order's favour in various stages, and of which Langstrother was appointed collector in Britain and Ireland.[29] Shortly before Langstrother was sent to the West as collector Passmere was dispatched to various places in the world as the convent's nuncio on 'arduous', but unspecified, 'business of great importance' concerning both the Order and all other Christians.[30] The trust in which he was held is further illustrated by his appointment in 1459 as scribe of the common treasury in England, making him arguably the most important lay officer in the priory.[31] Like Anthony Tonge, Passmere was a probable relative of Hospitaller brethren active in Rhodes, one of whom, Nicholas Passmere, was castellan of Lindos in 1467.[32]

Passmere was not the only man who held a position in England after serving in Rhodes. Service 'beyond the sea' was remembered in several grants of corrodies or offices by the provincial chapter of the priory of England, although it is conceivable that some of this service had been performed in continental Europe rather than in the Dodecanese. Christopher Newton, appointed bailiff of the manor of Highbury in 1524, had served the Order beyond the sea, as had Edmund Travar, who was granted custody of the Hospital's chapel at Islington in 1515, and Robert Coldale, who was granted an annuity from the issues of the preceptory of Dingley in 1496.[33] In 1524 the provincial chapter made John Chamber, a former domestic servant of the prior, who had retired to a hermitage in Northamptonshire, a grant of winter fuel in consideration of his service 'whether beyond the sea in war or elsewhere and in all business and causes'.[34] Some Hospitallers may themselves have begun their careers in the service of more senior brethren. The Thomas West who had become a professed knight of the Order by May 1440 was likely the man of the same name who had served Hugh Middleton in the 1430s.[35]

Besides these seemingly all-purpose lay servants, several preceptors took secular priests with them to serve as their or the *langue*'s chaplain while they were in Rhodes. Other *langues* certainly had chapels within or adjacent to the auberges which served as their meeting halls and dining rooms and appointed chaplains to serve in them.[36] It is possible that a chapel in Knights' Street, in Rhodes town, which bears various fourteenth-century arms including those of England quartered with France, was associated with the *langue* in some way, although it was some distance

---

archeio ton Ionniton Ippoton (Rhodes, 1995), pp. 318–19.

29 Sarnowsky, *Macht und Herrschaft*, p. 172n; *Cal. Papal Letters*, 10, pp. 261–3, 265; *Foedera*, 5/2, p. 57.

30 Passmere's original passport was issued on 27 October 1454. Another followed on 25 February 1455. Malta, Cod. 365, ff. 183r–v, 257r.

31 Malta, Cod. 369, f. 198v.

32 Malta, Cod. 283, f. 54v.

33 London, British Library (hereafter BL) MS Cotton Claudius E.vi, ff. 254r, 136v–7r; BL MS Lansdowne 200, f. 36v.

34 BL MS Cotton Claudius E.vi, f. 254v.

35 Malta, Cod. 361, ff. 240r–v.

36 Luttrell, *Town of Rhodes*, p. 117; S. Fiorini and A.T. Luttrell, 'The Italian Hospitallers at Rhodes, 1437–1462', *Revue Mabillon* 68 (1996), pp. 209–231, at pp. 211, 216, 223; Bonneaud, *Catalogne*, p. 166.

away from the later English auberge.[37] While the *langue* at times lacked an English-speaking chaplain,[38] there were some English priests in Rhodes who might have fulfilled this function. John Newton, who was licensed to return to England in 1475 on condition he received the permission of the turcopolier, had also been on the island in 1459, when he had perhaps completed a translation of Vegetius' *De re militari*.[39] The other man involved in the translation, John Clifton, is presumably the John Clifton who can be found acting for Brother Richard Pauley on Rhodes in April 1442.[40] Another English priest, William More, was granted letters of passage five weeks after Newton; as was a chaplain of the bailiff of Eagle, then resident on Rhodes, in 1516.[41] The Scottish preceptor Andrew Meldrum also took a secular priest, John de Kindeloch, with him on at least one of his visits to Rhodes in the 1430s and 1440s.[42] The humanist William Lily, who according to his son visited Rhodes so that he might learn Latin and Greek, and certainly stayed on the island for a number of years, was an associate of the turcopolier John Kendal during his stay in Rome in the 1480s, was granted a benefice in the Order's gift on his and Kendal's return to England in 1492, and in 1496 was accused of complicity in the latter's plots to poison Henry VII.[43] Another English scholar linked with the island was the Augustinian canon, physician and alchemist George Ripley, who was reported in the seventeenth century to have stayed on Rhodes. Ripley was certainly abroad during the 1460s, when he spent several years in Italy, and also expressed a wish to visit the Holy Places in the mid-1470s.[44] Not all English-speaking clerics necessarily served the English *langue* or its members while they were in Rhodes. An Irish priest, William Lacy of the diocese of Ferns, was received as a magistral chaplain in 1456,

37 Luttrell, *Town of Rhodes*, pp. 27–9, 110–11. Documentary evidence, however, suggests that the chapel might have belonged to the *langue* of France. Luttrell, *Town of Rhodes*, pp. 282–4.

38 *Book of Deliberations of the Venerable Tongue of England 1523–67*, ed. H. P. Scicluna (Malta, 1949), pp. 14–16. The Italian *langue* employed a French chaplain in 1441. Fiorini and Luttrell, 'Italian Hospitallers', pp. 215, 225.

39 Malta, Cod. 75, f. 79r; Flynn, 'Intellectual Life', p. 247.

40 Flynn, 'Intellectual Life', p. 247; Malta, Cod. 355, f. 169r. A Sir John Clifton had died at Rhodes in 1388. C. Tyerman, *England and the Crusades* (Chicago, 1988), p. 293.

41 Malta, Cod. 382, f. 235r; Cod. 404, f. 230v.

42 *Foedera*, 5/2, p. 56; Malta, Cod. 357, f. 236v; Cod. 358, ff. 227v–8v; *The Knights of St John of Jerusalem in Scotland*, ed. I.B. Cowan, P.H.R. Mackay and A. Macquarrie (Edinburgh, 1983), pp. xlii, 165.

43 Flynn, 'Intellectual Life', pp. 239–40; *The Register of John Morton Archbishop of Canterbury 1486–1500*, ed. C. Harper-Bill, 3 vols (York, 1985, Woodbridge, 1987, 2000), 2, no. 186; 'Documents Relating to Perkin Warbeck', ed. F. Madden, *Archaeologia* 27 (1838), pp. 153–210, at p. 177; O'Malley, *English Langue*, p. 289; I. Arthurson, *The Perkin Warbeck Conspiracy 1491–1499* (Stroud, 1994), p. 137.

44 E. Ashmole, *Theatrum Chemicum Brittanicum* (London, 1652), p. 458; J. Hughes, *Arthurian Myths and Alchemy. The Kingship of Edward IV* (Stroud, 2002), pp. 202–3, 57, 85–6, 288. Ashmole derived his information from an English gentleman who had visited Malta and claimed to have seen records there stating that Ripley had given the master the figure of £100,000 per annum towards the war against the Turks. I am grateful to Dr Helen Nicholson for the reference to Ashmole.

perhaps because James Keating, the only Irish Hospitaller in convent, was too poor to maintain him.[45]

Like Lacy, other natives of Britain and Ireland are referred to in the Order's registers as having held offices or pensions from the Hospital or its master rather than from members of the *langue*. Some of them had probably come to Rhodes in the train of a professed Hospitaller but remained there after their master had died or returned home. One such was 'Duguethus le Scot', who probably came to Rhodes in the train of Andrew Meldrum in the 1430s, had been granted two pensions from the Order's revenues in Scotland in recognition of his service by 1442, and was described in 1454 as a magistral servant who had served the Order by land and sea for many years.[46] Others may have originated as crusading volunteers or stipendiary soldiers, like the Patrick Kelly of the diocese of Kildare who had spent more than seven years on Rhodes and at the castle of St Peter by 1479, at a time when no Irish brethren are known to have been serving in the East.[47]

Most of the British and Irish residents of the Dodecanese mentioned in the Order's archives but not specified as being servants of individual Hospitallers were soldiers or sailors. There are few references to them even so. Most of the material relating to the military activities of the English *langue* concerns the responsibility of the turcopolier for organizing the coastguard, but the banneret, turcopoles and coastguards who served under him appear to have been Rhodians, whether Greek or Latin in origin.[48] Yet the *langue* was also responsible for manning a section of the walls of Rhodes town, and had a part to play in garrisoning Bodrum and supplying brethren for galley service. Unfortunately these activities have generated very little documentation referring to non-brethren, but there is enough to show that at least some of the soldiers and sailors serving in the Dodecanese were from Britain and Ireland. There were certainly times when soldiers from Britain might have considered entering the Order's service. The general demobilizations that accompanied the breaks in the Anglo-French wars from 1392 to 1415, 1444 to 1448 and after 1453 left many who had earned their living in arms without an income, and some may have been attracted by the prospect of service in Rhodes, with English or Gascon Hospitallers presumably acting as recruitment agents. The employment of Stephen Ward as master of the arsenal on Rhodes in 1456 certainly suggests a previous military or naval career, as does William Radcliffe's appointment to be bailiff of the Order's chief fortress on Kos, Narangia, sometime before 1454.[49] It is conceivable that Radcliffe served under his namesake Sir John, the seneschal of Gascony between 1423 and 1436, and one of the most vigorous and successful

45 Malta, Cod. 366, f. 116r. In 1461 Keating promised pensions to two English knight-brethren who had aided him in his 'necessities', while another English brother paid for 'writings of the prior of Ireland', presumably the bulls appointing Keating prior of Ireland. Malta, Cod. 371, ff. 144r, 144v.

46 *Knights of St John in Scotland*, ed. Cowan et al., pp. xliii, 62–4, 168; Malta, Cod. 355, f. 197r; Cod. 365, f. 120r; A. Macquarrie, *Scotland and the Crusades* (Edinburgh, 1983), pp. 94–5.

47 Malta, Cod. 387, f. 202r.

48 O'Malley, *English Langue*, pp. 307–8.

49 Malta, Cod. 366, f. 174v; Cod. 364, f. 175r.

captains of the Lancastrian dynasty.[50] It has also been suggested that another Englishman with military experience in France, Sir Thomas Malory, the author of *Le Morte d'Arthur*, served in Rhodes with his uncle Robert, the Hospitaller prior of England between 1433 and 1439. This hypothesis rests on the possibility that the prior, who was certainly not averse to employing relatives, took Sir Thomas with him when he visited Rhodes with a considerable company in 1435, and on a passage in the *Morte* describing a castle and harbour with loosely similar characteristics to Rhodes.[51]

Even given the English crown's claims on the exclusive service of its subjects, some Englishmen and Irishmen served in the Dodecanese while their monarch was waging war elsewhere. The dispatch of 200 longbows, 200 palettes, 200 'wire hattes' [coifs?] and twelve dozen bracers to Rhodes in 1427 suggests that the English or Anglo-Welsh contingent there may have been relatively substantial, despite the fact that the war in France was at its height.[52] Given that a military career in France was highly dangerous and often irregularly paid,[53] transfer to the Eastern Mediterranean may have appeared an attractive prospect, especially in the period before the 1440s, when the Order's conventual islands were relatively free from attack. That is not to say that the Britons and Irishmen in the garrison did not see action. According to family tradition, the Scot Sir Colin Campbell of Glenorchy spent some time in the Order's service before 1448 and 'fought in battle at the Rhodes against the Turks', perhaps a confused reference to the Mamluk siege of the island in 1444.[54] The sectors of the walls controlled by the English *langue* came under extremely heavy assault during the Turkish sieges of 1480 and 1522, and there were both persons from the British Isles and Rhodians among those defending the post of England during the later action.[55] After the siege a Scot who had served during it was admitted into the Order in reward for his service,[56] while two Englishmen who became brother knights shortly after the evacuation from Rhodes, and the Sussex gentleman John Shelley, who was apparently killed during the siege, may also have been volunteers,

50 R.A. Griffiths, *The Reign of King Henry VI* (repr. Stroud, 1998), pp. 86–7, 183–4, 202, 205–6.

51 *Cal. Patent Rolls 1429–36*, p. 452; C. Hardyment, *Malory. The Life and Times of King Arthur's Chronicler* (London, 2005), pp. 172–90, 181. See also P.J.C. Field, 'Sir Robert Malory'; P.J.C. Field, *The Life and Times of Sir Thomas Malory* (Cambridge, 1993), pp. 72–3, 78–82, 116, 130.

52 *Cal. Close Rolls, 1422–9*, p. 280. A more modest shipment of 46 pairs of knives, 15 other knives and four gross of arrowheads in 1408 seems likely to have been for the use of the brethren of the *langue* and perhaps their turcopoles. *Cal. Close Rolls, 1405–8*, p. 411.

53 A point made with especial force in N. Wright, *Knights and Peasants: The Hundred Years' War in the French Countryside* (Woodbridge, 1998).

54 *Knights of St John in Scotland*, ed. Cowan et al., pp. xlvi–xlvii; Macquarrie, *Scotland and the Crusades*, pp 93–4.

55 The Rhodian Francisco Galliardetto was granted a corrody in 1533 in recognition of his service 'on the island of Rhodes, especially in the siege of Rhodes town, or on our departure from Rhodes and in England'. London, The National Archives: Public Record Office, LR2/62, f. 122v.

56 *Knights of St John of Jerusalem in Scotland*, ed. Cowan et al., pp. l, 177, 180.

although family tradition had Shelley as a knight-brother.[57] Other soldiers appear occasionally in fifteenth-century records. Robert Gay, who had taken a vow to fight the Turks but served at Bodrum during a period of truce, was licensed to return home in 1474.[58] Gay had only served for a few months, but several others had done so for years and may have been professional soldiers, although Robert Patrison, a Scottish *bombarderius* pardoned of homicide in 1504, is the only man who can unequivocally be described as such.[59] Besides Patrison, William Brereton, a possible servant of John Langstrother, had served at Bodrum before being granted letters of passage to England in 1458.[60] Thomas Ruth, who had been admitted as the master's familiar and servitor by 1457 on account of his many services at Bodrum, on the galleys and elsewhere, had served for a long time, as had William Bathcote of Herefordshire, who had sailed on the galleys of the kings of Cyprus and Aragon during the 1440s and early 1450s, as well as on the Hospitaller galleys then commanded by the preceptor of the Herefordshire house of Dinmore, William Dawney.[61] Bathcote and Brereton were probably soldiers serving on the galleys rather than sailors, but at least one English sailor, Gervase Roger or Roger Jervis, is said to have fought at the Turkish siege of Rhodes in 1480.[62] In addition to those serving the Order, soldiers and sailors from the British Isles who had joined the crusading expeditions against the Turks or Mamluks must also have stopped at Rhodes, as had their fourteenth-century forebears.[63] There were English soldiers with the fleet that Gonsalvo de Cordoba mustered against the Turks in Sicily in 1500, and others may have taken part in the Aragonese, Burgundian, Italian and French campaigns in the Eastern Mediterranean, many of which called at Rhodes.[64]

Unsurprisingly, given that most references to them are licences to depart, very few of these men can be shown to have put down roots in the Dodecanese. An Englishman, Thomas, who in November 1500 was granted a safe-conduct for two

57 *Book of Deliberations of the Venerable Tongue of England 1523–1567*, ed. H.P. Scicluna (Valletta, 1949), p. 5; *The History of Parliament: The House of Commons, 1509–1558*, ed. S.T. Bindoff (London, 1982), 1, p. 414. *The Visitations of the County of Sussex, Made and Taken in the Years 1530 by Thomas Benolte, Clarenceux King of Arms, and 1633–4 by John Philipot, Somerset Herald, and George Owen, York Herald*, ed. W. Bruce Bannerman (London, 1905), p. 37, describes Shelley as a 'knight of the Rhodes, slaine at the winning of the same'.

58 Malta, Cod. 382, f. 138r–v.

59 Malta, Cod. 395, f. 196r.

60 Malta, Cod. 367, f. 201v.

61 Malta, Cod. 366, f. 119v; Cod. 363, f. 259r. The commendation to Bathcote or Boycott is published in Tsirpanlis, *Anekdota*, pp. 318–19. He was perhaps a relative of William Bacichot or Bathcote, preceptor of Halston between 1442 and 1454. Malta, Cod. 355, f. 177r; Cod. 365, f. 116r.

62 R.A. de Vertot d'Aubeuf, *Histoire des chevaliers hospitaliers de S. Jean de Jérusalem*, 5 vols (Paris, 1726), 3, pp. 112–13.

63 A.T. Luttrell, 'Chaucer's Knight and the Mediterranean', *Library of Mediterranean History* 1 (1994), pp. 127–160, at pp. 131–2, 145, 149.

64 *Calendar of State Papers and Manuscripts existing in the Archives and Collections of Milan, 1385–1618* (London, 1912), 1, p. 137; Tyerman, *England and the Crusades*, p. 435.

years so that he might come to terms with his creditors, had got married at Rhodes, and may also have been a companion at Bodrum.[65] The English commander slain at the siege of Rhodes, and whose Rhodian mistress supposedly slew their children in grief before hurling herself against the Turkish lines, may have been the turcopolier John Bouthe, but may also have been an unprofessed soldier serving at the post of England.[66] In 1454 William Radcliffe, the bailiff of Narangia, was granted a pension of 20 florins per annum and three *modia* of corn to maintain his *familia*, which may conceivably have meant his family as well as his household.[67] None of these references proves anything more than that a few English residents had settled on a long-term basis, but one document suggests not only that its recipient intended to stay, but also that he expected his heirs to do so as well. Before July 1456, the English *protomagister* of the Arsenal, Stephen Ward, vowed to turn one of his work buildings into a chapel dedicated to St Michael if God should spare Rhodes from the plague. Ward secured a grant remitting any magistral right in the chapel, forbidding the *papates* from interfering in it, and reserving to him and his descendants the right to appoint priests to serve in it.[68] Ward at least had come to stay, and perhaps even intended to leave behind him an institution that would cater for English visitors to and residents in Rhodes, but there are no further references to his chapel in the context of the activities of the *langue*, so that it may be presumed that if this is what he had in mind, he failed.

Most British and Irish persons who visited Rhodes, as opposed to residing there, and whose names can be recovered, were pilgrims on their way to Jerusalem. Evidence for their journeys derives from a variety of sources, of which the most important are travel or export licences, wills and pilgrim diaries. Pilgrimages to the Holy Land required papal licence and while their issue was often delegated to legates or bishops, a number of English and Scots pilgrims combined a pilgrimage to Rome with travel to the Holy Land, so that their petitions for licence to visit Jerusalem and papal protection when doing so are sometimes recorded in the papal registers. Pilgrims leaving England and Scotland also required royal licence to take bullion out of the country besides, if they were of high status, permission to leave the realm. Leaving aside Hospitallers and their servants, and those who commuted their vows without leaving the British Isles, I have come across at least 73 named persons recorded as having vowed to visit, set off towards or actually set foot in the Holy Land in the period between 1409 and 1522. More than 320 more people are recorded as having travelled, or been licensed to travel, in their company, and these figures do not include the parties of noblemen and clerics who were licensed to take unspecified numbers of attendants with them.[69]

---

65 Malta, Cod. 78, f. 142r–v; Cod. 79, f. 11v.

66 Vertot, *Histoire des chevaliers hospitaliers*, iii, pp. 342–3.

67 Malta, Cod. 364, f. 175r.

68 Malta, Cod. 366. f. 174v. Ward's foundation is noticed in Butler, 'Port of Rhodes', p. 342.

69 Partial lists in Macquarrie, *Scotland*, pp. 93, 95, 105–6; Tyerman, *England*, pp. 282–8, 309–11; G.J. O'Malley, 'The English and the Levant in the Fifteenth Century', unpublished M. Phil dissertation (University of Cambridge, 1994), pp. 97–102. I have found notices of further named fifteenth- and sixteenth-century pilgrims in *Select Cases in Chancery*

Although most Jerusalem pilgrims stopped at Rhodes, which was a regular resort of Venetian sailings to Jaffa, few appear in the Order's archives as having done so. No register of visitors or vessels calling at Rhodes has survived and very few pilgrims engaged in activities of sufficient importance to leave a trace in the records of the Hospitaller chancery, not least because the patrons of the pilgrim galleys were contractually bound not to remain in any port for longer than a few days.[70] That does not mean that Rhodes was merely a convenient stopping place on the way to Jerusalem. The Order had not only not forgotten its origins in the Holy Land, but had long since embellished them with legends designed to lend them greater antiquity and lustre. It maintained its connection with the Holy Land in various ways: through linking its continued practice of holy war with the recovery of Jerusalem, through the dispatch of brethren on pilgrimage, through attempts to maintain the functions and fabric of the hospital in Jerusalem and even, in 1403, through an attempt to secure the guardianship of the Holy Places from the Mamluk sultan.[71] From the pilgrims' point of view, however, the most obvious of these connections, and the ones that the Order was most keen to publicize, were, first, its possession of important relics such as the thorn from Christ's crown which flowered annually on Good Friday and the arm of St John the Baptist, and second, the hospital in which it continued to care for sick pilgrims. All visitors to the island were encouraged to see both relics and hospital, and many were taken on tours of the treasury, the fortifications and the arsenal as well.[72] The Order's care to create a favourable impression was further demonstrated by the quality of the hospitality it provided, which encompassed formal

A.D. 1364 to 1471, ed. W.P. Baildon (London, 1896), pp. 113–14; R.M. Haines, *Ecclesia anglicana. Studies in the English Church of the Later Middle Ages* (Toronto, 1989), p. 189; *Victoria County History of Wiltshire*, 3, ed. R.B. Pugh and E. Crittall (London, 1956), p. 299; A. Heales, 'The Church of Stanwell and its Monuments', *Transactions of the London and Middlesex Archaeological Society* 3 (1867), pp. 105–37, at p. 120; D.M. Owen, *Church and Society in Medieval Lincolnshire* (Lincoln, 1971), p. 125; V. Davis, *William Waynflete, Bishop and Educationalist* (Woodbridge, 1993), p. 135; *The Visitation of Yorkshire in the Years 1563 and 1564, made by William Flower, Esquire, Norroy King of Arms*, ed. C.B. Norcliffe (London, 1881), pp. 363–4; *The Visitation of Suffolk, 1561, made by William Henry, Clarenceux King of Arms*, ed. J. Corder, 2 vols (London, 1981–84), p. 211. Two knights of the Holy Sepulchre noticed in *Tudor Royal Proclamations*, ed. P.L. Hughes and J.F. Larkin, 3 vols (New Haven, 1964–9), 1, nos. 82, 84, may not have been from the British Isles.

70 *Canon Pietro Casola's Pilgrimage to Jerusalem in the Year 1494*, ed. and trans. M.M. Newett (Manchester, 1907), p. 42.

71 Luttrell, 'Hospitallers' Historical Activities, 1400–1530'; A. Calvet, *Les Légendes de l'Hôpital de Saint-Jean de Jérusalem* (Paris, 2000); Sarnowsky, *Macht und Herrschaft*, pp. 461–2; A.T. Luttrell, 'The Hospitallers' Medical Tradition: 1291–1530', in Luttrell, *The Hospitaller State on Rhodes and its Western Provinces, 1306–1462* (Aldershot, 1999), no. X, pp. 64–81, at p. 70; Luttrell, 'Rhodes and Jerusalem: 1291–1411' in Luttrell, *Mediterranean World*, art. X, pp. 189–207.

72 A.T. Luttrell, 'The Rhodian Background of the Order of St John on Malta', in Luttrell, *Mediterranean World*, no. XVIII, pp. 3–14, at 12–13; Luttrell, *Town of Rhodes*, pp. 222–4, 279–81; M. Balard, 'The Urban Landscape of Rhodes as perceived by Fourteenth- and Fifteenth-Century Travellers', *Mediterreanean Historical Review*, 10 (1995), pp. 24–34.

welcome, shelter, food, drink and divine service.[73] Brethren would lay on meals and entertainments for distinguished visitors, especially if they were their countrymen or women. In 1458, for example, the rich English castellan of Rhodes, Brother John Langstrother, held a banquet in honour of the English nobleman John Tiptoft, earl of Worcester, in his garden at Malipassi, a few miles outside Rhodes town. A number of Italian noblemen were also invited, including the diarist Roberto da Sanseverino, who recorded his 'great delight' at the abundance, ordering and magnificence of the feast, which he thought would have been a 'great ornament' even to a royal court.[74] Another Italian, canon Pietro Casola, recorded in 1494 that he had enjoyed a banquet every night on the return leg of his pilgrimage, and made similar remarks on the quality of the fare provided.[75]

Unfortunately the fifteenth- and sixteenth-century English pilgrim diaries have relatively little to say about Rhodes. The most remarkable and idiosyncratic, the *Book of Margery Kempe*, does not mention it.[76] Other writers noted information that was almost entirely conventional. William Wey, the fellow of Eton who visited Jerusalem in 1458 and 1462, recorded the relics displayed to pilgrims, made some brief notes on the operations of the hospital, and spoke of the dogs kept at Bodrum to guard the castle and guide Christians fleeing Turkish captivity into it. He also recorded seeing the punishments inflicted on some of the Turks and apostates captured by the Order in 1458, and mentioned that in 1462 the Order had had a *Te Deum* sung to celebrate an Ottoman defeat in Wallachia.[77] The conventional picture was completed by the author of the *Information for Pilgrims*, first published in 1498, who spoke briefly of Rhodes town's fair haven, double walls and windmills, and by Richard Guildford's chaplain, who mentioned the 'good cheer and well intreating' that he and his fellow Englishmen had received at the hands of the *langue*.[78] Most disappointing of all is the Norfolk priest Richard Torkington, who spent six weeks convalescing in Rhodes following his return from Jerusalem in 1517, but could add no more to the Guildford account than that those of his party who had been sick had been especially cheered and well treated.[79] It is unfortunate that an account the Carmelite Richard Scrope

73 Vatin, *L'ordre*, pp. 53–5.

74 R. da Sanseverino, *Viaggio in Terra Santa*, ed. G. Maruffi (Bologna, 1888; reprinted Bologna, 1969), pp. 57–9. This event is discussed in R.J. Mitchell, *The Spring Voyage: The Jerusalem Pilgrimage in 1458* (London, 1965), pp. 80–1. Mitchell was unaware that the castellan was Langstrother. On his garden see O'Malley, *English Langue*, pp. 284–5.

75 *Canon Pietro Casola's Pilgrimage*, ed. and trans. Newett, pp. 307, 207.

76 Kempe did, however, meet 'knights of Rhodes' on the road between Assisi and Rome. *The Book of Margery Kempe*, ed. B. Windeatt (Woodbridge, 2004), p. 181.

77 W. Wey, *Itineraries*, ed. G. Williams (London, 1857), pp. 78, 94–5, 99–101.

78 *Information for Pilgrims unto the Holy Land*, ed. E.G. Duff (London, 1893), p. 27 (c. iv verso); *The Pylgrymage of Sir Richard Guylforde to the Holy Land*, ed. H. Ellis, Camden Society, Original Series 51 (London, 1851), pp. 57–8.

79 R. Torkington, *Ye Oldest Diarie of Englysshe Travell*, ed. W.J. Loftie (London, 1884), p. 27.

apparently left of a journey to Rhodes which probably took place in the late 1460s has not survived.[80]

Ill-served though they have been by their countrymen with literary leanings, some Holy Land pilgrims from the British Isles did more than stay for a few days and see the sights. As Anthony Luttrell has pointed out, Cardinal Henry Beaufort, who visited the Holy Land in 1418, arranged for the dispatch of considerable quantities of timber to Rhodes for use in the construction of Bodrum as soon as he arrived in Venice on the return leg of his journey.[81] Another contributor was Henry, lord FitzHugh, who sent arrows, bows and bowstrings to Rhodes for use at Bodrum in 1409.[82] The noble escutcheons placed on the English tower at Bodrum, possibly representing contributors to its construction, suggests that it was conceived of partly as a project to uphold national honour, possibly in the face of the attempts of the *langue* of Spain to appropriate the building.[83] Although many of the arms at Bodrum represented members of noble families who are not known to have visited Rhodes or the Holy Land in this period, the arms of Beauchamp, Montague and Fitzhugh do appear, as do those of others with earlier crusading traditions.[84] Richard Beauchamp, earl of Warwick had undertaken a pilgrimage to Jerusalem in 1408, and Thomas Montague, earl of Salisbury at some stage before 1426.[85] Fitzhugh need not necessarily have travelled to the island with his gift in 1409, but his grandson Henry probably did set off for Jerusalem in 1468, perhaps in part to confer with John Langstrother, a fellow ally of Richard Neville, earl of Warwick.[86] Although the Lancastrian dynasty had an affection for the Order which dated back to Henry IV's visit to Rhodes while still earl of Derby, it was still concerned to protect the investments made by it and its subjects in the Dodecanese, and several of the prominent pilgrims who visited the Holy Land in this period may have been instructed to check that English monies were being spent properly and that the honour and pre-eminence of the *langue*

80 Information kindly communicated by Fr. R. Copsey, O. Carm. According to Bale, the first writer to mention his visit to Rhodes, Scrope was dispatched there as a legate 'sub nescio quo'. It was likely that he was sent either by Eugenius IV, who appointed him bishop of Dromore, or by Nicholas V.J. Bale, *Illustrium Maioris Britanniæ scriptorum, hoc est, Angliæ, Cambriæ ac Scotiæ Summarium* (London, 1548), f. 214r; L. Stephen and S. Lee (eds), *Dictionary of National Biography*, 63 vols (London, 1885–1900), 51, pp. 148–9.

81 Luttrell, 'English Contributions', p. 167. For the political significance of Beaufort's pilgrimage see G.L. Harriss, 'Henry Beaufort, "Cardinal of England"' in D. Williams (ed.), *England in the Fifteenth Century* (Woodbridge, 1987), pp. 111–27.

82 Luttrell, 'English Contributions', pp. 166–7.

83 Luttrell, 'English Contributions', pp. 168–70. Dr Luttrell suggests that the arms were placed there in conjunction with the visit of the two lords Scrope to the Dodecanese in 1435. Ibid, p. 169.

84 Ibid, pp. 171–2; Tyerman, *England and the Crusades*, pp. 314–15.

85 *Pageant of the Birth, Life and Death of Richard Beauchamp Earl of Warwick 1389–1439*, ed. H.A. Dillon (London, 1914); *Cal. Papal Letters*, 7, pp. 439–40, 468.

86 He was licensed to visit the Holy Land on 18 February 1468. *Complete Peerage*, ed. G.E. Cockayne, V. Gibbs et al., 13 vols (London, 1910–59), 5, p. 429. For his alliance with Warwick see M. Hicks, *False, Fleeting, Perjur'd Clarence: George, Duke of Clarence, 1449–1478*, 2nd ed. (Gloucester, 1992), p. 73.

was being respected by the Order's authorities. Cardinal Beaufort's pilgrimage can probably be seen partly in this context, and John, lord Scrope of Bolton, who was the only formally appointed ambassador certainly sent by the English crown to Rhodes after 1409, may have been instructed to ensure that the English tower at Bodrum did not pass out of the *langue*'s control and was also charged with restoring the turcopoliership to its rightful dignity and pre-eminence, which it had lost under Antoni de Fluvià.[87] Similarly, given that his master had recently dispatched artillery to be used by the *langue*, Henry VII's servant Sir Richard Guildford, who visited Rhodes during his pilgrimage to Jerusalem in 1506, may also have been charged with seeing that his master's gift was being properly employed.[88] It is also conceivable that a royal interest in trade with or crusading against Mamluk Egypt may have lain behind the decision of John Wykes and William Brereton to use Rhodes as a base from where to visit Egypt and Syria in 1458.[89]

Few British or Irish pilgrims who visited Jerusalem in the period between 1409 and 1522 can be shown to have had a personal or family connection with the order of St John. Among those who did were Sir Alexander Seton of Gordon, who was descended from or related to a similarly named fourteenth-century Hospitaller and Reginald West, lord de la Warre. Seton not only died in the Hospital on Rhodes, but also bequeathed his movable goods to the Order, from which the Order had extracted 1700 ducats by 1451.[90] Having been granted royal licence to leave England in October 1439, de la Warre had set off for the Holy Land in company with Robert, lord Willoughby but had been seized, robbed, held to ransom and otherwise mistreated somewhere in Germany before being released in the following year through the auspices of the archbishop of Cologne.[91] Understandably enough, Willoughby commuted his vow soon afterwards, but de la Warre was made of sterner stuff.[92] He not only appears to have proceeded to Jerusalem to fulfil his vow upon his release, for he is to be found supplicating on behalf of a citizen of Rhodes in March 1442, but in late 1446 or 1447 he set out for Jerusalem again, bolstered by royal letters demanding the rulers of the Rhineland grant him safe-conduct.[93] That de la Warre involved himself in local matters while on Rhodes is interesting and suggests that he stayed on the island longer than the few days customary for pilgrims. It seems likely that his pilgrimage was actively encouraged by the Order. Besides his possible kinship with the Hospitaller Thomas West, the family had ties with the Hospital reaching back to at least the first half of the fourteenth century and the perpetuation of these can only have been encouraged by the fact that the Wests' ancestral home of Swallowcliffe abutted the preceptory of Ansty, whose incumbent,

87 Luttrell, 'English Contributions', p. 169.

88 Malta, Cod. 78, f. 95r–v.

89 Malta, Cod. 367, ff. 201v, 215v; G.J. O'Malley, 'Pilgrimage, Crusade, Trade and Embassy: Early English Contacts with the Ottoman Turks', *Crusades* 3 (2004), 153–70, at pp. 160–1.

90 Malta, Cod. 354, ff. 219v–20r; Cod. 363, f. 217v.

91 *Foedera*, 5/1, p. 167; T. Bekynton, *Official Correspondence*, ed. G. Williams, 2 vols (London, 1872), 1, pp. 93–4.

92 *Cal. Papal Letters*, 9, p. 84.

93 Malta, Cod. 355, f. 232v; *Foedera*, 5/1, p. 175.

Robert Botill, was elected prior of England just before de la Warre's departure on his first expedition.[94] Family ties with the Order perhaps also lay behind the decision of the 80-year-old widow Alice Skipwith, probably the sister-in-law of the long-dead turcopolier Thomas Skipwith, to undertake the Jerusalem pilgrimage in about 1439. Having reached Rhodes, she was unable to continue further, due to old age and infirmity, perhaps because her compatriots on the island persuaded her to desist.[95]

From the 1480s English merchants also begin to appear in the Order's records as factors for members of the *langue*, or as creditors of the conventual common treasury. John Millet (or Miller) in 1487, and two members of the Shelley family and a John Thomas in 1513 appear in one of these capacities.[96] The Hugh Ball who was sent to England with gifts for the king in 1515 was perhaps also a merchant.[97] Given that most English merchants in the Eastern Mediterranean traded in Cretan wine or in alum, it is unlikely that many settled in Rhodes, particularly given the fuss which their export of Turkish alum to Western Europe provoked at the curia in the early years of the sixteenth century.[98] Even so, it is possible that from the 1460s onwards dozens of English merchants and sailors called at Rhodes, even if only briefly.

With the possible exception of the 1450s, when references to them are fairly numerous, the British and Irish inhabitants of Rhodes and the Dodecanese cannot be proved to have constituted anything approaching a community except in the context of their service to members of the English *langue*. Nevertheless it is clear that persons from many parts of Britain and Ireland made their way to and settled in Rhodes and the Dodecanese, so that their presence there cannot have been regarded as in any way unusual or exotic.

94 *The Knights Hospitallers in England: Being the Report of Philip de Thame to the Grand Master Elyan de Villanova*, ed. L.B. Larking, with a historical introduction by J.M. Kemble (London, 1857), p. 8; *Victoria County History of Wiltshire*, 13, ed. D.A. Crowley (London, 1987), pp. 178, 180–1; *Complete Peerage*, ed. Cockayne, Gibbs et al., 12/2, pp. 517–18; O'Malley, *English Langue*, p. 137, n. 161.

95 M.M. Harvey, *England, Rome and the Papacy 1417–64* (Manchester, 1993), pp. 108–9. Earlier pilgrimages to Jerusalem by Englishwomen are discussed in A.T. Luttrell, 'Englishwomen as Pilgrims to Jerusalem: Isolda Parewastell, 1365', in J. Bolton Holloway, C.S. Wright and J. Bechtold (eds), *Equally in God's Image. Women in the Middle Ages* (New York, 1990), pp. 184–97.

96 Malta, Cod. 389, f. 162r; Cod. 402, ff. 175r–v.

97 Malta, Cod. 404, f. 234v; Sarnowsky, *Macht und Herrschaft*, p. 501; O'Malley, *English Langue*, p. 164.

98 C. Singer, *The Earliest Chemical Industry: An Essay in the Historical Relations of Economics and Technology illustrated from the Alum Trade* (London, 1948), pp. 158–9; G. J. O'Malley, 'Pilgrimage, Crusade, Trade and Embassy', pp. 153–170, at pp. 157–8.

PART 3
The Military-Religious Orders in the West

PART 3

The Military-Religious Orders in the West

Chapter 15

Scribes and Notaries in Twelfth- and Thirteenth-Century Hospitaller Charters from England

Michael Gervers and Nicole Hamonic

A search through over 3,000 charters from the surviving cartularies of the Order of St. John of Jerusalem in England produces a meagre list of twenty-five individuals from the witness lists who are designated as being in one way or another responsible for the preparation of the document in question (Table 1).[1] For the purposes of comparison, a similar search through the 10,300 dated English charters in the DEEDS[2] database at the University of Toronto, covering the period 1100–1307, produced twenty-six names in a similar context (Table 2). For the most part, these individuals are clearly scribes, whose responsibility it was to compose and copy the record to which they attached their names. Those who "hanc brevem/cartam/convencionem/quietam clamanciam *scripsit*" seem to have been on a par with those "qui hanc cartam *fecit*"[3] or "*composuit*".[4] On occasion, from the third quarter of the thirteenth century, an ecclesiastic identifies himself as the *notarius*.[5] With the exception of the notaries[6], however, there are no references to scribes in the witness lists in either Hospitaller or

---

1 Note that full bibliographical references for the short titles or abbreviations used throughout to identify sources, both published and unpublished, appear at the end of this paper.

2 The Documents of Early England Data Set, or DEEDS Project, was established at the University of Toronto in 1975 (http://www.utoronto.ca/deeds). During the course of the past decade, its main objective has been to develop a computer programme for dating undated private charters. To this end, a database of dated charters has been established for the period 1066–1307, when approximately 92% of all private charters were issued without dates. Dates are determined from a comparison of vocabulary in the undated document with dated counterparts in the database. The authors encourage others to test Michael Margolin's beta version of the programme, which can be accessed at <http://res.deeds.utoronto.ca:49838/research/bin/chroneval.html>.

3 *St Paul's*, no. 198; *St John, Oxford,* v. 2, no. 621; *PC,* nos. 19, 70; *SC*, nos. 698, 940; *Oseney*, v. 2, no. 986.

4 Nero E VI, fo. 172*v*; Nero C IX, fo. 39*v.*

5 Nero E VI, fo.158*v* (? c. 1250); *PC* no. 95 (1269); *Reg. Ant.*, v. 8, no. 2366 (1272/3); *Finchale*, no. 80 (1279).

6 The office of notary first occurs in the DEEDS database in 1188, when Robert, "notario decanis" witnesses a charter of John of Oxford, bishop of Norwich (*Dodnash*, no. 4, pp. 35–7), and among the Hospitaller charters c. 1250 (Nero E VI, fo. 158*v*). See also

database sources after c. 1272.[7] The date[8] corresponds to the beginning of the reign of Edward I, whose revisions to the common law were extensive.

The charters provide very little information about the scribes, other than their names and occupation. Among the Hospitaller documents, they appear only in the witness lists, sometimes identified with their occupation, sometimes not. The DEEDS database finds two occurrences of scribes issuing charters; one in 1233 conveying a house and land in Oxford, owing an annual fee of 10s, in exchange for £9/9/8[9], and another in 1276, also in Oxford, concerning an annual rental of 4s.[10] Other non-Hospitaller documents find scribes referred to as holders or previous holders of tenements, always in major towns[11], from before 1141 to before 1278.[12] Clerics identifying themselves as notaries appear in the same context.[13] The town-based domicile of these individuals points to the urban setting of their trade.

Eighteen of the twenty-nine charters in the Hospitaller cartularies which mention scribes are either grants to, or directly concern, that Order. Two others were issued to the Templars.[14] The rest refer almost certainly to property which belonged, or eventually came, to the Hospitallers.[15] Sixteen of the scribes bear the title *capellanus, clericus* or *diaconus*. Walter de Hull witnesses a Bumpstead Helion (Hinckford Hd., Essex) charter as "clerico magistri" c. 1185 and may, in fact, have been the clerk of the English prior[16], but there is no sure proof that he, or any of the scribes recorded as having written Hospitaller charters, were themselves members of the Order. Answers to the question "Who, then, were they?" will remain partly hypothetical, but context provides some insights.

Stephanus de Esseleia (Esseleya/Essele), "qui hoc scripsit", appears as the final witness in an authentication issued in London by William of Oxford, bishop of London, to the Hospitallers in 1219.[17] He is very likely the scribe of the bishop rather than of the Order, however, as he is also witness to a number of other charters

---

C. R. Cheney, *Notaries Public in England in the Thirteenth and Fourteenth Centuries*, Oxford: Clarendon Press, 1972, esp. p. 23.

7 *PC* no. 103 for the latest Hospitaller reference; *Reg. Ant.,* v. 8, no. 2366 for non-Hospitaller, dated 1272–73. Expanded non-Hospitaller: *St John, Oxford* v. 2, no. 897 (1271–72).

8 Of the Hospitaller charters in which a scribe is mentioned, only four can be securely dated: *PC* no. 95 (1269); *SC* no. 46 (1200–1204); Nero E VI, fo. 84*v* (1219); Nero E VI, fo. 172*v* (1257–58). Dates for the rest have been determined from internal evidence and through the use of the DEEDS interactive Dating Program (see supra n. 2).

9 *Oseney*, v. 1, no. 329.

10 *St John, Oxford*, v. 2, no. 863.

11 Derby, Gloucester and Oxford [Oxford: *St John, Oxford*, v. 1, nos. 31, 127].

12 *St John, Oxford*, v. 1, no. 292; *Oseney,* v. 1, no. 371, v. 2, no. 924; *Sancti Petri*, v. 2, no. 807; *Hereford*, no. 5; *Darley*, p. 505.

13 *St John, Oxford*, v. 1, no. 129 (Oxford, 1287–88).

14 *PC* no. 19 (c. 1190–1200), no. 103 (c. 1270–80).

15 *SC* no. 707 is a grant to Simon of Odewell, who, in 1242, granted the bulk, if not all of his lands and rents to the Hospitallers. See also *SC* xlii–xliii.

16 The clerk Walter de Hull is the scribe of *SC* no. 538.

17 Nero E VI, fo. 84*v*.

issued by Bishop William concerning, and issued at, Waltham Holy Cross in 1218[18], and at St. Osyth in 1220[19], which have nothing to do with the Order. Another fairly obvious outsider is Master Phillip, "medicus", the scribe of an early thirteenth-century document concerning the annual rent of 6s/8d owed by the Hospitallers for the manor of "Nortoft" (Northants).[20]

While some of the scribes who copied for the Order or its benefactors were probably garnered locally, the appearance of others serving as scribes or witnesses to documents concerning places at considerable distances from each other suggests either that they were itinerant, or that scribal activity was centralized and that they worked in established scriptoria. C. 1240, Robert of Stisted (Hinckford Hd., Essex) copies a Gestingthorpe (Hinckford Hd., Essex) charter, and witnesses nearly contemporary charters for Gestingthorpe and neighbouring Halstead.[21] Towards the middle of the thirteenth century, the chaplain Peter of Codham (Essex) occurs as a witness to a charter concerning Gestingthorpe, written by Peter of Halstead who is also a chaplain, and local.[22] In what appears to be an approximately contemporary document, the same Peter of Codham is recorded as the scribe for a charter conveying land and a messuage in Hampton (Middlesex).[23] Similarly, c. 1255 William son of Derkin copies both a Bumpstead Helion (Essex) document and another which deals with a grant to the Order in Harefield (Middlesex).[24] This latter Peter, and William, had a wider scope and may have worked in the London area.

The twenty five scribes appearing in the Hospitaller cartularies are all found in charters which concern only the counties of Cambridgeshire (2), Essex (17)[25], Lincolnshire (1), Middlesex (6), Surrey (2) and Sussex (1). This rather limited geographical distribution points to a concentration of scribal activity in the counties around London, and to a group of professionals who were identified with their trade. None of the charters bearing names of scribes give any indication that they were copied at the Order's head priory in the London suburb of Clerkenwell. The expression "datum apud" ("issued at") does not occur in the database before 1198[26], or among the Hospitaller charters before 1205[27], suggesting a significant development in diplomatic procedure at the very end of the reign of Richard I. It does not occur in the context of Clerkenwell until 1312[28], an indication, perhaps, that the Order did not maintain a scriptorium there before the fourteenth century. Earlier dates appear

18 *Waltham*, no. 216.

19 *St John, Colchester*, v. 1, pp. 89–90.

20 Nero E VI, fo. 118*r-v*.

21 *SC* nos. 708, 734, 787.

22 *SC* no. 541.

23 Nero E VI, fo. 171*r*.

24 William son of Derkin occurs five more times as witness to Essex charters in Cotton MS Nero E VI, concerning Bumpstead Helion (*SC* nos. 462, 465, 466), Radwinter (*PC* no. 170) and Gestingthorpe (*SC* no. 699).

25 Essex holdings represent about a third of all the documents in BL Cotton MSS Nero C IX and E VI, hence the apparently large number of scribes appearing among them.

26 *Oseney*, v. 4, no. 425b; *Constance*, Appendix, p. 91 (1199–1200).

27 Nero E VI, fo. 181*r*.

28 Nero E VI, fo. 14*r*.

in conjunction with the Order's Chapter meetings in the provincial preceptories: at Hampton (Middx.) in 1257–60[29], and Melchbourne (Beds.), in 1277 and 1281[30], and with the northern Essex preceptory of Little Maplestead (Hinckford Hd., Essex), from 1275[31], suggesting that a significant activity of the Chapter meeting, held twice yearly, was the issuance of charters. But, if "datum apud" means that the charter was physically issued at the place mentioned, the numerous cases in which charters were issued in parishes beside a preceptory, rather than at it, confirm that there was no need for the parties concerned to be present at a Chapter meeting, or at one of the Order's rural administrative centres, to have the document written. Taking the Little Maplestead preceptory as an example, we find charters being "datum apud" the neighbouring parishes of Gestingthorpe in 1297[32], Halstead in 1274[33], Hedingham Castle in 1260–72,[34] and Toppesfield in 1294.[35] It is, however, in the witness lists of charters concerning Gestingthorpe/Little Maplestead and Hampton/Tolworth that the names of scribes occur most frequently. Five scribes each lend their names to Gestingthorpe/Little Maplestead documents from c. 1225 to 1245[36], and to those for Hampton/Tolworth from c. 1240 to 1258.[37] It is during these periods that two-thirds of the references to scribes appear among the charters from the Hospitaller cartularies.

Only twice, among all the charters both Hospitaller and non-Hospitaller, is any person involved in its preparation cited in a document in which the place of issue is specified:

1. *Iohanne clerico qui hanc cartam composuit et aliis; datum apud Hampton in die Sancti Michaelis anno ab incarnacione Domini millesimo cc lvii et anno regni Regis Henrici filii Iohannis xlii* (1257/8).[38]
2. *Stephano de Esseleia qui hoc scripsit et aliis; datum London' anno domini millesimo ducentesimo nonodecimo* .... (1219).[39]

Were the scribes of a lesser level of legal competence than the notaries who, from the mid-thirteenth century, appear increasingly in the role of those who wrote,

29 Nero E VI, fo. 172*r*; Nero E VI fo. 172*v*; Nero E VI, fos. 172*v*-173*r*.

30 *SC* nos. 250, 480. The Hospitallers held Chapter meetings at Melchbourne from at least the mid-thirteenth century, probably twice yearly at Michaelmas and Easter (*PC* no. 204 and p. lxxii).

31 *SC* nos. 41, 136, 140, 144–45, 187, 551, 642.

32 *SC* no. 819.

33 *SC* no. 638.

34 *SC* nos. 37, 49, 149.

35 *SC* no. 27.

36 Peter of Halstead, chaplain (*SC* no. 541), Reginald, clerk (*SC* no. 698), Robert of Stisted (*SC* no. 734), William de Rendfr' (*SC* no. 707) and William of Selston (*SC* no. 155).

37 John, clerk (Nero E VI, fo. 170*r*, 172*v*), Peter of Codham, chaplain (Nero E VI, fo. 171*r*), Thomas, clerk (Nero E VI, fo. 179*v*), Walter, clerk (Nero E VI, fo. 180*r*), William, chaplain (Nero E VI, fo. 173*v*-174*r*).

38 Nero E VI, fo. 172*v*.

39 Nero E VI, fo. 84*v*.

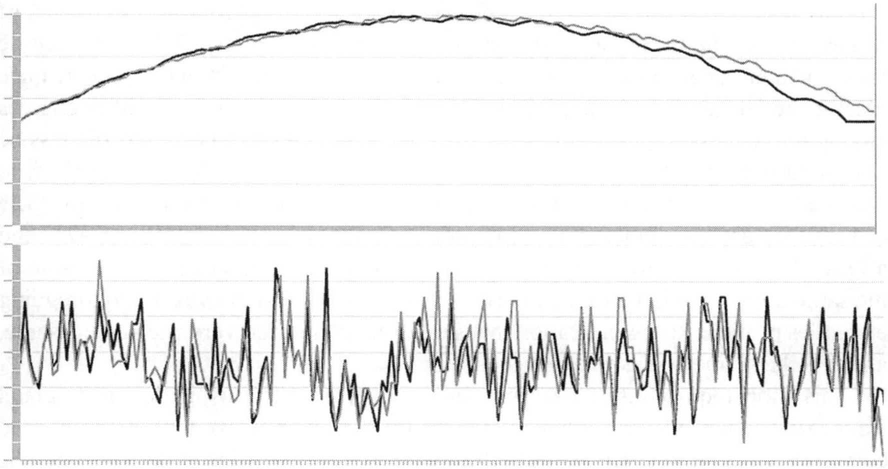

Graph 1 QSUM and EMCL results for William son of Derkin

made or composed charters? As we have seen, the association of the scribe with the preparation of the charter is replaced by that of the notary after 1272. Scribes are sometimes, but by no means always, clerks or chaplains. Notaries are always identified as ecclesiastics, indicating in general a higher degree of learning and preparation. One would imagine that notaries had more responsibility than scribes for drawing up conveyances, although a reference in a non-Hospitaller charter from Oxford in 1258 to the notary Thomas de Sancto Germano "fideliter transcripsi nichil addens" indicates that he was, in this case at least, no more than a copyist.[40]

The trail is difficult to follow, but the application of computational stylometry techniques to Hospitaller charters produces additional evidence of scribal identity.[41] A combination of two independent authorship attribution techniques, Cumulative Sum (QSUM) and Entropy for Markov Chains of Letters (EMCL), was applied to groups of Hospitaller documents bearing references to the same scribes. As an example, the congruence of QSUM (85%) and EMCL (91%) for William son of Derkin (Fig. 1), who c. 1255 is the scribe of a Hospitaller charter concerning Bumpstead Helion (Essex) and the last witness of another (Appendix: 1 and 2)[42], is a strong indicator of common authorship.[43]

40 *Oseney,* v. 5, no. 625a.

41 The main assumption of stylometric studies is that authors have an unconscious as well as a conscious aspect to their style. Measuring and counting stylistic traits captures variations which are specific to a given author's style. See D. V. Khmelev, "Disputed Authorship Resolution through Using Relative Empirical Entropy for Markov Chains of Letters", *Journal of Quantitative Linguistics*, 7/3(2000), pp. 201–207; Jill M. Farringdon, with contributions by A. Q. Morton, M. G. Farringdon, and M. D. Baker, *Analyzing for Authorship: A Guide to the Cusum Technique*, Cardiff, 1996.

42 *SC* nos. 462 and 512.

43 The scribal attribution programme for medieval Latin charters uses lexically based techniques paired with statistical analyses to identify the "richness" and "diversity" of a

Similar results (EMCL: 67% and QSUM: 63%) occur c. 1230–40 for Robert of Stisted, the scribe of *SC* no. 734 and the last witness in *SC* no. 787.[44] Stephen de Esseleia, mentioned above as a scribe working for the bishop of London, occurs once among the Hospitaller cartularies as the scribe,[45] and three times in other sources among the witnesses, but never as the final witness. Authorship can nevertheless be attributed to him in three of the four cases.[46] The numbers for John the clerk, who was the "scriptor" of Nero E VI, fo. 170r and who "composuit" Nero E VI, fo. 172v c. 1255–60, are less indicative of common authorship, with an EMCL of 97% and a QSUM of 66%. Unfortunately, we have no two documents bearing the name of the same notary available for comparison. For the most part, however, the foregoing examples provide strong indication that scribe and composer were one and the same, and that the scribe was not merely a copyist.

This short inquiry into the scribes who worked for the Hospitallers in England leads to the conclusion that although few, if any, were members of the Order, they had composed what they copied. None of the documents issued by the Order itself include references to scribes or notaries, yet those charters are more likely to have issued from the Hospitallers' own scriptorium, wherever that might have been. Individuals who made grants to the Order, or conveyed property in some way connected to it, would seem to have used the services of local scribes working independently. What that service comprised, however, remains a moot question. One might think that they were working from formularies,[47] but each document is so unique in itself that there was clearly a significant degree of original composition included in each. It seems sure that, at least for the charters in the Hospitaller cartularies, scribes and notaries were not just filling in the blanks.

---

scribe's vocabulary. A beta version of the programme for the attribution of scribal identity in medieval English charters using stylometry has been developed by Michael Margolin at the DEEDS Project. It may be consulted and used at: <http://res.deeds.utoronto.ca:49838/research/bin/anlw.html>

44 Robert of Stisted also occurs as the final witness in *SC* no. 708, for which the stylometric evidence is less indicative of common authorship.

45 Nero E VI, fo. 84*v*.

46 Nero E VI, fo. 84*v* and *St. John, Colchester* nos. 89 and 90; but not *Waltham* no. 216.

47 H. Hall, *A Formula Book of English Official Historical Documents*, vol. 1: *Diplomatic Documents*, Cambridge, 1908; T. Madox, *Formulare Anglicanum*, London: Tonson and Knaplock, 1702; S. C. Ratcliff, A. J. Collins, B. Schofield (eds), *Legal and Manorial Formularies / edited from originals at the British Museum and the Public Record Office: in memory of Julius Parnell Gilson*, Oxford, 1933.

Table 1: Scribes Appearing in the Hospitaller Cartularies

Date	Name	Location	Phrase	Reference
1250 c.*	Adam diaconus de Angemare	Angmering, Sx	presentis scripti notario	Nero E VI, fo. 158*v*
1180 c.	Adam scriptor	Whitewell, Ess	scriptore	*SC* no. 294
1250 c.*	Edmundus	Ely, Ca	qui hanc cartam scripsit	Nero C IX, fo. 31*r*-*v*
1190 c.	Hamelinus clericus	Roydon, Ess	qui hanc cartam fecit	*PC* no. 19
1200–1204	Hugo capellanus	Hatfield Peverel, Ess	presentis carte scriptore	*SC* no. 46
1155 c.	Hugo scriptor	Henham, Ess	scriptore	*SC* no. 394
1240 c.	Iohannes clericus	Aveley, Ess	qui hanc quietam clamanciam fecit	*PC* no. 70
1255 c.*	Iohannes clericus	Hampton, Middx	scriptore huius carte	Nero E VI, fo. 170*r*
1257–1258	Iohannes clericus	Hampton, Middx	qui hanc cartam composuit	Nero E VI, fo. 172*v*
1255 c.*	Iohannes de Shryneham clericus	Chippenham, Ca	qui presens scriptum composuit	Nero C IX, fo. 39*v*
1205 c.*	Philippus medicus, magister	Nortoft, Northants	qui hanc cartam scripsit	Nero E VI, fo. 118*r*-*v*
1269 –	Nicholaus clericus	Wennington, Ess	huius scripti notario	*PC* no. 95
1250 c.*	Petrus capellanus de Codham	Hampton, Middx	qui hanc cartam scripsit	Nero E VI, fo. 171*r*
1235–1245	Petrus capellanus de Halstede	Gestingthorpe, Ess	qui hanc cartam scripsit	*SC* no. 541
1280 c.	Radulphus de Boughton	Farringdon, Ess	presencium scriptore	*PC* no. 103
1245 c.	Reginaldus clericus	Gestingthorpe, Ess	qui hanc cartam fecit	*SC* no. 698
1230 c.	Robertus de Stistede	Gestingthorpe, Ess	qui hanc cartam scripsit	*SC* no. 734
1255 c.	Simon clericus	Great Sampford, Ess	qui hanc cartam fecit	*SC* no. 940
1219 –	Stephanus de Esseleia	Harefield, Middx	qui hoc scripsit	Nero E VI, fo. 84*v*
1250 c.*	Thomas clericus	Tolworth, Sr	qui hanc cartam scripsit	Nero E VI, fo. 179*v*
1190–1200	Walterus	Sawbridgeworth, Ess	qui cartam scripsit	*SC* no. 319
1230 c.	Walterus clericus	Bumpstead Helion, Ess	huius scripti scriptore	*SC* no. 523
1255 c.*	Walterus clericus	Tolworth, Sr	scriptore huius carte	Nero E VI, fo. 180*r*
1185 c.	Walterus de Hull clerico magistri	Great Baddow, Ess	qui hanc cartam scripsit	*SC* no. 538
1240 c.*	Willelmus capellanus	Hampton, Middx	qui hanc cartam scripsit	Nero E VI, fo. 173*v*-174*r*
1225 –	Willelmus de Rendfr'	Gestingthorpe, Ess	scriptore huius carte	*SC* no. 707
1220–1230	Willelmus de Salsetun	Little Maplestead, Ess	qui scripsit hanc cartam	*SC* no. 155
1255 c.*	Willelmus filius Derkini	Harefield, Middx	qui hanc cartam scripsit	Nero E VI, fo. 85*v*-86*r*
1255 c.*	Willelmus filius Derkini	Bumpstead Helion, Ess	qui hanc cartam scripsit	*SC* no. 512

Note: Dates followed by an asterisk were calculated through the Dating Programme developed at the DEEDS Project by Michael Margolin (http://res.deeds.utoronto.ca:49838/research/bin/chroneval.html); the rest were determined from internal information.

Table 2: Scribes Appearing in the DEEDS Database

Date	Name	Location	Datum apud	Phrase	Reference
1188–1189	A. capellanus	?		qui scripsit hanc cartam	*Sandford,* v. 1, no. 448.
1163	Adam	Shiplake, O	Creendon?	presentis carte scriptore	*Missenden,* v. 1, no. 667.
1176–1182	Alexander de fonte clericorum	?		qui hanc cartam scripsit	*St Mary,* no. 228.
1224	David filius Asseri	Hampton Gay, O		fecit hanc convencionem	*Oseney,* v. 2, no. 986
1234	Galfridus capellanus	Eccles, La	Susam?	qui has literas scripsit	*Whalley,* v.1, p. 37
1190	Henricus clericus	Benning-borough, YN	Leicester, Le	qui hanc cartam scripsit	*Yorkshire,* no. 551
1272–73	Henricus de Romes clericus	Oxford, O		qui hanc cartam fecit	*St John, Oxford,* v. 2, no. 621
1177–78	Iohannes clericus	?		scriptore videlicet carte	*St Bees,* no. 2202.
1279	Iohannes clericus	Giggleswick, YW		huius scripti notario	*Finchale,* no. 80.
1208	Lodovicus clericus	North Luffenham, Ru		qui hanc cartam scripsit	*Beauchamp,* no. 226.
1174–76	Godardus scriptor, magister	Oxendon, Np		scriptore huius carte	*Cirencester,* v. 2, no. 709
1191	Iohannes de Uffenton, magister	?	Lichfield, St	qui hanc cartam scripsit	*Burscough,* no. 164
1189–1191	Robertus, magister	Isle of Wight		qui hanc cartam scripsit	*Devon,* no. 66
1192	Nicholaus de Well'	Little Packington, Wa	Coventry, Wa	qui hanc cartam scripsit	*Worcester,* no. 310
1197–1198	Ricardus	Essex		qui hoc scripsit	*Colne,* no. 104
1189–1191	Ricardus Aaron	[General confirmation]	Bristol, Gl	qui scripsit hec	*St Augustine's,* no. 23.
1272–73	Robertus clericus	Lincoln, Li		presencium notario	*Reg. Ant.,* v.8, no. 2366
1218	Rogerus	Lambourne, Ess	Waltham, Ess	qui hoc scripsit	*Waltham,* no. 216.
1167	Rogerus capellanus	Broughton, Bk	Gurnay, Bk	qui hanc cartam scripsit	*Missenden,*v. 1, no. 556.
1167	Rogerus capellanus	Broughton, Bk		qui hanc cartam scripsit	*Missenden,*v. 1, no. 561.
1192	Salomon	Periton?		qui cartam scripsit	*Malmesbury,* no. 137.
1106	Simon scriptor	London		scriptor qui brevem fecit	*St Paul's,* no. 198.
1175	Walterus capellanus de Stoch	Holford, So		qui hanc cartam scripsit	*Stogursey,* no. 12
1191–1192	Willelmus clericus	?		qui hanc cartam scripsit	*St Denys,* no. 336.
1243	Willelmus de Gertinton, clericus	Rothwell, Np		presentis scriptore	*Cirencester,* v. 2, no. 698

Date	Name	Location	Datum apud	Phrase	Reference
1258	Willelmus de Cokebyr, capellano	Mercer Row, Gl		huius carte scriptore	*St Peter's, no. 301.*
1238–39	Willelmus de Notingham, clerico	Ampleforth, YN		qui hoc cyrographum scripsit	*York Minster,* no. 17

Short Title Bibliographical References for Primary Sources

Beauchamp	E. Mason, ed. *Beauchamp Cartulary, 1100–1268*. London: Pipe Roll Society, N.S., v. 43, 1980.
Burscough	A. N. Webb, ed. *An edition of the cartulary of Burscough Priory*. Manchester: Published for the Chetham Society by Manchester University Press, 1970.
Cirencester	C. D. Ross, ed. *The Cartulary of Cirencester Abbey, Gloucestershire*. 3 vols. London: Oxford University Press, 1964.
Colne	J. Fisher, ed. *Cartularium Prioratus de Colne*. Colchester: Essex Archaeological Society, Occasional Publications; no. 1, 1946.
Constance	J. Everard and Michael Jones, (eds) *The Charters of Duchess Constance of Brittany and her Family, 1171–1221*. Suffolk, England; Rochester, NY, USA: Boydell Press, 1999.
Darley	Reginald R. Darlington, ed. *The Cartulary of Darley Abbey*. Highgate: Kendal, 1945.
Devon	R. Bearman, ed. *Charters of the Redvers family and the Earldom of Devon, 1090–1217*. Exeter, England: Devon and Cornwall Record Society, 1994.
Dodnash	Christopher Harper-Bill, ed. *Dodnash Priory Charters*. Woodbridge: Boydell & Brewer, Suffolk Records Society, Suffolk Charters, XVI, 1998.
Finchale	James Raine, ed. *The Charters of Endowment, inventories, and account rolls of the Priory of Finchale*. London: J.B. Nichols and Son, 1837.
Hereford	David Walker, ed. *Camden Miscellany, vol. XXII. Charters of the Earldom of Hereford, 1095–1201*. London: Royal Historical Society, 1964.
Malmesbury	J. S. Brewer, ed. *The Register of Malmesbury Abbey*. London: Longman, 1879–80.
Missenden	J. G. Jenkins, ed. *Cartulary of Missenden Abbey*. 3 vols. London: Buckinghamshire Records Society, 1938–62.
Nero C IX	British Library Cotton MS. Nero C IX.
Nero E VI	British Library Cotton MS. Nero E VI.
Oseney	J. E. Salter, ed. *Cartulary of Oseney Abbey*. 6 vols. Oxford: Oxford Historical Society, 1929–36.
PC	Michael Gervers, ed. *The Cartulary of the Knights of St. John of Jerusalem in England, Part 2, Prima Camera*. London: The British Academy, 1996.

Reg. Ant.	C. W. Foster, ed. *Registrum Antiquissimum of the Cathedral Church of Lincoln*. 10 vols. Hereford: Lincoln Record Society, 1931.
SC	Michael Gervers, ed. *The Cartulary of the Knights of St. John of Jerusalem in England, Part 1, Secunda Camera*. London: The British Academy, 1982.
Sancti Petri	William Henry Hart, ed. *Historia et Cartularium Monasterii Sancti Petri Gloucestriae*. 3 vols. London: Longman, 1865.
Sandford	Agnes M. Leys, ed. *Sandford Cartulary*. 2 vols. Oxford: Oxfordshire Record Society, 1938.
Stogursey	T. D. Tremlett and Noel Blakiston, (eds) *Stogursey Charters*. Frome, England: Butler & Tanner, 1949.
St Augustine's	David Walker, ed. *The Cartulary of St Augustine's Abbey, Bristol*. Gloucester, England: Bristol and Gloucestershire Archaeological Society, 1998.
St Bees	J. Wilson, ed. *The Register of the Priory of St Bees*. Durham: Surtees Society, v. 126, 1915.
St Denys	E. O. Blake, ed. *Cartulary of the Priory of St. Denys near Southampton*. 2 vols. Southampton, England: University Press, 1981.
St John, Colchester	S. A. Moore, ed. *Cartularium Monasterii Sancti Johannis Baptiste de Colecestria*. 2 vols. London: Chiswick Press, 1897.
St John, Oxford	H. E. Salter, ed. *A Cartulary of the Hospital of St. John*. 3 vols. Oxford: Oxford Historical Society, 1914–17.
St Mary	W. O. Hassal, ed. *Cartulary of St Mary Clerkenwell*. London: Royal Historical Society, 1949.
St Paul	Marion Gibbs, ed. *Early Charters of the Cathedral Church of St. Paul, London*. London: Royal Historical Society, 1939.
St Peter's	R. Patterson, ed. *The Original Acta of St Peter's Abbey, Gloucester, 1122–1263*. Gloucester, England: Bristol and Gloucestershire Archaeological Society, 1998.
Waltham	Rosalind Ransford, ed. *The Early Charters of the Augustinian Canons of Waltham Abbey, Essex, 1032–1230*. Woodbridge, Suffolk ; Wolfeboro, N.H., USA: Boydell Press, 1989.
Whalley	W. A. Hulton, ed. *The coucher book or chartulary of Whalley Abbey*. 4 vols. Manchester: Printed for the Chetham Society, 1847–49.
Worcester	R. R. Darlington, ed. *The cartulary of Worcester Priory Cathedral, Register I*. London: Pipe Roll Society, 1968.
York Minster	C. T. Clay, ed. *York Minster Fasti*. The Yorkshire Archaeological Society, Record Series v. 123, 1958–9.
Yorkshire	William Farrer, ed. *Early Yorkshire Charters*. Edinburgh: Ballantyne, Hanson, 1914–16.

Appendix
Documents Displaying Common Authorship Using EMCL and QSUM Techniques

1. William son of Derkin as Last Witness and Scribe (SC no. 512)

Sciant presentes et futuri quod ego Thomas Merveile dedi, concessi et hac carta mea confirmavi Simoni filio Gilberti, pro homagio et servicio suo et pro duodecim solidis sterlingorum quos ipse michi dedit in gersummam, unam acram et dimidiam terre sicut iacet in Webecroft de feodo hospitalis Ierusalem et extendit se de essarto Michaelis filii Iocii usque ad cheminum quod iacet ante portam Reginaldi agricole. Habendas et tenendas illi et heredibus suis vel cuicumque dare vendere assignare vel delegare voluerit et heredibus suis preter religionem de me et heredibus meis in feodo et hereditarie, libere et quiete, bene et in pace. Reddendo inde annuatim michi et heredibus meis ille et heredes sui vel eius assignati quatuor denarios et obolum ad duos terminos anni, scilicet ad festum sancti Michaelis duos denarios et unum quadrantem et ad Pascha duos denarios et quadrantem, pro omnibus serviciis, consuetudinibus et demandis ad me et heredes meos pertinentibus. Et ego Thomas et heredes mei warantizabimus predictum tenementum prenominato Simoni et heredibus suis vel cuicumque dare, vendere, assignare vel delegare voluerit, et heredibus suis preter religionem, contra omnes gentes imperpetuum per predictum servicium. Et in huius rei testimonium presentem cartam sigilli mei signo consignavi. Hiis testibus Ricardo de Canne, Ricardo filio Arnulfi, Roberto fratre eius, Simone de Bobelawe, Waltero coco, Galfrido Tempernoyse, Roberto de Berdfeld', Gilberto le moyne, Alano filio Galfridi, Waltero de Hewre, Iohanne de Cruce, **Willelmo filio Derkini** qui hanc cartam scripsit et multis aliis tam clericis quam laicis.

2. William son of Derkin as Last Witness (SC no. 462)

Sciant presentes et futuri quod ego Hunricus filius Galfridi Brichwold' de Hamsted', beneplacito et consensu fratris Hugonis de Fancote custodis domus hospitalis Ierusalem in Essex', dedi et quietum clamavi Willelmo filio Radulphi et heredibus suis totum ius et clamium quod habui in tribus acris terre arabilis cum mesuagio in villa de Bumsted' sicut iacent in longitudine et latitudine inter duas terras Willelmi de Hoo cum pertinentiis et abuttant super magnum cheminum ex opposito domus Galfridi Tempernoyse; preterea quietum clamavi prenominato Willelmo totum redditum cum homagio quem tenui de domo hospitalis Ierusalem in Essex in villa scilicet de Bumsted'. Habendas et tenendas has predictas acras terre arabilis cum redditibus et homagiis et omnibus consuetudinibus ad eas pertinentibus de domo hospitalis Ierusalem, illi et cui assignare voluerit in feodo hereditarie, libere et quiete; reddendo inde annuatim predicte domui pro omnibus serviciis, consuetudinibus et demandis viginti et quinque denarios ad duos terminos scilicet ad Pascha 12d et ad festum sancti Michaelis 13d. Pro hac autem donacione et reddituum cum homagio, quieta clamancia dedit michi predictus Willelmus duas marcas argenti de recognicione. Et ego prefatus Hunrichus predictam terram et predictum redditum cum homagio et omnibus pertinentiis suis pro me et pro omnibus illis qui aliquid iuris in illis per me poterunt clamare in perpetuum abiuravi. Hiis testibus domino Willelmo de Heliun, Gilberto de Bailloll', Helya de Bailloll', Philippo de Bello campo, Roberto filio Radulphi, Galfrido novo homine, Willelmo de Hoo, Gilberto de Heliun, Rogero le Utlaghe, Michaele filio Ioce, Rogero filio Bernardi, **Willelmo filio Derkini** et multis aliis.

Chapter 16

The Military Activity of the Hospitallers in the Medieval Kingdom of Hungary (Thirteenth to Fourteenth Centuries)

Zsolt Hunyadi

The following survey is based on a recently completed doctoral thesis on the Hungarian-Slavonian Hospitaller Priory up to 1387.[1] One of the main goals of the thesis was to investigate whether the sources justify the common scholarly assumption that the Hospitallers in Hungary performed significant military activities during the thirteenth and fourteenth centuries. The aim was to collect and analyse possible sources of such military activities and either to confirm this belief or to redefine it as necessary.

Although the survey traced the activities of the Hungarian-Slavonian Hospitaller Priory from the mid twelfth century onwards, the first palpable, albeit still indirect, information comes down to us from as late as the first phase of the Fifth Crusade. Before his armed pilgrimage to the Holy Land, King Andrew II (1205–35) sent the Hospitaller prior of Hungary to Venice to prepare for his embarkation in the late summer of 1217.[2] However, there is no clear sign of the participation of the Hospitallers in the Hungarian ruler's campaign. During the king's stay in the Holy Land no Hungarian Hospitallers were recorded as being present either in his entourage or in his army. His remarkable donations made in the Latin East concerned the castles of Crac des Chevaliers and Margat[3] and had no immediate reference to Hospitallers stationed in Hungary. After his return from Syria, Andrew II asked the pope to commission the Hospitallers and the Templars to guard his son, who had been sent to Armenia in 1219, but this request did not particularly concern the brethren of these military-religious orders in Hungary.[4]

1 Zs. Hunyadi, 'Hospitallers in the medieval Kingdom of Hungary, c. 1150–1387', Ph.D. thesis (Budapest, 2004). Its revised version is forthcoming.

2 *Codex diplomaticus Hungariae ecclesiasticus ac civilis*, 11 vols, ed. G. Fejér (Buda, 1829–44) (hereafter Fejér, *CD*), vol. 7/4, p. 73; *Árpádkori új okmánytár. Codex diplomaticus Arpadianus continuatus*, 12 vols, ed. G. Wenzel (Pest, 1860–74) (hereafter: *ÁUO*), vol. 6, pp. 380–3.

3 *Vetera Monumenta Historica Hungariam Sacram Illustrantia, 1216–1352*, 2 vols, ed. A. Theiner (Romae, 1859–1860), vol. 1, pp. 14–18; *ÁUO*, vol. 1, pp. 156–8; *Cartulaire général de l'Ordre des Hospitaliers de Saint-Jean de Jérusalem, 1100-1310,* ed. J. Delaville le Roulx, 4 vols (Paris, 1894–1906) (hereafter *CH*), nos. 1613–1616.

4 Fejér, *CD*, vol. 3/1, pp. 250–4; Theiner, vol. 1, pp. 20–21.

What sort of military support the Hospital provided to King Béla IV (1235–70) during the 1241–42 Mongol invasion of Hungary is also obscure.[5] It is likely that the report of Master Rogerius, in its known form, is not completely reliable as it reads that 'Upon the Mongols' retreat, King Béla came to Hungary from the coastal areas with the help of the knights of the Island of Rhodes'.[6] Other contemporary sources, however, indicate Hospitaller participation in these events. Béla IV complained in a letter to the pope, most likely in 1247,[7] that at the appearance of the Mongol menace he received help *a nullo christianorum Europe principe, nisi a domo Hospitalis Iherosolimitani, cuius fratres ad requisitionem nostram nuper arma sumpserunt contra paganos*. It is likely that the Hospitallers accompanied the king when he fled from the Mongols, down to Trau on the Dalmatian coast.[8] This hypothesis is supported by two indirect pieces of evidence. The corroborating formula of the first extant charter (1243) issued by the Székesfehérvár Hospitaller preceptory reads: *proprium sigillum nostrum erat in maritima propter metum tartarorum*; that is, the personnel of the preceptory took their common seal and perhaps their archives to the safety of the coast when the Mongols came in 1241.[9] Another charter reveals that Raimbaud of Voczon, the Hungarian-Slavonian prior, was in Trau on the Dalmatian coast as

5 Hungarian scholarly literature often cites Hospitallers who fought in the battle of Muhi but the sources clearly refer to the Templars. See, for instance, Chapter 36 of *Thomas archidiaconus, Historia Salonitana*, in A.F. Gombos (ed.), *Catalogus fontium historiae Hungariae 800–1301*, 3 vols (Budapest, 1937–43), p. 2235; J. Długosz, *Annales seu Cronicae incliti regni Poloniae. Liber septimus et octavus*, Annales Poloniae (Varsaviae, 1975), pp. 33–4.

6 '... *rex Bela marittimis de partibus per cruciferos de insula Rodi [...] de recessu Tartarorum in Hungariam venit* ...' 'Rogerii carmen miserabile,' in *Scriptores Rerum Hungaricarum*, 2 vols, ed. E. Szentpétery (Budapest, 1937–38), vol. 1, p. 596. It is clearly an anachronism to associate the Hospitallers with Rhodes in the mid-thirteenth century. Thus this is an obvious interpolation of a later hand, and noted by László Juhász, the editor of the text. It cannot be ruled out, however, that in the 'original' version *cruciferos* referred to the Hospitallers without using the phrase 'de insula Rhodi', as the Hospitallers were not present in Rhodes before 1309/10. See also P. Jackson, 'The Crusade against the Mongols (1241)', *Journal of Ecclesiastical History*, 42 (1991), 15.

7 On the dating and the background of the letter, see T. Senga, 'IV. Béla külpolitikája és a IV. Incéhez intézett "tatár-levele"' [The Foreign policy of Béla IV and his 'Mongol letter' sent to Pope Innocent IV], *Századok,* 121 (1987), 606–9.

8 E. Reiszig, *A jeruzsálemi Szent János lovagrend Magyarországon* [The Order of the Knights of St John of Jerusalem in Hungary], 2 vols (Budapest, 1925–28), vol. 1, p. 56. For the flight of the royal court, see J.R. Sweeney, '"Spurred on by the fear of Death": Refugees and Displaced Population during the Mongol Invasion of Hungary', in M. Gervers and W. Schlepp (eds), *Nomadic Diplomacy, Destruction and Religion from the Pacific to the Adriatic* (Toronto, 1994), pp. 46–8.

9 *ÁUO*, vol. 7, pp. 144–5; cf. Zs. Hunyadi, 'A székesfehérvári johannita konvent hiteleshelyi tevékenysége az Árpád-korban' [The Székesfehérvár Hospitaller convent as a place of authentication in the Árpád Age], in L. Koszta (ed.), *Capitulum I. Tanulmányok a középkori magyar egyház történetéből* (Szeged, 1998), pp. 40–1.

late as November 1243, since he witnessed a transaction there.[10] This may account for the fact that the Order appointed a general proctor in the person of a canon of the Buda collegiate chapter.[11] In the defence against the Mongols the Order must have played some kind of military role,[12] since as late as the summer of 1247 the king, perhaps remembering his father's plans between 1211 and 1225 for the Teutonic Order in the Barcaság,[13] wanted to have the Hospitallers as defenders of the south-eastern frontiers of the kingdom. Béla IV tried to settle the Hospitallers in the region called Severin as far as the River Olt. According to a letter issued in November 1247, the Hospital partially occupied it: *quos [fratres] iam partim collocavimus in loco magis suspecto, videlicet in confinio Cumanorum ultra Danubium et Bulgarorum.*[14] It is obscure, however, why the Order left the region shortly after 1250,[15] wrecking the king's defensive plans. It should be emphasized that the grant was not a genuine one, but rather a concession for occupying and populating the region, and it included the usual exemptions for would-be settlers. It resembles a contract, as it clearly sets out the military obligations of the Order: where and how many armed men they were expected to provide in case of an attack against the kingdom. The Hospitallers were to provide 100 armed brethren in the event of an attack by pagans, Bulgars and schismatics; 50 armed brethren were to be stationed in Pozsony, Moson, Sopron, Vasvár and Újvár or other places against Christian invaders; while against the Mongols they were to provide 60 *fratres* for the defence of the frontiers.[16] Some scholars regard this as a manifest military role played by the Hospital, although it is not clear whether the above plans were ever executed. Nonetheless, Pope Innocent IV provided further evidence for possible or planned Hospitaller military activities

---

10 '*Testes sunt Rambaldus preceptor domus Hospitalis per totam Hungariam ...*' *Codex diplomaticus regni Croatiae, Dalmatiae ac Slavoniae.* Diplomatički zbornik kraljevine Hrvatske, Dalmacije i Slavonije, 18 vols, ed. M. Kostrenčić and T. Smičiklas (Zagreb, 1904–98) (hereafter Smičiklas), vol. 4, pp. 205–6.

11 *ÁUO*, vol. 7, pp. 144–5.

12 For a general observation, see H. Nicholson, 'The Knights Hospitaller on the Frontiers of the British Isles', in J. Sarnowsky (ed.), *Mendicants, Military Orders, and Regionalism in Medieval Europe*, (Aldershot, 1999), p. 55.

13 See A. Forey, *The Military Orders from the Twelfth to the Early Fourteenth Centuries* (London, 1992), pp. 34–5; see also H. Zimmermann, 'Der deutsche Ritterorden in Siebenbürgen', in J. Fleckenstein and M. Hellmann (eds), *Die geistlichen Ritterorden Europas*, Vorträge und Forschungen 26, (Sigmaringen, 1980), 261–98; J. Fleckenstein and M. Hellmann, *Der Deutsche Orden im Burzenland: eine diplomatische Untersuchung*, Studia Transylvanica 26 (Köln-Weimar-Wien, 2000); J. Laszlovszky and Z. Soós, 'Historical Monuments of the Teutonic Order in Transylvania,' in Zs. Hunyadi and J. Laszlovszky (eds), *The Crusades and the Military Orders: Expanding the Frontiers of Medieval Latin Christianity* (Budapest, 2001), pp. 319–36.

14 Fejér *CD*, vol. 4/1, pp. 447–54; *Erdélyi okmánytár. Codex diplomaticus Transsylvaniae 1023–1300*, vol. 1, ed. Zs. Jakó (Budapest, 1997), p. 191; *CH*, no. 2445.

15 Pope Innocent IV confirmed Béla IV's grant in 1250. Fejér *CD*, vol. 4/2, pp. 75–6; Theiner, vol. 1, pp. 208–11; Jakó, *Codex diplomaticus Transsylvaniae*, p. 195.

16 For comparison, see the case of Charles of Anjou with the Hospital in 1262: D. Selwood, *The Knights of the Cloister: Templars and Hospitallers in Central-Southern Occitania, 1100–1300* (Woodbridge, 1999), p. 109.

when, unusually in European practice, he granted to both the Hospitallers and those who joined them fighting against the Mongols in Hungary the same indulgence that had been granted to the crusaders who won martyrdom against the infidel in the Holy Land.[17]

A few years later, following the fall of the Latin Empire, Emperor Baldwin II sought to win Pons de Fay, the Hungarian-Slavonian prior, to provide military assistance for the recovery of Constantinople in 1267. But there is no evidence that a Hungarian contingent was ever sent to or stationed *in frontaria Grece.*[18]

After the turmoil that followed the extinction of the Arpadian dynasty in 1301, a long-lasting consolidation of royal power started with the triple coronation (1301, 1309, 1310) of the Angevin King Charles (Caroberto) I (1301–42).[19] It is obscure what role the Hospitallers played in this process, but there is no doubt that Pope Boniface VIII put pressure upon them to support the Angevin claimant against the Bohemian Wenceslas.[20] The Battle of Rozgony in 1312 provides another piece of evidence. According to the chronicle, after the royal standard-bearer was killed the king continued to fight under the banner of certain *cruciferi*[21] who – subsequent to the dissolution of the Templars – may have been either the Hospitallers or the

---

17 '*...familie vestre ac omnibus aliis, qui vobiscum signo crucis assumpto in Ungariam contra Tartarorum processerint feritatem, illam indulgentiam idemque privilegium elargimur, que transeuntibus in terre sancte subsidium in generali concilio sunt concessa...*', Fejér *CD*, vol. 4/1, pp. 465–7; Theiner, vol. 1, p. 206; *ÁUO*, vol. 2, pp. 205–6; *CH*, no. 2477. About the importance of the indulgence, see Luttrell, 'The Hospitaller Province of Alamania to 1428', in *Ritterorden und Region*, Ordines militares – Colloquia Torunensia Historica VIII, ed. Z.H. Nowak (Toruń, 1995), p. 29. See also Luttrell, 'The Military Orders: Further Definitions,' *Sacra Militia,* 1 (2000), 10–11; A. Forey, 'Military orders and secular warfare in the twelfth and thirteenth centuries', *Viator*, 24 (1993), p. 85.

18 *CH* no. 3252; A. Forey, 'The Military Orders and Holy wars against Christians in the thirteenth century', *English Historical Review,* 104 (1989), 3; Luttrell, 'The Hospitaller Province of *Alamania*', 29; Luttrell, 'The Hospitallers in Hungary before 1418: Problems and Sources', in Zs. Hunyadi and J. Laszlovszky (eds), *The Crusades and the Military Orders: Expanding the Frontiers of Medieval Latin Christianity* (Budapest, 2001), p. 272.

19 P. Engel, 'Az ország újraegyesítése. I. Károly küzdelmei az oligarchák ellen (1310–1323)' [The reunion of the country. The struggle of Charles I against the oligarchs (1310–1323)], in P. Engel, *Honor, vár, ispánság. Válogatott tanulmányok*, ed. E. Csukovits (Budapest, 2003), pp. 320–408; See also Gy. Kristó, 'I. Károly király harcai a tartományurak ellen' [The struggles of Charles I against the oligarchs], *Századok*, 137 (2003), 297–347.

20 Theiner, vol. 1, pp. 401–2; *Anjou-kori oklevéltár. Documenta res Hungaricas tempore regum Andegavensium illustrantia*, 22 vols. Praeside J. Kristó (Budapest–Szeged, 1990–2005) (hereafter *AOkl*), vol. 1, p. 220.

21 '*... Gurke sub vexillo regis vexillarius existens occisus est: rex sub vexillo cruciferorum pugnavit...*' *Johannes de Thurocz, Chronica Hungarorum, I, Textus*. Bibliotheca Scriptorum Medii Recentisque Aevorum, Series nova VII, ed. Gy. Kristó and E. Galántai (Budapest, 1985), chapter 117; cf. Gy. Kristó, *A rozgonyi csata* [The battle of Rozgony] (Budapest, 1978), pp. 80, 84; Gy. Kristó,, *Az Anjou-kor háborúi* [Wars of the Angevin period] (Budapest, 1988), pp. 37–8. In the former work (1978), Kristó mentions Hospitallers, while in the latter (1988) he uses the literary translation of *cruciferi* ('keresztesek'), but later in the book he still seems to identify them with the Hospitallers.

canons regular of St Stephen, that is, the Stephanites.[22] If the Hospitallers rendered effective military services to Charles I, the king would probably have supported the Order in acquiring possessions. Yet in 1317 or 1318 Charles I supported his relative, Prince Miesco of Beuthen, as prospective prior of the Hungarian-Slavonian priory against Filippo of Gragnana, the candidate of the Hospital, or more precisely of Pope John XXII.[23] Moreover, it was a difficult period for both the Hungarian king and the Hospital. Charles I still struggled against provincial *potentates*, and his 'Slavonian war' proved to be lengthy. Perhaps this situation, and/or the absence of a legal prior, induced Pope John XXII to commission the archbishop of Kalocsa to appoint judges for the custody of the Hospitallers' property.[24] Difficulties proved to be ceaseless for the time being. Although the king had consolidated his position against the great provincial nobles by 1322–1323, Vrana – the former Templar headquarters now held by the Hospitallers – was besieged by the Croatians (*crohati*) in (or just before) 1328. Owing to the help of laymen, the resident brethren survived, but the fortification and the building complex suffered serious damage.[25]

Just as for the Arpadian period (up to 1301), there is much discussion about the role played by the Hospital in Hungary during Angevin rule with regard to fighting the infidel and its other military–defensive functions. There are sources that indicate that in the first third of the fourteenth century the Hospitallers took up arms not against the infidel but against the enemies of the king or in favour of their own properties (1312, 1319–20, 1328). The Hospitallers also ceased to fight against the infidel in other parts of Europe after 1320. Only in 1334 did the Hospitallers show some inclination to again play a more active role in the crusading movement. Anthony Luttrell has pointed out that this moment can be regarded as a turning point in the history of the Hospital.[26]

This change, however, did not convince either the public or the papal curia. As for the public, both royal and private land donations virtually ceased in the fourteenth century.[27] The series of secular privileges also faltered in Hungary during the reign

22 In contrast to the Western European situation, Hungarian and many Central European written sources in Latin very often use the term *crucifer* instead of the appropriate *frater hospitalis, miles Templi*, conceivably with reference to the cross they wore on their habits. This led to confusion: many scholars treated the houses and the landed properties of other orders, for instance the Order of St Anthony or the Order of the Holy Spirit, as belonging to the Hospital or the Temple, and vice versa.

23 *Registres de Jean XXII, Lettres communes analysées d'après les registres dits d'Avignon et du Vatican*, ed. G. Mollat and G. de Lesquen (Paris, 1904–20), no. 6549. See also K. Borchardt, 'The Hospitallers, Bohemia, and the Empire, 1250–1330', in J. Sarnowsky (ed.), *Mendicants, Military Orders, and Regionalism in Medieval Europe* (Aldershot, 1999), p. 225.

24 *Registres de Jean XXII*, no. 10462; *AOkl*, vol. 5, p. 232.

25 Fejér *CD*, vol. 8/3, pp. 341–3; *AOkl*, vol. 12, p. 146.

26 A. Luttrell, 'The Hospitallers of Rhodes: Prospectives, Problems, Possibilities', in J. Fleckenstein and M. Hellmann (eds), *Die Geistlichen Ritterorden Europas*, Vorträge und Forschungen 26 (Sigmaringen, 1980), p. 244.

27 Cf. the Polish situation: M. Starnawska, 'Crusade Orders on Polish Lands during the Middle Ages. Adaptation in a Peripheral Environment', *Quaestiones Medii Aevi Novae,*

of Charles I. It would be irrational to expect private gifts, which were infrequent even in the Arpadian period, to be given to an Order that was gradually losing its popularity. At the same time, papal discontent was manifest. In 1342, Pope Clement VI threatened to replace the Hospitallers with a newly founded military-religious order, if they were still reluctant to support a general papal crusade against the Turks.[28]

The calls to fight against the Turks also reached Hungary and those Hospitallers stationed here, but this was already another period: the reign of King Louis I (1342–1382). Although the new ruler also belonged to the Angevin dynasty, his accession to the throne marked the beginning of a new era in many respects, including changes in the life of the Priory. These changes became manifest during the wars against Venice and the Kingdom of Naples.[29]

There was a peculiar triangular relationship between Venice, Louis I and the Hospital in rivalry for the Dalmatian coast.[30] In July 1345 the Hungarian prior obtained the Venetians' permission to acquire oars *apud Jadram* (sc. Zara/Zadar in Dalmatia) and to export them to the Master of the Hospital (most likely to Rhodes), who had asked for these oars, on a ship that he hired from Venice, because it was stated that *ipse Prior non teneatur facere venire contra litteras a dicto Magistro, quomodo dicti remi illuc sint conducti.*[31] By the time the transaction was made, war had broken out in the Dalmatian coastal area, including Zara.[32] During this war the Venetians believed that they were on the same side as the Hungarian Hospitallers. Their error was based on the fact that the Hungarian-Slavonian Priory belonged to the Italian *langue* and was thus linked to the Priory of Venice.[33] The 'good relations' were spoiled when the Croatian Mladen Subić (III) – who had been a citizen of Venice

2 (1997), 124–5, 137; M. Starnawska, *Między Jerozolimą a Łukowem. Zakony krzyżowe na ziemiach polskich w średniowieczu* [Between Jerusalem and Łuków. Military-religious orders in Medieval Poland] (Warszawa, 1999), p. 70.

28 A. Luttrell, 'The Hospitallers at Rhodes, 1306–1421', in *Crusades*, vol. 3, p. 294; Luttrell, 'The Hospitallers of Rhodes: Prospectives, Problems, Possibilities,' p. 244; H. Nicholson, *The Knights Hospitaller* (Woodbridge, 2001), p. 52.

29 As far as the Neapolitan wars are concerned, King Louis I encroached on the autonomy of the Priory (and that of the Order) by, most likely, giving the prioral title to the infamous Montreal du Bar, also known as Frà Moriale. Reiszig, vol. 1, pp. 100–12; cf. I. Miskolczy, *Magyar-olasz összeköttetések az Anjouk korában. Magyar-nápolyi kapcsolatok* [Hungarian-Italian relations in the Angevin period. Hungarian-Neapolitan relations] (Budapest, 1937), pp. 250, 252.

30 Kristó, *Az Anjou-kor háborúi*, pp. 97–115; P. Engel, *The Realm of St Stephen: A History of Medieval Hungary 895–1526* (London and New York, 2001), pp. 161–2.

31 *Diplomácziai emlékek az Anjou-korból. Acta extera Andegavensia*, 3 vols, ed. G. Wenzel (Budapest, 1874–76), vol. 2, pp. 75–6. Apparently the prior received a special licence to export oars, although generally it was prohibited to sell oars abroad.

32 Zara was under Hungarian control in 1311–12, 1345–46 and in the period 1357–1401.

33 Cf. Zs. Hunyadi, 'Hospitaller Officials of Foreign Origin in the Hungarian-Slavonian Priory: thirteenth–fourteenth century', in H.J. Nicholson and J. Burgtorf (eds), *International Mobility in the Military Orders (Twelfth to Fifteenth centuries): Travelling on Christ's Business* (Cardiff, 2006), p. 145.

since 1343[34] – was prompted by the Venetians to besiege Vrana during the winter of 1345.[35] Without adequate sources, it cannot be determined whether the Hungarian prior Pierre Cornuti (1335–48) or his lieutenant, Giovanni Latini of Perugia, made any arrangements for Vrana's defence, or whether any of them stayed at Vrana during the siege. King Louis I led his army to Zara against Venice but in 1346 he suffered an unexpected defeat, which he wanted to repair quickly.[36] This had to be postponed, however, since in the meantime Prince Andrew, the younger brother of Louis, was assassinated in Naples and Hungary reorientated its foreign policy immediately. Not much attention was paid to the report sent by the Hungarian-Slavonian vice-prior, Baudoin Cornuti (1348–74), to Nicholas of Lendva, warden of Slavonia, concerning the Venetians' military preparations against Zara in the spring of 1348.[37] By that time Pierre Cornuti was away from Hungary, although it is not known whether he left for Rhodes or if he ever arrived there. The affair with Venice in the coastal areas came to an end in 1358 through the Treaty of Zara, which in a certain respect concluded the debate over this region not only among the secular parties but also in relation to the role played by the Hospital. The Hungarian-Slavonian prior was among the witnesses on behalf of the Hungarian king,[38] while the head of the Priory of Venice, Napoleone de Tibertis, witnessed the oath of the Venetian party in San Marco in the same year.[39]

Returning to the fight against the infidel, it can be observed that, although the leaders of the Order made efforts to involve the Hungarian Hospitallers, the local brethren followed the policy of the Hungarian ruler. A full assessment of King Louis I's anti-Turkish policy would exceed the scope of the present survey, but it is worth summarizing briefly its major characteristics. During the first decade and a half of Louis I's reign the Turks were not an important concern for him. If he planned wars against the infidel, he meant the heathen Lithuanians. Fighting against the Lithuanians established Louis's fame as *rex bellator*, *athleta domini*, and *zelator fidei christianae*. These wars, nonetheless, did not involve the Hospital, as opposed to the Teutonic Order. Similarly, the first measures of Louis I against the Turks in the 1360s did not involve the Hospitallers either. Royal policy did not favour direct military activities but tried to impede Turkish expansion into the Balkans by shaping buffer zones under Hungarian control. As Ferenc Szakály has pointed out, the problem was not with Louis I's plans but rather with their implementation.[40] Western scholars have charged the *rex bellator* with the abuse of religious enthusiasm and

---

34 Wenzel, *Acta extera*, vol. 2, pp. 34–5.

35 Wenzel, *Acta extera*, vol. 2, p. 124.

36 Kristó, *Az Anjou-kor háborúi*, pp. 97–115.

37 '... *Veneti die noctuque non cessant civitatem Jadre fortificare et munire*', Smičiklas, vol. 11, pp. 444–5; *A római szent birodalmi széki Teleki család oklevéltára* [The cartulary of the Teleki family], 2 vols, ed. S. Barabás (Budapest, 1895), vol. 1, pp. 84–7.

38 Wenzel, *Acta extera*, vol. 2, pp. 501–4.

39 Wenzel, *Acta extera*, vol. 2, pp. 513–18.

40 F. Szakály, 'A török-magyar küzdelem szakaszai a mohácsi csata előtt (1365–1526)' [The periods of the Turkish-Hungarian struggle prior to the battle of Mohács (1365–1526)], in L. Rúzsás and F. Szakály (eds), *Mohács. Tanulmányok a mohácsi csata 450. évfordulója alkalmából* (Budapest, 1986), p. 15.

misuse of financial support originally dedicated to crusading activity. Louis I used the subsidies against the Turks for his own purposes expansionary by pretending to make efforts to uproot the heresy spreading in the Balkans.[41] The popes from Clement VI to Gregory XI prevailed upon the Hungarian ruler – either by bringing pressure to bear on him or by feather-bedding[42] – to become a leading figure of a *passagium generale*. In the early 1370s, Pope Gregory XI used all the means in his power to induce Louis I to fight against the infidel. Instead, the king turned against Venice in 1372–73, allying with Padua.[43] In addition, a disagreement arose between Louis I, the pope and the Hospital concerning the succession of the Hungarian prior in 1373, although Baudion Cornuti was still in office![44] This was not the only reason that prevented Louis I from providing effective help against the Turks, but it certainly made diplomatic relations tenser than before. Eventually, the pope seemed to lose hope over the participation of the Hungarian ruler in a land crusade. Gregory XI again began to prefer the organization of a naval force in which the Hospitallers had a share. He called the Order in December 1375 to recruit a contingent of more than 400 knights, including one and a half dozen brethren from the Hungarian-Slavonian Priory.[45] It is not known, however, whether they played an active role, that is, whether they took part in any *passagium* at all. All that is known is that Hesso Schlegelholtz, preceptor of Rottweil and Freiburg-im-Breisgau, was sent to Hungary to advance the crusading movement, but in the end he failed to reconcile the quarrel between the pope and Louis I over the succession of the Hungarian-Slavonian prior. Thus the cooperation was cancelled.[46] Perhaps it was because of this situation that King Louis I did not encourage the local Hospitallers to fight against the infidel. The menace of the Turks was still far from the frontiers of Hungary in the first half of Louis's rule, and the issue did not belong to the main problems of Hungarian foreign policy.

Perhaps Hungarian Hospitallers participated in crusades by joining a *passagium* individually or in smaller groups. According to a recently discovered letter from Rhodes, Hungarians served in the army of King Peter I of Cyprus at the siege of Antalya in 1361.[47] In this letter, James of Panyit mentions that he had received news from Hungary. Thus it is likely that there were other Hungarians arriving in Rhodes. From 1351 at the latest, there may have been a hospice of the Hungarian prior at their

41 N. Housley, 'King Louis the Great of Hungary and the Crusades, 1342–1382', *The Slavonic and East European Review*, 62 (1984), 207–8.

42 For example, Theiner vol. 1, pp. 658, 697–8.

43 Cf. A. Luttrell, 'Gregory XI and the Turks: 1370–1378', *Orientalia Christiana Periodica*, 46 (1980), 395–6.

44 Hunyadi, 'Hospitaller Officials', p. 146.

45 Theiner, vol. 2, pp. 155–6; J. Delaville Le Roulx, *Les Hospitaliers à Rhodes jusqu'à la Mort de Philibert Naillac: 1310–1421* (Paris, 1913; reprint: London, 1974), p. 188; Luttrell, 'The Hospitallers at Rhodes', p. 301; Luttrell, 'Gregory XI and the Turks', p. 409.

46 A. Luttrell, 'Intrigue, Schism, and Violence among the Hospitallers of Rhodes: 1377–1384', *Speculum*, 41 (1966), 35; Luttrell, 'Gregory XI and the Turks', p. 408.

47 P. Engel, 'A török-magyar küzdelmek legrégebbi fejezete? (Egy magyar lovag levele Rhodoszról 1361-ból)', [The earliest chapter of the Turkish-Hungarian struggle? The letter of a Hungarian knight from Rhodes] in F. Glatz (ed.), *Szomszédaink között Kelet-Európában. Emlékkönyv Niederhauser Emil 70. születésnapjára* (Budapest, 1993), pp. 33–40.

disposal.[48] Moreover, Ede Reiszig explained Prior Baudoin's long absence by stating that he left the priory for Rhodes in July 1364 and came back as late as the beginning of 1370. This explanation cannot be confirmed as Reiszig referred to the exact date of the charter of 1364 but, unusually for him, he did not give the signature or the shelf-mark of the charter of Louis I in which he found this information.[49] Neither the inventory of the National Archives of Hungary[50] nor the source publications contain any charter of Louis I issued on 24 July 1364. Not even the central administration of the Order recorded the presence of Baudoin on Rhodes. On the contrary, Reiszig's theory can be refuted with the help of other extant written sources. According to a charter issued in February 1365, Baudoin stayed in the County of Dubica when he – as the count of Dubica – exempted the folk of the Pauline monastery of Dubica from various forms of taxation.[51] He also appeared in Slavonia at the end of May 1367, when he issued a charter at the preceptory of Pakrac.[52] Admittedly, there are several hiatuses in his prioral itinerary (24 June 1361–12 February 1365 and 22 May 1367–12 December 1371), but they do not include the one long hiatus suggested by Reiszig. The prior's absence could have had many different reasons, although the possibility of the war against the Turks should not be ruled out entirely.

Last but not least a certain Barraxius de Barrax should be mentioned, who applied for *ancianitas* in 1392.[53] According to this charter of the Master of the Order, Barraxius – who was most likely of Provençal origin[54] – accompanied Raymond de Beaumont not only to the Priory of Hungary but *etiam partes alias cismarinas se contulerit in eis residens*. It is hopeless to reconstruct either the exact pursuits of Barraxius in Hungary or whether he was provided a *stagia* at any of the local preceptories. The fact that he appealed for *ancianitas* implies that as a senior brother he served the Order as *miles*. Raymond de Beaumont acted as prior between 1374 and 1381,[55] and in a certain respect up to 1384. So it is probable that his compatriot stayed in the Hungarian-Slavonian priory and went to *partes alias cismarinas*, for instance, to fight the infidel at this time.[56]

---

48 For the *hospicium*, see A. Luttrell, *The Town of Rhodes, 1306–1356* (Rhodes, 2003), pp. 115, 249.

49 Reiszig, vol. 1, pp. 116–17.

50 Gy. Rácz, *A középkori Magyarország levéltári forrásainak adatbázisa. (DL-DF 4.2)* [Database of Archival Documents of Medieval Hungary], CD-ROM edition (Budapest, 2003).

51 *Alsó-Szlavóniai okmánytár (Dubicza, Orbász és Szana vármegyék). Codex diplomaticus partium regno Hungariae adnexarum (Comitatuum Dubicza, Orbász et Szana) 1244–1718,* ed. L. Thallóczy and S. Horváth (Budapest, 1912), pp. 82–3.

52 National Archives of Hungary, Budapest, *Collectio Antemohacsiana* (hereafter: MOL), Dl.8617.

53 Malta cod. 325, fol. 61v–62r.

54 B. Beaucage, *Visites générales des commanderies de l'Ordre des Hospitaliers dépendantes du Grand Prieuré de Saint-Gilles: 1338* (Aix-en-Provence, 1982), p. 200.

55 Hunyadi, 'Hospitaller Officials', pp. 146–7.

56 During the priorship of Raymond, in 1376, two other Hospitallers of unknown origin turned up: '*Philipus de Czamana magister domorum, Blvsnis magister domorum.*' I could not identify their affiliation in Hungary; MOL Df.230580.

From the written sources, therefore, there is rather limited evidence for defensive-military functions of the Hospitaller brethren in the Hungarian-Slavonian priory. Finally, the castles and fortifications pertaining to this priory should be taken into consideration. In this respect the organization of the preceptories has to be discussed.[57] On the basis of my research and critical survey, I found that the prevailing view in Hungarian scholarship[58] concerning the Hospitaller fortified sites is highly coloured. In the Arpadian period, only one fortification clearly belonged to the Order. It may have been built just after the Mongol invasion. The castle was situated at the southern corner of Margitsziget,[59] if what King Béla IV said in his letter to Pope Innocent IV is accepted, that the king – due to fear that the Mongols would return – had built castles along the Danube River before ca. 1247.[60] It is not clear where, exactly, these fortifications were situated, although scholarly literature seems to identify the one built on Margitsziget. The king also states in his letter that he gave the Hospitallers control of some of these *castra* since 'our people is inexperienced in such matters'. The above data and Béla IV's special 'devotion' toward the island support the interpretation that it was the Hospital which indeed controlled that castle for a while. The Hospitallers may have been more experienced in this respect than the majority of the Hungarians, but there are no palpable signs of their castle-building activity in Hungary.[61] In the Angevin period there was no radical change either, although there was a 'new' castle of the Priory at Bela in 1303, and another fortification was located near Pakrac (Szentiván, Trnava), though the first information about this is from the 1320s. The Hospital also took over the former Templar headquarters in Vrana, which no doubt was a huge and splendid fortification, by 1328 at the latest. These three examples still do not indicate a fundamental change in the basic activities of the Order. Several secular lords had more castles even after the consolidation of the Angevin rulership and the recovery of the royal domain. Really important changes took place only around the end of the fourteenth century. These were partly in connection with the changes in the leadership of the Priory, but, first of all, they reflected the Turkish menace. The striking increase in the number

57 For details, see Hunyadi, *Hospitallers in the medieval Kingdom of Hungary*, chapter VI.

58 Originally stated by Ede Reiszig and then by those who have based their ideas on his 2-volume monograph.

59 Margaret's Island, in the Middle Ages: *Insula Leporum* (island of the rabbits) (today Budapest).

60 Fejér *CD*, vol. 4/2, pp. 218–24; Theiner, vol. 1, pp. 230–2; Senga, 'IV. Béla külpolitikája', pp. 590–605; *A tatárjárás emlékezete* [Memory of the Mongol invasion] ed. T. Katona (Budapest, 1981), pp. 341–4; B. Nagy, ed. *Tatárjárás* [Mongol invasion] (Budapest, 2003), p. 197.

61 Accordingly, Miklós Horler's theory concerning the application of the 'knowledge' of the Hospitallers in castle building in Hungary is unfounded: cf. M. Horler, 'A johanniták és a korai magyar vártípus' [The Hospitallers and the early Hungarian castle-type], in L. Horváth (ed.), *Castrum Bene 1989, Várak a 13. században* (Gyöngyös, 1990), p. 138.

of *castra* from the second third of the fifteenth century onwards directly reflects the reaction of the Order to the growth of Ottoman power in the Balkans.[62]

62 Cf. P. Engel, 'The Estates of the Hospitallers in Hungary at the end of the Middle Ages', in Hunyadi and Laszlovszky (eds), *The Crusades and the Military Order*, pp. 293–9.

Chapter 17

The Valencian Bailiwick of Cervera in Hospitaller and Early Montesian Times, ca. 1230–ca. 1330

Luis García-Guijarro Ramos

The foundation of the Order of Montesa by papal charter on 10 June 1317 and its effective establishment in the kingdom of Valencia two years later marked a turning point in the history of the military orders in the crown of Aragon. The formal dissolution of the Temple at the Council of Vienne in 1312 posed the immediate question of the future of the Templar territories in Eastern Iberia, but the reluctance of King Jaime II of Aragon to allow the Hospitallers to increase their weight in Aragon, Catalonia and Valencia by adding Templar lands and rights to their own delayed for some years the answer to such a question. After long negotiations, Pope John XXII agreed to found a new order, which was to be centred in the kingdom of Valencia at the southern castle of Montesa, and was to receive Templar and Hospitaller properties there, while the Order of St John would be compensated with the rights and territories that the extinguished institution had held in Aragon and Catalonia.[1]

The importance of the Montesian early years lay not only in the deep restructuring of the military orders that took place in the different parts of the crown of Aragon after the extinction of the Temple, nor in the undeniable monarchical control over the new order. The great number of documents relating to Montesa produced in the order's early period has made possible a minute knowledge of different aspects of the life of this institution at the time;[2] some of the sources also provide a precious insight into the near or distant past of the areas in the kingdom of Valencia that had been in the hands of the Templars or the Hospitallers[3] (see Map 16.1). One example

1 Alan Forey, *The Fall of the Templars in the Crown of Aragon* (Aldershot, 2001), pp. 162–178; Enric Guinot Rodríguez, 'La fundación de la orden militar de Santa María de Montesa', *Saitabi*, 35 (1985), 73–86. In the kingdom of Valencia, the Hospitallers kept Torrente and their properties and rents in the city of Valencia.

2 The ample information on the number of brethren and their responsibilities form the basis of a study of the order's administrative structure at this time: Luis García-Guijarro, 'The Development of a System of Commanderies in the Early Years of the Order of Montesa, 1319–1330', in Anthony Luttrell and Léon Pressouyre (eds), *La Commanderie, institution des ordres militaires dans l'Occident médiéval* (Paris, 2002), pp. 57–73.

3 For a general view of the Hospitallers in the Kingdom of Valencia up to 1317 see: Robert I. Burns, *The Crusader Kingdom of Valencia: Reconstruction on a Thirteenth-Century*

is a valuable report dated 25 March 1320 and ordered by the recently elected second master of the order, Arnaldo de Soler.[4] Montesa had been officially launched on 22 July 1319. The first months after that date were devoted to the cumbersome processes of taking possession of the different territories and receiving the allegiance of their inhabitants.[5] This task had been perturbed by the untimely death in late September or early October 1319 of the first master, Guillermo de Eril. Nevertheless, when a Hospitaller brother, Arnaldo de Soler, was elected master in February 1320, the order was already in control of a significant part of its territories.[6] He was not an outsider; he had been Hospitaller commander of the Valencian district of Cervera in the mid 1290s.[7] Nonetheless, a general estimate of the financial basis of Montesa was required. A more or less accurate count of the new dependants, as well as a precise description and estimate of the rents they paid, were urgently needed. The report written on 25 March 1320 contained all this information. The details it provided offered not just a 'snapshot', limited to the early months of 1320, but presented relevant facts regarding the Templar and Hospitaller past of the recently acquired territories. This valuable source is well known and has been transcribed, but still deserves a systematic study to relate its content to what is already known about Templar and Hospitaller lands and rights in the kingdom of Valencia in the thirteenth and early fourteenth centuries.

Frontier, vol. 1 (Cambridge Mass., 1967), pp. 183–90; Eugenio Díaz Manteca 'Notas para el estudio de los antecedentes históricos de Montesa', *Estudis Castellonencs*, 2 (1984–85), 246–64; Enric Guinot Rodríguez, 'La Orden de San Juan del Hospital en la Valencia medieval', *Aragón en la Edad Media*, 14–15 (1999), 723–38.

4 'Registre de tots los castells, vilas e lochs quel orde de Muntesa ha en lo Regne de Valencia': Archivo Histórico Nacional [AHN], Sección de Órdenes Militares [SOM], Libros Manuscritos [LM], Montesa, 871 C. It was transcribed by Eugenio Díaz Manteca in 'Notas para el estudio', 288–305.

5 Luis García-Guijarro Ramos, 'Los orígenes de la Orden de Montesa', in *Las Órdenes Militares en el Mediterráneo Occidental (siglos XII–XVIII)* (Madrid, 1989), pp. 69–83.

6 The first two masters of Montesa have been studied by Vicente García Edo: 'El efímero mandato de Guillem d'Erill, primer maestre de la orden de Montesa (22 julio/4 octubre 1319)', in Ricardo Izquierdo Benito and Francisco Ruiz Gómez (eds), *Las Órdenes Militares en la Península Ibérica*, vol. 1, *Edad Media* (Cuenca, 2000), pp. 589–606; Vicente García Edo, 'Arnau de Soler, segon mestre de l'orde de Montesa (1320–1327) (itinerari i altres noticies del seu temps)', in *Actes de les primeres jornades sobre els ordes religioso-militars als països catalans (segles XII– XIX)* (Tarragona, 1994), pp. 555–66.

7 4 September 1294: AHN, SOM, Pergaminos [Perg.], Montesa, Particulares [P] 509; 5 May 1295: ibid., P 522; 31 March 1296: ibid., P 527.

Map 1 Hospitaller districts and possessions in the kingdom of Valencia at the time of the foundation of the Order of Montesa. Based on the map by E. Guinot Rodriguez, 'La Orden de San Juan', p. 742. The maps could not have been drawn without the help of Elizabeth López Orduin.

The data on the population and rents of the different territories that were assigned to Montesa by the papal charter of 1317 offer a clear idea of their weight and relative importance. The most important asset given to the new order was the bailiwick of Cervera, a group of eight villages around the castle of Cervera at the extreme north of the kingdom of Valencia[8] (see Map 16.2). This area was donated to the Hospital by King Jaime I on 23 December 1235.[9] The survey of 1320 estimated its population at 2,029 hearths, the highest number by far of all the recorded inhabitants of the lands received by Montesa.[10] The neighbouring old Templar territories of Cuevas, Peñíscola and Chivert had only 910, 540 and 324 hearths respectively,[11] and the nearby districts of Culla and Ares, also in the hands of the Templars when they were dispossessed by King Jaime II, had 1,035 and 250 hearths respectively.[12] In other parts of the kingdom only Onda showed figures clearly exceeding 200 hearths.[13] Within the bailiwick of Cervera three villages had reached that demographic level: Cervera, the centre of the district, had 250 hearths; Traiguera 300; while San Mateo outstripped the rest with 900 hearths. The expansion of this village had been truly remarkable, bearing in mind that less than a century before it had been given by the Hospitallers to just three settlers.[14] A charter of 12 March 1326 reckoned that San Mateo was the largest of the order's villages, and that it had recently doubled its population due to the privileges bestowed by Montesa and by the Order of St John in previous times. The Master Arnaldo de Soler was thus inclined to agree to the villagers' petition for freedom from certain dues, in the belief that this concession would further increase the village's population.[15] In the Hospitaller period, on 18 January 1308, the castellan of Amposta Pedro de Soler had used a similar argument

8 Cervera, San Mateo, Traiguera, Canet, Chert with Molinar and Barcella, Calig, La Jana with Carrascal, and Rosell. The bailiwick of Cervera's limits were the River Cenia to the east, which marked the border between Valencia and Catalonia, the castles of Peñíscola and Chivert to the south, the castle of Cuevas to the west, and the castle of Morella to the north.

9 AHN, SOM, Perg., Montesa, Reales [R] 50, R 51, R 52, R 53; transcription from the text kept in Archivo del Reino de Valencia [ARV] by Ambrosio Huici Miranda and María Desamparados Cabanes Pecourt (eds), *Documentos de Jaime I de Aragón*, vol 1 (Valencia, 1976), no. 226, p. 372.

10 AHN, SOM, LM, Montesa, 871 C, fols 69 and 71–77. Although it is not possible to establish reliable total numbers, the population of the bailiwick of Cervera may have amounted at that time to just under a third of that of all the Montesian lands.

11 Ibid., fols 33, 35, 37–9, 41, 64–66 55, 57–8 and 60–1.

12 Ibid. fols 46–8, 50–3 and 44.

13 Namely 780 hearths (600 Christians, 180 Muslims): ibid. fol. 22.

14 The population charter was given on 17 June 1237: AHN, SOM Perg., Montesa, P 8; ibid., LM, Montesa, 542 C, fols 3v–4v. Transcription by Manuel Betí Bonfill in *Boletín de la Sociedad Castellonense de Cultura* [hereafter cited as *BSCC*], 35 (1959), 264–265, and by Eugenio Díaz Manteca, *El 'Libro de Poblaciones y Privilegios' de la Orden de Santa María de Montesa (1234–1429)* [hereafter cited as *LPP*] (Castellón, 1987), pp. 183–4.

15 *Attendentes etiam et considerantes villam nostram Sancti Mathei que maior est et unum ex honorabilioribus membris aliis locis dicioni nostri subiectis a brevi tempore citra pretextu graciarum et libertatum per nos et predecessores nostros habitatoribus eiusdem ville hactenus indultarum quasi in duplo augmentatam et populatam fuisse ...*: AHN, SOM, LM, Montesa, 542 C, fols 169v–170; transcription by E. Díaz Manteca, *LPP*, p. 408.

when he agreed to the villagers' petition for an oven; he reckoned that the growth of San Mateo made this demand reasonable.[16]

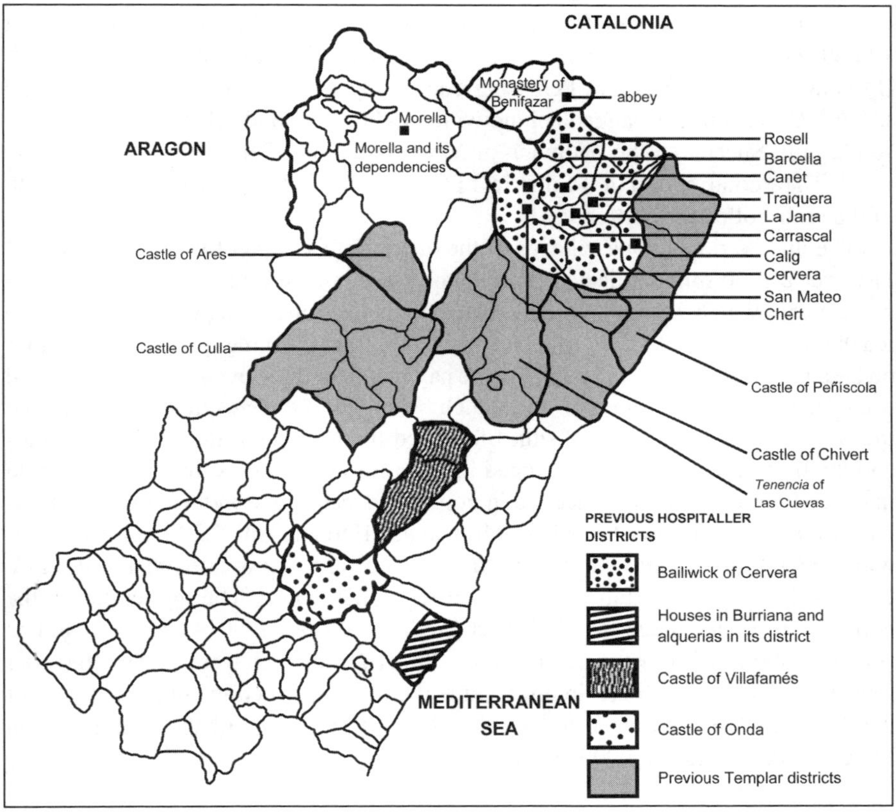

Map 2 The bailiwick of Cervera and other former Hospitaller and Templar territories in the northern part of the kingdom of Valencia belonging to the Order of Montesa after 1319 (modern village limits are shown). Based on the map of E. Díaz Manteca.

The great importance of the bailiwick of Cervera in terms of population in relation to all the other lands that Montesa received in 1319 was also reflected in the rents that the new order collected in its different territories. The survey provided information about the leasing of the rents in each commandery between 1317 and 1320. The data for every village in the bailiwick of Cervera covered only 1320, as was the case for other sources of income in that area that were sold separately by the order. As was also the case in the information provided from other territories, these were minimum

16 Elena Sánchez Almela (ed.), *El Llibre de Privilegios de la Villa de Sant Mateu (1157–1512)* (Castellón, 1985), p. 269.

figures because there were payments received directly by the order – judicial fines for instance.[17] The combined figure of the rents obtained from the bailiwick of Cervera can be compared with those paid by other territories of the order in the same year. Montesa was supposed to receive from the district of Cervera more than 36,000 *solidi*, 24,140 *solidi* coming from the leasing of the rents of the different villages and 12,600 *solidi* from other sources of income not attached to any village in particular.[18] By comparison, Cuevas and Peñíscola could only offer 17,600 *solidi* and 17,350 *solidi*;[19] Culla and Ares lagged behind with 14,400 *solidi* and 7,150 *solidi*.[20] Further south, only Sueca and the bailiwick of Moncada could offer figures above 10,000 *solidi*.[21] The contribution of the district of Cervera would have been around one-fifth of the rents collected by Montesa.

The distribution among villages of the district of Cervera of the total amount of just over 24,000 *solidi* collected from them showed the different economic strength of each unit, which was undoubtedly related to their demographic weight. San Mateo led the way with 9,720 *solidi*, which came mainly from the three-quarters of the tithes on bread, wine, oil, linen and hemp, while payments for three ovens, the butchery and use of the local legal weight or *pes*, which belonged to the Hospitallers, completed the sum.[22] Such distribution of tithes followed the agreement that the Hospitallers and the bishop of Tortosa had reached in 1243 for all the lands that the Order held in the bishopric.[23] Traiguera, second in population, came next in the ranking of rents with 4,000 *solidi*, followed by Chert, Molinar and Barcella with 2,200 *solidi*, Cervera with 2,130 *solidi*, Canet with 2,000 *solidi*, La Jana and Carrascal with 1,720 *solidi*, Calig with 1,650 *solidi* and finally Rosell with 720 *solidi*.[24] The figures reflect the populations of the villages in the district. To the total sum of 24,140 *solidi* should be added 12,600 *solidi*, mostly grazing and milling rights, which were sold by the order separately.[25] These numbers do not include the rents provided by all the parishes of the district, which amounted to 11,300 *solidi*.[26] The income of the church of San Mateo was estimated at 4,000 *solidi*.[27]

---

17 In the reference to the leasing of rents in each village of the district of Cervera *quarts, bans e calonies* were always excluded.

18 AHN, SOM, LM, Montesa, 871 C, fols 69–70 and 72–78.

19 Ibid., fols 41 and 67.

20 Ibid., fols 54 and 44.

21 Ibid., fols 8 and 16. The estates in Burriana offered only 7,500 *solidi* and not 12,500 *solidi* as deemed by E. Díaz Manteca: 'Notas para el estudio', p. 295. Later information supports the lower figure. On 3 May 1320 the order of Montesa sold the rents of Burriana for a year for the sum of 7,500 *solidi*: ARV, Clero, legajo [leg.] 95, caja [c.] 2357, Protocolo de Pedro López de Balaña [PPLB], no. 115, fols 96r–96v.

22 AHN, SOM, LM, Montesa, 871C, fol. 70.

23 Ibid., LM, Montesa, 543 C, fols 67–69.

24 Ibid., LM, Montesa, 871C, fols 76, 72, 69, 74, 75, 77 and 73.

25 Ibid., fols 77–78.

26 Traiguera and La Jana-Carrascal, 3,000 *solidi*; Cervera, 1,400 *solidi*; Chert, Molinar and Barcella, 1,300 *solidi*; Calig, 800 *solidi*; Rosell, 500 *solidi*; Canet, 300 *solidi*: ibid., fols 76, 69, 72, 77, 73 and 74.

27 Ibid., fol. 71.

These figures are reliable because they come from a precise report, intended to inform Arnaldo de Soler about the economic and financial background of the new order. They appear even more trustworthy when compared with the information provided by two charters, the first dealing with the selling of the rents of the district of Cervera for six years in 1313, and the second with the readjustments made on the previous contract in 1316. On 6 November 1313 Raimundo de Ampurias, Castellan of Amposta, sold the rents of the bailiwick of Cervera to Simón Negro, citizen of Tortosa, for six years beginning on 1 July 1314, for a price of 18,000 *solidi* to be paid yearly in three instalments (at Michaelmas, January and May) plus 9,000 *solidi* for the expenses that the commander of Cervera and other Hospitaller brethren should incur.[28] The annual sum of 27,000 *solidi* was fixed, but each year Simón Negro would present the real account of incomes and expenditures. If it was positive, that is, above the agreed sum of 27,000 *solidi*, the Hospitallers would retain a quarter of the surplus; if it should be negative, the order would contribute a quarter of the losses. The charter clearly specified those aspects that were excluded from the contract.[29] It also stated that Simón Negro should pay 100 *solidi* as hospitality payments (*cenas*) if the Hospitaller authorities, the bishop or the archbishop were present in the district.

On 16 February 1316 the Castellan of Amposta, Martín Pérez de Oros, reached an agreement with Simón Negro and his partners regarding some details about the contract of 6 November 1313 that had been interpreted differently by the two parties.[30] Simón Negro agreed to renounce the rents of the bailiwick of Amposta, which had also been sold to him in 1313, and restricted to the district of Cervera his claims to the tax known as *monedaje*. The price fixed in 1313 for this area was increased to 20,000 *solidi* a year plus the already accorded 9,000 *solidi* (*pro custodia seu expensis castri Cervarie*) and the addition of 36 *cafizes* of wheat for the parish priests of the bailiwick. The Hospitallers reduced their participation in the benefits above or the losses below the accorded sum to one-tenth instead of the previous one-quarter The contract was extended for two more years, so was due to end on 1 June 1322.

When the report of March 1320 was produced, the rents of the bailiwick of Cervera were thus in the hands of Simón Negro and others, although the transition period from the Hospitallers to the order of Montesa had seen the growth of tension between the Montesian authorities and the lessees of the rents. Simon Negro and Aparicio Sadaho refused to pay the third due in September 1319 until the master's delegate, the *clavero* Eriman de Eroles, had demonstrated his powers and compelled some debtors to pay rents they had refused to pay.[31] Some people seemed to have taken advantage of the interregnum months to avoid handing over the rents. The Michaelmas instalment was eventually paid, but Eriman de Eroles notified Aparicio Sadaho on 5 November 1319 that, in spite of having received and accepted the

28 AHN, SOM, Perg., Montesa, P 674.

29 *A predicta autem vendicione excipimus calonias tam civiles quam criminales, banna, quarta curiarum dictorum locorum in quibus se obligant debitores suis creditoribus sub pena quarti si debita eis non solvant in comprensis terminis inter eos*: ibid.

30 AHN, SOM, Perg., Montesa, P 687.

31 ARV, Clero, leg. 895, c. 2357, PPLB, no. 48, fols 63v–65.

September payment, the order refused to recognize the contracts of 1313 and 1316 because Montesa, which had received from the pope all the rights over its lands and inhabitants, should be free to decide and should not be hampered by any previous agreements.[32] The order received the January and May 1320 payments, but on 19 July 1320 Jaime de Anglesola, delegate of Arnaldo de Soler, informed Simón Negro and Aparicio Sadaho that the master had decided to break the previous agreements with the lessees on the grounds that Montesa owned those rents, as stated in the papal bulls.[33] The fact that Simón Negro and his partner were informed the day after the master had signed the receipt for the May instalment, showed that Arnaldo de Soler had thought about this move for a long time. In fact, on 9 March 1320, he had appointed Fr. Arnaldo de Pedriza and Jaime de Anglesola as delegates in the northern territories of the order, including the bailiwick of Cervera.[34] Among the powers they received was the capacity to sell the rents and rights of these places *prout assueta sunt vendi temporibus retroactis*. The dispute between Simón Negro and the order dragged on for three years. It ended on 10 August 1323, when Arnaldo de Soler gave Simón and his partners 10,000 *solidi* and the lessees abandoned any further claims to the rents.[35]

The contention did not prevent an agreement over the rents of Traiguera, which were sold by the order to Simón Negro on 10 March 1322 for three years at the price of 4,000 *solidi*, the same price that appeared in the report of March 1320 and probably the amount that had been estimated when the contracts of 1313 and 1316 were signed for the entire bailiwick of Cervera.[36] The coincidence shows that Montesa was ready to sign of its own accord contracts with the old lessees, but that it had not been happy to fully honour previous Hospitaller agreements. This attitude was surely not limited to the district of Cervera. There is only very scanty previous information on the selling of rents in other Hospitaller or former Templar Valencian areas after 1307, but we have several new contracts arranged by Arnaldo de Soler for prices that if not identical were quite similar to those appearing in the report of 1320. We do not know if they were continuing agreements signed before 1318–19 or if they were new ones accorded after the expiry of the previous contracts. On 13 May 1321 the rents of the old Hospitaller commandery of Villafamés were sold for a year to Arnaldo Celoni for 5,500 *solidi*, which was the amount referred to in the report for 1319 and also for 1320.[37] On 30 May 1322 a new contract was signed for three years at the price of 7,000 *solidi*.[38]

The survey of 1320 probably stated the value of the rents of the villages and of those not assigned to any particular place, taking into account existing contracts or others that had expired recently. The price of 29,000 *solidi* fixed for the entire

32 AHN, SOM, Perg., Montesa, P 743 = ARV, Clero, leg. 895, c. 2357, PPLB, doc. 50, fol. 65r–65v.

33 Ibid., no. 83, fol. 79v, no. 137, fol. 109, and no. 138, fols 109–110.

34 Ibid., no. 74, fols 74–75.

35 Ibid., no. 304, fol. 228r–228v.

36 Ibid., no. 253, fols 202–203.

37 Ibid., no. 207, fol. 170.

38 Ibid., no. 267, fol. 210r–210v.

bailiwick of Cervera in 1316 – which, it must be remembered, was an economic guess and not the real rent obtained from the district – fits well into the data provided by the report of March 1320. It was roughly half way between the assessment for the rents of all the villages, 24,140 *solidi*, and the total sum of 36,000 *solidi*, which included additional incomes.

The information on population and rents provided by the survey is confirmed by other contemporary charters and shows the key role played by the bailiwick of Cervera in the Hospitaller past, as well as the dominant position that it enjoyed after 1319. No wonder that in the Middle Ages San Mateo became the real centre of the order of Montesa. The southern castle and village that gave its name to the order was no demographic or economic match for the district of Cervera, and specifically for San Mateo, which, on the other hand, was nearer to the centres of power under the crown of Aragon.[39] San Mateo was severely hit by the late medieval crisis, as the estimated drop in population shows: by 1429 the number of the village's inhabitants had almost halved; between 1320 and 1463 the population fell by 70.5 per cent.[40] This reduction must have made it a less attractive place to establish the order's central government. The fact that the court was far away in Habsburg times must have deprived the bailiwick of Cervera of another of its main assets. From the sixteenth century onwards the castle of Montesa and the city of Valencia became the centre of an order that had been absorbed by the Habsburg monarchy in the late sixteenth century, nearly a hundred years later than its Castilian counterparts.[41]

The survey of 1320 showed the success of a northern Valencian district but of course it did not explain how it came to be so in the previous hundred years. It is interesting to view the history of the bailiwick of Cervera in Hospitaller and early Montesian times from the perspective of the information assembled in March 1320. The sources accumulated from the time of the Christian conquest onwards are not as rich as historians would like, but at least they give indications of how that district became the most important Hospitaller territory in the kingdom of Valencia. The order of Montesa evidently benefited from that legacy.

The bailiwick of Cervera was given to the Hospitallers long before the area was taken from the Muslims in 1233. In 1157 Ramón Berenguer IV offered the order either the castle of Cervera or that of Cullera, south of the city of Valencia, after

39 Bernardo de Bellavista gave Montesa and Vallada to 120 settlers in the settlement charter signed on 16 October 1289: AHN, SOM, LM, Montesa, 542 C, fols 1r–2r; transcription by E. Díaz Manteca, *LPP*, pp. 179–81. The survey of 1320 referred to 200 warriors, a number related more to the capacity of the castle than to the demographic value of Montesa and its surrounding *alquerías*: AHN, SOM, LM, Montesa, 871 C, fol. 4. The rent of the district of Montesa was valued in 1320 at 1,280 *solidi* for the year 1319: ibid.

40 Luis García-Guijarro Ramos, *Datos para el estudio de la renta maestral de la Orden de Montesa en el siglo XV* (Valencia, 1978), Table XXI, pp. 162–63.

41 Fernando Andrés Robres, 'Galcerán de Borja, Felipe II y la tardía incorporación del maestrazgo de la Orden de Montesa a la Corona. Los hechos (1492–1592)', in Enrique Martínez Ruiz and Vicente Suárez Grimón (eds), *Iglesia y Sociedad en el Antiguo Régimen. III Reunión Científica de la Asociación Española de Historia Moderna (Las Palmas, 1994)* (Las Palmas de Gran Canaria, 1995), pp. 409–20.

they had been conquered.[42] In April 1171 Alfonso II confirmed the donation of one of the two castles by his father and granted the second.[43] In October 1192 he also gave to the Hospitallers Barcella, a small village not far away from Cervera.[44] The latter strongpoint was still in the hands of the Muslims, but apparently Barcella was not. There was no reference to a future conquest in the charter granted to the order, and the king wished the brethren to populate the area and build a castle, so the place must have been briefly conquered by Alfonso II. These endowments were tacitly reaffirmed by Pedro II in his general privilege bestowed on the Hospitallers on 9 September 1208, and by Jaime I in a similar privilege granted in the last stages of the siege of Burriana on 15 July 1233.[45] The long-standing pre-conquest grant impelled the Castellan of Amposta, Hugo de Fullalquer, to impose surrender on the Muslims defending the castle of Cervera in the autumn of 1233, once Burriana and Peñíscola had been taken in the summer and early autumn of that year.[46] Jaime I explicitly mentioned it in his chronicle.[47]

The Hospitallers did not delay action in the district that had just been conquered. By 12 July 1234 there was already a commander at Cervera. On that day the Castellan of Amposta, Hugo de Fullalquer, granted to Pedro de Balaguer and Bernardo de Puig a settlement charter for the villages of Cálig and Ali, in the eastern part of the district.[48] On 8 October 1235, the castellan gave to four settlers a charter for the whole bailiwick of Cervera with the exception of the lands given to Pedro de Balaguer and others in 1234.[49] Previously, in April 1235, Hugo de Fullalquer and Blasco de Alagón had agreed on the boundaries between the castles of Morella and Cervera.[50] All these signs of effective rule by the order preceded the official royal

42 E. Sánchez Almela (ed.), *El Llibre de Privilegis*, p. 266.

43 AHN, SOM, Perg., Montesa R 4, R 5, and R 6.

44 Ibid., R 11 and R 12; transcription by Eugenio Díaz Manteca in *BSCC*, LXIII (1987), pp. 371–2.

45 9 September 1208: AHN, SOM, Perg., Montesa, inserted in R 279, in R 280, in R 281, in R 282 and in R 283; transcription by E. Sánchez Almela (ed.), *El Llibre de Privilegis*, pp. 177–9. 15 July 1233: AHN, SOM, Perg., Montesa, inserted in R 151 and in R 152; transcription in A. Huici Miranda and M.D. Cabanes Pecourt (eds), *Documentos de Jaime I de Aragón*, vol 1, no. 182, pp. 313–15.

46 Miguel Gual Camarena, 'Reconquista de la zona castellonense', *BSCC*, 25 (1949), 434–7.

47 Ferran Soldevila (ed.), *Cronica del rei Jaume I*, in Soldevila, *Les Quatre Grans Cròniques*, 2nd edn (Barcelona, 1983), section 185, p. 83.

48 AHN, SOM, LM, Montesa, 542 C, fols 4v–5v; transcription by Manuel Ferrandis Irles in *BSCC*, XX (1944), pp. 103–4; and by E. Díaz Manteca, *LPP*, pp. 184–6. Angel Sánchez Gozalbo, 'Cálig y Alí del Castillo de Cervera', *BSCC*, 23 (1947), pp. 105–7.

49 AHN, SOM, Perg., Montesa, P 6; ibid., LM, Montesa, 542 C, fols 2–3; transcription by Manuel Betí Bonfill in *BSCC*, 23 (1947), pp. 389–90; and by E. Díaz Manteca, *LPP*, pp. 181–2; Manuel Betí Bonfill, 'La población del término de Cervera', ibid., pp. 391–3.

50 Manuel Beti Bonfill, *Rosell. Pleito que por su dominio sostuvieron en el siglo XIII la Orden de San Juan de Jerusalén y el Real Monasterio de Benifazá* (Castellón, 1920), no. XII, pp. 80–82.

donation of the territory, which took place on 23 December 1235.[51] Until that date the order had governed the area on the authority of the pre-conquest grants.

In 1237 the order settled Guillermo Colón, Guillermo Forner and Pedro Claver at San Mateo, and Guillermo de Pellaga, Pedro Soler and Guillermo Gras at Rosell.[52] The small village of Carrascal, which was soon to be absorbed by La Jana, received a settlement charter on 17 April 1239.[53] All these privileges, as well as that given specifically to the village of Cervera on 21 March 1250,[54] were based on the general charter given to the district in October 1235. These communities followed the customs of Lérida and did so in the following decades. On 24 September 1274 the customs of Lérida were confirmed as the usages that should govern life at San Mateo, after the inhabitants had asked the castellan to unify the different legal systems that coexisted in the village.[55]

Due to the sparsity of the sources, the development of the different villages of the district of Cervera in Hospitaller times can be traced only in general lines. One exception is the legal dispute over Rosell between the Hospitallers and the Cistercian monastery of Benifazar.[56] This abbey considered that it was entitled to Rosell as a result of Jaime I's donation to the mother house of Poblet, on 22 November 1233, of several localities, among them Rosell, with the obligation of setting up a daughter monastery in the area.[57] The lawsuit lasted more than 20 years, from 1246 till 1268. Both parties reached an agreement on 14 September 1268 by which the monastery renounced claims to Rosell; it received in return a Hospitaller estate by the River Ebro.[58] It is not surprising that almost daily information was kept about a dispute that affected the possession of a significant part of the bailiwick.[59]

The district of Cervera was well populated in Muslim times. Most of the places settled by Christians had existed before the conquest, but the case of San Mateo is uncertain. The classical Valencian historians, Pedro Antonio Beuter, Martín de Viciana and Gaspar de Escolano, assumed that the village did not exist in Muslim times, and that it was established after the conquest of the area in the autumn of

51 See above, note 9.

52 San Mateo, 17 June 1237: see above, note 14. Rosell, 17 June 1237: AHN, SOM, Perg., Montesa, P 9; ibid., LM, Montesa, 542 C, fols 5v–7; transcription by Manuel Betí Bonfill in *BSCC*, 37 (1961), 127–9, and by E. Díaz Manteca, *LPP*, pp. 186–7.

53 AHN, SOM, LM, Montesa, 542 C, fols 47v–48; transcription by Manuel Ferrandis Irles in *BSCC*, 44 (1968), 234–5, and by E. Díaz Manteca, *LPP*, pp. 250–1. Angel Sánchez Gozalbo, 'El poblado de Carrascal', *BSCC*, 44 (1968), pp. 235–7.

54 AHN, SOM, LM, Montesa, 542 C, fol. 3r–3v; transcription by Manuel Ferrandis Irles in *BSCC*, 45 (1969), pp. 32–3, and by E. Díaz Manteca, *LPP*, pp. 182–3.

55 AHN, SOM, LM, Montesa, 542 C, fols 168v–169; transcription by Eugenio Díaz Manteca in *BSCC*, 59 (1983), pp. 141–3, and by E. Díaz Manteca, *LPP*, pp. 405–6.

56 Manuel Beti Bonfill's little book remains the only study of that conflict: see above, note 50.

57 M. Beti Bonfill, *Rosell*, no. XI, pp. 77–9. A. Huici Miranda and M.D. Cabanes Pecourt (eds), *Documentos de Jaime I de Aragón*, vol 1, no. 191, pp. 324–5.

58 M. Beti Bonfill, *Rosell*, no. XV, pp. 91–8.

59 AHN, SOM, Perg., Montesa, P 107 (12 December 1246), P 122 (15 March 1249–9 February 1250), P 128 (13 June 1248–9 February 1250) and P 299 (12 April 1268).

1233. Their narrative included the usual prodigious discoveries that, according to them, had favoured the foundation. But their arguments in favour of a new settlement fundamentally relied on a passage of Jaime I's *Llibre dels feyts*. In the late summer of 1233 Jaime I had travelled across the plain of San Mateo on his way from Teruel to Peñíscola in a second, and this time successful, attempt to conquer the castle. When later he recalled this journey he explicitly mentioned that the area was either barren or uninhabited, depending on later interpretations of the text: 'and we crossed the plain of San Mateo which then had no population/was barren, and reached the river Sec which runs above Cervera'.[60] The key word is *erm*.[61] The sixteenth- and seventeenth-century Valencian historians mentioned above thought that it meant 'void of population'. Martín de Viciana, who was the most restrained and trustworthy of the three, relied on this reading for his consideration of San Mateo as a new foundation.[62] His contemporary Jerónimo Zurita also followed this line.[63] Much later, in 1911, Manuel Betí Bonfill interpreted it in the sense of 'uncultivated' land.[64] His reasoning was based on a privilege granted by Alfonso II to the cathedral chapter of Tortosa in April 1195. In the donation of the castle of Benifazar the king mentioned the road from San Mateo to the River Cenia as one of the boundaries of the new estate.[65] This reference led Manuel Betí to conclude that the village had existed before the final Aragonese conquest, although he did not explain how the Christian settlers could have survived in such barren surroundings. As has been pointed out in relation to Barcella, the area may have been briefly under the control of Alfonso II, who could have established a new settlement, giving it an unmistakable Christian name. If that had been the case, the region would have reverted quickly to Muslim hands until the final conquest of 1233. San Mateo would have then been abandoned, and so it would have been uninhabited when Jaime I crossed the plain in that year. Other alternatives, such as the persistence of Christian Mozarabic population under Muslim control, are possible but not probable. In any case, even if San Mateo had existed before the Hospitallers took control of the district of Cervera, it surely must have been a minor place, significantly less important than Cervera itself.

The striking later success of San Mateo, regardless of whether the village was strictly a new settlement or not, owed much to the site that the original Christian

60 Ferran Soldevila (ed.), *Cronica del rei Jaume I*, section 183, p. 82.

61 A recent English translation of the chronicle reads *erm* as 'wasteland': Damian Smith and Helena Buffery (eds), *The Book of Deeds of James I of Aragon: A Translation of the Medieval Catalan 'Llibre dels Fets'* (Aldershot, 2003), p. 173.

62 *E caminando el rey desde Teruel para peniscola, passo por los campos que hoy nombromos de sant Matheo, aunque entonces en estos campos no havia poblacion alguna, antes todo era yermo*: Martín de Viciana, *Crónica de la ínclita y coronada ciudad de Valencia*, Book III (Valencia, 1564), ed. Sociedad Valenciana de Bibliófilos (Valencia, 1882), p. 127.

63 *... enderezando [Jaime I] al llano de sant Mateo que entonces era despoblado*: Jerónimo Zurita, *Anales de la Corona de Aragón*, Book III.VII (Zaragoza, 1585), ed. Ángel Canellas López (Zaragoza, 1998), p. 490.

64 Manuel Beti Bonfill, 'Fundación de San Mateo', *Lo Rat Penat*, 1 (1911), p. 150; reproduced in Bonfill, *Morella y el Maestrazgo en la Edad Media* (Castellón, 1972), p. 128.

65 Ana Isabel Sánchez Casabón, *Alfonso II Rey de Aragón, Conde de Barcelona y Marqués de Provenza. Documentos (1162–1196)* (Zaragoza, 1995), no. 638, p. 833.

populatores either chose or revitalized. San Mateo was situated beside the highway that had connected southern Catalonia to the city of Valencia since Roman times. Martín de Viciana was well aware of this advantage: 'The new settlers took much care in placing the village just by the royal highway, and they chose well, because the traffic is intense along that way and the village greatly benefits from it.'[66] The chronicler Ramón Muntaner described this route on the occasion of the visit to Valencia of the king of Castile, Alfonso X, and his subsequent journey to Catalonia at the end of 1274: 'leaving Valencia they reached Santa María del Puig, and from Santa María del Puig to Morvedre, and from Morvedre to Burriana, and from Burriana to Castellón, and from Castellón to Cabanes, and from Cabanes to Las Cuevas, and from Las Cuevas to San Mateo, and from San Mateo to Ulldecona, and from Ulldecona to the city of Tortosa'.[67] San Mateo was also on the east–west route that connected the coast to Morella and eventually to Zaragoza, as the *Crònica de Pere el Ceremoniós* briefly related.[68] The strategic setting of San Mateo made it an ideal place for assembling the *Cortes*; Pedro IV did so in 1370, Alfonso V in 1421 and 1429, and Fernando II in 1495.[69]

Martín de Viciana also attributed San Mateo's growth to the agricultural and livestock development of the locality from the time of the first settlers 'because the fields and municipal area of this village are highly convenient for that'.[70] Wool manufacture was also another economic factor that favoured the site's expansion. 'For all these reasons the village became the best and the biggest in the whole region', Viciana concluded.[71] These statements by a historian who lived more than three hundred years after the developments he was recording are difficult to check against contemporary sources, which not only are scarce but also give no direct information about the growth of San Mateo or the reasons for that growth.[72] There are only hints that the village was growing, perhaps the most relevant being charters related to the leasing of the rights to sell meat and fish. On 22 May 1252 the Hospitallers gave Arnaldo Zapater and his wife and family these rights after

66 *Los nuevos pobladores advertieron mucho en el assentar el lugar en el camino real y acertaron en ello, porque el passaje es muy grande por aquel camino, del qual la villa recibe grandes aprovechamientos*: Martín de Viciana, *Crónica ...*, Book III, p. 128.

67 Ferran Soldevila (ed.), *Crònica de Ramon Muntaner*, in Soldevila, *Les Quatre Grans Cròniques*, chapter 23, p. 686. This section is not included in a recent English translation of part of the chronicle: Robert D. Hughes (ed.), *The Catalan Expedition to the East: From the 'Chronicle' of Ramon Muntaner* (Woodbridge, 2006).

68 Ferran Soldevila (ed.), *Crònica de Pere el Ceremoniós*, in Soldevila, *Les Quatre Grans Cròniques*, section 40, p. 1142.

69 M. Beti Bonfill, 'Fundación de San Mateo', *Lo Rat Penat*, 1 (1911), p. 146; reproduced in Bonfill, *Morella*, p. 124.

70 *... pues el campo y termino de esta villa es para todo ello muy conveniente*: Martín de Viciana, *Crónica*, Book III, p. 128.

71 *Delos quales vino que esta villa fue la mejor e mayor de toda la comarca*: ibid.

72 The *Llibre de Privilegis de la Villa de Sant Mateu* contain only 54 documents from the period 1157–August 1319; very few of them are relevant in one way or another to the expansion of the village.

an entry payment of 40 *solidi* had been given.[73] The rights must have returned to Hospitaller control, because in 1280 the commander of Cervera sold them to Novella, widow of Guillermo Colón, for a price of 1,040 *solidi*, which contrasted with the modest entry payment of 1252.[74] Novella must have soon arranged the sale of one-third of the rights to Berenguer Pellicer and his wife. On 18 January 1281 Berenguer resold this third to Bernardo Torner, citizen of Barcelona, for a price of 280 *solidi*.[75] On 7 April 1288 the order regained control over these rights by buying the one-third in possession of Bernardo Torner, and the two-thirds that Novella had kept.[76] The joint price paid by the Hospitallers was 1,000 *solidi*, which was only slightly less than the sum received in 1280. Three aspects of these sales may have reflected the demographic growth of San Mateo and the greater importance of any retailing activities in the village: the considerable difference between the entry payment of 1252 and the price received by the order in 1280 may be a sign of increase in population, and therefore in consumers in the village; the fact that a citizen of Barcelona was ready to invest in one of the activities of San Mateo may also have reflected the village's increasing economic importance. Finally, the order's desire to recover control of the rights to sell meat and fish could reflect the order's interest in retaining control over the rents deriving from that occupation, in accordance with the growth of the village and the subsequent increasing sales.

Hospitaller rule over the bailiwick of Cervera and other territories in the kingdom of Valencia was not immediately affected by the extinction of the Temple in 1312. As has been pointed out, the Order was free to arrange the selling of the rents of the district in February 1316. The bull of 10 June 1317 which founded the new order of Montesa changed things, and Jaime II required the Hospitallers to hand over to him all their territories in Valencia as a preliminary step to passing them to Montesa once the institution had been established. On 22 November 1317 Jaime II informed the castellan of Amposta that he should transfer the lands north of the River Guadalaviar into the hands of Pedro Boil, a royal counsellor.[77] The castellan delegated this responsibility to Sancho de Oros, his representative in the bailiwick of Cervera and commander of Calatayud, and Pedro Boil delegated likewise to his son Ramón Boil.[78] On 3 December 1317, and after having on the same day absolved the different communities of the district from their homage and fidelity to the order, Sancho de Oros officially passed the castle of Cervera into royal hands.[79]

73 AHN, SOM, Perg., Montesa, P 151.

74 Ibid., P 404.

75 Ibid., P 1. The notary writing the document missed the hundreds in the date, and so it read: *anno Domini Millessimo octuagesimo*. This obvious error has been overlooked by archivists since the eighteenth century. The date 18 January 1180/81 is absurd since San Mateo did not exist at that time and the whole district of Cervera was held by the Muslims. The only possible alternative year in which San Mateo was ruled by the Hospitallers is 1281.

76 Ibid., P 461 and P 462.

77 Ibid., R 195.

78 Ibid., inserted in P 691.

79 Ibid., P 691. A pre-eighteenth-century title at the back of the document mentioned the *tinença de sent matheu*, a clear sign of the idea of predominance of San Mateo over Cervera

In Barcelona, a fortnight after the order of Montesa's establishment on 22 July 1319, Ramón de Boil gave the castle of Cervera to the first master, Guillermo de Eril, although the official ceremony was delayed until the end of August.[80] On the following day, 8 August 1319, Jaime II, who was still in control of the bailiwick because the transfer had not been completed, ordered the village of San Mateo and all other places of the district to elect delegates to swear homage to Montesa.[81] On 30 August all of them chose their representatives, and the following day Vidal de Vilanova, in the king's name, put all the villages of the bailiwick into the possession of Eriman de Eroles, *clavero* of the order, who acted as the master's deputy because the latter was already ill.[82] On that day too, the delegates swore homage to the order, and Eriman de Eroles, jointly with Vidal de Villanova and the abbot of the Cistercian monastery of Valldigna, provisionally confirmed the privileges of the different communities of the district. The village of Cervera itself seems not to have been transferred jointly with the other communities, but in independent ceremonies.[83] In the case of San Mateo, at the request of the authorities of the village, on 17 September 1319 the master, Guillem de Eril, ratified its privileges.[84] The handover of the bailiwick of Cervera from the king's to the order's control had been concluded.

The new authorities soon realized the true importance of the district of Cervera and of the village of San Mateo within it. Although the castle of Montesa held some general chapters in the 1320s, the centre of gravity moved swiftly to San Mateo. The momentous chapter that established the final structure of the order in commanderies, after a decade of adjustments, took place in that same village on 25 May 1330. From then on the master kept direct control of the bailiwick of Cervera, which thus became the most important part of his magistral *camera*. The central administrative and personal lodgings of the master were not located at the castle of Cervera but at San Mateo, where a new set of buildings for that purpose was erected. If, in Hospitaller times, that district had been the main asset of the order in the kingdom of Valencia, when Montesa took over, the bailiwick, and specifically San Mateo, became the centre of the new institution. Once again, Martín de Viciana clearly summarized the master's preference for this village: 'When the very reverend master of Montesa, lord of the magistral *camera*, realized the advantages and superiority of the village of San Mateo over the castle of

in later minds.

80 ARV, Clero, leg. 895, c. 2357, PPLB, no. 3, fol. 2.

81 AHN, SOM, Perg., Montesa, inserted in P 707, and in P 709; reference in P 703 = ARV, Clero, leg. 895, c. 2357, PPLB, inserted in no. 10, fol. 5v.

82 30 August 1319: AHN, SOM Perg., Montesa, P 703. 31 August 1319: ibid., P 704 and P 706 = ARV, Clero, leg. 895, c. 2357, PPLB, no. 11, fols 9v–10v. 31 August 1319: ibid., no. 10, fols 5–9v.

83 AHN, SOM, Perg., Montesa, P 701 (24 August 1319); ibid., P 705 (31 August 1319) = ARV, Clero, leg. 895, c. 2357, PPLB, no. 14, fols 12v–13v; AHN, SOM, Perg., Montesa, P 708 (31 August 1319) = ARV, Clero, leg. 895, c. 2357, PPLB, no. 15, fols 13v–14; ibid., no. 13, fols 11v–12v (31 August 1319).

84 AHN, SOM, Perg., Montesa, P 740.

Cervera because it was far more pleasant and attractive, he ordered a palace and a house to be built as accommodation for the master.'[85]

85 *E como el reverendissimo maestre de Montesa, señor dela mesa maestral vido el avantage y mejoria que tenia la villa de sant Matheo al castillo de Cervera por ser mas aplazible y graciosa para habitar. Mando edificar un palacio y casa para apossiento del maestre*: Martín de Viciana, *Crónica* ..., Book III, p. 129.

Chapter 18

La règle de l'*ancianitas* dans l'ordre de l'Hôpital, le prieuré de Catalogne et la *Castellania de Amposta* aux XIVe et XVe siècles

Pierre Bonneaud

A partir de 1420 les maîtres de l'Hôpital, en particulier le Catalan Antoni de Fluvià (1421–37), entreprirent une remise en ordre des règles du couvent de Rhodes et des prieurés occidentaux par une intense législation statutaire. Après l'époque troublée du schisme pontifical et face à la menace accrue des Ottomans et des Mamelouks dans le Levant, l'heure était venue pour Rhodes de renforcer sa défense afin de conserver sa position de bastion de la Chrétienté face à l'Islam. Des contingents stables et importants de frères étaient indispensables et dès 1418 les 'passages' d'Hospitaliers devinrent plus nombreux, en particulier depuis le prieuré de Catalogne et la *Castellania de Amposta.* Les dispositions que firent adopter Fluvià puis son successeur Lastic (1437–54) visèrent en particulier à mieux organiser la vie collective des frères, appelés à demeurer au couvent pendant de longues périodes, et à mieux les motiver dans l'exercice de leurs devoirs. Parallèlement le rôle des langues dans les auberges et au conseil du maître s'accompagnait d'initiatives des frères eux-mêmes pour défendre leurs intérêts avec l'encouragement et, dans la mesure du possible, sous le contrôle du maître.[1]

---

1 Citons parmi les ouvrages qui évoquent les règles de carrière des Hospitaliers et en particulier celle de l' *ancianitas* aux XIVe et XVe siècles, A. Luttrell, 'Rhodes: base militaire, colonie, métropole de 1306 à 1440' , in M. Balard et A. Ducellier (eds), *Coloniser au Moyen Age* (Paris, 1995), pp. 235–40 et 244–5; Luttrell, *'El Priorat de Catalunya: el Segle XIV' , L Avenç*, 179 (1994)1–10; Luttrell, The Italian Hospitallers at Rhodes: 1437–1462 , *Revue Mabillon*, 68 (NS 7) (1996), 209–31 (ces trois articles sont repris dans Luttrell, *The Hospitaller State on Rhodes and its Western Provinces, 1306–1462* (Aldershot, 1999), et seront dorénavant cités comme Luttrell, 1999, VII, XV et XVIII); J. Sarnowsky, *Macht und Herrschaft in Johanniterorden des 15. Jahrhunderts, Verfassung und Verwaltung der Johanniter auf Rhodos (1421–1522)* (Münster, 2001); Sarnowsky, The Oligarchy at Work, The Chapter General of the Hospitallers in the XVth Century (1421–1522), in M. Balard (ed.), *Autour de la première croisade* (Paris, 1996), pp. 267–76; Sarnowsky, Der Konvent auf Rhodos und die Zungen (*lingue*) im Johanniterorden (1421–76) , in Z.H. Novak (ed.), *Ritterorden und Region: Politische, soziale und wirtschaftliche Verbindungen im Mittelalter* (Toruń, 1995), pp. 43–65; M. Bonet Donato, *La orden del Hospital en la Corona de Aragón. Poder y Gobierno en la castellania de Amposta (SS. XII–XV)* (Madrid, 1994); P. Bonneaud,

Dans un tel contexte, la règle de l'*ancianitas* dans le déroulement des carrières se précisa et s'imposa. L'ancienneté, décomptée à partir du premier 'passage' et prenant prioritairement en compte la durée des séjours des frères en Orient, devint le critère exigé pour accéder aux commanderies et aux offices réservés à chaque langue. Il ne s'agissait pas vraiment d'une nouveauté car depuis le début du XIVe siècle la notion d'*ancianitas* cheminait au fil des statuts et des décisions de l'ordre mais avec un contenu et des modalités imprécis.

L'examen de l'évolution vers la généralisation de l'*ancianitas* au cours du XIVe siècle puis pendant les magistères de Fluvià et Lastic éclaire la gestion par l'Hôpital des carrières des frères et, par voie de conséquence, les ambitions, les motivations et le comportement de ceux-ci. Les deux prieurés de la Langue d'Espagne dépendant de la Couronne d'Aragon, le prieuré de Catalogne et la *Castellania de Amposta*, nous sont apparus comme un cadre privilégié pour étudier le développement de la règle jusqu'à son aboutissement au milieu du XVe puis ses conséquences et ses difficultés d'application au cours des magistères de Jacques de Milly (1454–61) et Pere Ramon Sacosta (1461–67). D'une part les frères des deux prieurés furent particulièrement nombreux à Rhodes et actifs, voire remuants, au sujet de l'*ancianitas* à l'auberge d'Espagne; d'autre part, les deux textes les plus complets que nous ayons pu consulter aux archives de Malte sur la mise en forme de la règle sont des bulles concernant le prieuré de Catalogne, en 1442, et la *Castellania de Amposta* en 1446.

En 1301 et 1304, peu après l'abandon de la Terre Sainte, deux chapitres généraux tenus à Limassol sous la présidence de Guillaume de Villaret prirent quelques dispositions annonçant l'*ancianitas*.[2] En 1301, le maître se vit reconnaître le droit de retenir en sa compagnie '*deça mar*', c'est-à-dire au couvent, quelques 'prud'hommes' anciens et d'accorder à chacun une commanderie dans leur prieuré d'origine, avec le conseil du chapitre.[3] Les commanderies attribuées n'échappaient pas au contrôle et au droit de visite des prieurs, non plus qu'aux devoirs habituels des commandeurs en matière de responsions. En 1304 il fut interdit aux prieurs d'attribuer des commanderies à qui n'aurait pas été reçu dans l'ordre depuis au minimum trois ans ou cinq s'il s'agissait d'un château fort.[4] Ces deux statuts traitaient donc de la compétence des prieurs, habilités à attribuer les commanderies dans leur prieuré, et de celle du maître qui disposait d'un même droit en faveur des frères 'anciens' qu'il retenait au couvent.

Au cours du chapitre général présidé par Hélion de Villeneuve en 1330 à Montpellier il fut déclaré qu'à la mort de commandeurs 'retenus à la main du maître', chaque prieur était autorisé à couvrir ces vacances 'sauf que ledit maistre retient des dites commanderies qui vagueront ou d'autres chascun an de X ans ii en

Le prieuré de Catalogne, le couvent de Rhodes et la couronne d Aragon, 1415–1447 (Millau, Bez-et-Esparron, 2004).

2 Nous avons eu recours pour les textes des différents statuts aux sources suivantes: 1301–67, Archives municipales de Perpignan, ms. 29, dorénavant Arch. mun. Perpignan, ms 29; 1410–46, Archives départementales de la Haute-Garonne, H13 et H14, dorénavant Arch. dép. Haute-Garonne; 1462, Archives de l Ordre de St Jean, National Library of Malta, La Valette, Cod. 282, dorénavant Malta, Cod.

3 Arch. mun. Perpignan, ms. 29, fol. 52r–v, Statut XXIX de Guillaume de Villaret.

4 Ibid., fol. 58r–v, Statuts LXVIII et LXIX de Guillaume de Villaret.

chaque prieuré pour donner aux frères qui seront outre mer les quelles baillies et commandeurs soient au commandement des prieurs aussi comme les autres ou le maistre en fera mention en ses lettres'. Nous citons le texte publié par Charles Tipton dans la version chronologiquement la plus proche du chapitre général, car cette décision de 1330, quelque peu ambiguë, devint fréquemment citée par les maîtres lorsqu'ils accordaient une commanderie à un frère du couvent. Le même chapitre autorisa le maître à retenir 'en sa main' dans chaque prieuré un, deux ou trois frères selon l'importance du prieuré.[5]

Le chapitre général de 1344 vint assurer un contrôle des dispositions précédentes: avant toute provision, les prieurs devraient faire connaître au maître les commanderies vacantes afin que celui-ci, avec l'avis de son conseil, puisse exercer annuellement son droit d'attribuer l'une d'entre elles 'au plus digne des frères qui sera au couvent'.[6] En 1353, il fut ajouté que si les prieurs omettaient de communiquer la liste des vacances le maître et à son conseil attribueraient celles-ci dans leur totalité.[7]

Le chapitre général suivant, tenu à Rhodes par Pierre de Corneillan en 1354, déclara qu'il appartenait au maître de pourvoir en son conseil toutes les commanderies des commandeurs mourant au couvent.[8]

Ces premières dispositions, qui évoquaient par intermittence l'ancienneté des frères du couvent, semblent plutôt avoir eu pour but de préciser les compétences des prieurs et du maître dans l'attribution des commanderies, en donnant de plus en plus de poids au maître qui, informé préalablement de toutes les vacances, pouvait pourvoir par grâce magistrale chaque année une ou plusieurs commanderies dans chaque prieuré.

Mais en 1367, un statut du chapitre général d'Avignon, présidé par le maître Raymond Bérenger innova en reconnaissant un rôle important aux langues dont les 'prud'hommes' furent appelés à donner conseil au maître tous les ans lorsque celui-ci exercerait son droit de donner une commanderie à l'un des frères les plus anciens et méritants du couvent.[9] Cependant le droit du maître d'attribuer des commanderies par grâce magistrale n'était pas remis en question puisque au cours du même chapitre parmi les 'retentions' de Bérenger figurait le droit de 'donner les commanderies qui deviendraient vacantes dans les prieurés de Toulouse, Auvergne, Aquitaine, Catalogne, Campanie et les autres prieurés'.[10]

Lors du chapitre général d'Aix-en-Provence de 1410, présidé par Raymond de Lescure, lieutenant du maître Philibert de Naillac, hors la présence de ce dernier, le principe d'*ancianitas* se vit enfin confirmé et précisé de façon lapidaire: 'Il est établi par ce chapitre général que tous les frères anciens quand ils demeurent au couvent,

5 Ch. Tipton, 'The 1330 Chapter General of the Knights Hospitallers at Montpellier', *Traditio*, 24 (1968), 293–308, qui utilise comme source NLM 280. Les documents cités apparaissent parmi les *Recordia* et non parmi les *Statuta*. Remarquons que le chapitre ayant lieu à Montpellier, le terme 'outre mer' se rapporte à Rhodes et au Levant, alors que, utilisé depuis Rhodes, il se réfèrerait à l Occident.

6 Arch. mun. Perpignan, ms. 29, fol. 70, Statut LXXIIII d Hélion de Villeneuve.

7 Ibid., fol. 75r–v, Statut VIII de Dieudonné de Gozon.

8 Ibid., fol. 78v–79, Statut VIII de Pierre de Corneillan.

9 Ibid., fol. 87r–v , Statut XXIII de Raymond Bérenger.

10 Ibid., fols 88v–89, Statut XXXIII de Raymond Bérenger.

comme il faut entendre par cela les frères les plus anciens et méritants, doivent être pourvus selon leur tour, outre mer ou '*deça mar*', d'une commanderie ou d'un priorat ou d'un baillage capitulaire.'[11] La notion de tour ou de rang était énoncée pour la première fois ainsi que la prise en compte de l'ancienneté pour l'accès aux dignités de prieur et de bailli capitulaire. Enfin les droits préférentiels des frères résidant au couvent furent soulignés par un second statut fixant le temps de présence dans l'ordre pour obtenir une première commanderie à trois ans au couvent, contre cinq en Occident.[12]

Les deux statuts d'Aix-en-Provence nous semblent consacrer un démarrage antérieur et déjà acquis de la règle de l'*ancianitas*. Cette évolution n'était probablement pas étrangère à la multiplication des 'passages' groupés de frères vers Rhodes au départ d'Aigues-Mortes ou de Marseille au cours de la deuxième moitié du XIVe siècle, en raison des menaces croissantes de l'expansion ottomane dans la région.[13] Le séjour de certains frères à Rhodes se prolongeait pendant des années comme dans les cas, en 1408, du frère Joan de Mur et du futur maître Antoni de Fluvià qui y résidaient depuis vingt cinq ans pour le premier et vingt ans pour le second.[14] Malgré une certaine désaffection à l'égard du couvent provoquée par le schisme pontifical et l'absence de Rhodes de Naillac entre 1409 et 1420, il demeurait à Rhodes suffisamment de frères pour se rassembler dans les auberges de leurs langues et veiller à la défense de leurs intérêts. Ces assemblées autorisées par le maître ou son lieutenant au cas par cas débattaient des carrières des frères et en particulier de leur ancienneté au couvent.

Ainsi, en 1385, les frères de la langue d'Espagne avaient réclamé au lieutenant du maître l'attribution de la commanderie de Tortosa, dans le prieuré de Catalogne, à Berenguer Batlle, au couvent depuis huit ans.[15] En 1399, 63 frères de la langue de Provence signèrent dans leur auberge un engagement individuel de remettre en état leurs logements à Rhodes lorsque leur ancienneté leur permettait d'en obtenir de

11 Arch. dep. Haute-Garonne, H 13, fol.74r, Statut XXIII de Philibert de Naillac (Traduction en français du texte catalan). Il faut entendre par baillages capitulaires les importantes commanderies ne faisant pas partie d un prieuré et représentées au chapitres généraux en tant que telles (par exemple, en Italie, San Stefano de Monopoli et Venosa).

12 Ibid., fol.74v, Statut XXIV.

13 Par exemple, 60 frères en 1358 (Malta, Cod. 316, fol.142), 100 en 1366 (A. Luttrell, 1992, II, p. 95), 390 en 1377 selon les souhaits de Heredia et de Grégoire XI qui ne furent certainement pas suivis d'effets (J. Delaville Le Roulx, *Les Hospitaliers à Rhodes jusqu'à la mort de Philibert de Naillac, 1310–1421* (Paris, 1913), pp. 188 et 189, et A. Luttrell, 'Papauté et Hôpital: l'enquête de 1373, in A.M. Legras (ed.), *L'enquête dans le prieuré de France* (Paris 1987), pp. 3–41), puis des contingents divers en 1391, 1393 et 1395 (Malta, Cod. 324, fol. 172v–173, Malta, Cod. 327, fol. 2 et Malta, Cod. 329, fol. 10v). En 1401, le maître Naillac réclama au prieur de Toulouse d admettre d urgence vingt chevaliers et dix sergents pour les envoyer au couvent (Malta, Cod. 331, fol.162v).

14 Archivo de la Corona de Aragón, Barcelone, Registro de Cancelleria (dorénavant, ACA RC) 2184, fol. 107v et ACA RC 2171, fol. 77v.

15 ACA RC 1374, fol. 104r.

meilleurs.[16] En 1404, dix-huit frères de la langue de France dont le premier dignitaire de la langue, l'hospitalier, proposèrent de maintenir pendant trois ans l'ancienneté d'un frère de la langue qui s'absentait pour se rendre en mission en Occident; en 1409, trente trois frères de la langue d'Auvergne émirent une déclaration devant notaire pour exiger que quatre commanderies vacantes dans leur prieuré fussent concédées à des frères anciens et méritants résidant au couvent.[17] En 1415, les frères de la langue de France avaient réclamé une commanderie pour un sergent au nom de son ancienneté et ils s'opposèrent au lieutenant du maître qui donnait raison à un chevalier, le quel avait recouru contre le choix de la langue. Le maître, saisi de la question, se réserva la décision finale.[18] Le recours à l'*ancianitas* pouvait aussi concerner les dignités supérieures réservées à la langue comme l'enseigne la requête des frères du prieuré de Catalogne, réunies en 1410 à l'auberge d'Espagne, de désigner comme prieur Garcia de Mahissens, drapier de l'ordre et *antiquior* de la langue.[19]

Les décisions des assemblées de frères étaient soumises à la ratification du maître, prise en son conseil, et consignées dans les registres de chancellerie. Le maître Fernandez de Heredia invoquait déjà en 1385 le principe de l'*ancianitas* pour résister à la demande du roi d'Aragon, Pierre le Cérémonieux, de pourvoir des commanderies d'Avinyonet et Castelló de Empuries le frère Arnau de Biure, parent de la reine. Le roi s'adressa alors, directement aux frères catalans du couvent pour leur demander d'accepter cette exception à la règle.[20]

Après le règlement définitif du schisme pontifical en 1417 et le retour de Naillac à Rhodes pour y tenir le chapitre général de 1420, l'*ancianitas* allait constituer l'un des principaux instruments pour assurer le maintien à Rhodes d'effectifs permanents et stables. Le chapitre général de 1420 marqua le début d'un afflux régulier et constant de chevaliers de l'ordre au couvent, en particulier de frères de la langue d'Espagne. En 1418, Naillac convoqua une vingtaine de commandeurs et de frères du prieuré de Catalogne à se rendre à Rhodes et donna licence au prieur ou à des commandeurs de recevoir vingt-quatre nouveaux frères chevaliers invités à faire leur 'passage' au couvent avec armes et chevaux.[21] Après sa mort en 1421 Naillac fut remplacé par un 'ancien' du couvent, le Catalan Antoni de Fluvià, élu à Rhodes par ses pairs selon les règles de l'ordre. Les chapitres généraux de 1420, 1428, 1433 et 1440, ce dernier présidé par Jean de Lastic, successeur de Fluvià, apportèrent des compléments essentiels aux règles de l'*ancianitas* et de l'accès aux dignités.

Tout d'abord, l'*ancianitas* fut clairement définie comme une ancienneté au couvent. Le chapitre de 1420 déclara qu'elle devait être calculée à partir du premier passage à Rhodes avec harnais et cheval où, à défaut de ceux-ci, du paiement au

16 Malta, Cod. 330, fols 36v–37v. A. Luttrell, 1999, VII, p. 239, fait état de cette réunion ainsi que de celles mentionnées dans les trois notes suivantes.

17 Ibid., 332, fol. 6v et 339, fols 199v–201.

18 Ibid., 338, fol. 240r–v.

19 Ibid., 339, fols 201v–204.

20 ACA RC 1385, fol. 86v.

21 Bonneaud, pp.120 à 124.

Trésor d'un *passagium* fixé à 2000 livres tournois pour un chevalier et 1500 pour un sergent.[22] En 1428, afin de ne pas porter préjudice à qui tomberait aux mains d'un ennemi lors de son 'passage', il fut précisé que l'ancienneté serait décomptée au jour du départ. Mais fallait-il apprécier la durée même de l'*ancianitas* en fonction du seul temps de présence au couvent? Un statut de 1440 établit que tous les frères 'partant du couvent pour aller aux armées combattre les infidèles et ennemis de la foi chrétienne par ordre et licence de leur souverain ou par commandement gardent leur ancienneté et leurs droits au couvert et au salaire comme s'ils résidaient continuellement au couvent'.[23] Hors de tels cas, d'autres motifs d'absence n'interrompaient pas toujours l'ancienneté. Ainsi, en 1427, celle du frère de la *Castellania*, Pedro Sarnes, fut maintenue pendant la durée de sa résidence à Chypre.[24] En 1433, une décision du maître et de son conseil accorda que les frères accompagnant les ambassadeurs au concile de Bâle conserveraient leur ancienneté.[25] En 1434, à la demande des frères du prieuré de St Gilles qui réclamaient sa présence en raison des difficultés du prieuré, le commandeur Pierre d'Uzès fut autorisé à regagner la Provence sans perdre son *ancianitas*.[26] Enfin, en 1437, les frères de la langue de Provence concédèrent la même faveur pendant trois ans à un frère du couvent qui se rendait en pèlerinage à Jérusalem.[27] Toutefois de telles décisions étaient prises au cas par cas.

D'autres dispositions capitulaires précisèrent le rôle de l'ancienneté dans l'accès aux commanderies. Un statut de 1428 rappela clairement les deux modes d'accès, le *cabimentum*, c'est-à-dire l'octroi d'une première commanderie en raison de l'ancienneté, et le *melioramentum*, c'est-à-dire l'obtention d'une meilleure commanderie, après avoir renoncé à la première. Ce statut imposait aux frères d'aller administrer personnellement pendant trois ans leurs commanderies de *cabimentum* avant de pouvoir en obtenir ensuite de meilleures selon leur rang. Toutefois, s'ils étaient retenus au couvent par le maître, ils pouvaient prétendre au *melioramentum* sans être allés administrer leurs commanderies de *cabimentum*.[28] En 1433 il fut décrété qu'un frère qui bénéficierait d'une recommandation d'une tierce personne dans l'attribution d'une commanderie ou d'un autre office non seulement se verrait privé de ceux-ci mais perdrait à jamais son *ancianitas*. L'exposé des motifs de ce statut mettait en avant le droit légitime des frères venus à Rhodes pour la défense de la foi et du couvent de recevoir sous forme de biens et de dignités la rémunération de leur 'travail'.[29]

La législation adoptée entre 1420 et 1440 donnait donc forme au principe de l'*ancianitas*, qui demeurait pourtant soumis à certaines limites et à des interprétations divergentes, sources de conflits entre les frères au sein des langues. L'accès aux commanderies par 'grâce magistrale' laissait au maître un vaste champ d'intervention.

---

22 Arch. dép. Haute-Garonne, H 13, Statut 33, fol. 87.
23 Ibid., H 14, fol. 136. Traduction du catalan.
24 Malta, Cod. 347, fol. 80v.
25 Ibid., 350, dos de page de garde du registre.
26 Ibid., 351, fol. 35r–v.
27 Ibid., 352, fol. 38v.
28 Arch. dép. Haute-Garonne, H 13, Statut 18, fol. 98v.
29 Ibid., Statut 55, fol. 111v.

Le maître décidait seul des nominations de commandeurs à ses chambres magistrales, comme Masdeu dans le prieuré de Catalogne et Aliaga dans la *Castellania.* Avec l'avis de son conseil il disposait des commanderies du Levant, comme Cos et Chypre, et de celles devenues vacantes lorsque leurs détenteurs mouraient au couvent, situation de plus en plus fréquente avec l'allongement de la durée des séjours outre-mer. Il pouvait aussi recourir aux 'rétentions' que lui reconnaissaient les chapitres généraux. Enfin, en se référant étrangement au 'record' du chapitre général de Montpellier de 1330, le maître se reconnaissait le droit d'accorder une deuxième commanderie à des frères méritants demeurant au couvent, ce qui lui permettait en fait d'en gratifier des dignitaires qu'il souhaitait favoriser.[30]

Il arrivait fréquemment qu'un frère bénéficiât d'une commanderie par grâce magistrale avant d'avoir reçu son *cabimentum* au titre de son *ancianitas.* Il n'en perdait pas pour autant ses droits au *cabimentum* auquel il pouvait toujours prétendre sans renoncer à la commanderie reçue par grâce magistrale. En 1436 Pere Ramon Sacosta, bailli de Rhodes, obtint avec l'accord des frères de sa langue la commanderie de Torrent de Cinca comme *cabimentum* sans devoir renoncer à celle d'Horta qu'il tenait du maître. Le précédent commandeur de Torrent, Azbert de Vilamari, avait au cours de la même réunion vu reconnaître son droit à la commanderie d'Ambel au titre de son *melioramentum* et Fluvià avait ratifié ces deux mouvements.[31] Cependant, l'affaire ne fut pas réglée pour autant car quatre ans plus tard Vilamari, après la mort de Fluvià, recourait au nouveau maître Lastic: il n'avait pu prendre possession d'Ambel qui avait été, au même moment, attribuée par le *castellan*, Joan de Vilagut, à Pedro de Linyan.[32] Le *castellan*, en tant que prieur, disposait en effet statutairement chaque année des commanderies vacantes, par *cabimentum* ou *melioramentum*, une fois exercée par le couvent sa préséance, limitée en principe à une seule vacance. Or en 1436 le maître, avec l'accord de la langue, avait accordé à Pedro Sarnes la commanderie de Villel pour son *cabimentum* et le *castellan* s'estimait en droit de pourvoir en son chapitre provincial les autres vacantes, dont Ambel, point de vue que ratifia Lastic.

Les différends les plus fréquents étaient dus aux disputes entre les frères eux-mêmes au sujet de leur ancienneté. Au sein du prieuré de Catalogne, Joan de Vilafranca, châtelain de Rhodes et commandeur de Vilafranca, Selma et Vallmoll, ne cessa de protester et de faire porter ses doléances dans les registres de chancellerie en alléguant que les frères Rafel Saplana et Felip d'Hortal comptaient moins d'ancienneté que lui lorsqu'ils lui furent préférés, l'un après l'autre, par les frères de leur langue comme drapiers ou pour d'autres dignités.[33] Certains cas étaient particulièrement ardus: en 1434, Pere Ramon Sacosta et Galceran de Sentmenat qui prétendaient tous les deux à la commanderie de Torrent de Cinca reconnurent devant l'assemblée des frères de leur langue qu'ils avaient la même ancienneté car tous les deux avaient

30 Par exemple, Malta, Cod. 350, fol. 124v (1434: attribution d une deuxième commanderie à Lluis de Mur, sénéchal du maître).

31 Ibid., 352, fols 69v–70.

32 Ibid., 354, fol. 113r–v (1441).

33 Ibid., 350, fols 141v–144 (1434), 351, fols 79v–80 (1434), 354, fol. 129 (1440), 357, fol. 94r–v.

fait leur 'passage' sur le même bateau et, arrivés à Rhodes, avaient pris l'habit le même jour au cours d'une messe solennelle à l'église St Jean.[34] La multiplication des disputes et conflits entraînait parfois le recours aux *esgards*, tribunal arbitral de l'ordre, et rendait nécessaire de procéder à une mise au point supplémentaire dans l'application de la règle de l'ancienneté.

Pendant le magistère de Lastic deux bulles vinrent mettre de l'ordre dans l'application de l'*ancianitas*, la première d'entre elles prise le 21 novembre 1442 par le maître lui-même pour les frères du prieuré de Catalogne,[35] la seconde émise le 25 avril 1446 pour ceux de la *Castellania de Amposta*, lors du chapitre général tenu à Rome en l'absence de Lastic, par les trois présidents du chapitre, le prieur de France, Foulcauld de Rochechouart, le prieur d'Angleterre Robert Botyll et le *castellan de Amposta*, Pere Ramon Sacosta.[36] Les deux textes présentent certaines différences et il convient de les examiner l'un après l'autre.

En 1442, dans le long exposé des motifs par lequel débute le texte de la bulle le maître dressait un tableau alarmant de l'état d'abandon des commanderies catalanes et des 'scandales, controverses et litiges' qui entachaient leur possession en raison, indiquait-il, de leur éloignement.[37] Afin de remédier à cette situation il était indispensable que les commanderies n'échappent plus aux frères anciens et méritants résidant au couvent au service de la religion. En conséquence, 'après mûre délibération', le maître et de son conseil avaient décidé que les frères du prieuré, réunis selon l'usage en leur auberge, devaient désigner comme bénéficiaires des commanderies vacantes les frères les plus anciens et les plus méritants, après avoir déclaré leur ordre d'ancienneté compté à partir de leur premier 'passage' au couvent. La véritable nouveauté consistait en l'émission par la chancellerie de lettres d'ancienneté, sous la forme de bulles magistrales remises à leurs bénéficiaires qui iraient, le moment venu, les présenter personnellement ou par l'intermédiaire de leurs procureurs au prieur ou à son lieutenant. Deux frères du prieuré, désignés au couvent par leurs pairs, seraient délégués auprès du prieur afin de faire respecter le rang, après examen des lettres d'ancienneté, lorsqu'une vacance se produirait. Ces deux frères percevraient un salaire annuel de quarante florins payé par la caisse du prieuré.

L'accès aux dignités de prieur de Catalogne et de bailli capitulaire de Majorque n'échappait pas à cette procédure mais dans tous les cas les droits du Trésor en matière de vacances devaient être respectés. L'accès à une commanderie de *melioramentum* devait être précédé de l'abandon par le bénéficiaire de sa précédente

34 Ibid., 352, fol. 69v.

35 Ibid., 355, fols 107v–109.

36 Ibid., 359 fol. 73r–v et 362 fols 67v–68v. Sur les circonstances particulières du chapitre général de Rome, convoqué par le pape Eugène IV sans la présence du maître Lastic voir R. Valentini, 'Un capitolo generale degli Ospitalieri di S: Giovanni tenuto in Vaticano nel 1446', *Archivio storico di Malta*, 7, Fasc.II (1936), 136–68 et Bonneaud, p. 317.

37 En fait, après la mort du prieur de Gualbes en 1439 le roi d Aragon, Alfonse le Magnanime, avait fait occuper plusieurs importantes commanderies pour y installer des Hospitaliers ayant sa faveur sans tenir compte des attributions décidées au couvent. Voir Bonneaud, pp. 293–9 et 312–31.

commanderie, de *cabimentum* ou d'un antérieur *melioramentum*. Si un frère refusait d'exercer son droit à un *melioramentum*, la commanderie vacante serait attribuée par le maître à un frère du couvent, en respectant l'ordre d'ancienneté. Le maître rappelait que ces dispositions n'affectaient en rien son droit de pourvoir par grâce magistrale sa 'chambre' de Masdeu non plus que d'exercer les prérogatives qui lui étaient reconnues par les statuts en matière de collations de commanderies. Il se réservait le droit d'annuler à tout moment toutes ces résolutions.

La bulle de 1446 concernant l'*ancianitas* dans la *Castellania* proclamait les mêmes principes. Toutefois elle limitait les déclarations d'ordre d'ancienneté par les frères du couvent, à un moment donné, aux deux ou au maximum aux trois frères les plus anciens, les suivants étant évidemment déclarés au fur et à mesure que les commanderies étaient pourvues. Il n'était pas prévu de déléguer auprès du *castellan* des frères du couvent choisis par leurs pairs. Le maître adresserait directement les bulles d'*ancianitas* au *castellan* ou à son lieutenant qui devraient en tenir compte dans l'attribution des commanderies vacantes, avec le conseil de deux ou trois commandeurs de la *Castellania*, et s'exposeraient à perdre une de leurs propres commanderies s'ils agissaient autrement. Une fois en possession de leurs commanderies les bénéficiaires devaient recevoir une bulle de confirmation du maître dans un délai non supérieur à un an et demi.

Comme en 1442 le maître voyait réaffirmés avec force ses droits en matière de collations par grâce magistrale. Ses décisions étaient toujours préférentielles et si un commandeur pourvu par le *castellan* voyait ensuite sa commanderie attribuée par le maître à un autre frère il devait s'effacer et même restituer les rentes qu'il aurait perçues. Il était même prescrit au *castellan* d'exiger une caution de la part de celui qu'il aurait désigné afin de faire face aux frais de telles restitutions.

Aucun document général ni aucun statut ne vinrent semble t'il concerner l'ensemble des frères de l'ordre sur le 'mode d'emploi' de l'*ancianitas*. Nous n'avons pas non plus trouvé dans les archives de Malte de bulles comparables pour les autres prieurés. Mais la pratique observée dans l'accès aux commanderies, ailleurs qu'en Catalogne et en Aragon, faisait partout appel à la déclaration des rangs d'ancienneté par les frères de la langue, suivie en général par des bulles de confirmation du maître et de son conseil,[38] et à l'examen par les assemblées des collations autres que celles réservées au maître.

De quelle manière les deux bulles de 1442 et 1446 furent-elles appliquées dans le prieuré et la *Castellania* dans les vingt années qui suivirent leur adoption? Les informations à ce sujet proviennent, en dehors des archives de Malte, de celles du prieuré à Barcelone, de la *Castellania* à Madrid et également de la chancellerie royale à Barcelone. En raison de leur abondance nous nous limiterons à évoquer les grandes lignes des évolutions constatées.

Pendant cette période les frères de la langue se réunirent très fréquemment au sujet de l'*ancianitas*. A l'auberge d'Espagne les assemblées se faisaient séparément pour chaque prieuré, lorsqu'il ne s'agissait pas de sujets communs à tous ceux de la langue, généralement sous la présidence du drapier ou de son lieutenant et

38 Sarnowsky, *Macht und Herrschaft*, p. 217.

avec l'autorisation du maître à qui il était ensuite rendu compte des débats. Les déclarations d'ancienneté, conformément aux décisions de 1442 et 1446, pouvaient concerner une dizaine de frères à la fois dans le prieuré mais seulement deux ou trois dans la *Castellania*.[39] Un frère du couvent, le commandeur Despilles, fut envoyé en 1445 en Catalogne pour représenter ses pairs auprès du prieur lors des vacances de commanderies.[40]

La procédure des bulles nominatives d'*ancianitas* semble avoir été scrupuleusement suivie. Le *castellan* en était destinataire et se voyait enjoindre par le maître d'attribuer les vacances aux bénéficiaires désignés.[41] Lorsque ces derniers se trouvaient hors du couvent le caractère et la cause de leur absence étaient parfois déclarés mais il était de plus en plus fréquemment indiqué sans aucune réserve qu'ils bénéficieraient de l'ancienneté pendant leurs séjours en Occident comme s'ils demeuraient au couvent.[42] Une bulle d'*ancianitas* fut émise en 1456 en faveur de Jaume de La Geltru, bailli de Majorque, précisant qu'en raison de son rang d'ancienneté, présent ou non au couvent, il pourrait accéder au prieuré de Catalogne et à d'autres dignités et honneurs. Lors de la mort du prieur, Gilabert de Loscos, en 1460, La Geltru se prévalut de cette bulle pour réclamer et obtenir le prieuré de Catalogne.[43]

Les difficultés dans l'application des règles étaient souvent d'ordre interne. Les conflits entre les frères et les protestations consignées dans les registres de chancellerie au sujet des rangs d'ancienneté étaient monnaie courante. Les commanderies ne constituant plus les lieux de vie collective des frères qu'elles avaient été aux siècles précédents, elles étaient mises en fermage avec l'autorisation du maître. Les rentes qu'elles produisaient se transformaient en liquidités pour les commandeurs qui en faisaient bénéficier des membres de leurs familles si, retenus au couvent, ils ne les percevaient pas eux-mêmes. Au nom de l'*ancianitas* les frères du couvent se disputaient avidement l'accès aux vacances Ils prétendaient parfois que l'ancienneté d'un frère ne pouvait lui être accordée parce qu'il n'avait pas payé son passage ou parce qu'il n'avait pas, en arrivant au couvent, l'âge requis pour partir en caravane, des preuves devant alors être fournies.[44] En 1462, les frères demeurant au couvent se plaignirent au prieur de France, qui exerçait les pouvoirs du maître entre la mort de Milly et l'arrivée à Rhodes de son successeur Sacosta, de l'utilisation frauduleuse par des frères résidant en Catalogne de leur première bulle d'*ancianitas*. Il fut alors décidé que de tels documents ne pouvaient être présentés qu'une seule fois et qu'il était obligatoire de retourner au couvent pour prétendre à une nouvelle commanderie.[45]

39 Voir entre autres, pour le prieuré, Malta, Cod. 357, fol. 92v (1445) et 377, fol. 84rv (1468), pour la *Castellania*, 361 fol. 102v (1448) et 368, fol. 74v (1459).

40 Ibid., 356, fol. 87v.

41 Ibid., 361, fol. 102v (1448), 364, fols 56–57 (1453), 369, fol. 60 etc.

42 Ibid., 375, fol. 70v (1455).

43 Ibid., 366, fol. 73 et ACA, Archivo del Gran Priorato, 573, fol. 28r–v.

44 Ibid., 363, fol. 86 et 369, fol. 89r–v.

45 Ibid., 371, fol. 84r–v. Voir également, Sarnowsky, *Macht und Herrschaft*, p. 166, note 102.

L'attribution de commanderies par grâce magistrale et l'existence des chambres prieurales limitaient les disponibilités ouvertes aux frères au titre de l'ancienneté. Dans le prieuré de Catalogne, en 1445, huit commanderies relevaient de l'attribution du maître et quatre autres constituaient les chambres du prieur.[46] Il n'en demeurait que treize à distribuer au fil des vacances.

Des interventions extérieures à l'ordre rendaient par ailleurs précaires l'exercice des droits de l'*ancianitas*. Le roi d'Aragon, Alphonse le Magnanime, multiplia les pressions, jusqu'à sa mort en 1458, pour faire attribuer les commanderies aragonaises et catalanes à ses protégés qui étaient rarement les frères les plus anciens du couvent. Comme le roi n'hésitait jamais à faire saisir par ses officiers les commanderies pour y installer ses candidats et à recourir au pape Nicolas V pour obtenir des collations qui s'imposaient alors à l'ordre, le maître et les frères de la langue devaient accepter de composer avec les exigences du monarque. Deux ans après la mort du Magnanime une situation de troubles et de guerre civile déchira la Catalogne et l'Aragon à un moindre degré. Alors que les frères du couvent et le maître continuaient à réclamer et à attribuer des commanderies au nom de l'ancienneté, la mise en possession de celles-ci par leurs attributaires devenait impossible car dans bien des cas elles étaient aux mains de détenteurs illégitimes.

Devant de telles difficultés, l'attente d'une commanderie au titre de l'ancienneté pouvait s'avérer fort longue. Pour parvenir à leurs fins certains frères occupaient sans droit, souvent avec l'appui du roi, la commanderie qu'ils convoitaient, parfois en dédommageant son détenteur légitime. Ainsi, le frère Bernat Guillem de Foxa fut plusieurs fois convoqué à Rhodes par le maître car il occupait sans droit la commanderie de La Senia et Alcanar dont avait été pourvu Alfonso Diez d'Aulx. Il se maintint néanmoins en possession illégitime de cette commanderie jusqu'à la négociation d'un accord avec Diez d'Aulx qui renonça à ses droits, moyennant paiement d'une rente annuelle de 50 florins, avec l'agrément des frères de la *Castellania*.[47] D'autres s'unissaient par des pactes de solidarité à l'instar des trois frères de la *Castellania*, Luis d'Azagra, Alfonso de Linyan et Carles de Torelles, qui avaient la même ancienneté et s'engagèrent, en faisant consigner leur accord par la chancellerie, à se partager les fruits des commanderies qu'ils obtiendraient jusqu'à ce que chacun d'entre eux ait effectivement été pourvu. Peu importait, déclaraient-ils, de qui ils tiendraient ces commanderies: des frères de la langue en tant que *cabimentum*, du maître par grâce magistrale, du *castellan de Amposta*, du pape ou du roi.[48]

En 1449, Lastic, lors du chapitre général, prit la décision d'ériger en commanderies certains 'membres' de celles-ci ou de mettre un terme à la politique d'union entre des commanderies de faible rendement, dans le prieuré comme dans la *Castellania*.[49] Cette nouvelle politique de morcellement qui diminuait les revenus de chaque commandeur permettait évidemment de satisfaire un plus grand nombre d'aspirants, mais Lastic argumentait que devant les occupations illégitimes il serait plus facile

46 Ibid., 357, fol. 96.

47 Ibid., 366, fol. 64 (1456), 367, fol. 62 (1457), 368, fol. 82v (1458), 370, fols 72r–73.

48 Ibid., 361, fol. 101v (1448).

49 Ibid., 361, fols 130–131 (Prieuré) et 126v–127v (*Castellania*).

aux frères issus du couvent d'administrer et de conserver des bénéfices plus restreints et moins dispersés. En 1462, un autre chapitre général décida de mettre un terme à une pratique trop développée des grâces magistrales, en évoquant les nombreux litiges dus à la confusion des statuts sur les collations de commanderies par grâce magistrales, *quolibet decennio*. Ces statuts antérieurs, coutumes et usages (issus du chapitre général de Montpellier de 1330) étaient donc annulés, le maître n'étant plus autorisé à pourvoir par grâce magistrale qu'une seule commanderie tous le cinq ans à des frères rèsident au convent.[50]

La généralisation de la règle de l'*ancianitas* au XVe siècle ne doit pas être considérée comme le simple choix d'une formule plutôt qu'une autre dans le mode de déroulement des carrières, sinon comme une des pièces clefs d'une nouvelle stratégie de l'ordre visant à accroître le nombre et le temps de présence des frères chevaliers au couvent. Marquant le même tournant, deux autres pratiques étaient au service de la même politique. Le développement des autorisations de mise en fermage permit aux commandeurs de s'éloigner de leurs commanderies et de financer leur séjour à Rhodes, alors que l'exigence renouvelée d'une origine noble ou chevaleresque pour les frères chevaliers devait contribuer à mieux préparer ceux-ci à la défense de l'archipel. Par ailleurs, la règle de l'*ancianitas* eut pour conséquence directe de renforcer le rôle des langues et de leurs frères dans le gouvernement de l'ordre.

50 Ibid., 282, fol. 115r–v.

Chapter 19

Los Hospitalarios y los últimos reyes de Navarra (1483–1512)

Carlos Barquero Goñi

Introducción

Como muestra de mi profunda admiración y respeto al Dr. Anthony Luttrell en su 75 cumpleaños, me he decidido a redactar el siguiente trabajo. Se trata de un pequeño artículo que trata el tema de la Orden del Hospital u Orden de San Juan al final de la Edad Media, materia sobre la cual he aprendido mucho en las numerosas publicaciones del profesor Luttrell al respecto.

Como es bien conocido, al llegar el fin de la Edad Media Navarra era el reino más pequeño de todo el Occidente Europeo.[1] Sin embargo, según vamos a tener ocasión de comprobar a continuación, los hospitalarios mantuvieron unas relaciones muy estrechas con los últimos reyes de Navarra como reino 'independiente', Juan III de Albret y Catalina de Foix. Como es bien sabido, Catalina de Foix se convirtió en reina de Navarra tras la muerte de su hermano, el monarca navarro Francisco Febo, en 1483. Al año siguiente se casó con Juan de Albret, que se convirtió así en rey consorte. Sin embargo, en la práctica no pudieron iniciar su gobierno efectivo en el reino hasta que Francia y España no se pusieron de acuerdo para que, bajo protección de tropas de ambos países, viajaran a Navarra y se coronaran en Pamplona en 1494.[2] Después de más de medio siglo de continua guerra civil entre los bandos nobiliarios de los agramonteses y de los beaumonteses, el reinado conjunto de Juan III de Albret y Catalina I de Foix significó para Navarra hasta su brusco final en 1512 un periodo de relativa paz y de incipiente recuperación del poder real.[3] Por entonces las relaciones de los monarcas navarros con los hospitalarios y, más concretamente, con el prior de San Juan en Navarra se intensificaron.

Desde los siglos XII y XIII existía en Navarra un priorato hospitalario que era, además, uno de los señoríos más importantes del reino.[4] Durante la Baja Edad

---

1 B. Leroy, *Le royaume de Navarre à la fin du Moyen Age* (Aldershot, 1990), I, p. 79.

2 P. Boissonnade, *Histoire de la réunion de la Navarre a la Castille. Essai sur les relations des princes de Foix-Albret avec la France et l'Espagne (1479–1521)* (París, 1893), pp. 32–99.

3 J.M. Lacarra, *Historia política del reino de Navarra. Desde sus orígenes hasta su incorporación a Castilla* (Pamplona, 1972–73), 3, pp. 396–402. E. Ramírez Vaquero, *Estudios sobre la realeza navarra en el siglo XV* (Pamplona, 2005).

4 S. García Larragueta, *El gran priorado de Navarra de la Orden de San Juan de Jerusalén (siglos XII–XIII)* (Pamplona, 1957), 2 volúmenes.

Media su importancia social y política no disminuyó sino que, por el contrario, se incrementó.[5] En consecuencia, el prior de San Juan se convirtió en una figura relevante en la corte navarra. De hecho, habitualmente era un estrecho colaborador de los reyes. Sólo a mediados del siglo XV, durante el priorazgo de Juan de Beaumont (1435–87), mostró una postura levantisca frente a la corona. Sin embargo, a fines de la centuria sus inmediatos sucesores en el cargo, Pedro de Espinal (1487–91) y sobre todo Berenguer Sanz de Berrozpe (1491–1513), habían retomado la política tradicional de proximidad a la monarquía.[6]

Protección real del patrimonio hospitalario

En efecto, los reyes de Navarra parecen mantener unas relaciones bastante cordiales con los hospitalarios durante esta época. No efectúan donaciones a la Orden, pero sí se preocupan por mantener la integridad del patrimonio y rentas sanjuanistas en el reino durante una época en la que los navarros experimentaban una situación económica delicada, en la que de forma incipiente comenzaban a recuperarse de la profunda crisis del periodo inmediatamente anterior.[7] Las medidas que los reyes de Navarra tomaron en este sentido fueron muy diversas. Así, los monarcas repetidamente ordenaron la devolución a los hospitalarios de todas las propiedades de la Orden de San Juan cuyos usufructuarios no pagasen el censo estipulado a la Orden en 1498, 1504 y 1509.[8] También mandaron a sus oficiales en 1492 que devolvieran al prior del Hospital en Navarra la posesión de las encomiendas de Aberin, Echávarri, Melgar y Cogullo, las cuales se encontraban ocupadas ilegalmente por Jacobo Velaz.[9] Además, en 1499 los monarcas junto con los alcaldes del tribunal de la Cort sentenciaron a favor del convento sanjuanista de Puente la Reina un pleito que enfrentaba a dicho cenobio con el Hospital de Roncesvalles por unas propiedades en Puente la Reina.[10] En 1502 la reina Catalina de Foix prometía al prior de Navarra, Berenguer Sanz de Berrozpe, la futura concesión de una licencia para exportar trigo fuera del reino.[11] Posteriormente, en 1503 los monarcas reconocieron al prior una rebaja en la fiscalidad real que debía abonar el señorío hospitalario de Ribaforada.[12] Finalmente,

5 C. Barquero Goñi, *La Orden de San Juan de Jerusalén en Navarra. Siglos XIV y XV* (Pamplona, 2004).

6 C. Barquero Goñi, 'The Hospitallers and the Kings of Navarre in the Fourteenth and Fifteenth Centuries', *The Military Orders. Volume 2. Welfare and Warfare*, ed. H. Nicholson (Aldershot, 1998), pp. 349–54. C. Barquero Goñi, *La Orden de San Juan de Jerusalén en Navarra*, pp. 37–61 y 94–106.

7 P.J. Monteano, *Los navarros ante el hambre, la peste, la guerra y la fiscalidad. Siglos XV y XVI* (Pamplona, 1999).

8 Archivo Histórico Nacional, Madrid [ANH], Órdenes Militares [OO.MM], carpeta 850, no. 31; legajo 8538, no. 3^2; legajo 8569, nos 5 y 7.

9 AHN, OO.MM, legajo 8533, no. 33.

10 Archivo General de Navarra, Sección de Clero, Convento del Crucifijo de Puente la Reina, legajo 6, no. 55.

11 AHN, OO.MM, carpeta 847, no. 15.

12 AHN, OO.MM, carpeta 847, no. 21.

los reyes facilitaron a los freires sanjuanistas la obtención de copias de cualquier documento que necesitasen para la defensa de su patrimonio en Navarra.[13]

Es importante señalar que la monarquía preservó los derechos señoriales de la Orden en el reino. En 1498 los reyes Juan III de Albret y Catalina de Foix mandaron a sus oficiales que dieran las cantidades derivadas de las multas por delitos en Fustiñana y en los otros lugares de la Orden de San Juan al prior del Hospital en Navarra, Berenguer Sanz de Berrozpe.[14] Posteriormente, en 1504 los mismos monarcas pronunciaron una sentencia a favor del comendador hospitalario de Fustiñana, en la que le reconocieron el disfrute de la jurisdicción baja y media en su encomienda.[15] Se trata de los mismos derechos señoriales que la Orden de San Juan tradicionalmente venía gozando en sus dominios de Navarra al menos desde el siglo XIV, ya que la monarquía siempre se había reservado celosamente el ejercicio de la alta jurisdicción criminal.[16]

Proximidad del prior del Hospital a los monarcas

Por su parte, el prior del Hospital en Navarra a fines del siglo XV y principios del siglo XVI, Berenguer Sanz de Berrozpe, aparece en las fuentes como una figura bastante cercana y próxima a los reyes. Se conserva una interesante correspondencia dirigida por los monarcas al prior en la que le manifiestan mucha familiaridad e intimidad. En primer lugar, sabemos que el prior del Hospital frecuentemente hace pequeños regalos, consistentes sobre todo en fruta, a Catalina de Foix. La reina siempre agradece cortésmente al prior por carta todos estos obsequios.[17] El rey Juan III de Albret también recibió en alguna ocasión un presente del prior.[18]

Además, los monarcas escriben al prior para informarle de acontecimientos familiares, como el nacimiento de un hijo de la pareja en 1507[19] o el nuevo embarazo de la reina en 1510.[20] Las cartas de los reyes de Navarra a frey Berenguer Sanz de Berrozpe también tratan de cuestiones de política exterior, especialmente de las relaciones de los monarcas navarros con Fernando el Católico.[21] Asímismo, la correspondencia alude a problemas de política interna, como la rebelión del conde de Lerín en 1507.[22] Finalmente, a veces los reyes solicitan la colaboración del prior con la administración real.[23]

---

13 AHN, OO.MM, carpeta 914, no. 43; legajo 8488, no. 33; carpeta 899, no. 51 y carpeta 889, no. 313.

14 AHN, OO.MM, legajo 8516, no. 18.

15 AHN, OO.MM, carpeta 899, nos 38 y 39.

16 C. Barquero Goñi, *La Orden de San Juan de Jerusalén en Navarra*, pp. 47–8.

17 AHN, OO.MM, carpeta 847, nos 14, 24, 26, 27, 28, 38, 43 y 44.

18 AHN, OO.MM, carpeta 847, no. 11.

19 AHN, OO.MM, carpeta 847, no. 30.

20 AHN, OO.MM, carpeta 847, no. 35. Publicado por A. Millares Carlo, *Tratado de Paleografía Española* (Madrid, 1983), III, no. 374.

21 AHN, OO.MM, carpeta 847, nos 29, 33 y 36.

22 AHN, OO.MM, carpeta 847, no. 25.

23 AHN, OO.MM, carpeta 847, nos 40 y 41.

También conocemos que la cabeza de los hospitalarios navarros actúa como consejero de los monarcas en determinadas ocasiones. Tradicionalmente, el prior de San Juan había formado parte del Consejo Real de Navarra durante la Baja Edad Media. Sin embargo, durante este reinado parece que el prior no formaba parte formalmente de él, al igual que la mayoría de los personajes importantes del reino porque el Consejo ya estaba bastante profesionalizado.[24] No obstante, todavía ocasionalmente los monarcas requerían su asesoramiento. Por ejemplo, el 23 de agosto de 1498 la reina Catalina de Navarra escribió a Berenguer Sanz de Berrozpe, prior de San Juan en Navarra, para que acudiera a Pamplona el día 2 de septiembre siguiente con el fin de hablar con ella antes de que Catalina partiera de allí para visitar a sus señoríos del otro lado de los Pirineos. La reina llega a calificar al prior en su carta como 'fiel consejero'.[25] Otro caso bastante similar lo encontramos en 1506, cuando los monarcas Catalina de Foix y Juan III de Albret solicitaron al prior de la Orden de San Juan que retrasase su proyectado viaje a Castilla ya que su presencia les era necesaria para aconsejarles en ciertos asuntos.[26]

La influencia del prior Berenguer Sanz de Berrozpe cerca de los reyes de Navarra llegó hasta el punto de llegar a situar a un pariente suyo cercano dentro del Consejo Real. Como es bien conocido, se trataba de un organismo dotado de mucho poder dentro de la monarquía navarra de la época.[27] A principios del siglo XVI el prior presentó un sobrino suyo a los monarcas como candidato para cubrir la vacante producida en el Consejo por la muerte de Fernando de Baquedano. Los reyes inicialmente rechazaron la propuesta en agosto de 1502.[28] Sin embargo, al mes siguiente finalmente la aceptaron.[29]

Participación del prior del Hospital en las reuniones de las Cortes navarras

No obstante, la actividad política del prior del Hospital junto a la monarquía navarra se encauzó en buena parte mediante su participación en las Cortes del reino. Como es bien conocido, durante la Baja Edad Media y la Edad Moderna el prior de San Juan asistía regularmente a las reuniones de Cortes de Navarra dentro del brazo eclesiástico.[30] Hay que recordar también que durante el reinado de Juan III de Albret y Catalina de Foix, las Cortes conservaban un poder bastante notable en Navarra, a diferencia de lo que ocurría en otros reinos por la misma época.[31] Por eso es destacable que los monarcas navarros continuamente convoquen al prior de San

24 J.J. Salcedo Izu, *El Consejo Real de Navarra en el siglo XVI* (Pamplona, 1964), pp. 19–40.

25 AHN, OO.MM, carpeta 847, no. 8.

26 AHN, OO.MM, carpeta 847, no. 23.

27 Salcedo Izu, pp. 33–40.

28 AHN, OO.MM, carpeta 847, no. 18.

29 AHN, OO.MM, carpeta 847, no. 19.

30 M.P. Huici Goñi, *Las Cortes de Navarra durante la Edad Moderna* (Madrid, 1963), pp. 13–48.

31 Boissonnade, pp. 180–3. Lacarra, 3, p. 399.

Juan en Navarra a las reuniones de las Cortes. Sabemos que así lo hicieron de forma repetida en los años 1500, 1507, 1510 y 1511.[32]

Durante la celebración de las Cortes, el prior del Hospital gozaba de un asiento preferente dentro del brazo eclesiástico. Precisamente en esta época se produjo una agria disputa entre el prior de San Juan y el prior de Roncesvalles por la preferencia de asiento en las Cortes inmediatamente después del obispo de Pamplona. En 1499 la infanta doña Catalina, lugarteniente general de los reyes de Navarra, ordenó que el entonces prior de Roncesvalles, Juan de Egües, tuviera un asiento en Cortes preferente al del prior de San Juan mientras viviese. No obstante, después de su muerte sería el prior de San Juan quien tendría dicho asiento.[33] El mandato de la infanta correspondía, en realidad, a una sentencia del Consejo Real de Navarra emitida en la misma fecha y con idéntico contenido.[34] La disposición de doña Catalina fue confirmada por los propios monarcas navarros en 1500.[35] Sin embargo, no fue la solución definitiva al conflicto y el pleito se prolongó durante unos años más. Finalmente, en 1505 el Consejo Real decidió que el prior de Roncesvalles y el prior de San Juan se alternasen en ocupar el segundo asiento en el brazo eclesiástico de las Cortes de Navarra.[36]

Dentro de las reuniones de las Cortes, el papel del prior del Hospital parece que fue bastante activo. Por ejemplo, en 1501 las Cortes a propuesta de los reyes nombraron una comisión para entender en la reforma del patrimonio real.[37] Uno de los elegidos para formar parte de dicha comisión fue precisamente el prior de San Juan, Berenguer Sanz de Berrozpe.[38] La citada comisión fue uno de los antecedentes de la posterior Diputación del Reino.[39] Parece que tuvo alguna vida efectiva.[40] Por lo menos sabemos que en febrero de 1502 los reyes de Navarra, Juan III de Albret y Catalina de Foix, mandaron al prior de San Juan en Navarra que el primer domingo de Cuaresma siguiente estuviera en la villa de Olite para entender en la negociación de la reforma junto con las otras personas diputadas para ello, según había sido acordado en las últimas Cortes anteriores celebradas en Pamplona.[41]

El prior del Hospital en Navarra no sólo participaba en las reuniones de las Cortes, sino que también era convocado a otras asambleas de diferente naturaleza. Es lo que ocurrió con una junta de eclesiásticos que el vicario general del obispado de Pamplona pretendió reunir en 1503 con el apoyo del rey de Navarra. El 12 de junio de dicho año el monarca Juan III de Albret escribió al prior de Navarra, Berenguer

---

32 AHN, OO.MM, carpeta 847, nos 13, 31, 34, 37 y 39. Millares Carlo, III, no. 375.

33 AHN, OO.MM, carpeta 850, no. 32. Publicado por C. Barquero Goñi, *La Orden de San Juan de Jerusalén en Navarra*, pp. 300–2.

34 AHN, OO.MM, carpeta 850, no. 33.

35 AHN, OO.MM, carpeta 850, no. 34 y legajo 8496[1], no. 1.

36 J. Ibarra, *Historia de Roncesvalles* (Pamplona, 1936), pp. 387–90. F. Miranda García y E. Ramírez Vaquero, *Roncesvalles* (Pamplona, 1999), pp. 63–5.

37 Lacarra, III, pp. 396–7.

38 M.P. Huici Goñi, *La Cámara de Comptos de Navarra entre 1328–1512 con precedentes desde 1258* (Pamplona, 1988), p. 169.

39 Huici Goñi, *Las Cortes de Navarra*, p. 361.

40 P.J. Monteano, pp. 295–6.

41 AHN, OO.MM, carpeta 847, no. 16.

Sanz de Berrozpe, para informarle de que dicha junta finalmente no había podido celebrarse precisamente porque habían faltado el propio prior de San Juan y el abad del monasterio de La Oliva. En consecuencia, se les citaba de nuevo a ambos para una nueva convocatoria el día 16 de junio siguiente.[42] Sin embargo, en la fecha prevista el prior del Hospital volvió a faltar, al igual que otros prelados. Por ello el 28 de junio de 1503 el rey de Navarra pidió al prior Berenguer Sanz de Berrozpe que por lo menos enviara a un representante suyo al sínodo, que se pretendía reunir el día 1 de agosto siguiente en Pamplona.[43] Desconocemos si esta asamblea finalmente se celebró o si acudió a ella algún procurador del prior de San Juan, aunque sí que llama poderosamente la atención el gran interés de la monarquía navarra porque el prior participase en ella. No parece que se trate de un sínodo diocesano, pues en esta época tan sólo tenemos noticia de uno reunido por el vicario general de la diócesis de Pamplona, Juan de Monterde, en la propia ciudad de Pamplona en abril de 1499.[44]

Intervencionismo de los reyes de Navarra en los asuntos internos del priorato hospitalario

La contrapartida del respaldo general de los reyes de Navarra a los hospitalarios fue su intervencionismo sobre el priorato de la Orden en su reino. Dicho intervencionismo formaba parte de una política más global de control de la Iglesia navarra por parte de la monarquía, en la que obtuvo un relativo éxito a fines del siglo XV y principios del XVI. Los reyes perseguían, en especial, que todos los cargos eclesiásticos de su reino fueran ocupados por navarros y no por extranjeros. Además, en la medida de lo posible, los monarcas también procuraban influir en los nombramientos, presentando ellos a los candidatos.[45] Sabemos que el propio prior de San Juan colaboró activamente con los reyes en esta política. En 1500 y por expreso encargo del monarca navarro, el prior Berenguer Sanz de Berrozpe hizo gestiones con el deán de Tudela, Juan Cabañas, para que los oficiales de la iglesia de Tudela que éste designara fueran naturales del reino y no extranjeros.[46]

En el caso de la Orden de San Juan, el grado de influencia obtenido por los reyes Juan III de Albret y Catalina de Foix en los asuntos internos del priorato navarro fue bastante grande. El control de la monarquía se hizo especialmente evidente en las designaciones de los principales cargos de la Orden en el reino por parte del maestre del Hospital o del Papa.

El intervencionismo de la realeza ya se manifestó a la hora del nombramiento de un nuevo prior de San Juan en Navarra tras la muerte de Pedro de Espinal en 1491. Entonces los monarcas navarros, Juan III de Albret y Catalina de Foix, procedieron a secuestrar el priorato para evitar la designación de un prior que no fuera natural de su reino. Afortunadamente, el papa Inocencio VIII nombró entonces para el puesto a

42 AHN, OO.MM, carpeta 847, no. 20.

43 AHN, OO.MM, carpeta 847, no. 22.

44 J. Goñi Gaztambide, *Historia de los obispos de Pamplona. II. Siglos XIV–XV* (Pamplona, 1979), pp. 662–5.

45 Boissonnade, pp. 174–7.

46 AHN, OO.MM, carpeta 847, nos 11 y 12.

un hospitalario navarro, Berenguer Sanz de Berrozpe, cuya elección fue del gusto de los reyes. En consecuencia, en septiembre de 1491 los reyes de Navarra ordenaron levantar la aprehensión del priorato del Hospital y mandaron a sus oficiales que dieran posesión de él a Berenguer Sanz de Berrozpe.[47]

La monarquía navarra también pretendió influir en las designaciones de los comendadores sanjuanistas en su reino. En 1496 los reyes Juan III de Albret y Catalina de Foix solicitaron al maestre del Hospital, Pedro d'Aubusson, que nombrara comendador de Apat a Juan de la Lana, capellán de los monarcas.[48] Simultáneamente, los reyes rogaron al prior de San Juan en Navarra, Berenguer Sanz de Berrozpe, que realizara todas las gestiones oportunas para que dicha designación se verificase efectivamente.[49] La monarquía también interfería en los nombramientos de priores o vicarios de los templos hospitalarios. Por ejemplo, en 1499 el rey de Navarra, Juan III de Albret, encargó al prior de San Juan que designara vicario de la iglesia de Esparza a don Juan.[50] Parece que era necesaria siempre por lo menos la aprobación previa de la monarquía para el candidato a ocupar el puesto. Así, en 1502 la reina de Navarra, Catalina de Foix, comunicó al prior de San Juan en Navarra que tanto ella como su marido habían acogido favorablemente su petición de que la vacante del priorato de Caparroso fuera para un sobrino del prior.[51] En este mismo caso se comprueba que la monarquía podía llegar a intervenir para forzar al prior a acatar nombramientos efectuados directamente por el Papa, ya que en 1507 el rey de Navarra mandó al prior Berenguer Sanz de Berrozpe que obedeciera la designación de vicario de Caparroso efectuada por el pontífice Julio II en favor de Pedro de Peralta y en contra de los deseos del prior, que ya conocemos.[52]

El caso del convento hospitalario del Crucifijo en Puente la Reina es especialmente elocuente a la hora de constatar el severo control de la monarquía navarra sobre los nombramientos de cargos de la Orden en Navarra. Aquí sabemos que cuando el priorazgo del cenobio quedó vacante en 1511, los reyes Juan III de Albret y Catalina de Foix encargaron a frey Juan de Lizarazu que se hiciera cargo del priorato del convento de forma interina mientras se procedía a la elección de un nuevo prior.[53] Sin embargo, cuando el prior de Navarra finalmente nombró prior del convento a frey Carlos de Ayanz en detrimento de frey Íñigo de Caparroso, los monarcas navarros procedieron a embargar los bienes del priorato del monasterio del Crucifijo. Dicho embargo no fue levantado hasta 1515, ya después de la conquista del reino por Fernando el Católico.[54]

Otra manifestación del intervencionismo de los reyes de Navarra en los asuntos del priorato sanjuanista de su reino fue su papel como árbitros en las disputas internas

47 AHN, OO.MM, carpeta 850, no. 29.

48 AHN, OO.MM, carpeta 847, no. 6. C. Gutiérrez del Arroyo, *Catálogo de la documentación navarra de la Orden de San Juan de Jerusalén en el Archivo Histórico Nacional. Siglos XII–XIX* (Pamplona, 1992), 1, p. 24.

49 AHN, OO.MM, carpeta 847, no. 7.

50 AHN, OO.MM, carpeta 847, no. 9.

51 AHN, OO.MM, carpeta 847, no. 17.

52 AHN, OO.MM, carpeta 847, no. 32.

53 AHN, OO.MM, legajo 8568, no. 114.

54 AHN, OO.MM, legajo 8568, no. 14.

entre los principales hospitalarios navarros. A principios del siglo XVI éstos eran el prior de Navarra, Berenguer Sanz de Berrozpe, y el comendador de Induráin, Juan López de Eulate. Sabemos que mantuvieron, por lo menos, dos enfrentamientos que fueron dirimidos por la monarquía con resultado alterno. El primero de ellos en 1504 fue resuelto en favor del prior.[55] La decisión real en el segundo conflicto resultó ser favorable a los intereses de Juan López de Eulate en 1506.[56]

Conclusión: los hospitalarios y la conquista del reino de Navarra por Fernando el Católico

La invasión y ocupación de Navarra por las tropas de Fernando el Católico en 1512 pusieron un brusco final a las relaciones de los reyes Juan III de Albret y Catalina de Foix con los hospitalarios navarros. A pesar de los subsiguientes contraataques de los monarcas y sus descendientes, apoyados por Francia, no volvemos a tener noticia de posteriores contactos suyos con la Orden de San Juan.[57] Tan sólo el abandono de la parte del territorio del antiguo reino situada al norte de los Pirineos por las tropas españolas a partir de 1527,[58] ocasionó que dos encomiendas hospitalarias situadas en la zona, las de Apat e Irisarry, volvieran a quedar sujetas a la jurisdicción de los descendientes directos de Juan III de Albret y Catalina de Foix durante el siglo XVI, a pesar de que siguieron formando parte del priorato sanjuanista de Navarra.[59]

Para finalizar, puede ser conveniente dedicar algunas líneas para analizar las interesantes relaciones establecidas Fernando el Católico con el priorato hospitalario de Navarra. Como es bien conocido, el monarca conquistó e incorporó Navarra a sus reinos a partir de 1512.[60] Sin embargo, los Reyes Católicos habían mantenido contactos previos con el entonces prior del Hospital en Navarra, Berenguer Sanz de Berrozpe. Ya en 1488, cuando todavía era sólo comendador de Santa Catalina, el Consejo Real de Castilla había mandado al alcaide de Los Arcos, Lope de Porras, que no ocupase las rentas y bienes de la Orden de San Juan en las encomiendas de Berenguer Sanz de Berrozpe.[61] Posteriormente, tras ascender al puesto de prior de Navarra, los Reyes Católicos le habían prestado su ayuda en 1492 a la hora de tomar

55 AHN, OO.MM, carpeta 904, no. 17.

56 AHN, OO.MM, carpeta 889, no. 311.

57 Boissonnade, pp. 321–560. L. Suárez Fernández, *Fernando el Católico y Navarra* (Madrid, 1985), pp. 236–44. A. Floristán Imizcoz, *La monarquía española y el gobierno del reino de Navarra, 1512–1808* (Pamplona, 1991), pp. 13–92. M.P. Huici Goñi, *En torno a la conquista de Navarra* (Pamplona, 1993). M.I. Ostolaza Elizondo, 'El Reino de Navarra en el dilema de su incorporación a Castilla o su fidelidad a los Albret. Agramonteses y beamonteses entre 1512–1524', *Huarte de San Juan. Geografía e Historia*, 1 (1994), 55–81. P. Esarte Muniain, *Navarra, 1512–1530. Conquista, ocupación y sometimiento militar, civil y eclesiástico* (Pamplona, 2001).

58 S. Herreros Lopetegui, *Las tierras navarras de Ultrapuertos (siglos XII–XVI)* (Pamplona, 1998), pp. 123–45.

59 AHN, OO.MM, legajo 8572, no. 74–83; carpeta 943, no. 10; carpeta 944, no. 5; legajo 8573, no. 17.

60 Suárez Fernández, pp. 242–4. Floristán Imizcoz, pp. 15–62.

61 Archivo General de Simancas, Registro General del Sello, 1488, febrero, fol. 235.

posesión de las encomiendas anejas a su cargo.[62] Además, en 1499 el rey Fernando escribía al prior de San Juan en Navarra para agradecerle los servicios que le estaba prestando y para rogarle que siguiera haciéndoselos.[63]

Así pues, dadas estas buenas relaciones previas, no es de extrañar que la conquista de Navarra en 1512 no resultara traumática para el priorato navarro del Hospital. De hecho, en el mismo momento de producirse la invasión, el jefe de las tropas de Fernando el Católico por el sector aragonés, Alonso de Aragón, llegó a otorgar un salvoconducto para los señoríos sanjuanistas del Sur de Navarra.[64] Por su parte, el prior Berenguer Sanz de Berrozpe parece que se adaptó sin problemas a la nueva situación y en septiembre de 1512 juró obedecer y servir fielmente como a su rey y señor natural a Fernando el Católico.[65] Al mes siguiente, sabemos que el monarca le consideraba efectivamente como un servidor leal y procuraba que recibiera un buen tratamiento.[66]

En 1513 Fernando el Católico convocó al prior del Hospital para que acudiera a la primera reunión de Cortes de Navarra que se iba a celebrar en Pamplona después de la conquista.[67] Sabemos que, en efecto, el prior Berenguer Sanz de Berrozpe asistió a aquella importante reunión de Cortes.[68] De hecho, el prior de San Juan fue uno de los tres embajadores de las Cortes navarras que acudieron a Valladolid en 1513 para que el monarca ratificara el juramento prestado por su virrey a dichas Cortes de respetar las leyes, ordenanzas, usos, costumbres y franquezas del reino.[69]

Tan sólo los contraataques posteriores, tanto franceses como castellanos sí que ocasionaron algunos daños en el patrimonio de la Orden en Navarra. En concreto sabemos que la casa y fortaleza sanjuanistas de Aberin fueron ocupadas transitoriamente en noviembre de 1512 y que una viña de la encomienda hospitalaria de Cizur Menor sufrió algunos daños en 1513 y 1514.[70]

Sin embargo, lo más interesante de todo es que parece que Fernando el Católico practicó una política consciente y deliberada de atracción de los principales hospitalarios navarros en esta época. En 1513 el rey nombró consejero suyo al prior de San Juan en Navarra, Berenguer Sanz de Berrozpe, y le asignó una renta anual de 400 libras.[71] En ese mismo año el mismo monarca también otorgó al comendador hospitalario de Induráin, Juan López de Eulate, la concesión de una renta anual de 5.000 maravedís.[72] Además, Fernando el Católico tomó otras disposiciones favorables a la Orden. En 1513 confirmó los privilegios de los hospitalarios en el

62 Archivo General de Simancas, Registro General del Sello, 1492, septiembre, fol. 87.

63 AHN, OO.MM, carpeta 847, no. 10.

64 AHN, OO.MM, legajo 8510, no. 38.

65 Archivo General de Simancas, Patronato Real, Caja 13, documento 50.

66 Esarte Muniain, pp. 130–1.

67 AHN, OO.MM, carpeta 847, no. 42.

68 V. Pradera, *Fernando el Católico y los falsarios de la historia* (Bilbao, 2003), p. 291.

69 Archivo General de Navarra, Sección de Comptos, cajón 168, no. 27. Citado por Boissonnade, p. 400.

70 Esarte Muniain, pp. 126 y 131. AHN, OO.MM, legajo 8521^1, no. 34.

71 AHN, OO.MM, legajo 8488, no. 35.

72 AHN, OO.MM, legajo 8555^1, no. 16.

reino.[73] También en ese mismo año mandó devolver a la Orden las propiedades sanjuanistas que hubieran sido enajenadas ilegalmente.[74] Finalmente, hizo levantar en 1515 el embargo que los últimos reyes privativos de Navarra habían impuesto sobre la abadía de Aoiz y otros bienes del convento sanjuanista del Crucifijo de Puente la Reina.[75] De esta forma debió de granjearse el apoyo y la lealtad de los hospitalarios navarros.

Apéndice documental

1512, septiembre, 21. Logroño.

El prior de la Orden de San Juan en Navarra, Berenguer Sanz de Berrozpe, presta juramento de fidelidad a Fernando el Católico como nuevo monarca del reino.

A. Archivo General de Simancas, Patronato Real, legajo 13, documento 50 (original en papel. Buen estado de conservación).

Regesta:

A. Prieto Cantero, *Archivo General de Simancas. Catálogo V. Patronato Real (834–1851)* (Valladolid, 1946–49), I, p. 178.

Cita:
M. Huici Goñi, *En torno a la conquista de Navarra* (Pamplona, 1993), p. 134.

Yo fray Belenguer de Berrozpe, prior de San Juan de Navarra, juro a Dios y a la cruz + y a los santos evangelios en que pongo mi mano en presencia del católico Rey don Fernando, Rey de Aragón y de Navarra, nuestro señor, que daquí adelante le obedeceré y serviré leal y fielmente con toda obediencia y reverencia como a mi Rey y señor natural y guardaré su real persona y estado y la tierra y pueblos del dicho Reyno de Navarra. Y donde viere su bien y servicio gelo allegaré, y donde viesse o supiesse lo contrario gelo arredrare, y quando por mi persona no pudiere gelo faré saber por mis cartas y mensajeros ciertos a su alteza o a la persona que estuviere o residiere en el dicho Reyno en su lugar, y le ayudaré a mantener los fueros, leyes, usos y costumbres del dicho Reyno de Navarra conforme a las leyes y fueros dél.

Y en señal de obediencia beso la mano a su alteza.
(Al dorso): Juramento del prior de Navarra en Logroño XXI de setiembre de DXII en manos de Diego Degui, nuestro capellán. Testigos el tesorero Hontañón, Tello repostero.

73 AHN, OO.MM, carpeta 850, nos 34 y 35.
74 AHN, OO.MM, carpeta 847, no. 45.
75 AHN, OO.MM, legajo 8568, no. 14.

Chapter 20

Friesland under the Teutonic Order? A Fantastic Plan from 1517 by Grand Master Albrecht of Brandenburg-Ansbach

Johannes A. Mol

The year 1517 is indelibly printed on many people's memories as an important year in European history. It certainly was an *annus memorabilis* for the Dutch province of Friesland, not because of Martin Luther's actions but because, after two consecutive years of war, plague and flooding, the region was once again exposed to all forms of misery imaginable. In May 1515, George, duke of Saxony, who was hard pressed for money, transferred his title to this difficult-to-govern region to Charles of Habsburg, who had just become the ruler of Burgundy and the Netherlands. At the same time Charles, duke of Guelders, the traditional enemy of the House of Burgundy–Habsburg, invaded the southern part of the region with a band of mercenaries and a civil war ensued, the end of which was nowhere in sight.[1] With hindsight, the area of Friesland between the Vlie and Lauwers was never ravaged as badly as it was in the years 1515–17. It was not only Friesland that suffered; the region of Groningen, which was comprised of the city of that name and the area to the north and west of the city, the so-called (Frisian) Ommelanden, also fell victim to the war. The unprotected countryside, in particular, had to endure all sorts of violence from the evenly matched parties and their hundreds of badly paid mercenary soldiers. No monastery escaped destruction, and nearly every village church was mercilessly looted.

The longer the stalemate between Habsburg and Guelders lasted in Friesland, the more other parties became interested in the situation. If two dogs are fighting for a bone, a third one may have an opportunity to run away with it.... One interested party, at any rate an unexpected one for the Frisians and the Groningers, went so far as setting out on paper his ideas for a possible assumption of power. This was Albrecht of Brandenburg-Ansbach, since 1511 grand master of the Teutonic Order, who, in 1525, would cause a stir throughout Europe by transforming the Teutonic

1 For an outline of the political events in the Frisian lands, see Jonathan I. Israel, *The Dutch Republic. Its Rise, Greatness and Fall 1477–1806* (Oxford, 1995), p. 29ff. More detail in A.F. Mellink, 'Territoriale afronding der Nederlanden', in *(Nieuwe) Algemene Geschiedenis der Nederlanden*, vol. 5 (Haarlem, 1980), pp. 492–505. The (German) East Frisian perspective in: H. Schmidt, *Politische Geschichte Ostfrieslands* (Leer, 1975), p. 129ff.

state of Prussia into a duchy under vassalage to Poland. In early 1517, he drafted a plan to bring the area of Friesland west of the Ems under the rule of the Teutonic Order, and subsequently instructed his brother Johann and several other diplomats to sound various parties to find out whether it had any chance of success.

Albrecht's plan turned out to be a castle in the air, but nevertheless it is worthwhile paying it some attention because it shows the ease with which the young grand master, who had little respect for the order's traditions, devised and dropped new political ideas for Prussia. This article also demonstrates that Friesland, in spite of its peripheral position on the North Sea coast, was at least a square on the chessboard of the European dynasts. The plan in question has been discussed indirectly in the older literature on the Teutonic Order,[2] but was never noted in the Netherlands nor in East Friesland and so could not be analysed in light of knowledge of the balance of power in Friesland. In this article, I will hold the plan briefly up to the light, basing my analysis on documents that were published by Erich Joachim in his monumental study (1892–94) of the politics of Albrecht, the last grand master of the Teutonic Order in Prussia.

The Grand Masters of the Teutonic Order and Poland, 1466–1517

Almost all the projects of Albrecht of Brandenburg-Ansbach were underpinned by the ambition to develop Prussia, which was initially ruled by the Teutonic Order, into a powerful principality of the size it enjoyed before 1453.[3] The civil war that broke out in 1453 and ended only 13 years later when the Treaty of Thorn was concluded, made Prussia and the Teutonic Order strongly dependent on Poland, at the same time as more than halving the territory of the order in terms of sources of income and area. The order retained only East Prussia, a poor region with the city of Königsberg as its centre. It has often been emphasised that the Prussian branch of the order set out to strengthen its position by abandoning its tradition of appointing a leader from among its own members, who were generally recruited from the lower nobility. Upon the death of Grand Master Hans von Tiefen in 1498, the order's leadership, for the first time, attracted the son of a prince as its new superior, anticipating that he would receive support from his own dynastic network. The choice fell on Frederick, the second son of Albrecht of Saxony and the brother of George, who was 'gubernator' of

---

2 See E. Joachim, *Die Politik des letzten Hochmeisters in Preussen Albrecht von Brandenburg*, vols 1 and 2: 1510–17; 1518–21 (Stuttgart, 1892/94, reprint Osnabrück, 1965), 1, pp. 154–5; 2, p. 17; A.H. Eggers, 'Hochmeister Albrecht und dessen Plan zur Gewinnung Frieslands für den deutschen Orden', *Altpreussische Monatschrift*, 43, 'Sitzungsberichte' 1906, pp. 135–6; W. Reese, 'Gesamtdeutsche und territoriale Zusammenhänge in der Geschichte des Deutschritterordens der Niederlande', *Blätter zur Deutsche Landesgeschichte*, 83 (1936/37), pp. 223–72, p. 264; W. Hubatsch, *Albrecht von Brandenburg-Ansbach. Deutschordens-Hochmeister und Herzog in Preussen 1490–1568* (Heidelberg, 1960), p. 64.

3 The literature on Albrecht is extensive. A useful introduction to his reign as grand master is offered by P. G. Thielen, 'Albrecht von Brandenburg-Ansbach', in Udo Arnold (ed.), *Die Hochmeister des Deutschen Ordens 1190–1994* (Marburg, 1998), pp. 160–5. The above-mentioned biography by Walter Hubatsch is still worth reading.

Friesland as well as being duke of Saxony.[4] Frederick's policies more or less fulfilled their expectations. He refused to take the oath of allegiance to the king of Poland, which had been compulsory since 1466, and withdrew to Saxony to forge alliances from there, so that he could prevent the Teutonic Order state from becoming a Polish dependency. This, in a way, connected Prussia and Friesland, as both regions were governed from Saxony for a period after 1498 by brothers who were in close contact with each other.

When this first 'princely' grand master, Frederick of Saxony, died at the end of 1510, Poland's pressure on Prussia was undiminished. To prevent the Polish king, Sigismund, from forcing his own candidate on the Teutonic Order, the order's leadership and dynasts sympathizing with the order thought it advisable to find a new grand master again of high birth, as soon as possible. In fact, plans were already circulating in Poland to remove the Teutonic Order as a whole to Podolia (in the western Ukraine) to fight the Tatars and other enemies of Poland. Although the Teutonic Order was still prepared to expend military efforts for the benefit of Christendom, it was no longer the flexible crusading body it had once been. By this time, its leaders and patrons regarded the order as a life-long care institution for the younger sons of the German nobility, befitting their estate. Therefore, it was unthinkable to give up the order's own state of Prussia (or the state of Livonia), even if there were no heathens left to fight in that region.

The architect of the grand magisterial election held in 1511 was George, duke of Saxony, who had been closely involved in the administration of the order up to that time as the adviser of his brother Frederick.[5] He chose Albrecht, who was 20 years old at the time and the third son of Margrave Frederick of Brandenburg-Ansbach, in Franconia, whose brother Johann ruled from Berlin the large electorate of Brandenburg, which adjoined Saxony. Like Albrecht of Saxony, Margrave Frederick had served the Holy Roman Emperor, Maximilian of Austria, as one of his army commanders in Flanders. The families were in-laws and knew each other well. At this time, young Albrecht of Brandenburg had for some time been destined for an ecclesiastical career and had already received four ordinations. He seemed a suitable candidate and indeed, in spite of his youth, proved to be so.

During his first years as the head of the Teutonic Order, Grand Master Albrecht continued the policy of Frederick of Saxony under the supervision of George of Saxony, but with much greater energy. He avoided paying homage to the Polish king, and undertook extensive diplomatic activities, employing many specially appointed advisers. At first, he operated from Ansbach, but at the end of 1512, with some show of power, he established himself in Königsberg, where he set up a more or less secular court. His main goal was to achieve autonomy vis-à-vis Poland and to reunite East and West Prussia. He was prepared to go to war for this, if he had to. But because the order had nothing like the resources necessary for conducting a war on its own, Albrecht's only way out was to forge as many alliances as he

4 M. Biskup, 'Friedrich von Sachsen', in U. Arnold (ed.), *Die Hochmeister des Deutschen Ordens*, pp. 155–60.

5 Hubatsch qualifies Albrecht as a 'Schützling' of Duke George: Hubatsch, *Albrecht von Brandenburg*, p. 40.

could. First, he played the card of the Holy Roman Empire, tried to interest the king of Denmark, sought the support of Saxony and Brandenburg, put pressure on the German master, Dietrich Cleen, and the master of Livonia, Wolter von Plettenberg, and even successfully contacted the grand prince of Moscow – which, however, was not appreciated by most rulers in Central and Eastern Europe.

Albrecht's policy initially appeared to be successful, but halfway through 1515 he suffered a setback when Emperor Maximilian, who wanted to have his hands free in the East to be able to carry out his Italian plans, concluded in Vienna a comprehensive treaty of alliance with King Sigismund of Poland. This treaty reiterated the provisions of the Treaty of Thorn (1466) regarding Prussia, and so the grand master was back where he had been in 1511. In future he would have to manage without the support of the emperor; but he did not give up. Tirelessly, he kept sending new proposals to his relatives and neighbours, aided by the brilliant, but also erratic, 'broker diplomat' Dietrich von Schönberg, whom he took into his service in late 1515. Schönberg continued Albrecht's war preparations and succeeded in obtaining many pledges to supply troops, from inside as well as outside the Empire, and also in Moscow. A large part of his activities in 1516 and 1517 consisted of making agreements about the raising of, and the rights of passage for, a sufficient number of horsemen, foot soldiers and military supplies.

It was during these frantic war preparations that the Frisian plan was drafted. The first to comment on the plan, after Joachim, was the medievalist Adolf Eggers, who said that the plan was intended to create a new territory under the rule of the order, to which the Teutonic Order state could be transplanted in an emergency.[6] However, this does not seem very likely when seen in the light of the developments outlined above. Albrecht's main goal had always been, and still was, to develop Prussia into a viable and independent principality, if possible, in its existing ecclesiastical form. But if this is true, what did he intend to achieve in Friesland?

George of Saxony inspires the plan

The first document in the file is an undated draft of a note from Grand Master Albrecht to his cousin and ally Joachim, the elector of Brandenburg. It probably dates from early 1517.[7] Alas, it contains only a few details. It says, literally, that Albrecht gives his support (*seinen Beifall*) to the proposal (*der Vorschlag*) made by the Duke of Saxony for the acquisition of Friesland by the Teutonic Order, and that, for this purpose, Albrecht has sent the jurist Johannes Oed to his brother Johann as '*Sollizitato*r', apparently to provide legal and diplomatic support. He asks the Elector Joachim to promote this cause. It is important to know in this connection that

6 According to Eggers the basic idea of the plan was 'den Orden durch Verpflanzung in ein anderes Land vor dem drohenden Untergange durch polnische Übermacht zu bewahren': Eggers, 'Plan zur Gewinnung Frieslands', p. 135. This judgement was followed by Reese, 'Gesamtdeutsche und territoriale Zusammenhänge', p. 264, who states that 'die bedrohliche Gefährdung Preussens hiess Hochmeister Albrecht von Brandenburg nach einem neuen Herrschaftsbereich Ausschau zu halten'.

7 Joachim, *Politik des letzten Hochmeisters*, 1, no. 125.

Albrecht's younger brother, Johann of Brandenburg-Ansbach, lived in Brussels at the court of Charles V, where he not only received a suitable education as a courtier and member of the higher nobility, but was also expected to protect the interests of the whole Brandenburg-Ansbach family.

The most important statement in the document is that the proposal originated from George of Saxony. There is no reason to doubt the validity of this statement. George of Saxony had succeeded his father, Albrecht, in 1500 as ruler of Friesland and, as such, in the period 1504–14 had endeavoured to turn the area of Friesland between the Vlie and Ems into a vigorous principality. This proved to be too tall an order, for two reasons. First, one should realize that Friesland was only introduced to princely rule in 1498.[8] In that year, Albrecht of Saxony, acting as Emperor Maximilian's general and governor of the Netherlands, and adroitly profiting from a power vacuum in the area of Friesland west of the Lauwers, easily conquered and subjected the region, aiming to pass it on to one of his sons as a second principality besides Saxony-Meissen, with a view to expansion in the direction of the Frisian lands to the east.[9] The drawback of this 'land-stealing' was that it concerned a region that was totally unfamiliar with princely or, in fact, any kind of central government.[10] It proved to be difficult to impose regular taxation on Friesland's peasant population, or its elite, and this impeded the duke's military ambitions. Eventually, in 1514, George discovered, to his loss, that he could not raise enough troops to militarily subdue the city of Groningen, which enjoyed the support of Edzard, count of East Friesland. Because his intended successor proved to lack the capabilities of a ruler George decided to turn over his title to the area of Friesland west of the Lauwers to Charles V, who was the heir of Philip the Fair, duke of Burgundy. After some hesitation on the part of his councillors, the young prince agreed to the transfer in May 1515 for a compensation of 100,000 guilders.

At the end of 1516, the Saxon duke was consulted by Dietrich von Schönberg, who was seeking support for Albrecht's war plans. Eggers writes that it was Albrecht's intention to get hold of the artillery left behind in Friesland by Duke George.[11] Nothing is known about the outcome of the negotiations, but it is likely that Duke George, although he had distanced himself from Albrecht to some extent by this time, provided information about Friesland to Schönberg. He knew the balance of

8 For the political structure of Friesland before 1498, see O. Vries, 'Die Friesische Freiheit: ein Randproblem des Reiches', in H. van Lengen (ed.), *Die Friesische Freiheit des Mittelalters – Leben und Legende* (Aurich, 2003), pp. 266–93.

9 On the 'Frisian adventure' of Albrecht of Saxony, see P. Baks, 'Albrecht der Beherzte als erblicher Gubernator und Potestat Frieslands – Beweggründe und Verlauf seines friesischen Abenteuers', in A. Thieme (ed.), *Herzog Albrecht der Beherzte (1443–1500). Ein sächsischer Fürst im Reich und in Europa* (Cologne, 2002), pp. 103–41.

10 There is reason enough to maintain that the Saxon dominion of Friesland in the period 1498–1514 was a form of occupation, albeit not a harsh one: P. Baks, 'Modernisierung durch Okkupation. Die sächsische Besatzungsherrschaft in Friesland, 1498–1515', in M. Meumann and J. Rogge (eds), *Die besetzte* res publica. *Zum Verhältnis von ziviler Obrigkeit und militärischer Herrschaft in besetzten Gebieten vom Spätmittelalter bis zum 18. Jahrhundert* (Berlin, 2006), pp. 129–66.

11 Eggers, 'Plan zur Gewinnung Friesland', p. 135.

power in Friesland better than anybody else and, at that time, was acutely aware that the Habsburg family would have the greatest difficulty in asserting their power in Friesland against the Duchy of Guelders, which was allied with France. As it was, Charles of Guelders had taken the city of Groningen 'into his protection' and, from there, had infiltrated Friesland, west of the Lauwers, to thwart his traditional enemies, the House of Habsburg–Burgundy. George's advice to Grand Master Albrecht that he should explore the possibilities in Friesland must have matured from information about the stalemate between Habsburg and Guelders, which arose halfway through the year 1516 when the Guelders troops took up strong positions not only in the city of Groningen but also in the area of Friesland west of the Lauwers. They had the support of redoubtable local fighters such as Jancko Douwama and 'Great Pier', the nickname of Pier Gerlefs Donia, who strove to restore the communal political system that existed before 1498. Under the slogan *Vrij en Fries, sonder schattinge ende exciis* ('Free and Frisian, no taxation') Guelders and these allies acquired a great following, which they used to press the Habsburg soldiers hard in 1516. As a result, at the beginning of 1517 the Habsburgers possessed little more than the fortified cities of Harlingen, Franeker and Leeuwarden. If Charles V, by now crowned king of Spain, was thinking of selling his Frisian shares at a bargain price, this seemed a good time to negotiate with him.

Initial rejection in Brussels

However, Margrave Johann and *magister* Johannes Oed did not get much response from the policy makers at the Habsburg court in Brussels. This appears from a letter from Johann to Albrecht dated 23 April 1517.[12] In this letter, Johann wrote that the instructions given by his brother in respect of the project were not yet feasible (*zur Zeit unthunlich*). The grand master, he continued, would be wise to remember that King Charles had already incurred great expenses (*schweren grossen Kosten*) because of Friesland and was tenaciously trying to connect the region, which he controlled only partially at the time, with his other lands. In Johann's opinion, it would therefore be better to stop the negotiations for a while and to wait and see how the king's grip on Friesland developed. For the time being, Johann would keep an eye on the situation and do his part at the appropriate time. He also reminded his brother of the losses incurred by the duke of Saxony because of Friesland. The fact that his massive investments had never yielded any results demanded that prudence be shown before embarking on such an adventure. To satisfy the king, who had also expended much money on Friesland already, he would have to be given a considerable sum of money (*die ungezweivelt nit klein zu achten sein*). Such a sum was not available in advance. It could only be raised, with exceptional difficulty, by the Teutonic Order's state of Prussia. Apportioning the amount within Friesland itself, in the form of an annual ground rent or excises, seemed impossible without coercive measures being taken that would automatically lead to higher costs for the war. Anyway, Margrave Johann observed acutely at the end of his letter, if King

12 Joachim, *Politik des letzten Hochmeisters*, 1, no. 132.

Charles – who was the lawful ruler of Friesland and did have a foothold there – was not able to subject the Frisians, how much more difficult would it be for others (*so wird das anderen noch unmöglicher sein*)? He advocated that proper consideration be given to all the options, in consultation with expert advisers.

The Margrave's letter appears to contain a correct and sober assessment of the situation, which should have made Albrecht give up his plan immediately. But the energetic grand master, being who he was, persisted in pursuing his goal with some tenacity, in the same way that he pursued his other plans. There were more cards to play. Didn't the city of Groningen and Count Edzard of East Friesland also have interests in the area which might be compatible with his? At any rate, it seemed worthwhile to send a separate mission to find out how the land lay, and thus Albrecht decided, in early September of 1517, to send a diplomat to Groningen, where he was to visit the pastor of St Martin's Church, Wilhelmus Frederici, who pulled all the strings in the city and the surrounding lands, to interest him in voluntary acceptance of the rule of the Teutonic Order in the event that the House of Habsburg was prepared to transfer its rights. The confidant who was entrusted with this task was no less a person than Wilhelm von Isenburg, former marshal of the order in Prussia. He originated from the Rhine area and was, therefore, supposed to be familiar with the political balance of power in north-west Germany. We can comment upon his intended actions because his instructions have been preserved in Albrecht's correspondence.[13]

The instructions for Isenburg's mission to Groningen

The document in question is not easy to understand because it is written in 'telegram' style using catchwords that Isenburg undoubtedly understood without difficulty, but which may puzzle the modern reader. One should also note that instructions for diplomatic use, such as this document, are usually full of disguised terms.

The introduction, however, poses no problems. Albrecht expects Isenburg to explain that the grand master is very concerned about the situation in Friesland: the grand master is aware that the country has been ravaged by war for a long time, and to excess, and that the common people are suffering severely from pillaging and arson. Because no end to the war is in sight, Isenburg is to explain that 'matters would not become worse' if the grand master and the order could find ways of acquiring the title and the positions of power which the Habsburg family possesses in respect of Friesland. Perhaps negotiations could be conducted in such a way that France and Guelders would not offer any resistance. To introduce this intention, Isenburg is to explain to the pastor of Groningen that the grand master is an ecclesiastic who rules on Christian principles and only wants to 'conquer' land by winning the hearts of the inhabitants, so that they will of themselves accept the order's benevolent co-government (*menschliche gütige midtregirung*). The reason why Isenburg is approaching Wilhelmus Frederici – so the instruction continues – is because he is aware of the great reputation that Frederici has gained by overcoming

13 Ibid., 1, no. 140.

difficulties, endangering his own life, and by his courage and loyal counsel, in the city of Groningen as well as in all the surrounding parts of Friesland. Furthermore, Frederici is the right person to confide in because he is an ecclesiastic, like Isenburg (who had indeed taken monastic vows), who is acting on behalf of his ecclesiastic superior.

The next section contains a veiled request for advice and cooperation in the matter: could the Groningen pastor indicate how he felt about the Habsburgers transferring the country to the order under certain conditions, so that it would have a 'respectable' government? Here, Isenburg had to emphasise that, in that case, no estate, whether city-dwellers or farmers, needed to fear loss of livelihood or food shortages, and that the clergy and the nobility would be involved in decision making.

Isenburg is instructed only to listen to Frederici's response at first. If the pastor puts forward too many unsuitable considerations and only appears to want peace for the time being, and if he does not offer executive powers but keeps the possibility open that the land will secede again as soon as it is convenient, then Isenburg must stick to his guns (*sal her wol wider part halten*). He must not do this too stubbornly, or else he may scare his interlocutor or make him suspicious. For example, he should not demand a fortified house or a stronghold in Groningen in advance. He may not claim the Ommelanden and should not demand an annual tribute from Groningen. It is also important to emphasize that, if it should come to negotiations, the order would let itself be received according to the subjects' wishes, because 'it is led by nought but God's word, love and good will'.

The instruction then takes into account that the pastor may want to involve the count of East Friesland, Edzard. There was no objection to this in itself, because the grand master and the order were completely neutral with regard to the count. In addition, the elector of Brandenburg was on excellent terms (*in sunderlicher einickeit*) with him. It was important, however, to know whether the pastor wanted to involve one of the count's confidants, and if so, whom. In this event, Isenburg had to prevent people from Münster or Utrecht becoming involved in the transaction. He also had to beware of Doctor *Harcke*, Knight *Boluff* and *Klaws van Werp*, the count's marshal. The people whom he could trust were Master *Hicke* and Squire *Ulrich*, who were considered to be the most loyal and sensible members of the count's council.

In case the bishop of Münster, who, apparently, was also to be honoured by a visit from Isenburg, would assist him in contacting the count of East Friesland, a short itinerary is included. Isenburg had best travel to Emden via Aschendorf, and sail along the Ems, visiting Leerort on the way because the chancellor of Münster, *Sturczekop*, worked there as a priest.

Finally, Isenburg is urged to be careful in all the discussions, to rely on himself alone, and to obtain information secretively. He must act on his own judgement and proverbially 'sail with the wind' as much as possible. If, however, the pastor asks him for more information, for example, about the organization of the order, this should be provided to him in an agreeable manner, of course. He could explain, for example, that the order could attach a commander, who would owe obedience to the grand master, and a convent to each of the present fortified houses. Noblemen might join these communities as knight-brothers of the Teutonic Order: 'Oberländer' (from southern Germany), Dutchmen, Frisians or others. Secular priests interested in joining the order could also be accepted into the brotherhood. Secular fiefs might be given to, or incorporated in, the order. Thus, the whole country could be governed by the advice of commanders and priests of the Teutonic Order, in a manner agreeable to the inhabitants.

Basic information proves to be outdated

At first sight, the document appears to have been composed thoughtfully. Apart from the questionable assumption that the House of Habsburg could be persuaded to vacate its Frisian positions, it is cautious, stating many ifs and buts. After all, it was only intended to be a first exploration by the grand master. Also, of all the powerful men east of the Lauwers, Wilhelmus Frederici was definitely the most appropriate one to approach. The contemporaneous Frisian chronicler Worp van Thabor wrote, in so many words, that Frederici ruled the city of Groningen: 'everything went through his hands, and whatever he advised or wanted, was what happened in Groningen'.[14]

On closer inspection, however, the document proves to be very weakly underpinned. In 1515, Groningen had placed itself under the protection of Charles, duke of Guelders. This meant that Wilhelmus Frederici could hardly consider any 'trade' with the Teutonic Order without involving the duke. It is also curious that Albrecht thought that the count of East Friesland might be interested, because Count Edzard had become the enemy of Groningen at the time when Wilhelm of Isenburg should have set out. Edzard had governed the city of Groningen more or less independently between 1506 and 1514, but, in the latter year, under pressure from the patriciate, had had to vacate the castle of Groningen for the benefit of Guelders. By the end of 1515 he had lost all of his power in Friesland west of the Ems, and was under threat in his own East Frisian territory from the duke of Oldenburg and other greedy neighbours.[15] In 1517, instead of turning to Guelders and Groningen, he turned to Charles V, to whom he even gave his lands in fief. Although the document text presumes that Habsburg and Guelders may be reconciled with each other, it is odd that the relationship between Frederici and Edzard is supposed to (still) be a very close one.

The impression one has, that Albrecht based himself on outdated information when issuing his instructions to his diplomat, is confirmed by checking the names of Edzard's advisors.[16] *Doctor Harcke* can be identified as Dr Harko Aepken von Suurhusen; *ritter Boluff* has to be Edzard's army commander Foleff von Inn und Knyphausen; *Klaws von Werp* may have been the bailiff of Emden, Clawes Hatte; and *Hicke* and *juncker Ulrich* can be identified unmistakably as the brothers Hicko and Ulrich von Dornum. We know that all these men were confidants of Edzard in 1517, with the exception of Hicko von Dornum. He had advised Edzard on many

14 *Worp van Thabor, Kronijk van Friesland, Book V*, ed. J.G. Ottema (Leeuwarden, 1871), p. 119.

15 H. Reimers, *Edzard der Grosse* (Aurich, 1910), pp. 109–22.

16 Chr. Lamschus, *Emden unter der Herrschaft der Cirksena* (Hildesheim, 1984), pp. 322–3, 345.

matters since he accompanied him on a pilgrimage to Jerusalem in 1491, and would still have been his confidant in 1517, but he had died in 1515!

Another noteworthy omission in the instructions is that they completely ignore the existing infrastructure of the Teutonic Order in the North.[17] The Order possessed at least three establishments: the commanderies of Nes (near Akkrum), Schoten (south of Heerenveen) and Bunne (in North Drenthe). All three were manned by priest-brothers and were accountable to a provincial commander, who resided in the Teutonic House (*Duitse Huis*) in Utrecht and who, in turn, was subordinate to the German master in South Germany. Grand Master Albrecht apparently did not bother checking the existing connections of the order with Friesland in his own documentation in Königsberg. For this reason alone, Hubatsch's assertion that Albrecht wanted to model the administration of the order in Friesland on the bailiwick of Utrecht ('*in Anlehnung an die Ballei Utrecht*') does not seem tenable.[18] This fact makes it clear that the Prussian branch of the Teutonic Order acted completely independently of the order's branch in the Holy Roman Empire at this time. In view of the fact that the many Groningen and East Frisian establishments of that other important order of knights, the Order of St John,[19] which Wilhelmus Frederici knew well, are not mentioned in the instructions, we must conclude that the idea of a provincial government run by commanders and knight-brothers must also have seemed a fantasy to the grand master himself.

Purpose of the plan; the outcome

This brings us back to the purpose of the plan. What, in heaven's name, did Grand Master Albrecht hope to achieve by it? First, we may establish that Wilhelmus Frederici was never apprised of it,[20] because Wilhelm of Isenburg never undertook the journey to Groningen. There were two reasons for this, according to a communication of 14 September 1518.[21] First, the route to Groningen seemed too insecure to Wilhelm, who was an old man. Secondly, he was advised not to undertake the mission by the steward of Charles V, whom he had in the meantime spoken to. The steward, listing the same objections which he had mentioned to Margrave Johann, advised him that nothing could come of it as far as the 'House of Brabant' was concerned. This is understandable because, should a conflict arise between Habsburg/Spain on the one hand and France/Guelders on the other, Charles V could do little else than continue

---

17 J.A. Mol, *De Friese huizen van de Duitse Orde. Nes, Steenkerk en Schoten en hun plaats in het middeleeuwse Friese kloosterlandschap* (Leeuwarden, 1991); a German translation of this book is due to appear in the series *Quellen end Studien zur Erforschung des Deutschen Ordens*.

18 Hubatsch, *Albrecht von Brandenburg*, p. 64 ff.

19 On the many Frisian houses of the Order of St John, see J.A. Mol, 'The Hospitaller sisters in Frisia', in A. Luttrell and H.J. Nicholson (eds), *Hospitaller Women in the Middle Ages* (Aldershot, 2006), pp. 179–207.

20 No mention is made of Isenburg in the biography of this influential politician by W. Zuidema, *Wilhelmus Frederici, persona van St. Maarten te Groningen* (Groningen, 1888).

21 Joachim, *Politik des letzten Hochmeisters*, 2, p. 7.

his northern adventure. He needed to drive the troops of Guelders out of Friesland, Groningen and the rest of the north-eastern Netherlands once and for all, and unite these regions with his other Dutch principalities. To allow a vacuum by indulging a weak ecclesiastical state would have been political foolishness.

We have already seen that Grand Master Albrecht could never have wanted to transplant the whole Teutonic Order state from Prussia to the area of Friesland between the Vlie and the Ems. The only thing that he could have had in mind was to acquire a kind of colony, a land that he could use in the long term to provide money and men to support his Prussian ambitions. The plan was born ad hoc, at the instigation of Duke George, and was based on his assessment of the insecure situation that had arisen after his departure from Friesland. Because George's own mission had failed, his advice about building up power in Friesland can only have been given discreetly, but this probably did not bother Albrecht of Brandenburg. Together with his adviser Dietrich von Schönberg, he thought up various other fantastic plans, only to drop them just as rapidly after properly assessing them. Still, this speculative element in his political life had a function. In the end, one idea – which would have been regarded as a castle in the air by most people beforehand – did materialise: the surprising transformation of the Teutonic Order's state of Prussia into a Protestant secular duchy in 1525, and this in vassalage to a Catholic king whose ancestors had, for centuries, been the arch-enemies of the Teutonic Order.

Chapter 21

The Hospitaller Castiglione's Catholic Synthesis of Warfare, Learning and Lay Piety on the Eve of the Council of Trent

David Frank Allen

Although they will be mentioned, Baldassare Castiglione [1478–1529] and his *Il libro del cortegiano* [1528] are not the focus of this essay. This 'most representative book of the Renaissance'[1] along with the writings of Machiavelli, provoked a Catholic reaction from Baldassare's younger cousin, Frà Sabba da Castiglione, who spent his long life [ca. 1480–1554] serving his religious, military and Hospitaller Order of St John of Jersualem. Frà Sabba deserves better than to be interpreted as standing in the shadows of his cousin Castiglione and Machiavelli.[2] The twofold charism of his Order of St John – fighting the Muslim infidel and tending the poor and sick – shaped Frà Sabba's experiences as a Knight of Rhodes and as the *commendatore* of the Hospitaller estates at Magione di Faenza in Lombardy, where he matured as a Christian humanist and exemplified Catholic lay piety on the eve of the Council of Trent.

Before detailing Frà Sabba as the representative ideal of the *cavaliere di belle lettere e di santa vita* in the Order of St John, an apparent incongruity must be confronted. Why should connoisseurship of the arts, scholarship and science have been juxtaposed with the vocation of a religious, military order? How can killing or mutilation in battle relate at all with the intellectual and artistic pursuits of mankind? Besides his sword, why should any soldier wield his pen? Through the ages, warfare has been both a destructive activity, improving its efficiency via its knowledge of mathematics and applied sciences, as much as it has been a subject for creative artists who have idealized or lamented its necessary contribution to society. Whether with Renaissance humanists or with the Enlightenment's *philosophes*, warfare enjoyed an ambiguous reputation. Humanists had sold their pens to legitimize the *condottieri* of Renaissance Italy just as *philosophes* later taught 'enlightenment' to such warlike rulers as Frederick II of Prussia or Catherine II of Russia. Applicable to any period between the fifteenth and eighteenth centuries was this comment by the Cardinal de Bernis and as gilded by the *philosophe* Algarotti: 'A nation's reputation in the arts is usually linked to its reputation in warfare and its pen is seldom esteemed

1 George Bull's phrase in his introduction to his English translation of Baldassare Castiglione, *The Book of the Courtier* (Harmondsworth, 1967), p.12.

2 The meagre historiography of Frà Sabba da Castiglione is summarized conveniently by Claudio Scarpati, *Studi sul cinquecento italiano* (Milan, 1982), pp. 27–8.

when its sword is not feared.'[3] The supranational Order of St John, whose knights also fought in the armies of their respective natural monarchs or princes, was a cockpit of experiments in warfare. Brethren were expected to understand enough of mathematics and what today we would call certain applied sciences in order to fight effectively.

Beyond that, once the valiant Knight of St John had graduated from his *carovane* and obtained his commandery for service in the Convent at Rhodes or Malta, he became, in effect, a bachelor prince within his seigneurial jurisdiction. And the income from his commandery might support the Knight of St John in his literary, botanical or geological pursuits as readily as it might pay for soldiering in the service of his prince, or for the expenses of an embassy at the courts of Catholic Europe.[4] Indeed there was one Italian knight who refused his grand master's order to return to Malta at the time of the Great Siege in 1565, saying that he was too old, lacking teeth to bite the Turks or eyes to see them. Probably his eyes had been ruined by too much study, since Annibale Caro was better known as a translator of Aristotle and Virgil. As secretary to Cardinal Alessandro Farnese, Caro had more to do with his master's patronage of artists and scholars than he ever had with fighting.[5] Although exceptional in the Order of St John, Caro was not alone in his humanist orientation, as we know from his contemporary, Frà Sabba da Castiglione. In that period of the late Renaissance and on the eve of the Council of Trent, Frà Sabba produced for his brethren a synthesis of warfare, learning and lay piety which was to influence all subsequent tracts on the awesome duties of a Knight of St John.

Unlike Baldassare Castiglione, who glorifies war in his celebrated work, the Hospitaller Castiglione describes it more realistically in his letters from Rhodes to the Gonzaga court at Mantua, and later in his book of *Ricordi*, a work which enjoyed 26 editions between 1546 and 1613, mostly at Venice but also at Bologna, Milan and Mantua.[6] Frà Sabba's whole life exemplified that integration of *armi* and *lettere*

3 F. Algarotti, *Pensieri diversi*, ed. G. Ruozzi (Milan, 1987), p. 48.

4 See David F. Allen, 'The Order of St John as a "School for Ambassadors" in Counter-Reformation Europe' in *The Military Orders*, vol. 2, ed. H. Nicholson (Aldershot, 1998) pp. 363–79.

5 Marchese di Villarosa, *Notizie di alcuni cavalieri del Sacro Ordine Gerosolomitano illustri per lettere e per belle arti* (Naples, 1841), pp. 79–80.

6 A. Luzio, 'Lettere inedite di Fra Sabba da Castiglione', *Archivio storico lombardo*, Series 2, vol. 3 (1886), pp. 91–112. For bibliographical analysis of Frà Sabba da Castiglione's *Ricordi*, see I. Massaroli, 'Fra Sabba da Castiglione e I suoi "Ricordi"', *Archivio storico lombardo*, Series 2, vol. 6 (1889), 375–92; Claudio Scarpati, *Studi sul cinquecento italiano* (Milan, 1982), pp. 83–125. Since the first two editions at Bologna are rarely available and cannot be dated respectively to 1546 and 1549 with absolute certainty, the commonly found third edition of 1554 at Venice is the version (annotated by an unknown hand) we have consulted in the National Library of Malta: *Ricordi overo ammaestramenti di monsignor Saba da Castiglione cavalier gierosolomitano ne' quali con prudenti e christiani discorsi si ragiona di tutte le materie honorate che si ricercano a un vero gentilhuomo / Con la tavola per alphabeto di tutte le cose notabili / Con privilegio / In Vinegia per Paulo Gherardo / MDLIIII*. Subsequent references to Frà Sabba's *Ricordi* are to this edition (upon which all successive editions were based) and to the numbered *ricordo* therein. There were 133 *ricordi*

which figures so airily in the conversations of his cousin Castiglione's characters at Urbino.[7] Frà Sabba declared that just as faith and works or grace and free will were properly linked in their being necessary to salvation, so too arms and letters, although not being necessary to salvation but being highly esteemed in the world, should never be separated, as they sadly were in the case of most soldiers of his time. The difference between a living and dead plant was like that difference between a lettered and ignorant warrior and the latter would always be at a disadvantage in his profession of arms.[8]

For Frà Bartolomeo, the younger Knight of St John who was his great-nephew and who would succeed him as *commendatore* of their Order's estates at Magione di Faenza, Frà Sabba composed his *Ricordi*, with the purpose of making him *un vero gentiluomo*. Such a paragon had to adapt himself to the diverse brethren he would encounter in their Order of St John. He should follow Dante's advice to fall in with saints at church and gluttons at the tavern, whilst remaining true to his personal combination of soldiering, learning and piety.[9] The older knight declared himself averse to writing amorous tales of Orlandos or Rinaldos, and he had no time for chronicles, the composition of which was commonly associated with the religious life. Frà Sabba's tone was urgent because he believed he was living through an Iron Age and that the world was nearing its end. He claimed to have heard as clearly as St Jerome 'the horrible sound of the celestial trumpet' summoning the dead to eternal judgement.[10] Since it was shameful for a monk or any religious not to know the rules and constitutions of his own order, Frà Sabba had struggled with his palsied hand to write down for his young kinsman the Christian principles of their Order of St John. In his now decrepit state, Frà Sabba compared himself to a whetstone, which itself cannot cut but which can sharpen knives.[11] In alerting Frà Bartolomeo to the vice of contemporary courts in the Italian peninsula, Frà Sabba demonstrated his own humanist credentials, albeit in his 'Lombard' style of Italian, less graceful and more repetitive than that of his cousin Baldassare Castiglione.

Some of Frà Sabba's readings in both the pagan classics (especially Heraclitus, Plato, Aristotle, Hesiod, Herodotus, Cicero, Livy, Caesar, Vergil, Horace, Ovid, Plutarch, and Seneca) and in masters of the *volgare* (Dante, Petrarch, Ariosto, Bembo, Machiavelli and Baldassare Castiglione himself) have been analysed by Dr Scarpati.[12] Work remains for other critics to scrutinize Frà Sabba's readings in the Fathers, especially Origen, Eusebius, Ambrose and Augustine. The latter was

in this edition, having been increased from 72 *ricordi* in the earlier Bologna edition of 1546, 72 having equated with the '72 disciples of Jesus Christ'.

7 For Baldassare Castiglione's unsuccessful experience of, and dislike for, actual warfare, see J.R. Hale, 'Castiglione's military career', *Italian Studies*, 36 (1981), 41–57.

8 *Ricordo* 73.

9 *Ricordi* 74, 80.

10 *Ricordi* 130, 133, 131.

11 *Ricordo* 133.

12 Claudio Scarpati, *Studi sul cinquecento italiano* (Milan, 1982), pp. 48–82. Dr Scarpati reinforces the historiographical tradition of interpreting Sabba da Castiglione in reaction to Baldassare Castiglione and Machiavelli rather than relating Sabba da Castiglione to his Order of St John. Scarpati has similarly influenced Claudio Donati, *L'idea di nobiltà in Italia. Secoli*

linked by Frà Sabba with St Gregory as 'the two acknowledged beacons of the Holy Church of Jesus Christ'.[13] Also Frà Sabba had a devotion to the hermit St Antony of Egypt, whose cult was to flourish in Hospitaller Malta. Frà Sabba believed that Christian scholarship was superior to the pagan learning of the classical Greek and Roman world, speaking of *santa verità, più cara che Socrate e Platone.*[14] This was because ancient philosophers had worn themselves out in finding the key to this life, remaining ignorant of that eternal life to which the Christian's death is the threshold.[15]

Frà Sabba's profile as a *soldier* has been obscured by his own self-deprecating emphasis on retirement from the camps and courts of Catholic Europe and precisely where many of his brethren Knights of St John were often to be found. Frà Sabba's devotion to St Antony of Egypt – 'exemplar of the solitary life' – plus the inscription on his own tomb – 'solitarius et parvo contentus vixi' – have tended to edit his reputation as a humanist and Catholic reformer rather than as a soldier who had lived through the loss of Rhodes to the Ottomans in 1523 as well as the Habsburg–Valois wars in Italy and the Sack of Rome in 1527. Underneath the Petrarchan form of Frà Sabba's youthful letters and behind his funerary monument so artfully modelled on the Platina tomb in Santa Maria Maggiore at Rome, there had been relish for the profession of arms, both in his successful career as a Knight of St John and in his book of *Ricordi* for his great-nephew.[16] A young knight like Frà Bartolomeo who was so self-consciously inhabiting the physical world would never have listened to his uncle's advice, unless Frà Sabba had demonstrated his experience of *armi* as well as of *lettere*.

Frà Sabba believed that his young Knight of St John needed counselling because all other mistakes could be put right except military ones, which (as Cato had asserted) always carry sorrow on their back. Frà Sabba believed warfare to be endemic in the urban society which he had known along the coasts of the Mediterranean. He highlighted that apprehension among primeval citizens for the security of their property and their hiring of soldiers to defend it.[17] Frà Sabba wanted to give his great-nephew 'a certain taste and feeling for warfare', which was undeniably a most dignified and noble calling, when conducted according to its own rules and conventions, as was evidenced by classical and scriptural authorities. Since the pagan Greeks and Romans had both understood and written elegantly about these rules of war, contemporary Christian captains of arms were even more obliged to be both religious and learned in their motivation.

XIV-XVIII (Rome–Bari, 1988), pp. 64–6, and Aldo Scaglione, *Knights at Court* (Berkeley, 1991), pp. 250–1.

13 *Ricordo* 131.

14 *Ricordo* 74.

15 *Ricordo* 83. Cf. *Ricordo* 81: *la morte, la quale alli buoni Cristiani è fine, termine e meta di tutte le miserie mondane, e incomminciamento della eterna felicità.*

16 *Ricordo* 80 (St Antony of Egypt). The correlation with the Platina tomb has been made by A. Campana, 'A. Blado e B. Platina', in *Miscellanea bibliografica in memoria di Don T. Accurti* (Rome, 1947), pp. 49–50.

17 *Ricordo* 130.

Scripture revealed how St John the Baptist had baptized soldiers and had not commanded them to give up their profession of arms, recognizing their necessary presence as peace-keepers in civil society. And Luke revealed how Christ had praised the faith of the Roman centurion who had requested the healing of his servant. Christ had not commanded the centurion to stop being a soldier, nor had Christ challenged the Roman military presence in Judaea, preferring to admonish 'Render unto Caesar that which is Caesar's'. Frà Sabba was certain, therefore, that it was possible to be both a soldier and a servant of God. He cited both scriptural and historical models for his great-nephew, namely, Abraham, David, Moses, the crusading Godefroi de Bouillon and Richard I of England. As for those who asserted that all warfare was evil, Frà Sabba declared that they had been answered once and for all by St Augustine. Sometimes it was necessary to seize the initiative in waging war, and King Wenceslas should have acted sooner against heretics in Bohemia! In order for a prince to wage a just war, he must have a just cause and must reflect soberly before ordering his soldiers into battle. Should a prince's cause be manifestly unjust, his subjects were not obliged to fight, because their greater obedience was to God, the King of Kings and Lord of the Universe.[18]

Frà Sabba asserted that because they were in constant danger of losing their lives, all soldiers had a greater need of God's grace. Their captains should set an example by confessing themselves and communicating at the start of every day's campaign. These should adopt as their devices not lions, bears, wolves, dragons or serpents but the Crucifix, which should be underlined on their standards, *Christus vincit, Christus regnat, Christus imperat*. Junior officers should dedicate their respective devices to Our Lady, St John the Baptist, St Peter, St Paul, St Michael or St George, according to their individual devotions.[19] Frà Sabba believed that the morals of a Christian army would always be tested by its treatment of women on the enemy side as well as by its tolerance of its own female camp-followers. From pagan times Alexander the Great's honourable treatment of Darius's women provided a powerful example to contemporary Christian commanders. Frà Sabba agreed that even greater problems might ensue if Christian armies were not allowed their female camp-followers, but he deplored their excessive numbers, especially in the armies of the Spanish monarchy.

Just as the honour of women on the opposing side should remain inviolate, so too holy places like churches, monasteries, convents and hospitals should never be looted by Christian captains of arms. Just as Pompey the Great had despoiled the Temple in Jerusalem before his own miserable death, so too the soldiers who had sacked Rome in 1527 certainly lost their immortal souls. Although sieges might well be necessary in contemporary warfare, they should be conducted with propriety. Any subsequent damage to bastions or ditches should be made good by the victorious party. Whether commanding on land or at sea, all captains of arms must keep their diverse forces united. And the best mariners, according to Frà Sabba (who had never visited Malta), were the Venetians, the Catalans, the Portuguese and the Genoese.[20]

18 *Ricordo* 130.

19 *Ricordo* 120.

20 *Ricordo* 120.

Frà Sabba da Castiglione's own military experience had begun at sea (after an abortive study of law at the University of Pavia) between 1505–8 during his *carovane* from his Order of St John's convent at Rhodes, as he had then written to Isabelle d'Este, the ornament of the Gonzaga court at Mantua:

> Let me tell Your Ladyship that I have abandoned gentle Apollo with his soothing lyre and I have adopted as my model the warlike Mars with his fearsome trumpet. Where once my hands held papers, quills, pens, ink and books, they now grasp only swords, lances, armour-pieces, mail-vests, shields, bows and arrows. What is even more pleasant is that, from having been the most scrupulous upholder of law, I have become a sea-pirate.[21]

In fact Frà Sabba had used his *carovane* from Rhodes not merely to fight the Muslim foe but also to locate amidst the islands of the Eastern Mediterranean remnants of classical statuary, which were eagerly anticipated by the court of Mantua. Alighting from his Order's galleys at Delos, Frà Sabba wept to see the desolate state of Apollo's temple, recognizing the smashed stones as the artefacts of a master sculptor – *uscite da bon martello*. None of these could be sent to Mantua, but in April 1507, Frà Sabba despatched to Isabella d'Este a statue from Naxos. Although this lacked its head and arms, Frà Sabba was confident that its remaining pointers to perfection would appeal to artists such as Andrea Mantegna and Giovanni Cristoforo Romano, who had been advising Isabella on her growing collection.[22] By means of Gonzaga patronage and a sympathetic grand master, Frà Sabba had been able to shrug off the imputations of 'idolater and heretic' which his connoisseurship might otherwise have attracted from his brethren at Rhodes.

That island fortress – so far removed from Renaissance Mantua – seemed to Frà Sabba in his melancholy mood to be 'an arid and uninhabited desert', where classical statues were far from being esteemed. Indeed those in the grand master's gardens were exposed to the wasting elements of wind and rain. Yet the new Academy founded by Frà Sabba at Rhodes had been located not in a magnificent house or in a richly decorated room like its equivalents in Renaissance Italy, but on a barren rock. Here this Knight of St John recited in the open and to a select audience his own sonnets alongside the tragedies, comedies, eclogues or satires of better-known classical authors. Frà Sabba's consolatory epistle to the widow Camilla Scarampi was his self-conscious working of a *topos*, in which the lady's love for her dead husband was compared to Portia's love for Brutus and Cornelia's for Pompey. The tone of Frà Sabba's *Consolatoria* is humanist rather than Christian. Yet it also contains an attack

---

21 Frà Sabba's undated letter was written from Rhodes to the Marchesa di Mantua sometime between 1505 and 1508. See Luzio, 'Lettere', p. 100. In respect of his earlier studies at Pavia, Frà Sabba's *Ricordo* 113 mentions how he had held in his hand Petrarch's Vergil at the library of Pavia established by the Visconti of Milan and which is now in the Ambrosian Library of Milan – MS S.P. Arm 10, scat. 27. Cf. *Francisci Petrarchae Vergilianus Codex*, ed. G. Galbiati (Milan, 1930).

22 Luzio, 'Lettere', pp. 102, 106. Cf. C.M. Brown, '*Lo insaciabile desiderio nostro de le cose antique*: new documents for Isabella d'Este's collection of antiquities', in C.H. Clough (ed.), *Cultural Aspects of the Italian Renaissance: Essays in honour of P.O. Kristeller* (Manchester, 1976), pp. 324–53.

on Julius II, the Order of St John's supreme protector, for turning upside down the peace of the Italian peninsula.[23] During his brief sojourn at Rhodes, Frà Sabba had been untouched by any manifestation of that encounter between Latin and Greek cultures which is now a commonplace in the historiography of Hospitaller Rhodes. Although Frà Sabba had boasted to Isabella d'Este that he was ready to serve her in the East or the West, he remained a Latin rather than a Greek.[24]

Besides learning techniques of amphibious warfare at Rhodes, Frà Sabba had begun compiling there the book of *Ricordi* which he would later address to his great-nephew at Magione di Faenza in the 1540s. At Rhodes Frà Sabba had asked his Castilian brethren in the convent for their definition of 'the true and good knight'. These Castilian influences on Frà Sabba's *Ricordi* remind us not only of Spain's dominant presence in the Italian peninsula throughout the sixteenth century but also of how Spain's 'golden century' witnessed that productive coupling of *armas y letras.*[25] The physical beauty of the human body as revealed by a talented sculptor was another link between Frà Sabba's youthful experience of Rhodes and his later moralizing in his *Ricordi*. Always employing in that work similes drawn from his appreciation of sculpture, Frà Sabba urged his young kinsman Frà Bartolomeo to be physically prepared for warfare.[26] Frà Sabba recommended that physical exercise was necessary for young knights, who were to take morning exercise after hearing Mass. Sword play was recommended and, precisely because Frà Bartolomeo was tall, he was urged to exercise with swords in both hands and also with the pike. Regular exercise with all kinds of weapons was essential, since Frà Bartolomeo would never be able to choose in the heat of battle which particular weapons to employ, for Fate would bring them into his hands.[27]

Because the Order of St John's forces were more often at sea than on land, Frà Bartolomeo was urged by his uncle to swim well, so that he might carry

---

23 Luzio, 'Lettere', pp. 98–100. Frà Sabba's *Consolatoria*, dated at Rhodes, 25 November 1517, was printed at pp. 132–6 of the 1554 edition of his *Ricordi*.

24 Luzio, 'Lettere', p. 111. At Malta the Order of St John remained a resolutely Latin institution, showing little understanding of Greek culture. Knights of St John regularly enslaved Greek Orthodox Christians, despite growing complaints both from Venice and the Holy See. In 1644 Grand Master Lascaris described Greek Orthodox Christians as 'enemies of our Roman faith and vassals of our Turkish enemies' (Malta, Cod. 1552, despatch of 17 July 1644). However, some Maltese subjects of the Order of St John went to study in the *Collegio Greco di Roma*, founded by Gregory XIII in 1576. After graduating, such Maltese often became pastors to the Greek Catholics in Malta and elsewhere in the Mediterranean or they entered religious orders like the Somaschi or the Jesuits. See S. Bottari, 'Studenti Maltesi nel Collegio Greco di Roma (1576–1640), *Melita Historica*, 9 (1993), 209–12.

25 I. Massaroli, 'Fra Sabba da Castiglione e I suoi "Ricordi"', *Archivio storico lombardo*, Series 2, volume 6 (1889), 368. Cf. A.R. Firpo, 'Realidad y ficción en el retrato de un caballero de la Orden de Alcántara', *Las Ordenes Militares en el Mediterráneo Occidental (S.XII-XVIII)* (Madrid, 1989), pp. 155–67.

26 Cf. *Ricordo* 44, where a sculptor is defined as a craftsman who improves upon nature in making a body more perfect and beautiful by taking from nature the most beautiful components of several human bodies.

27 *Ricordo* 40.

with him through the waves his own shield and sword, if not other weapons. The young knight should learn navigation and the use of the compass and the charts; he should familiarize himself with the harbours, creeks, islands, rocks and forts of the Mediterranean. Precisely because he was called a knight, Frà Bartolomeo was expected to know how to ride and look after his own horse. Horses were sly beasts and should not be overfed.[28] *Orlando Furioso* and similar tales were full of vanity whereas truer guides to military science were captains in the field, from whom Frà Bartolomeo might learn how to build bastions, how to mine or counter-mine, how to dig trenches or how to align cannon for bombardment. Reading classical authors of military treatises such as Caesar, Livy, Plutarch and Vegetius would also help the young knight.[29]

Similarly speaking from practical experience, Frà Sabba advised the younger Knight of St John who succeeded him at Faenza how to manage the business of his commandery. When residing there, the Knight of St John must know every inch of his domain, recalling Hesiod's remark that nothing makes a field grow faster than the footprints of its owner. The Knight-commander should not rely even on a faithful steward but must keep his own accounts. Similarly he must know all the animals, visiting them twice a week to check how his servants were feeding and grooming them. Riding across his estates on a suitable but not showy mount, the Knight-commander should supervise the condition of fences, pens and barns. New buildings should not be erected unless they were necessary, and certainly never out of caprice.[30] Prompt payment of servants and workmen was to be recommended and buying on credit was an evil.[31] In contrast to Frà Sabba's own stewardship of Magione di Faenza, the negligence of absent Knight-commanders had allegedly reduced to nothing many of the commanderies of the Order of St John's Italian *langue*.[32] Whether temporarily absent or in residence, the Knight-commander should never allow his relatives to live at his commandery because his obligations were not to them but to God, St John the Baptist and his Order. There was no greater madness in this world than to go to Hell for the sake of others! Commanderies had never been established to enrich relatives, as many ignorant people believed, but rather were somewhere to live for poor Knights of St John after many years of service had rendered them decrepit.[33] Frà Bartolomeo was reminded to pay promptly his commandery's annual responsions to the Common Treasury, without which his Order could not continue to serve the whole of Christendom by defending the holy Catholic faith against the infidel.[34]

To wear the habit of St John without doing good works was a dead religion and therefore Frà Sabba urged his great-nephew to hear Mass every morning, to say the prescribed prayers of the day, and to observe the feasts and vigils of the

28 *Ricordo* 39, 70.

29 *Ricordo* 38.

30 *Ricordo* 70.

31 *Ricordo* 53.

32 *Ricordo* 68.

33 *Ricordo* 69.

34 *Ricordo* 1.

liturgical year. He should confess and communicate at least four times a year. Once he had chosen his spiritual director, necessarily a priest of holy reputation, the young knight should retain him as his confessor, since frequent changes of confessor were as harmful to the soul as were changes of physician to the body. Certain prayers were recommended to be said, as the young knight rose from his bed and dressed himself in the morning. These prayers were:

(I) *Gratias ago tibi aterne omnipotens Deus, quia me hac nocte*;
(II) *Vias tuas Domine demonstra mihi*;
(III) *Illumina oculos nos*;
(IV) *Pater Noster*;
(V) *Credo*;
(VI) *Miserere me Deus secundum magnam misericordiam tuam*;
(VII) *Ave Maria*;
(VIII) *Salve Regina*;
(IX) *Ave Santissima Maria Mater Dei*;
(X) *In principio erat Verbum*;
(XI) *Qui habitat in adiutorio altissimi.*

Similarly these same prayers were recommended for the end of the day, when the young Knight of St John was undressing for bed.[35]

When praying to God, the young Knight of St John was recommended to ask for the intercession especially of four advocates: (i) the Blessed Virgin Mary, 'refuge of all sinners'; (ii) St John the Baptist, 'our great consul'; and of two female saints whom Frà Sabba described as being still 'advocates of our Order', namely, (iii) St Mary Magdalene, who had been both a disciple and apostle; and (iv) St Catherine of Alexandria, virgin and martyr.[36] Frà Sabba urged his young knight frequently to visit holy places such as churches, monasteries or hospitals and especially those to which an indulgence might be attached. The sermons preached by religious of holy example and of Catholic and sound doctrine were especially commended. The *spirit* of the sermon should then be acted upon. But if the preacher should preach Luther, the young Knight of St John should avoid his sermons like the plague, for Luther killed the soul as readily as the plague would kill the body.[37]

Frà Sabba urged his great-nephew always to show respect to priests, even bad ones, because of their supreme dignity of consecrating the Host. Bad priests should be left to be punished by their ecclesiastical superiors. Social order would be turned upside down, if lay people presumed to judge priests.[38] When choosing a chaplain for his commandery, the Knight of St John was obliged to appoint a mature, honest and experienced priest, whose function in celebrating Mass and looking after souls was 'an art above all other arts'. The Knight-commander must ensure that all adult

35 *Ricordo* 2.

36 *Ricordo* 3. The church of Frà Sabba's commandery at Magione di Faenza was dedicated to St Mary Magdalene, on which see Francesco Lanzoni, *Storia ecclesiastica e agiografia Faentina dal XI al XV secolo*, ed. Giovanni Lucchesi (Città del Vaticano, 1969), pp. 59, 68–9.

37 *Ricordo* 4.

38 *Ricordo* 37.

parishioners knew the prayers, *Pater Noster*, *Credo* and *Ave Maria*, and that they performed their Easter duties. Parishioners should not be permitted to keep changing their confessors. Lutherans among them were to be admonished, converted or expelled. The Knight-commander of St John could not leave all this to his chaplain, and if he ignored any of this, he would have to answer to Our Lord Jesus Christ on his deathbed and on the Day of Judgement, since, precisely because of his neglect, some parishioners might have 'strayed into mortal sin'.

Above all, the Knight-commander of St John must remember his Hospitaller vocation and help the poor and sick. Frà Sabba had a teleological view of poverty: *il povero si può salvare da se con la patienza, ma il ricco senza il povero mal si può salvare. Perche Nostro Signore Dio non fece il povero se non per salvare il ricco.*[39] Insofar as the Knight-commander of St John had credit and influence with secular magistrates, he must use his authority always to help, defend and succour poor and miserable people who might be unjustly abused or oppressed, for such an intercession on behalf of the poor was especially meritorious to God our Saviour. However, the Knight-commander of St John must not interpose his authority to rescue from just punishment thieves, assassins, traitors, forgers, sodomites or heretics. The latter especially were not to be assisted when they provided no hopes of amendment.[40]

Given the long gestation of Frà Sabba da Castiglione's *Ricordi* between his sojourn at Rhodes in the first decade of the sixteenth century and his sending them from Faenza to the press at Bologna in 1546, it is interesting to speculate how they might have been influenced by expectations of the Council of Trent, which began its deliberations in December 1545. Certainly Paul III's bull of November 1544, *Laetare Jerusalem*, contained oblique encouragement for Frà Sabba's Order of St John when the pope announced the purpose of the forthcoming Council to be the liberation of Christian people from the Turks, alongside the now better-remembered purposes of removing religious discord and of reforming the Church. In the words of the bull:

> Whilst we desired the commonwealth to be safe and protected against the arms and insidious designs of the infidels, yet, because of our transgressions and the guilt of us all, indeed, because of the wrath of God hanging over us by reason of our sins, Rhodes had been lost, Hungary ravaged, war by land and sea intended and planned against Italy, and against Austria and Illyria, since the Turk, our godless and ruthless enemy, was never at rest and looked upon our mutual enmities and dissensions as his fitting opportunity to carry out his designs with success.[41]

Frà Sabba always lamented his Order's loss of Rhodes and commiserated with the fate of both male and female Christians sold into slavery throughout the Ottoman empire and maltreated by Muslim 'wicked, faithless dogs without pity'.[42]

39 *Ricordo* 36.

40 *Ricordo* 35.

41 H.J. Schroeder, OP, *Canons and Decrees of the Council of Trent* (St Louis, Mo, 1960), pp. 1–2.

42 Cf. *Ricordo* 131.

Frà Sabba da Castiglione lived long enough to witness the first two periods of the Council of Trent (1545–47 and 1551–52), but died in March 1554 before the third period of the Council between 1562 and 1563.[43] For generations of Catholic lay nobles after Trent (whether or not they joined the Order of St John), Frà Sabba da Castiglione had demonstrated how they might fuse orthodox piety with two necessary attributes of their social function: how to govern in peacetime and how to conduct a just and successful war. How else to explain the reception of Frà Sabba's *Ricordi* (through its 26 editions between 1546 and 1613) by a readership which, by definition, could not all have possessed those proofs of nobility required so stringently for admission to the Order of St John? In the crowded literature of courtiers' manuals, alongside his more celebrated cousin Baldassare Castiglione or next to Antonio de Guevara, or Giovanni della Casa, Frà Sabba's voice was heard posthumously, expounding something more urgent than a reminder to the would-be gentleman that he should never spit into his handkerchief.[44]

Frà Sabba's best known *ricordi*, entitled *Cerca la cortegiania di nostri tempi* and *Qual deve essere il prencipe*, were relevant to his great-nephew Frà Bartolomeo and other Knights of St John who might find themselves in various courts of Catholic Europe, serving their Order or their own natural sovereign. Frà Sabba's advice how to behave at court contrasts with the prescriptions of Baldassare Castiglione or Machiavelli. Instead of the latter's tension between *virtù* and *fortuna*, Frà Sabba links *envy* and *ambition* at the Italian courts. He bemoans the passing of the courtier's purpose (as formerly defined by Dante and Boccaccio) to entertain the prince and to bring harmony between all others at court. Italy had entered its dotage, according to Frà Sabba, because of the idiocies of its *gallanti*, and a courtier's true purpose was altogether masked by perfumes and the absurdity of wearing gloves to eat salad.[45] As for the ideal prince, Frà Sabba defined this ruler as loving and fearing God above all. Such a prince should exhibit a truly Christian religion, not a dissimulated piety. The essence of a Christian prince consisted, besides, in punishing criminals and protecting the just and the virtuous. The prince should move quickly but show compassion in the exercise of justice. Justice and mercy were linked indissolubly, as were faith and works, grace and free will, honesty and use, poverty and humility. Especially, four vices were to be eradicated from the prince's domains: blasphemy, sacrilege, heresy, and abominations against nature. Frà Sabba projected onto his ideal prince the Hospitaller concerns of his own Order, by emphasizing how this prince must be concerned especially for orphans, widows and other wretched persons not able to defend their interests. A Christian prince should never sell offices because this evil practice abused poor people.

---

43 At the end of his *Ricordo* 124, Frà Sabba recorded how the Council of Trent still had much work to do: 'il Sacrosanto Concilio, il quale spero in Dio et nella bontà, santità, virtù et religion di quelli a chi tocca, che riformarà, reparará et instaurarà il vivere christiano, sì del chierico come del secolare, già tutto conquassato et roinato per le negligentie passate di sorte che meritamente ci potremo appellare veri christiani et veri servi di Dio'.

44 For a survey of this literature, see J.R. Woodhouse, *From Castiglione to Chesterfield* (Oxford, 1991); A. Scaglione, *Knights at Court* (Berkeley, 1991), pp. 248–62

45 *Ricordo* 82.

Just as Frà Sabba insisted on the fusion of *armi* and *lettere* for his brethren in the Order of St John, so too his ideal prince must be valiant when waging a just and necessary war, and he must be well read both in pagan, classical authors and in Christian scripture. Just as Frà Sabba urged his brethren to conduct war according to Christian principles and to observe the honour of women, so too his ideal prince must cherish the honour of his female subjects. He should never compel individual subjects to marry partners chosen by himself because to do so would be tyrannical. The prince should finance his wars by savings in his treasury and not by seizing the wealth of his subjects. King Alfonso of Naples's comment that an illiterate king was a crowned ass was cited by Frà Sabba in support of that necessary fusion of *armi* and *lettere* in his ideal prince. Frà Sabba's hierarchy of knowledge for his ideal prince was topped by the scriptures. Amongst secular knowledge, history, whether classical or modern, was especially useful to the prince, both for the present and the future. The prince should surround himself at court with the best moral and natural philosophers, historians, poets, cosmographers, painters, sculptors, architects, engineers, captains of war and travellers who had seen distant lands.

In peacetime the prince's recreations should be riding, hunting, archery and ball games – physical exercises similar indeed to those Frà Sabba prescribed for his own brethren in the Order of St John. St John the Evangelist and St Anthony of Padua were cited in support of Frà Sabba's plea for physical recreation as a necessary foil to contemplation. Games of cards or dice had no place at the prince's court for these were the recreations of fools and cheats. Chess was more of a cerebral game but princes were known to be bad losers and should avoid it. Because Plato had recommended music's power to induce harmony, Frà Sabba was eloquent about the function of music at the court of his ideal prince. Dances, balls, concerts or songs were all recreations dismissed by Frà Sabba as tending to demean the prince's majesty. In peacetime, the music of lutes, viols and lyres was the Devil's music, from which the prince should recoil and turn instead to music of the psalms, of hymns, and the organ, all of which served to elevate the prince's mind in service of God. In wartime, a prince should delight only in the sounds of trumpets and drums, instruments calculated to induce soldiers to disregard their own lives for the acquisition of honour and glory.

The correlation between Frà Sabba's ideal Knight of St John and his ideal prince was made explicit, when he praised Ferdinand of Aragon as the model for all other Christian princes. Ferdinand's crusading valour had driven the Muslims from Spain and the fame of his Christian exploits had made him worthy – according to Frà Sabba – of being king of the whole world. Also in his *virtù*, justice and generosity, Ferdinand had experienced no equal in his lifetime. Amongst living princes, Cosimo I of Florence was a fine prince in the making, worthy of his ancestors, Leo X and Clement VII. The latter, as Frà Sabba pointed out, had been a Knight of St John and Prior of Capua before his election to the papacy. Though resident in Lombardy after his brief sojourn in Rhodes, Frà Sabba identified Florence with virtue and Rome with vice. He prayed to be proved wrong by God that Rome could never atone for all its *molte colpe, errori, falli et peccati* and that it would merit a further terrible punishment from God beyond that of 1527.

Frà Sabba contrasted the effeminate dress and behaviour of many contemporary courtiers with the celibate Knight of St John in one of the longest of his *Ricordi*, entitled *Cerca il maritarsi*.[46] It is not obvious why a senior Knight of St John should write at such length about marriage. Either this was another *topos* for Frà Sabba's display of learning or it had been prompted by anxiety lest his great-nephew, Frà Bartolomeo, might be tempted to abandon their shared vocation. Frà Sabba was defending his Order of St John's vow of celibacy in the topsy-turvy times of which he disapproved. Frà Sabba recognized that a wife's love for her husband could transcend any other love between human beings, and that a happy marriage was blessed indeed. At the same time he highlighted so many drawbacks to marriage, and advocated celibacy for those young men who could exercise self-control. Theirs would be a more certain, freer and smoother path than that trodden by their married contemporaries. Frà Sabba linked martyrdom with marriage to 'a mad, bestial, unwilling and immodest wife, as one finds', adding that the torment of martyrs now in Heaven has been brief, whereas the continuous pain caused by an unsuitable wife made a battlefield of the marital bed and 'crucifies the body and soul'. Such husbands should be canonized as martyrs and enrolled in the list of saints, and addressed in litanies by the faithful. Frà Sabba thanked God for recognizing that he himself would never have been patient in such bondage to a wife and for having made him a Knight of St John. In between these forthright opinions, Frà Sabba scatters witticisms about the marital state, drawing his examples from literature and from what he had observed at the Italian courts.

In character, the ideal wife should be prudent, honest and retiring. She should be literate but, since the love of God was the best education for women, she should be able to read the Bible, the Little Office of Our Lady, and the lives of the saints and the Fathers of the Church rather than the sonnets of Petrarch or the *Filocolo* of Boccaccio. These latter were vain and unsuitable for women, who tended to use reading and writing, singing and playing, even the art of fencing, for bad purposes. Frà Sabba shuddered to remember from his youth a Lombard lady who defeated most rivals at fencing. Women were excluded from Frà Sabba's ideal fusion of arms and letters. Rather, his ideal woman was described in the Canticle, *like the lily and among the thorns so is my beloved among the daughters of Jerusalem*. Frà Sabba confessed that, in his own youth, he had praised the singing and dancing of women but now, in his old age, he condemned these so-called accomplishments as vanities. However much provoked, no husband should ever beat his wife, even when she had cuckolded him, but he should turn, in his misery, to Holy Mother Church, who wisely provided the remedy of separation in such cases.[47]

Before Frà Sabba da Castiglione had drawn his shutters against the world, he had moved in the circles of the Medici pontiffs Leo X and Clement VII and so had known Pietro Bembo, the poet, humanist and literary theorist portrayed by Baldassare Castiglione in book IV of *The Courtier*. Julius II had provided Bembo with one of the Order of St John's commanderies, which he had accepted, whereas Frà Sabba had declined this same pontiff's offer of a position in the papal household. Leo X later

46 *Ricordo* 121.
47 *Ricordo* 121.

made Bembo grand prior of Hungary in the Order of St John, but the poet put aside his Order's habit upon his appointment as cardinal in 1539. In short, Bembo was receiving income from the Order of St John's commanderies but, unlike Frà Sabba da Castiglione, was not linking his membership of the Order with all other facets of his personality. The exceptional nature of Frà Sabba da Castiglione's achievement was praised by Giacomo Bosio, the Order of St John's historian in the sixteenth century, especially because Frà Sabba had opened a library at his commandery for his brethren and other students. Bosio, a chaplain of his Order, recognized that not all Knights of St John could be philosophers but they should be conversant with literature and thereby bring some grace to their vocation in society. Bosio expected his brethren to be conversant with the teachings of Christianity and in proportion to the fact that they were not priests.[48]

48 G. Bosio, *La corona del cavalier Gierosolomitano* (Rome, 1588), p.133.

Chapter 22

Towards a History of Military-Religious Orders[1]

Jonathan Riley-Smith

Although there is a growing interest in the history of the military-religious orders,[2] agreement has yet to be reached on their nature. This paper, dedicated to Dr Anthony Luttrell, is in part my response to his challenge to provide a convincing definition of them. I argue here that they are to be found in two forms, to which I give the names 'Military Orders' and 'Christian Orders of Chivalry'.

Definition

Military Orders

Military orders are orders of the Roman Catholic Church, the brothers (and occasionally sisters) of which are professed religious, subject to the usual obligations of, and constraints in, canon law, except one: some of them had the right and duty to bear arms. Since priests are forbidden by canon law to use force, these orders were – and one of them still is – unusual in that they were run by their lay brothers, the knights. Many flourished in the central Middle Ages, ranging from international organizations such as the Temple, through smaller bodies like St Lazarus, to the Iberian Orders of Calatrava, Aviz, Santiago, Alcántara, Christ and Montesa, the German Brothers of the Sword and Knights of Dobrzyn, and the tiny English Order of St Thomas, but only two, the Hospital of St John of Jerusalem (the Sovereign Military Order of Malta) and Order of St Mary of the Germans (the Teutonic Order) survive today as orders of the Church, although they are no longer military in practice. The priests of the Teutonic Order run parishes and the members of the Order of Malta care for the sick poor.

Orders of the Church, military or otherwise, pass out of existence when they are absorbed by others, or cease to attract vocations, or fail in their mission and are suppressed, or have their natures altered by some external authority. Absorption was the fate of the brethren of some early Iberian orders and of the German Swordbrothers.

---

1 This is an elaboration of a lecture delivered at Emmanuel College, Cambridge, on 17 March 2005 at the launch, funded by Mr Stephen Klimczuk, of a campaign to establish a Centre for the Study of Military-Religious Orders.

2 Reliable if necessarily brief accounts are Alan J. Forey, 'The Military Orders, 1120–1312', in *The Oxford Illustrated History of the Crusades*, ed. Jonathan Riley-Smith (Oxford, 1995), pp. 184–216; Anthony T. Luttrell, 'The Military Orders, 1312–1798', in ibid., pp. 326–64.

The Templars experienced catastrophic failure. Transformation of some military orders by outside authority took the form of secularization, a step which became popular with étatist monarchies in the late fifteenth and sixteenth centuries.

Christian Orders of Chivalry

The model for these royal adaptations was provided by the secular orders of chivalry, the earliest of which had been established in the fourteenth century, two hundred years after the emergence of the military orders. The most important of them, 'Monarchical Orders' such as those of the Garter, the Collar or Annunciation, the Golden Fleece and St Michael, possessed, like the military orders, bodies of laws governing the lives of their members, but they were not subject to the Church and canon law (except insofar as their members were baptized Christians). They were subject to the sovereignty of princely founders and their constitutional or dynastic successors. In other words, they acquired legitimacy not through their recognition as religious orders by the Church, but through the acts of secular founts of honours. The professed brothers of a military order were, and are, knights by virtue of their profession, although there is some evidence that the Templars had played safe by having postulants – even boys as young as 11 years – dubbed immediately before admission.[3] The knights of a secular order of chivalry, on the other hand, were, and are, such by virtue of the action of a sovereign power or its successor, and although it was common for some private devotional obligations to be imposed on them their role was, and is, honorific. As one of their historians has written, 'The only goal common to all of these societies was the promotion and reward of loyal service'.[4]

The secularization of the Iberian military orders was well under way in the fifteenth century. In the sixteenth, *de facto* royal control gave way to the kings' assumption of government over them *de jure*, by means of papal grants, and the brothers were freed from restrictions relating to almost every aspect of the religious life.[5] In some orders, however, the transformation was only partial, because elements from their past were retained for a significant period of time. Their knights – particularly those of Santiago and Christ – continued to serve in North Africa or in Mediterranean galley fleets or in the Portuguese empire.[6] No longer orders of the Church, they

3 *Le procès des Templiers*, ed. Jules Michelet, 2 vols (Paris, 1841–51), 1, pp. 404, 417.

4 D'Arcy J.D. Boulton, *The Knights of the Crown* (Woodbridge, 1987), p. xviii and *passim*; Maurice Keen, *Chivalry* (New Haven and London, 1984), pp. 179–99.

5 The process is briefly described in Luttrell, 'The Military Orders, 1312–1798', pp. 348–50. See also Luis Adão Fonseca, 'The Portuguese Military Orders and the Oceanic Navigations: from piracy to empire' (forthcoming). In England King Henry VIII seems to have toyed with the idea of converting the grand priory of St John into an Order of the Crown with the function of defending Calais. Gregory O'Malley, *The Knights Hospitaller of the English Langue 1460–1565* (Oxford, 2005), pp. 179–84, 335.

6 See Luis Adão Fonseca, 'As Ordens Militares e a Expansão', *A Alta Nobreza e a Fundação do Estado da Índia* (Lisbon, 2004), pp. 325–47; Luis Adão Fonseca, 'La storiografia dell'espansione marittima portoghese (secc. XIV–XV)', *Bullettino dell'Istituto Storico Italiano per il Medio Evo* 106 (2004), 299–346; Isabel Morgado de Sousa e Silva and Maria

had become confraternities legitimized by secular founts of honours, but unlike secular orders of chivalry their membership continued to entail public, as opposed to private, obligations which related to the defence of Christendom or the Faith. These Iberian hybrids, combining within themselves elements from the constitutions both of military orders and of secular orders of chivalry, were the original Christian orders of chivalry.

They must have influenced a number of new creations which mirrored their nature. In 1562 Cosimo I of Medici, duke of Tuscany, founded the Order of St Stephen, which attracted a large body of recruits and ran an effective navy for nearly two centuries, with its galleys serving alongside the Hospitallers of St John in the relief of Malta in 1565, at Lepanto in 1571 and in the defence of Crete from 1645 to 1669.[7] In its turn St Stephen probably provided a model for St Maurice and St Lazarus, created in 1572 out of the union of an order founded by Duke Amadeus VIII of Savoy and the Italian branch of the almost moribund Order of St Lazarus, after an attempted merger of the latter with St Stephen had failed.[8] Others followed, including Our Lady of Mount Carmel and St Lazarus in 1609, incorporating the French brothers of St Lazarus, and the Constantinian Order of St George, an invention of early sixteenth-century Balkan adventurers which was taken over by the Farnese dukes of Parma in 1697.[9]

The active roles of the early Christian orders of chivalry faded away or were renounced in the eighteenth and nineteenth centuries, but they seem to have had an indirect influence on the development of others. These were generated by the Reformation, which hit the military orders hard but left in its wake some odd survivals in northern Europe. The bailiwick of Utrecht of the Teutonic Order adopted Calvinism and lived on as a charitable body in the Netherlands.[10] In northern Germany the brothers of the Hospital of St John, who had already been organized into a separate province, the bailiwick of Brandenburg, converted themselves into a Lutheran lay confraternity, which bought its freedom from the headquarters on Malta, although it sought partial reintegration in 1763 with the encouragement of Grand Master Manoel Pinto. After an interlude of 40 years as a secular order, its surviving knights provided the basis for its revival by the crown of Prussia in 1852 and today it is recognized by the Federal Republic of Germany.[11] Two of its foreign commanderies, in Sweden

---

Cristina Pimenta, 'As Ordens de Santiago e de Cristo e a Fundação do Estado da Índia. Uma Perspectiva de Estudo', *A Alta Nobreza e a Fundação do Estado da Índia* (Lisbon, 2004), pp. 349–87.

7 Luttrell, 'The Military Orders, 1312–1798', pp. 351–2.

8 Luttrell, 'The Military Orders, 1312–1798', p. 354.

9 See Desmond Seward, *Italy's Knights of St George* (Gerrards Cross, 1986), *passim*; David Marcombe, *Leper Knights* (Woodbridge, 2003), p. 23.

10 Jonathan Riley-Smith, 'Revival and Survival', *The Oxford Illustrated History of the Crusades*, ed. Jonathan Riley-Smith (Oxford, 1995), p. 390.

11 Walter G. Rödel, 'Catholic and Protestant Members of the German Grand Priory of the Order of St John: the Development of the Bailiwick of Brandenburg', in Malcolm Barber (ed.), *The Military Orders. Fighting for the Faith and Caring for the Sick* (Aldershot, 1994), pp. 34–41; Johannes Schellakowsky, 'The Bailiwick of Brandenburg and the Prussian Monarchy 1701–1810', in Helen Nicholson (ed.), *The Military Orders. Volume 2. Welfare*

and the Netherlands, transformed themselves into independent orders in 1946 under the patronage of their respective crowns.[12]

Meanwhile, a non-Catholic Order of St John had emerged in England out of the confusion that had followed the fall of Hospitaller Malta to Napoleon in 1798. French Knights of Malta, whose minds had been awash with a half-baked scheme to recover the island of Rhodes, lost three centuries before, entered into an alliance with some of the leaders of the Greek revolt against Ottoman Turkish rule. The French, who agreed to provide the Greeks with troops and funds, tried to raise money on the London market and planned to equip in England a naval expedition for service in the Eastern Mediterranean. In 1827 membership of the Order of Malta was offered to all financial subscribers and to all officers commissioned in the mercenary force, whether Roman Catholic or not. The body of English knights which resulted was never recognized as part of the Order of Malta by the grand magistry in Rome, but in 1888 it was converted into an order of the British Crown.[13]

The four non-Catholic Orders of St John and the non-Catholic Order of St Mary of the Germans are Christian confraternities, which stem in a variety of ways from the original military orders and are legitimized by secular authorities. They are, therefore, amalgams on the pattern of those in Iberia, France and Italy. At about the same time as they reached their mature form they were joined by others.

The origins of the Equestrian Order of the Holy Sepulchre are to be found in the creation of knighthoods from the fourteenth century onwards by the Franciscans, who had custody of the Holy Places and wanted to build up a body of lay support. In the sixteenth century there was an abortive attempt to make something more substantial out of the Holy Sepulchre knights scattered throughout Europe, but it was only in the nineteenth century that an order was created for them by the papacy in its secular persona as a fount of honours. In this case a Christian order of chivalry had come into being which had a powerful religious dimension, a close association with the Holy Land and a cardinal as grand master.[14]

Another example developed within the Sovereign Military Order of Malta itself. The professed brothers, whose numbers were in decline, were supplemented – and were eventually to be outnumbered – by knights (and later dames) of Honour and Devotion. These had occasionally been found before 1800 but had not been numerous.[15] They are not professed, have in religious terms a similar standing to tertiaries, and the grant of knighthoods to them is based on the sovereign authority of the order and the grand master. The order has recently described itself as being at the same time 'an Order of the Roman Catholic Church' and 'a body which by

---

and Warfare (Aldershot, 1998), pp. 381–8; Adam Wienand (ed.), *Der Johanniterorden, Der Malteserorden* (Cologne, 1970).

12 For Sweden, see Jan van Konow, 'Johanniterorden i Sverige', in *Johanniterorden i Sverige 1995* (Karlskrone, 1995), pp. 74–5.

13 Jonathan Riley-Smith, 'The Order of St John in England, 1827–1858', in Malcolm Barber (ed.), *The Military Orders. Fighting for the Faith and Caring for the Sick* (Aldershot, 1994), pp. 121–38.

14 Kaspar Elm, *Umbilicus Mundi* (Bruges, 1998); Kaspar Elm and Cosimo Damiano Fonseca (eds), *Militia Sancti Sepulcri. Idea e istituzioni* (Vatican City, 1998).

15 Henry Sire, *The Knights of Malta* (Newhaven and London, 1994), p. 251.

its constitution also declares itself to be an Order of Chivalry'.[16] I interpret this as meaning that it embodies within itself both an order of the Church, which comprises the professed knights and chaplains, together with all the lay *confratres* and *consorores*, and a Christian order of chivalry which is confined to the grand master and the same lay knights and dames in confraternity.

Function

A distinguishing feature of the military orders and the Christian orders of chivalry is that they were, and still are, religious or semi-religious institutes. This fundamental characteristic does not make them an easy subject for modern writers to come to terms with and the distaste with which they have been regarded helps to explain why they are absent from so many standard works on the religious life. The foundation in 1120 of the Temple as a religious institution, the members of which took familiar vows, said or heard the Office and then rode out to kill their enemies, was unprecedented in Christian history, but the ideal it expressed was attractive to contemporaries. Many commanderies were endowed by benefactors in return for the intercessory prayer of the communities to be established in them.[17] Although most sons of armsbearers entered the ranks of the secular clergy or became monks or friars, some of them found in the life of the military orders a positive way of expressing their vocations. Hugh of Bourbouton, a Provençal lord who entered the Temple in 1138 and became the master of a commandery created out of his own lands, probably never went to Palestine. He had been relatively old when he had responded to the spirituality of the new 'knights of Christ' and he remained, living a religious life he must have found satisfying, on his old estate, content to manage the lands there for the benefit of the fighting convent in the east.[18] The orders' military role was to remain attractive to recruits and benefactors for centuries. Its appeal was manifest, for example, in the 26 English coats-of-arms at the centre of which are the royal arms of Henry IV and six other members of his family, sculpted on the face of the English Tower at the south-eastern corner of the enceinte of the Hospitaller castle of Bodrum on the coast of Asia Minor.[19]

Men like Hugh of Bourbouton were needed, because the orders' commitments demanded money, men and matériel, and these could only be generated through the management of endowed land and investments. Warfare was hugely expensive and it got more so as time went by. The orders, moreover, chose, or were persuaded, to concentrate on fortifications and shipping: the most costly, because the most technological, forms of commitment. When the Templar castle of Safad in Palestine

16 In a statement to a joint committee of the Sovereign Military Order of Malta and The Alliance.

17 For example, *Cartulaire général de l'ordre du Temple 1119?-1150*, ed. Guigue A.M.J.A. d'Albon, (Paris, 1913–22), p. 99.

18 Jonathan Riley-Smith, *The First Crusaders* (Cambridge, 1997), pp. 164–5.

19 Anthony T. Luttrell, 'English Contributions to the Hospitaller Castle at Bodrum in Turkey: 1407–1437', H. Nicholson (ed.), *The Military Orders. Vol. 2: Welfare and Warfare* (Aldershot, 1998), pp. 167–72.

was rebuilt in the 1240s an estimate made within the order put the bill, over and above the income from the villages nearby, at 1,100,000 saracen besants. Thereafter the annual cost of maintenance ran to 40,000 besants.[20] Since mercenary knights were serving in Palestine for 120 besants a year,[21] the expenses of restoring this great fortress came to the equivalent of paying a year's wages to over 9,000 knights and thereafter bearing a permanent establishment of 333 knights. At the time, the Templars had six castles in the Levant of roughly this size. The master of the Hospitallers, who were responsible for another three, wrote in 1268 that more than 10,000 men were being fed by his order in the East, over and above the 300 brothers who were resident there.[22] Many of the 10,000 must have been the mercenaries required to man the garrisons and to contribute to the defence of the cities. The cost to the orders most have been enormous and the records of the interrogation of the Templars in the early fourteenth century include a graphic account of a revolt of mercenaries in Acre in the 1270s, because their wages were not being paid on time.[23] The fleets of the Hospitallers on Rhodes and Malta and the advanced fortifications constructed in both archipelagos and by the Teutonic Knights in Prussia and Livonia were a heavy burden,[24] as must have been the lesser commitments made by Santiago, Christ, St Stephen, St Maurice and St Lazarus and Our Lady of Mount Carmel and St Lazarus.

The burdens on the Teutonic Order and the Hospital of St John were, moreover, multiplied when they founded order-states in Prussia and Rhodes, and later on Malta, even if these were among their most significant achievements. The concentration of resources on Prussia and Rhodes was in part a response to the arrest of the Templars, about which more below. It cannot be a coincidence that in the same year, 1309, when the investigation into the Temple was at its height, the grand master of the Teutonic Knights took up residence at Marienburg in Prussia, where his order had been established for nearly a century, and the Hospitallers moved their headquarters to the island of Rhodes, which they had invaded three years before and which they were to hold until 1522. They went on to create another order-state on Malta, which they ruled from 1530 to 1798. After the conversion of Prussia and Livonia into Lutheran duchies in the sixteenth century, the headquarters of the Teutonic Knights lived on somewhat decoratively in southern Germany, where, from Mergentheim,

20 *De constructione castri Saphet : construction et fonctions d'un château fort franc en Terre Sainte*, ed. Robert Huygens (Amsterdam, 1981), p. 41.

21 Jonathan Riley-Smith, 'The Crown of France and Acre, 1254–1291', in Daniel Weiss and Lisa Mahoney (eds), *France and the Holy Land* (Baltimore and London, 2004), p. 48. A stipend of 40 *livres tournois* was the equivalent of 120 besants. Alphonse-Martial Chazaud, 'Inventaire et comptes de la succession d'Eudes, comte de Nevers (Acre 1266)', *Mémoires de la société des antiquaires de France*, sér. 4, 2 (1871), 176–7, 179–80.

22 *Cartulaire général de l'ordre des Hospitaliers de St Jean de Jérusalem*, ed. Joseph Delaville Le Roulx, 4 vols (Paris, 1894–1906) (henceforward *Cart. Hosp.*), 4:292, no 3308 (*Regesta regni Hierosolymitani*, comp. Reinhold Röhricht (Innsbruck, 1893–1904), (henceforward *RRH*), no 1358a).

23 *Le procès* 1 p. 46.

24 For Rhodes, see Jürgen Sarnowsky, *Macht und Herrschaft im Johanniterorden des 15. Jahrhunderts* (Münster, 2001), pp. 497–511, 525–82.

the grand masters ruled a tiny principality until 1809 and sent brothers to fight in the Habsburg wars against the Turks.[25]

Prussia had been a semi-sovereign principality since 1226 and the grand master carried his rights as prince to Mergentheim. Rhodes's standing was ambiguous[26] and Malta's was even more so, since it was a fief of the kingdom of Sicily. There was a political crisis as late as 1753 when King Charles VII of Naples claimed his rights as sovereign. Stage by stage, however, the grand masters of the Hospital assumed the attributes of sovereignty in a process that culminated in the adoption by Manoel Pinto (1741–73) of the closed crown.[27]

Having some similarities to the papal patrimonies in Italy and on the east bank of the Rhône, and to the Jesuit missionary settlements in South America, the order-states were theocracies governed by an elite class of celibate soldier-religious, who originated from outside the boundaries and isolated themselves from the indigenous populations. Established on Christian frontiers, their policies towards their non-Christian neighbours, while theoretically defensive, were highly aggressive in practice and were exemplified by the *Reysen* of the Teutonic Knights, the caravans

---

25 In general, see Udo Arnold, 'Eight Hundred Years of the Teutonic Order', in Malcolm Barber (ed.), *The Military Orders. Fighting for the Faith and Caring for the Sick* (Aldershot, 1994), pp. 223–32; Udo Arnold and Gerhard Bott (eds), *800 Jahre Deutscher Orden* (Gütersloh and Munich, 1990). For Prussia, see especially Hartmut Boockmann, *Der Deutschen Orden. Zwölf Kapitel aus seiner Geschichte* (Munich, 1981); Norman J. Housley, *The Avignon Papacy and the Crusades, 1305–1378* (Oxford, 1986), pp. 266–81; Norman J. Housley, *The Later Crusades, 1274–1580. From Lyons to Alcazar* (Oxford, 1992), pp. 322–75; Werner Paravicini, *Die Preussenreisen des europäischen Adels*, 2 vols (Sigmaringen, 1989–95); Michael Burleigh, *Prussian Society and the German Order* (Cambridge, 1984).

26 For Rhodes, see Pierre Bonneaud, *Le prieuré de Catalogne, le couvent de Rhodes et la couronne d'Aragon 1415–1447* (Millau, 2004); Anthony T. Luttrell, *The Hospitallers in Cyprus, Rhodes, Greece and the West (1291–1440)* (Aldershot, 1978); Anthony T. Luttrell, *Latin Greece, the Hospitallers and the Crusades, 1291–1400* (Aldershot, 1982); Anthony T. Luttrell, *The Hospitallers of Rhodes and their Mediterranean World* (Aldershot, 1992); Anthony T. Luttrell, *The Hospitaller state*; Luttrell, *The Town of Rhodes*; Sarnowsky, *Macht und Herrschaft*; Nicolas Vatin, *L'Ordre de Saint-Jean-de-Jérusalem, l'Empire Ottoman et la Méditerranée orientale entre le deux sièges de Rhodes (1480–1522)* (Paris, 1994); O'Malley, *The Knights Hospitaller*.

27 For Malta, see Alain Blondy, *Ordre de Malte au XVIIIe siècle: des derniers splendeurs à la ruine* (Paris, 2002); J. Quentin Hughes, *The Building of Malta* (London, 1956); Alison Hoppen, *The Fortification of Malta by the Order of St John, 1530–1798* (Edinburgh, 1979); Stanley Fiorini and Victor Mallia-Milanes (eds), *Malta. A Case Study in International Cross-Currents* (Malta, 1991); Victor Mallia-Milanes, *Venice and Hospitaller Malta 1530–1798. Aspects of a Relationship* (Marsa, 1992); Victor Mallia-Milanes (ed.), *Hospitaller Malta 1530–1798* (Msida, 1993); David Allen, 'The Order of St John as a "School for Ambassadors" in Counter-Reformation Europe', in Helen Nicholson (ed.), *The Military Orders. Vol. 2: Welfare and Warfare* (Aldershot, 1998), pp. 326–79; David Allen, '"A Parish at Sea": Spiritual Concerns aboard the Order of St John's Galleys in the Seventeenth and Eighteenth Centuries', in Malcolm Barber (ed.), *The Military Orders. Fighting for the Faith and Caring for the Sick* (Aldershot, 1994), pp. 113–20.

of the Rhodian and Maltese fleets and the Hospitallers' use of licensed piracy, the *corso*.

But aggression is expensive. The resources the orders needed for their activities in Palestine, Cyprus, Rhodes, Prussia, Livonia and Malta could only come from their Western estates, as we have seen, and there is ample evidence for the relative efficiency with which they managed their vast property portfolios.[28] It is not surprising that their economic role has been at the forefront of the minds of many of the historians who have written about them, particularly as the provinces and commanderies themselves generated masses of archival material.[29] The orders' hunger for cash was also largely responsible for the leadership they took very early in their history in paving the way for the creation of true orders of the Church.

Orders of the Church have supranational, or rather supradiocesan, structures. The brothers and sisters, wherever they are, share the same privileges, including that of exemption, which liberates them from the powers of local bishops, the same regular life and the same obedience to a common central authority which can transfer them from place to place. It is true that other congregations of religious evolved in the eleventh and twelfth centuries, but none of them initially showed the features of a true order. Either the monks, wherever they were, were pretended to be where they were not, so that a Cluniac monk at an overseas priory was treated as if he was within the walls of a virtual abbey, located at Cluny in Burgundy, or there was a confederation of independent abbeys, like the Cistercian ones. The Hospital was the first recognizable order of the Church. It was closely followed by the Temple; and the structures the Hospitallers and Templars established were to be the models for others, including the Franciscans and Dominicans.

The chief reason for their precocity was that they were institutions which had to focus not on some geographically convenient location within Europe but on the eastern fringe of Christendom. Their headquarters were therefore dependent on resources that were being generated a long way away from them. The early stage at which the Hospitallers began to evolve intermediate government suggests that they had been forced to delegate. There was no obvious model to follow and the provincial representatives had to work out, perhaps through trial and error, a means of controlling the dependencies. The first Hospitaller provincial chapter can be found meeting in 1123, and by the 1160s the terms of the relationship between the local houses and the provincial heads, who were now proliferating and could collectively

28 For the earliest period, see Pierre Gérard and Elisabeth Magnou, *Cartulaires des Templiers de Douzens* (Paris, 1965); Michael Gervers, *The Hospitaller Cartulary in the British Library (Cotton MS Nero E VI)* (Toronto, 1981); Michael Gervers, 'Pro defensione Terre Sancte: the Development and Exploitation of the Hospitallers' Landed Estate in Essex', in Malcolm Barber (ed.), *The Military Orders. Fighting for the Faith and Caring for the Sick* (Aldershot, 1994), pp. 3–20; Beatrice A. Lees, *Records of the Templars in England in the Twelfth Century. The Inquest of 1185* (London, 1935).

29 For recent examples, see Judith Bronstein, *The Hospitallers and the Holy Land. Financing the Latin East 1187–1274* (Woodbridge, 2005); Kristjan Toomaspoeg, *Templari e ospitalieri nella Sicilia medievale* (Taranto, 2003); Alain Demurger, *Les Templiers. Une chevalerie chrétienne au moyen âge* (Paris, 2005), pp. 273–344.

make decisions affecting all their brothers, was becoming clear.[30] The introduction of intermediate provinces made the Hospital and the Temple stand out until similar structures were adopted by the Premonstratensians and Cluniacs later in the twelfth century.

Ethos

The military orders were generated by the same movement to reform the religious life that gave birth to Cistercians, Carthusians, Premonstratensians, Augustinians, Franciscans, Dominicans and Carmelites.[31] The reformers were acutely aware of the sinfulness that they perceived to be encompassing them. In one response, the battle against sin was to be a private one, fought in an enclosed and contemplative environment. In the other, prayer was to precede a public confrontation with sin, either through pastoral care and works of mercy or through the bearing of arms, which was believed to be an expression of Christian love. 'Like true Israelites and warriors most versed in holy battle [wrote Pope Innocent II to the Templars], on fire with the flame of true love, you carry out in your deeds the words of the Gospel, in which it is said *Greater love than this no man hath, that a man lay down his life for his friends.*'[32]

The perception that love could be shown as much in the use of force as in pastoral or medical care was demonstrated in the transformation of the Hospital into a military order. The earliest Hospitallers were inspired by Christ's injunction to behave towards each person – whether hungry or thirsty or a stranger or naked or sick or in prison (Matt. 25:31–46) – as though he or she was God himself and they were genuinely original in the lengths to which they were prepared to go. They treated the 'holy poor' – 'Christ's poor' – with the exaggerated respect that at the time was given to secular lords[33] and they made their ideal a reality by ministering to them when they were sick and burying them, when they died, in their own charnel pit.[34]

30 Jonathan Riley-Smith, 'The Origins of the Commandery in the Temple and the Hospital', in Anthony Luttrell and Léon Pressouyre (eds), *La Commanderie, Institution des ordres militaires dans l'Occident médiéval* (Paris, 2002), pp. 9–18.

31 See especially, Giles Constable, 'The Place of the Crusader in Medieval Society', *Viator*, 28 (1998), pp. 390–403; also Demurger, *Les Templiers*, pp. 83–162; Simonetta Cerrini (ed.), *I Templari, la guerra et la santità* (Rimini, 2000); Alan J. Forey, *The Military Orders* (Basingstoke, 1992), pp. 188–203; Klaus Militzer, *Von Akkon zur Marienburg. Verfassung, Verwaltung und Sozialstruktur des Deutschen Ordens 1190–1309*, Quellen und Studien zur Geschichte des Deutschen Ordens, 56 (Marburg, 1999), pp. 79–109.

32 *Papsturkunden für Templer und Johanniter, Neue Folge*, ed. Rudolf Hiestand, Vorarbeiten zum Oriens Pontificius, 2 (Göttingen, 1984), p. 96.

33 Jonathan Riley-Smith, *The Knights of St John in Jerusalem and Cyprus 1050–1310* (London, 1967), pp. 41–52.

34 See Benjamin Z. Kedar, 'A Twelfth-Century Description of the Jerusalem Hospital', in Helen Nicholson (ed.), *The Military Orders. Vol. 2: Welfare and Warfare* (Aldershot, 1998), pp. 3–26; Susan Edgington, 'Administrative Regulations for the Hospital of St John in

Their great hospital in Jerusalem was at the centre of a widespread charitable enterprise, since they ran two other hospitals in the city, the burial ground just outside, an infirmary in the Judaean hills, a church nearby that was wrongly identified with Emmaus, a transportation service for pilgrims, a primitive ambulance service, a major almonry, particularly for nursing mothers, a large orphanage, to which a school was attached, and a mobile hospital, staffed by surgeons, which accompanied the Christian field armies. A feature of their nursing was this: because every poor man and woman *was* Christ, he or she should not just have good treatment, but the best and most luxurious treatment possible. This was a religious imperative, but it was also the application of a basic nursing principle that patients tended to get better if they were well fed, relatively clean and comfortable. The hospital in Jerusalem, the most famous of the day, was also remarkable in that it made no distinction in the religion of its patients. 'This holy House, knowing that the Lord, who calls all to salvation, does not want anyone to perish, mercifully admits men of the Pagan faith [Muslims] and Jews ... because the Lord prayed for those afflicting him, saying: "Father, forgive them for they know not what they do". In this blessed House is powerfully fulfilled the heavenly doctrine: "Love your enemies and do good to those who hate you'; and elsewhere: 'Friends should be loved in God and enemies on account of God".'[35]

This charitable institution, which extended its mission to those perceived to be the enemies of Christendom, took the first steps towards militarization within six years of the foundation of the Templars, was granted its first castle – a major one – in 1136 and nearly bankrupted itself with over-ambitious military initiatives in the 1160s. If the establishment of the Temple was a new departure, the adoption of military functions by the Hospital, an existing religious institute hitherto devoted to caring for the sick poor, was even more radical and there were those who were worried by it. But although Pope Alexander III tried at first to set limits to the order's participation in warfare, which he maintained was contrary to its customs and to the intentions of its founder,[36] a reference to a military wing, in the order's statutes of 1182, could not have put the association in the brothers' minds of fighting and love more succinctly. 'These are the special charities established in the Hospital, apart from the brothers-at-arms, which the House ought to support honourably, and many other charities which cannot be individually detailed.'[37] They saw no contradiction in an affective concentration on Christ's suffering humanity, which inspired them at the same time to care sympathetically for sick Muslim pilgrims to Jerusalem and to defend their Christian brothers and sisters with armed force.[38]

Jerusalem dating from the 1180s', *Crusades*, 4 (2005), 21–37; Adrian Boas, *Jerusalem in the Time of the Crusades* (London and New York, 2001), pp. 185–7.

35 Kedar, 'A Twelfth-Century Description', p. 18 (paraphrase).

36 Riley-Smith, *The Knights of St John*, p. 76. But see Hiestand in *Papsturkunden*, pp. 149–55

37 *Cart. Hosp.*, 1, p. 429, no. 627.

38 For their affective faith, see Thomas Licence, 'The Templars and The Hospitallers, Christ and the Saints', *Crusades*, 4 (2005), pp. 39–47.

Although military and naval expenses swallowed up much of the order's revenue thereafter – it looks as though about 9 per cent was spent on the hospital on Rhodes in the fifteenth century[39] – one can exaggerate the extent to which nursing became a subsidiary activity. The reputation of the hospital in thirteenth-century Acre seems to have been as high as the one in Jerusalem had been.[40] At Limassol, to where the Hospital had moved its headquarters in 1291, the brothers were building a hospital in 1296.[41] On their arrival on Rhodes in 1309 they at once established a temporary hospital, which between 1314 and 1356 was replaced by a purpose-built one. This gave way in 1440 to a magnificent new building.[42] Their first act in 1523 on being driven from Rhodes was to construct a tented hospital on a south Italian beach and their hospital in Valletta extended the range of its care to the Maltese population; at the same time they created a flourishing medical school, which was incorporated into their university in 1771.[43] The importance to them of nursing and the fact that it could coexist with the exercise of arms were reflected in their attitude towards their saints. If one leaves aside those in their calendar who were fabricated or appropriated from elsewhere, the vast majority – Gerard, Ubaldesca, Toscana, Hugh of Genoa and Fleur – were associated in some way with the care of the sick poor.[44]

Whether nursing the sick or engaging in warfare on land or at sea, the life of these professed religious warriors never lost its religious dimension. Underlying and justifying their existence was a philosophy that has still to be thoroughly researched. An early, and possibly the greatest, of the texts on the subject, St Bernard's *De laude novae militiae*, is well known, but much more attention will have to be given in future to the sermons of James of Vitry and others, to liturgy and to works by the brothers themselves and their employees, such as the histories of 'The Templar of Tyre', William of St Stefano, Peter of Dusburg, William Caoursin, Giacomo Bosio and René-Aubert de Vertôt, and the *Ricordi* of Sabba di Castiglione and the *Memorie de' Gran Maestri* of Paolo Maria Paciaudi.[45]

---

39 Luttrell, 'The Military Orders, 1312–1798', p. 343.

40 See Jonathan Riley-Smith, 'Further Thoughts on the Layout of the Hospital in Acre', *Chemins d'outre-mer. Études sur la Méditerranée médiévale offertes à Michel Balard*, 2 vols (Paris, 2004), 2, p. 758.

41 Riley-Smith, *The Knights of St John*, p. 198.

42 Anthony Luttrell, *The Town of Rhodes, 1306–1356* (Rhodes, 2003), pp. 99–100. See Anthony Luttrell, 'The Hospitallers' Medical Tradition', in Malcolm Barber (ed.), *The Military Orders. Fighting for the Faith and Caring for the Sick* (Aldershot, 1994), pp. 68–80; Fotini Karassava-Tsilingiri, 'The Fifteenth-Century Hospital of Rhodes', in ibid., pp. 89–96.

43 Luttrell, 'The Hospitallers' Medical Tradition', pp. 80–1; Ann Williams, '*Xenodochium* to Sacred Infirmary', in Malcolm Barber (ed.), *The Military Orders. Fighting for the Faith and Caring for the Sick* (Aldershot, 1994), pp. 97–102; Roger Ellul Micallef, 'The Maltese Medical Tradition', in Stanley Fiorini and Victor Mallia-Milanes (eds), *Malta. A Case Study in International Cross-Currents* (Malta, 1991), pp. 188–94.

44 See Luttrell, 'The Hospitallers' Medical Tradition', pp. 74–5; Licence, 'The Templars and the Hospitallers', pp. 55–7.

45 For Paciaudi, see David Allen, 'Upholding tradition: Benedict XIV and the Hospitaller Order of St John of Jerusalem at Malta, 1740–1758', *Catholic Historical Review*, 80 (1994), 29–34.

Although it is not easy to penetrate the brothers' interior lives,[46] a distinctive ethos can be identified. It built on crusade ideas and crusading's penitential nature provided St Thomas Aquinas with a justification of the orders' role – 'to make war in the service of God is imposed on some as a penance, as is evident from those who are enjoined to fight in aid of the Holy Land'[47] – but the brothers were not crusaders, being permanently, as opposed to temporarily, committed to the defence of Christianity, and they took vows that were not like those of crusaders and indeed varied from order to order. Chivalric ideas were exerting some influence on them from the late twelfth century, but on closer inspection that influence was very limited, although the Teutonic Knights had to pander to the tastes of European nobles and employ extravagant theatre to attract them to their *Reysen*.[48]

The fact is that the ethos of the military orders was *sui generis*. They remained first of all religious institutes in which, at least on the surface, the prevailing mood was penitential. Austerity was a dominant feature of the brothers' lives. It was visually expressed in the unshaven faces of the Templars – it is striking how often in the accounts of the interrogations there are references to brothers who had shaved off their beards to mark their abandonment of the order.[49] It also expressed itself in the simplicity of their buildings. The architecture favoured by the Hospitallers on Rhodes (ignoring the anachronistic vulgarity of the Fascist reconstruction of the grand masters' palace) and in the first century of their occupation of Malta has clean lines, the bareness occasionally broken by mouldings over windows or doorways, often carved for the auberges by masons imported from the home countries concerned. But it would be misleading to categorize Hospitaller architecture as minimalist. The chief decorative feature on all the buildings is a profusion of coats-of-arms. This tradition was later carried to extremes in the order's conventual church in Valletta, where the floor of what was originally a very simple building became carpeted with armigerous mosaic memorials.[50] On the whole, splendour was rejected in favour of a severe, almost puritanical, religion that was identified with nobility and expressed itself in prowess and charity. The message seems to have been that the brothers were embodiments of the ancient Roman virtues of piety and nobility.[51]

The ethos had weaknesses, among them the way middle-ranking but noble brother-knights tended to resist change and the authority of their superiors.[52] The history of the military orders, in fact, provides a very unusual example of an order

46 See, for example, Anthony Luttrell, 'The Spiritual Life of the Hospitallers of Rhodes', in Zenon Hubert Nowak (ed.), *Die Spiritualität der Ritterorden im Mittelater* (Toruń, 1993), pp. 75–96 (reprinted in Anthony T. Luttrell, *The Hospitaller State on Rhodes and its Western Provinces, 1306–1462* (Aldershot, 1999), article no IX).

47 Thomas Aquinas, *Summa Theologica, 2a2ae, qu. 188, art. 3.*

48 Paravicini, *Die Preussenreisen*; Axel Ehlers, 'The crusade of the Teutonic Knights against Lithuania reconsidered', in Alan V. Murray (ed.), *Crusade and Conversion on the Baltic Frontier, 1150–1500* (Aldershot, 2001), pp. 21–44.

49 *Le procès, passim.*

50 Hannibal P. Scicluna, *The Church of St John in Valletta* (San Martin, 1955).

51 Is it too fanciful to suggest that the flamboyance at Tomar partly reflects the fact that the Order of Christ was in the process of secularization?

52 See Riley-Smith, 'The Origins of the Commandery', pp. 15–16.

of the Church collapsing into anarchy and having to be closed down. This was so rare an occurrence that when in 1646 the Piarists lost their right to be members of a religious order, contemporaries thought that the event was unprecedented.[53] The common opinion that the Templars were innocent of all the charges levelled against them in 1307 is under discussion, with a few historians coming to believe that in some commanderies postulants were being forced into a blasphemous rite of passage involving the denial of Christ.[54] Whether they are right in their belief or not, it is indisputable that the order was in chaos. The inquiries into it demonstrated that its system of government had become old fashioned and inefficient. Decisions affecting the whole order were being made by the grand master and his convent in the East. This consisted of a few very senior brothers and many young ones of fighting age. It was so divided that it found it hard to agree on anything and it cannot have been *au fait* with events and developments in the Western provinces, because the masters hardly ever visited them and the provincials were not summoned to Eastern chapters-general. The grand master and his convent had total legislative power, but, as is so often to be found with autocracies, the result was spinelessness. One theme that runs through the responses of the Templar officials to interrogation is that they had habitually avoided monitoring the activities of their subordinates in case they should come across something inconvenient. Many brothers had never heard the Rule read to them and there was no hope whatever of their comprehending the order's supplementary legislation, even had it been available to them, because it was repetitious, muddled and archaic.[55]

The state of the Temple seems to have been so dire that one wonders how long it could have been allowed to remain in existence, with or without the scandal. It had failed to mature institutionally when compared to the Hospital and the Teutonic Order, the structures of which appear to have been much more open and up-to-date. Unlike them, it had no function other than the defence of Christians. Isolated from the mainstream interests of other professed religious, the Templars were not locked into the conventional patterns of church life which could have provided them with models for development.

Five centuries later, the fact that the Hospitallers had never lost touch with their obligations as nurses contributed in a major way to their salvation. They had played a minor part in the reformed Catholicism of the sixteenth century – the brother knight Sabba di Castiglione's touching little book of advice to a nephew who had also entered the Order, first published in 1549, is as spiritual and penitent as any work emanating from a Counter-Reformation institute[56] – but their standing as Christian heroes preying on Muslim shipping was undermined by the situation on

53 Karen Liebreich, *Fallen Order* (London, 2004, pbk edn), p. 232.

54 Jonathan Riley-Smith, 'Were the Templars Guilty?', in Susan Ridyard (ed.), *Medieval Crusade* (Woodbridge, 2004), pp. 107–24; Barbara Frale, *I Templari* (Bologna, 2004), pp. 140–4, 153. Demurger (*Les Templiers*, pp. 484–509) sits on the fence.

55 Jonathan Riley-Smith, 'The Structures of the Orders of the Temple and the Hospital in c. 1291', in Susan Ridyard (ed.), *Medieval Crusade* (Woodbridge, 2004), pp. 125–43.

56 Sabba di Castiglione, *Ricordi a Fra Bartholomeo di Castiglione suo nipote* (Bologna, 1549).

the frontiers once the Turkish empire was in retreat. They may already have been subconsciously reflecting the reality that their old role and the ethos that underpinned it were becoming anachronistic. Decorative fantasies – the achievement above all of Matteo Preti – softened the austere lines and covered the bare walls of the interior of their conventual church in Valletta in the late seventeenth century, while the auberge of Castile was rebuilt in flamboyant baroque in the eighteenth. By then they seem to have been losing their way as religious – however able and interesting some of the late eighteenth-century brothers were as individuals – and the loss of Malta in 1798, which had been preceded by the confiscation of much of their landed wealth, could have been a death blow. They were, however, saved by the fact that warfare on behalf of Christendom had never been their only function. Although it took some time for them to find their feet, they were able to abandon it in the middle of the nineteenth century and the initiatives taken by Gottfried von Schröter, August von Haxthausen and others revitalized their ancient mission of mercy.[57]

Modern History

The nineteenth century was a crucial period for the military-religious orders. It began with the surviving military orders demoralized, since they represented ideals that had become unfashionable and despised. Remembering his seizure of Malta, Napoleon icily commented: 'Si les fortifications, les moyens matériels de résistance étaient immenses, les ressorts moraux les rendaient nuls.'[58] The Teutonic Order was almost smothered to death by the Habsburg dynasty, but it continued in being, at least technically, as a religious order and this enabled it to survive the suppression of the Austrian orders of chivalry by the new republic.[59] The Hospital of St John had to endure the illegitimate and eccentric grand mastership of Tsar Paul I, who was not Roman Catholic, celibate, professed or recognized by the Holy See, anarchy in its provinces and the refusal of the papacy to allow any grand master to be appointed between 1805 and 1879. No one has satisfactorily explained how, from 1834 onwards, its government managed to preserve its claims to sovereignty and succeeded in so short a time in persuading its members to renounce the military role they had followed for seven centuries, to readopt the care of the sick as their principal activity and to rebuild the Order's provincial structure on a new basis. Pope Gregory XVI, the lieutenant grand masters Carlo Candida and Philippe di Colloredo-Mels, and the German knights to whom I have already referred played important parts in the revival,[60] but it is also clear that nineteenth-century romanticism and imperialism combined to create a favourable environment. It is hard to imagine, but it is a fact, that

57 Sire, *The Knights of Malta*, pp. 251–3; Maximilian Freiherr von Twickel, 'Die nationalen Assoziationen des Malteserordens in Deutschland', in Adam Wienand (ed.), *Der Johanniterorden, Der Malteserorden* (Cologne, 1970), pp. 471–8.

58 Napoleon I, *Mémoires et Oeuvres*, ed. Tancrède Martel (Paris, 1910), p. 246.

59 Arnold, 'Eight Hundred Years', pp. 232–5.

60 See Sire, *The Knights of Malta*, pp. 250–3; Twickel, 'Die nationalen Assoziationen', pp. 471–85; Michel de Pierredon, *Histoire politique de l'ordre de Malte depuis la Révolution française*, 3 vols (Paris, 1956–63).

the age of steam bred figures like Charles-Martial Allemand-Lavigerie, archbishop of Algiers from 1867 and cardinal from 1882 until his death ten years later, who drew up a Rule for a new military order that was to operate in North Africa, and proposed sending members of the surviving ones to protect Catholic missionaries in East Africa.[61] An extraordinarily large number of secular orders were being founded and it was now that the Holy Sepulchre, the English Order of St John and the bailiwick of Brandenburg all achieved formal legitimation. The English Order of St John, playing a role in empire-building that, if differently expressed, paralleled that of the Portuguese orders in the fifteenth and sixteenth centuries, was able to create out of ancient and, one would have thought alien, traditions a genuinely popular ambulance movement that attracted thousands of not only British but also indigenous volunteers throughout the British Empire.[62]

If the nineteenth century witnessed the renewal of the Orders of St John, the second half of the twentieth saw them coming together. In the seventeenth century there had been interesting institutional experiments – for a time the Teutonic Order contained Lutherans and Calvinists as well as Catholics[63] – and in the eighteenth century the bailiwick of Brandenburg was nominally reunited to Malta,[64] but, in spite of some other examples of collaboration, confessional differences had prevailed. Two factors led to closer relations. The first was the proliferation of unrecognized Orders of St John, most of which claimed to stem from a Russian Orthodox grand priory established by Tsar Paul I. This had been abolished by Paul's successor, but in nineteenth-century Russia there was considerable interest in its traditions among the descendants of its original commanders, in the imperial *corps des pages*, the headquarters of which were in the magnificent Priory of Malta building in St Petersburg, and even in the imperial family, although whatever concern the tsars may have shown was never translated into official recognition. Romantic interest manifested itself in foundations outside Russia after the Revolution, which through fission have multiplied into no less than 27 separate bodies, some of which are criminal. The five Orders of St John that regarded themselves as the legitimate inheritors of the traditions were forced to face collectively the challenge posed by these *soi-disant* cousins.

The second factor was the ecumenical movement. With the improvement of relations between the churches there came the realisation that the five Orders of St John collectively disposed of almost 50,000 members and 400,000 regular volunteers in 150 countries and the belief that they could act much more effectively in concert. In 1961 the four non-Catholic orders formed themselves into an *Alliance* and from 1963 the first steps towards a closer relationship with the Sovereign Military Order of Malta were taken in a series of 'Declarations of Mutual Esteem'. In 1975 the

61 Adam Knobler, 'Saint Louis and French Political Culture,' in Leslie J. Workman and Kathleen Verduin (eds), *Medievalism in Europe II. Studies in Medievalism*, 8 (Cambridge, 1996), pp. 165–6; Norman Daniel, *Islam, Europe and Empire* (Edinburgh, 1966), pp. 306–7.

62 For the ambulance movement, see Ronnie Cole-Mackintosh, *A Century of Service to Mankind* (London, 1986), pp. 81–7.

63 Arnold, 'Eight Hundred Years', pp. 231–2.

64 Sire, *The Knights of Malta*, p. 225.

first joint international committee was established and it was followed by others in 1988, 1996 and 2002. Meanwhile, an instrument of mutual recognition, the so-called 'London Declaration', was signed in 1987 by the heads of the five orders and the process culminated in 2004 in what was in effect a concordat, committing them to collaboration in those countries and projects where this would be practicable. An abiding feature of the history of the military-religious orders has been their ability to adapt to new circumstances.

Anthony Luttrell Bibliography

Monographs

1) *Medieval Malta: Studies on Malta Before the Knights*, ed. A. Luttrell (London, 1975), pp. xiii, 232.

2) *Ħal Millieri: A Maltese Casale, its Churches and Paintings*, ed. A. Luttrell (Malta, 1976), pp. 143 [articles 60 and 61]

3) *The Hospitallers in Cyprus, Rhodes, Greece and the West, 1291–1440: Collected Studies* (London, 1978), pp. iv, 394, reprinting 24 articles with introduction [hereafter Luttrell, *Hospitallers in Cyprus*].

4) *Gozo Citadel, Malta: Report Submitted to the Division of Cultural Heritage, UNESCO* (typescript: Malta, 1981), pp. 180 [reserved].

5) *Latin Greece, the Hospitallers and the Crusades, 1291–1440: Collected Studies* (London, 1982), pp. iii, 322, reprinting 16 articles with introduction [hereafter Luttrell, *Latin Greece*].

6) *The Later History of the Maussolleion and its Utilization in the Hospitaller Castle at Bodrum* = *The Maussolleion at Halikarnassos: Reports of the Danish Archaeological Expedition to Bodrum, 2 – The Written Sources and their Archaeological Background: Jutland Archaeological Society Publications*, 15 part 2 (Aarhus, 1986), pp. 114–214; pp. 143–161 = Luttrell, *Hospitaller State*, item VI.

7) with T. Blagg and A. Bonanno, *Excavations at Ħal Millieri, Malta* (Malta, 1991), pp. 152 [articles 128 and 129].

8) *The Hospitallers of Rhodes and their Mediterranean World: Collected Studies* (London, 1992), pp. ix, 324, reprinting 18 articles with introduction [hereafter Luttrell, *Hospitallers of Rhodes*].

9) with T. Blagg, *Le palais papal et autres bâtiments du XIVe siècle à Sorgues* (Sorgues, 1998), pp. 139.

10) *The Hospitaller State on Rhodes and its Western Provinces: 1306–1462* (Aldershot, 1999), pp. x, 430, reprinting 19 items with introduction [hereafter Luttrell, *Hospitaller State*].

11) *The Making of Christian Malta: From the Early Middle Ages to 1530* (Aldershot, 2002), pp. vi, 352, reprinting 20 items with introductory essay [hereafter Luttrell, *Christian Malta*].

12) *La commanderie: institution des ordres militaires dans l'occident médiéval*, ed. A. Luttrell and L. Pressouyre (Paris, 2002), pp. 361.

13) The Town of Rhodes: 1306–1356 (Rhodes, 2003), pp. xxiv, 304.

14) Hospitaller Women in the Middle Ages, ed. A. Luttrell and H. Nicholson (Aldershot, 2006), pp. xiv, 265.

15) Studies on the Hospitallers after 1306: Rhodes and the West (Aldershot, 2007), pp. xii, 384, reprinting 25 items with introduction [hereafter Luttrell, *Studies*].

Translation

1) S. Aurigemma, *Italy in Africa*: *Archaeological Discoveries (1911–1943), Tripolitania*, 1: *Monuments of Decorative Art*, part 1: *The Mosaics* (Rome, 1960), pp. 82.

Articles

Many of the following items have been reprinted in the six volumes of collected studies listed above; translated articles, many book reviews and other marginal writings are excluded.

1) 'The Knights Hospitallers of Rhodes and their Achievements in the Fourteenth Century,' *Revue de l'Ordre Souverain Militaire de Malte*, 16 (1958), 136–42.

2) 'Venice and the Knights Hospitallers of Rhodes in the Fourteenth Century', *Papers of the British School at Rome*, 26 (1958), 195–212 = Luttrell, *Hospitallers in Cyprus*, item V.

3) 'A Note on the Archives of the Order of St John of Jerusalem in Spain', *Melita Historica*, 2 no. 3 (1958), 182–5.

4) 'A Fourteenth Century List of the Barons of Achaea (1377?)', *Byzantinische Zeitschrift*, 51 (1958), 355–6.

5) 'Actividades económicas de los Hospitalarios de Rodas en el Mediterráneo occidental durante el siglo XIV', in *VI Congreso de la Historia de la Corona de Aragón* (Madrid, 1959), 175–83 = Luttrell, *Hospitallers in Cyprus*, item VII.

6) 'Interessi fiorentini nell'economia e nella politica dei Cavalieri Ospedalieri di Rodi nel Trecento', *Annali della Scuola Normale Superiore di Pisa: Lettere, Storia e Filosofia*, ser. 2, 28 (1959), 317–26 = Luttrell, *Hospitallers in Cyprus*, item VIII.

7) 'Greek Histories Translated and Compiled for Juan Fernández de Heredia, Master of Rhodes, 1377–1396', *Speculum*, 35 (1960), 401–7 = Luttrell, *Hospitallers in Cyprus*, item XX.

8) 'Venetians at Medieval Malta', *Melita Historica*, 3 no. 1 (1960), 74–80.

9) Review of works by F. Thiriet on Venetian *Romania*, in *Speculum*, 36 (1961), 182–5.

10) 'The Aragonese Crown and the Knights Hospitallers of Rhodes, 1291–1350', *English Historical Review*, 76 (1961), 1–19 = Luttrell, *Hospitallers in Cyprus*, item XI.

11) 'Emmanuele Piloti and Criticism of the Knights Hospitallers of Rhodes: 1306–1444', *Annales de l'Ordre Souverain Militaire de Malte*, 20 (1962), 11–17 = Luttrell, *Hospitallers in Cyprus*, item XXIV.

12) 'Aragoneses y Catalanes en Rodas: 1350–1430', in *VII Congreso de Historia de la Corona de Aragón*, 2 (Barcelona, 1962), 383–90 = Luttrell, *Hospitallers in Cyprus*, item XIII.

13) 'Jean and Simon de Hesdin; Hospitallers, Theologians, Classicists', *Recherches de Théologie ancienne et médiévale*, 31 (1964), 137–40 = Luttrell, *Hospitallers in Cyprus*, item XVIII.

14) 'The Principality of Achaea in 1377', *Byzantinische Zeitschrift*, 57 (1964), 340–5 = Luttrell, *Hospitallers in Cyprus*, item XXII.

15) 'Vonitza in Epirus and its Lords: 1306–1377', *Rivista di Studi Bizantini e Neoellenici*, n.s. 1 (1964), 131–41 = Luttrell, *Latin Greece*, item VII.

16) 'Federigo da Venezia's Commentary on the Apocalypse: 1393/1394', *Journal of the Walters Art Gallery*, 27–28 (1964–1965), 57–65.

17) 'The Crusade in the Fourteenth Century', in *Europe in the Late Middle Ages*, ed. J. Hale, J. Highfield and B. Smalley (London, 1965), 122–54 = Luttrell, *Latin Greece*, item XVI.

18) 'Fourteenth-Century Hospitaller Lawyers', *Traditio*, 21 (1965), 449–56 = Luttrell, *Hospitallers in Cyprus*, item XVI.

19) 'Malta and the Aragonese Crown: 1282–1530', *Journal of the Faculty of Arts: Royal Malta University*, 3 no. 1 (1965), 1–9.

20) 'Slavery and Slaving in the Portuguese Atlantic (to about 1500)', in *The Transatlantic Slave Trade from West Africa*, ed. Centre of African Studies: University of Edinburgh (Edinburgh, 1965), 61–79 [circulated in cyclostyle].

21) 'Intrigue, Schism, and Violence among the Hospitallers of Rhodes: 1377–1384', *Speculum*, 41 (1966), 30–48 = Luttrell, *Hospitallers in Cyprus*, item XXIII.

22) 'Giovanni Contarini, a Venetian at Oxford: 1392–1399', *Journal of the Warburg and Courtauld Institutes*, 29 (1966), 424–32.

23) 'The Hospitallers' Historical Activities: 1291–1400', *Annales de l'Ordre Souverain Militaire de Malte*, 24 (1966), 126–9 = Luttrell, *Hospitallers in Cyprus*, item XVII.

24) 'Los Hospitalarios en Aragón y la Peste Negra', *Anuario de Estudios Medievales*, 3 (1966), 499–514 = Luttrell, *Hospitallers in Cyprus*, item XIV.

25) 'The Latins of Argos and Nauplia: 1311–1394', *Papers of the British School at Rome*, 34 (1966), 34–55 = Luttrell, *Latin Greece*, item VIII.

26) 'The Hospitallers' Historical Activities: 1400–1530', *Annales de l'Ordre Souverain Militaire de Malte*, 25 (1967), 145–50 = Luttrell, *Latin Greece*, item II.

27) 'The Hospitallers' Historical Activities: 1530–1630', ibid., 26 (1968), 57–69 = Luttrell, *Latin Greece*, item III.

28) 'The *Decas Loyca* of Leonini de Padua', *Scriptorium*, 22 (1968), 272–3.

29) 'John Cantacuzenus and the Catalans at Constantinople: 1352–1354', in *Martínez Ferrando, Archivero: Miscelánea de Estudios Dedicados a su Memoria* (Madrid, 1968), 265–77 = Luttrell, *Latin Greece*, item IX.

30) 'Venezia e il Principato di Acaia: secolo XIV', *Studi Veneziani*, 10 (1968), 407–14 = Luttrell, *Latin Greece*, item X.

31) 'La Corona de Aragón y la Grecia catalana: 1379–1394', *Anuario de Estudios Medievales*, 6 (1969), 219–52 = Luttrell, *Latin Greece*, item XI.

32) 'Malta and Dubrovnik towards the Year 1380', *Melita Historica*, 5 no. 2 (1969), 158–64.

33) 'La Casa de Catalunya-Aragó i Malta: 1282–1410', in *Estudis d'Història Medieval*, 1 = *Estudis Dedicats a Ferran Soldevila*, 1 (Barcelona, 1969), 19–30.

34) 'The House of Aragon and Malta: 1282–1412', *Journal of the Faculty of Arts: Royal Malta University*, 4 no. 2 (1970), 156–68 [translated from the Catalan version, = article no 33].

35) 'Feudal Tenure and Latin Colonization at Rhodes: 1306–1415', *English Historical Review*, 85 (1970), 755–75 = Luttrell, *Hospitallers in Cyprus*, item III.

36) 'Coluccio Salutati's Letter to Juan Fernández de Heredia', *Italia Medioevale e Umanistica*, 13 (1970), 235–43 = Luttrell, *Hospitallers in Cyprus*, item XXI.

37) 'The Hospitallers' Hospice of Santa Caterina at Venice: 1358–1451', *Studi Veneziani*, 12 (1970), 369–83 = Luttrell, *Hospitallers in Cyprus*, item IX.

38) 'Notes on the Chancery of the Hospitallers of Rhodes: 1314–1332', *Byzantion*, 40 (1970), 408–20 = Luttrell, *Hospitallers in Cyprus*, item XV.

39) 'Aldobrando Baroncelli in Greece: 1378–1382', *Orientalia Christiana Periodica*, 36 (1970), 273–300 = Luttrell, *Latin Greece*, item XII.

40) 'La Corona de Aragón y las Ordenes Militares durante el Siglo XIV', in *VIII Congreso de Historia de la Corona de Aragón*, 2 (Valencia, 1970), 67–77 = Luttrell, *Hospitallers in Cyprus*, item XII.

41) 'Two Templar-Hospitaller Preceptories North of Tuscania', *Papers of the British School at Rome*, 39 (1971), 90–124 = Luttrell, *Hospitallers in Cyprus*, item X.

42) 'Juan Fernández de Heredia at Avignon: 1351–1367', in *El Cardenal Albornoz y el Colegio de España*, ed. E. Verdera y Tuells, 1 (Bologna, 1972), 289–316 = Luttrell, *Hospitallers in Cyprus*, item XIX.

43) 'A Hospitaller in a Florentine Fresco: 1366/8', *Burlington Magazine*, 114 (1972), 362–6.

44) 'The Hospitallers in Cyprus after 1291', in *Acts of the I International Congress of Cypriot Studies*, 2 (Nicosia, 1972), 161–71 = Luttrell, *Hospitallers in Cyprus*, item II.

45) with I. Adams and F. Toker, 'An Umbrian Abbey: San Paolo di Valdiponte: part I', *Papers of the British School at Rome*, 40 (1972), 146–95.

46) 'La datazione della ceramica medioevale', in *Atti: V Convegno Internazionale della Ceramica: Albisola, 31 maggio–4 giugno 1972* (Albisola, 1973), 139–46.

47) 'Malta nel periodo normanno', in *Atti del Congresso Internazionale di Studi sulla Sicilia Normanna* (Palermo, 1973), 467–76.

48) with D. Andrews, 'A Hospitaller Tower near Orte', *Annales de l'Ordre Souverain Militaire de Malte*, 31 (1973), 86–94.

49) 'Late Medieval Tuscania: the Notarial Registers', *Papers of the British School at Rome*, 41 (1973), 178–79.

50) Preface to the anastatical reprint of J. Delaville le Roulx, *Les Hospitaliers à Rhodes jusqu'à la Mort de Philibert de Naillac: 1310–1421* (London, 1974), i–vi = Luttrell, *Latin Greece*, item IV.

51) 'Crete and Rhodes: 1340–1360', in *Acts of the III International Congress of Cretological Studies*, 2 (Athens, 1974), 167–75 = Luttrell, *Hospitallers in Cyprus*, item VI.

52) 'A Maltese Casale: 1436', *Melita Historica*, 6 no. 3 (1974), 322–4.

53) 'Case Rupestri a Malta', *Notiziario di Archeologia Medievale* (December 1974), 2–3.

54) 'An Umbrian Abbey: San Paolo di Valdiponte: part II – Historical Postscript', *Papers of the British School at Rome*, 42 (1974), 174–8.

55) 'The Hospitallers at Rhodes: 1306–1421', in *A History of the Crusades*, ed. K. Setton, 3 (Madison, Wisconsin, 1975), 278–313 = Luttrell, *Hospitallers in Cyprus*, item I.

56) 'The *Servitudo Marina* at Rhodes: 1306–1462', in *Serta Neograeca*, ed. K. Dimaras and P. Wirth (Amsterdam, 1975), 50–65 = Luttrell, *Hospitallers in Cyprus*, item IV.

57) 'The Augustinians at Malta: 1413', *Analecta Augustiniana*, 38 (1975), 295–301 = Luttrell, *Christian Malta*, item XVI.

58) Review article on P. Toubert, 'Les Structures du Latium médiéval', in *Medieval Archaeology*, 19 (1975), 269–73.

59) 'Approaches to Medieval Malta', in *Medieval Malta: Studies on Malta before the Knights*, ed. A. Luttrell (London, 1975), 1–70 = Luttrell, *Christian Malta*, item II.

60) 'An Introduction to Ħal Millieri', in *Ħal Millieri: a Maltese Casale, its Churches and Paintings*, ed. A. Luttrell (Malta, 1976), 19–35 = Luttrell, *Christian Malta*, item XX.

61) with M. Buhagiar and D. de Luca, 'The Tal-Baqqari Churches', ibid., 90–6.

62) 'Capranica before 1342: Petrarch as Topographer', in *Studies in the Italian Renaissance: A Collection in Honour of P.O. Kristeller*, ed. C. Clough (Liverpool, 1976), 9–21.

63) 'Frederick II and Paolino de Malta: 1235', *Quellen und Forschungen aus italienischen Archiven und Bibliotheken*, 55–6 (1976), 405–9 = Luttrell, *Christian Malta*, item VIII.

64) 'La Campagna a Nord di Roma: Archeologia e Storia Medievale', in *Atti del Colloquio Internazionale di Archeologia Medievale: Palermo, 1974*, 1 (Palermo, 1976), 123–6.

65) 'L'Abitato Medievale a Malta: un Approccio Archeologico', ibid., 1, 274–83.

66) 'The Administration of Gozo: 1335', *Melita Historica*, 7 no.1 (1976), 61–4 = Luttrell, *Christian Malta*, item XIV.

67) 'Slavery at Rhodes: 1305–1440', *Bulletin de l'Institut Historique Belge de Rome*, 46–7 (1976–1977), 81–100 = Luttrell, *Latin Greece*, item VI.

68) 'Guglielmo de Tocco, Captain of Corfu: 1330–1331', *Byzantine and Modern Greek Studies*, 3 (1977), 45–56 = Luttrell, *Latin Greece*, item XIII.

69) 'The Christianization of Malta', in *The Malta Year Book 1977* (Malta, 1977), 415–21 = Luttrell, *Christian Malta*, item IV.

70) 'Late-Medieval Mediterranean Empires: the Catalan Example', in *Contributions to Mediterranean Studies*, ed. M. Vassallo = *Journal of the Faculty of Arts: University of Malta*, 6 no. 4 (1977), 109–15.

71) 'The Earliest Documents Transcribed in the Cathedral Archives, Mdina: 1316–1372', in *Archives of the Cathedral of Malta Misc. 32A: 1313–1529*, ed. J. Azzopardi (Malta, 1977), 29–51 = Luttrell, *Christian Malta*, item XII.

72) 'Hal Millieri', *Heritage* [Malta], no. 1 (1977), 9–12.

73) 'Girolamo Manduca and Gian Francesco Abela: Tradition and Invention in Maltese Historiography', *Melita Historica*, 7 no. 2 (1977), 105–32.

74) with T. Blagg and A. Bonanno, 'Hal Millieri, Malta', *Notiziario di Archeologia Medievale*, 21 (December 1977), 44–5.

75) 'The House of the Castellan of Malta', *Heritage* [Malta], no. 9 (1978), 161–5.

76) 'The Hospitallers' Interventions in Cilician Armenia: 1291–1375', in *The Cilician Kingdom of Armenia*, ed. T. Boase (Edinburgh, 1978), 111–38 = Luttrell, *Latin Greece*, item V.

77) 'The Sale of Gumerin on Malta: 1318', *Estudios Históricos y Documentos de los Archivos de Protocolos*, 6 (1978), 169–77 = Luttrell, *Christian Malta*, item XIII.

78) with A.-M. Legras, 'Les Hospitaliers autour de Gap: une Enquête de 1330', *Mélanges de l'École française de Rome: Moyen Âge–Temps Modernes*, 90 (1978), 627–42.

79) 'Malta Troglodytica: Ghar-il-Kbir', *Heritage* [Malta], no. 24 (1979), 461–4.

80) with T. Blagg and M. Lyttelton, 'Ligorio, Palladio and the Decorated Roman Capital from Le Mura di Santo Stefano', *Papers of the British School at Rome*, 47 (1979), 102–16.

81) 'Die gejstlige Riddere', *Sfinx* [Aarhus], 3 (1980), 83–7.

82) 'Roman Anguillara', in *Roman Villas in Italy; Recent Excavations and Research*, ed. K. Painter = *British Museum Occasional Paper*, no. 24 (London, 1980), 45–50.

83) 'Popes and Crusades: 1362–1394', in *Genèse et Débuts du Grand Schisme d'Occident: 1362–1394* (Paris, 1980), 575–85 = Luttrell, *Latin Greece*, item XIV.

84) 'The Hospitallers of Rhodes: Prospectives, Problems, Possibilities', in *Die geistlichen Ritterorden Europas*, ed. J. Fleckenstein and M. Hellmann (Sigmaringen, 1980), 243–66 = Luttrell, *Latin Greece*, item I.

85) 'Malta e Gozo: 1222–1268', in *Actas del X Congreso de Historia de la Corona de Aragón* (Zaragoza, 1980), 589–603 = Luttrell, *Christian Malta*, item X.

86) 'Gregory XI and the Turks: 1370–1378', *Orientalia Christiana Periodica*, 46 (1980), 394–417 = Luttrell, *Latin Greece*, item XV.

87) 'Late-Medieval Galley Oarsmen', in *Le Genti del Mare Mediterraneo*, ed. R. Ragosta, 1 (Naples, 1981), 87–101.

88) 'The *Cappella* of Birkarkara, 1402', *Melita Historica*, 8 no. 2 (1981), 156–60 = Luttrell, *Christian Malta*, item XVII.

89) 'Las Órdenes Militares en la Sociedad Hispánica – los Hospitalarios Aragoneses: 1340–1360', in *Las Órdenes Militares en la Peninsula durante de Edad Media* (Madrid, 1981) = *Anuario de Estudios Medievales*, 11 (1981), 591–6 = Luttrell, *Hospitallers of Rhodes*, item XVI.

90) 'Eighteenth-Century Malta: Prosperity and Problems', *Hyphen* [Malta], 3 no. 2 (1982), 37–51.

91) 'The Benedictines and Malta: 1363–1371', *Papers of the British School at Rome*, 50 (1982), 146–65 = Luttrell, *Christian Malta*, item XV.

92) 'The Fourteenth-Century *Capitula Rodi*', *Thesaurismata*, 19 (1982), 204–11 = Luttrell, *Hospitallers of Rhodes*, item VI.

93) 'The Madonna del Soccorso at Mdina', *Heritage* [Malta], no. 47 (1983), 927–32.

94) 'Le origini della parrocchia a Malta', in *Pievi e Parrocchie in Italia nel Basso Medioevo (secc. XIII–XV)*, 2 (Rome, 1984), 1187–98 = Luttrell, *Christian Malta*, item XVIII.

95) 'Malta e Gozo: 1268–1282', in *XI Congresso di Storia della Corona d'Aragona*, 3 (Palermo, 1984), 301–4.

96) 'Rhodes after 1204', in *Tenth Annual Byzantine Studies Conference: Abstract of Papers* (Cincinnati, Ohio, 1984), 43.

97) 'Malta before 870: Some Libyan Connections', *Hyphen* [Malta], 4 (1984), 127–33 = Luttrell, *Christian Malta*, item III.

98) 'Appunti sulle Compagnie Navarresi in Grecia: 1376–1404', *Rivista di Studi Bizantini e Slavi*, 3 (1984), 113–27 = Luttrell, *Hospitallers of Rhodes*, item VIII.

99) 'Notes on Foulques de Villaret, Master of the Hospital: 1305–1319', in *Guillaume de Villaret Ier Recteur du Comtat Venaissin 1274 Grand Maître de l'Ordre des Hospitaliers de Saint-Jean de Jérusalem, Chypre 1296* (Paris, 1985), 73–90 = Luttrell, *Hospitallers of Rhodes*, item IV.

100) 'Settlement on Rhodes: 1306–1366', in *Crusade and Settlement*, ed. P. Edbury (Cardiff, 1985), 273–81 = Luttrell, *Hospitallers of Rhodes*, item V.

101) with V. von Falkenhausen, 'Lindos and the Defence of Rhodes: 1306–1522', *Rivista di Studi Bizantini e Neoellenici*, 32–33 (1985–1986), 317–32 = Luttrell, *Hospitallers of Rhodes*, item VII.

102) 'Les exploitations rurales des Hospitaliers en Italie au XIVe siècle', in *Les ordres militaires, la vie rurale et le peuplement en Europe Occidentale (XIIe–XVIIIe siècles)* = *Flaran*, no. 6 (Auch, 1986), 107–20 = Luttrell, *Hospitallers of Rhodes*, item XII.

103) 'The Hospitallers of Rhodes and the Mausoleum at Halicarnassus', in *The Meeting of Two Worlds: Cultural Exchange between East and West during the Period of the Crusades*, ed. V. Goss (Kalamazoo, 1986), 161–65.

104) 'John V's Daughters: a Palaiologan Puzzle', *Dumbarton Oaks Papers*, 40 (1986), 103–12.

105) 'The Hospitallers in Cyprus: 1310–1378', *Kypriaki Spoudai*, 50 (1986), 155–84 = Luttrell, *Hospitallers of Rhodes*, item IX.

106) 'Dalle Carceri, Narzotto; Niccolò; Ravano', *Dizionario Biografico degli Italiani*, 32 (Rome, 1986), 73–8.

107) 'Le Schisme dans les prieurés de l'Hôpital en Catalunya et Aragón', in *Jornades sobre el Cisma d'Occident a Catalunya, les Illes i el País Valenciá* (Barcelona, 1986), 107–13 = Luttrell, *Hospitallers of Rhodes*, item XI.

108) 'The Hospitallers around Narni and Terni: 1333–1373', *Bollettino della Deputazione di Storia Patria per l'Umbria*, 82 (1987), 5–22 = Luttrell, *Hospitallers of Rhodes*, item XIII.

109) 'Papauté et Hôpital: l'enquête de 1373', in A.-M. Legras, *L'Enquête pontificale de 1373 sur l'Ordre des Hospitaliers de Saint-Jean de Jérusalem*, 1 (Paris, 1987), 2–42.

110) 'Rhodes and Jerusalem: 1291–1411', *Byzantinische Forschungen*, 12 (1987), 189–207 = Luttrell, *Hospitallers of Rhodes*, item X.

111) 'Templari e Ospitalieri in Italia', in *Templari e Ospitalieri in Italia: la Chiesa di San Bevignate a Perugia*, ed. M. Roncetti, P. Scarpellini and F. Tommasi (Perugia, 1987), 19–26 = Luttrell, *Hospitallers of Rhodes*, item I.

112) 'Greeks, Latins and Turks on Late-Medieval Rhodes', *Byzantinische Forschungen*, 11 (1987), 357–74.

113) 'Christian Slaves at Malta: 1271', *Melita Historica*, 9 no. 4 (1987), 381–3 = Luttrell, *Christian Malta*, item XI.

114) 'Ibn Hauqal and Tenth-Century Malta', *Hyphen* [Malta], 5 no. 4 (1987), 157–60.

115) 'Juan Fernández de Heredia and Education in Aragón: 1349–1369', *Anuario de Estudios Medievales*, 17 (1987), 237–44 = Luttrell, *Hospitallers of Rhodes*, item XVII.

116) 'The Hospitallers' Accounts for 1373/4 and 1374/5: an Aragonese Text', *Medievalia* [Barcelona], 7 (1987), 87–107.

117) 'Da Verona, Bonifacio' and 'Da Verona, Giberto', *Dizionario Biografico degli Italiani*, 33 (Rome, 1987), 121–3, 123–4.

118) 'English Levantine Crusaders: 1363–1367', *Renaissance Studies*, 2 no. 2 (1988), 143–53.

119) 'The Hospitallers of Rhodes Confront the Turks: 1306–1421', in *Christians, Jews and other Worlds: Patterns of Conflict and Accomodation*, ed. P. Gallagher (Lanham, 1988), 80–116 = Luttrell, *Hospitallers of Rhodes*, item II.

120) 'Del Carretto, Daniele', *Dizionario Biografico degli Italiani*, 36 (Rome, 1988), 394–7.

121) 'The Hospitallers of Rhodes at Treviso: 1373', in *Mediterraneo Medievale: Scritti in onore di Francesco Giunta*, 2 (Soveria Manelli, 1989), 755–75 = Luttrell, *Hospitallers of Rhodes*, item XIV.

122) 'The Latins and Life on the Smaller Aegean Islands: 1204–1453', *Mediterranean Historical Review*, 4 (1989), 146–57.

123) 'The Rhodian Background of the Order of St John on Malta', in *The Order's Early Legacy in Malta*, ed. J. Azzopardi (Malta, 1989), 3–14, and catalogue entries 16, 35, 38 = Luttrell, *Hospitallers of Rhodes*, item XVIII.

124) 'Hospitaller Life in Aragon: 1319–1370', in *God and Man in Medieval Spain: Essays in Honour of J.R.L. Highfield*, ed. D. Lomax and D. Mackenzie (Warminster, 1989), 97–115 = Luttrell, *Hospitallers of Rhodes*, item XV.

125) 'Gli Ospitalieri e l'eredità dei Templari', in *I Templari: Mito e Storia – Atti del Convegno Internazionale di Studi alla Magione di Poggibonsi – Siena (29–32 maggio 1987)*, ed. G. Minucci and F. Sardi (Sinalunga, 1989), 67–86 = Luttrell, *Hospitallers of Rhodes*, item III.

126) 'The Hospitallers' Western Accounts: 1373/4 and 1374/5', in *Camden Miscellany*, 30 = *Camden Fourth Series*, 39 (London, 1990), 1–21 = Luttrell, *Hospitaller State*, item XI.

127) 'Coins', in *Excavations at Ħal Millieri, Malta*, ed. T. Blagg, A. Bonanno and A. Luttrell (Malta, 1990), 81–3.

128) 'Hal Millieri: Historical and Architectural Postscript', ibid., 103–31 = Luttrell, *Christian Malta*, item XXI.

129) with T. Blagg, 'Notes on San Pawl Milqi', ibid., 147–52.

130) 'Englishwomen as Pilgrims to Jerusalem: Isolda Parewastell, 1365', in *Equally in God's Image: Women in the Middle Ages*, ed. J. Holloway, J. Bechtold and C. Wright (New York, 1990), 184–97.

131) 'The Military and Naval Organization of the Hospitallers at Rhodes: 1310–1444', in *Das Kriegswesen der Ritterorden im Mittelalter*, ed. Z. Novak (Torun, 1991), 133–153 = Luttrell, *Hospitallers of Rhodes*, item XIX.

132) with T. Blagg, 'The Papal Palace and Other Fourteenth-Century Buildings at Sorgues near Avignon', *Archaeologia*, 109 (1991), 161–92.

133) 'Medieval Malta: the Non-Written and the Written Sources', in *Malta: a Case Study in International Cross-Currents*, ed. S. Fiorini and V. Mallia-Milanes (Malta, 1991), 33–45.

134) 'Notes on Cyprus and Aragon: 1306–1386', *Epetiris tou Kentrou Epistemonikon Ereuvon*, 18 (1991), 129–36.

135) 'The Roots of Medieval Gozo', *Al-Masaq: Studia Arabo-Islamica Mediterranea*, 4 (1991), 51–7 = Luttrell, *Christian Malta*, item XIX.

136) [collaboration in] *The Atlas of the Crusades*, ed. J. Riley-Smith (London, 1991).

137) with S. Düll and M. Keen, 'Faithful unto Death: the Tomb Slab of Sir William Neville and Sir John Clanvowe, Constantinople 1391', *Antiquaries Journal*, 71 (1991), 174–90.

138) 'Slaves and Captives on Malta: 1053/4 and 1091', *Hyphen* [Malta], 7 no. 2 (1992), 97–104 = Luttrell, *Christian Malta*, item V.

139) 'The Hospitallers of Rhodes between Tuscany and Jerusalem: 1310–1431', *Revue Mabillon*, 64 = n. s. 3 (1992), 117–38 = Luttrell, *Hospitaller State*, item XVII.

140) 'Emphyteutic Grants in Rhodes Town: 1347–1348', in *Papers in European Legal History: Trabajos de Derecho Histórico en Homenaje a Ferran Valls i Taberner*, ed. M. Peláez, 5 (Barcelona, 1992), 1409–16.

141) 'Derek W. Lomax. In Memoriam', *Anuario de Estudios Medievales*, 22 (1992), 913–15.

142) 'Mdina Hoard of Muslim Coins: 1698', *Melita Historica*, 11 no. 1 (1992), 19–25 = Luttrell, *Christian Malta*, item VI.

143) 'The Greeks of Rhodes under Hospitaller Rule: 1306–1421', *Rivista di Studi Bizantini e Neoellenici*, n. s. 29 (1992), 193–223 = Luttrell, *Hospitaller State*, item III.

144) 'Les Hospitaliers à Chypre et à Rhodes: 1291–1522', in *L'Ordre de Malte dans les Pays-Bas Méridionaux (XIIe–XVIIIe siècles)*, ed. M. Forrier (Brussels, 1993), 19–29.

145) 'The Spiritual Life of the Hospitallers of Rhodes', in *Die Spiritualität der Ritterorden im Mittelalter*, ed. Z. Novak (Torun, 1993), 75–96 = Luttrell, *Hospitaller State*, item IX.

146) 'Malta and Rhodes: Hospitallers and Islanders', in *Hospitaller Malta 1530–1798: Studies on Early Modern Malta and the Order of St John of Jerusalem*, ed. V. Mallia-Milanes (Malta, 1993), 255–84.

147) 'Sugar and Schism: the Hospitallers in Cyprus from 1378–1386', in *The Sweet Land of Cyprus*, ed. A. Bryer and G. Georghallides (Nicosia, 1993), 157–66 = Luttrell, *Hospitaller State*, item IV.

148) 'Latin Responses to Ottoman Expansion before 1389', in *The Ottoman Emirate (1300–1389)*, ed. E. Zachariadou (Rethymnon, 1993), 119–34.

149) 'El Priorat de Catalunya en el segle XIV', *L'Avenç* [Barcelona], 179 (March 1994), 28–33 = 'The Hospitaller Priory of Catalunya in the Fourteenth Century', in Luttrell, *Hospitaller State*, item XV.

150) with J. Fuguet, 'Conversació amb Anthony Luttrell', *L'Avenç* [as no. 149], 40–3.

151) 'Gli Ospedalieri e un progetto per la Sardegna: 1370–1374', in *Società, Istituzioni, Spiritualità: Studi in onore di Cinzio Violante*, 1 (Spoleto, 1994), 503–8 = Luttrell, *Hospitaller State*, item XVI.

152) 'Timur's Dominican Envoys', in *Studies in Ottoman History in Honour of Professor V.L. Ménage*, ed. C. Heywood and C. Imber (Istanbul, 1994), 209–29.

153) 'The Order of St John from Acre to Malta', *St John's Historical Society: Proceedings*, 4 (1994), 1–6.

154) 'The Hospitallers' Medical Tradition: 1291–1530', in *The Military Orders: Fighting for the Faith and Caring for the Sick*, ed. M. Barber (Aldershot, 1994), 64–81 = Luttrell, *Hospitaller State*, item X.

155) 'Chaucer's Knight and the Mediterranean', *Library of Mediterranean History*, 1 (1994), 127–60.

156) 'The Hospitaller Priory of Venice in 1331', in *Militia Sacra: gli Ordini Militari tra Europa e Terrasanta*, ed. E. Coli, M. De Marco and F. Tommasi (Perugia, 1994), 101–43 = Luttrell, *Hospitaller State*, item XVIII.

157) 'The Structure of the Aragonese Hospital: 1349–1352', in *Actes de les Primeres Jornades sobre els Ordes Religioso-Militars als Països Catalans (Segles XII–XIX)* (Tarragona, 1994), 315–28 = Luttrell, *Hospitaller State*, item XIII.

158) 'L'effritement de l'Islam: 1091–1282', in *Le Carrefour Maltais*, ed. C. Vilain-Gandosi = *Revue du Monde Musulman et de la Méditerranée*, 71 (1994), 759–66 = Luttrell, *Christian Malta*, item VII.

159) 'The Economy of the Fourteenth-Century Aragonese Hospital', *Estudis Castellonencs*, 6 (1994–1995), 759–66 = Luttrell, *Hospitaller State*, item XIV.

160) 'The Hospitaller Province of *Alamania* to 1428', in *Ritterorden und Region: politische, soziale und wirtschaftliche Verbindungen im Mittelalter*, ed. Z. Novak (Torun, 1995), 21–41 = Luttrell, *Hospitaller State*, item XII.

161) 'The Military Orders: 1312–1798', in *Oxford Illustrated History of the Crusades*, ed. J. Riley-Smith (Oxford, 1995), 326–64.

162) 'Ta Stratiotika Tagmata', in *Istoria tes Kyprou*, ed. T. Papadopoullos, 4 part 1 (Nicosia, 1995), 733–58.

163) 'The Hospitallers in Cyprus after 1386', in *Cyprus and the Crusades*, ed. N. Coureas and J. Riley-Smith (Nicosia, 1995), 125–41 = Luttrell, *Hospitaller State*, item V.

164) 'The Earliest Documents on the Hospitaller Corso at Rhodes: 1413 and 1416', *Mediterranean Historical Review*, 10 (1995), 177–88 = Luttrell, *Hospitaller State*, item VIII.

165) 'Rhodes: Base militaire, Colonie, Métropole de 1306 à 1440', in *Coloniser au Moyen Âge*, ed. M. Balard and A. Ducellier (Paris, 1995), 235–40, 244–5 = Luttrell, *Hospitaller State*, item VII.

166) with J. Fuguet i Sans, 'Diaphragm Arches and Stone Slab Roofs', *Melita Historica*, 11 no. 4 (1995), 325–35.

167) 'The Muslim Cemetery at Rabat, Malta', in *North Africa from Antiquity to Islam*, ed. M. Horton and T. Wiedemann (Bristol, 1995), 33.

168) with B. Arbel, 'Plundering Ancient Treasures at Bodrum (Halicarnassus): a Commercial Letter Written on Cyprus, January 1507', *Mediterranean Historical Review*, 11 (1996), 79–86.
169) 'The Sugar Industry and its Importance for the Economy of Cyprus during the Frankish Period', in *The Development of the Cypriot Economy from the Prehistoric Period to the Present Day*, ed. V. Karageorghis and D. Michaelides (Nicosia, 1996), 163–73.

170) with S. Fiorini, 'The Italian Hospitallers at Rhodes: 1437–1462', *Revue Mabillon*, 68 = n. s. 7 (1996), 209–33 = Luttrell, *Hospitaller State*, item XIX.

171) 'Gli Ospitalieri di San Giovanni di Gerusalemme dal Continente alle Isole', in *Acri 1291: la Fine della Presenza degli Ordini Militari in Terra Santa e i Nuovi Orientamenti nel XIV secolo*, ed. F. Tommasi (Perugia, 1996), 75–91 = Luttrell, *Hospitaller State*, item II.

172) 'The Earliest Templars', in *Autour de la Première Croisade: Actes du Colloque de la "Society for the Study of the Crusades and the Latin East" (Clermont Ferrand, 22–25 June 1955)*, ed. M. Balard (Paris, 1996), 193–202.

173) 'The Earliest Hospitallers', in *Montjoie: Studies in Crusade History in Honour of Hans Eberhard Mayer*, ed. B. Kedar, J. Riley-Smith and R. Hiestand (Aldershot, 1997), 37–54.

174) 'El Final de la Dominació catalana d'Atenes: la Companyia navarresa i els Hospitalers', *L'Avenç*, 213 (1997), 30–5.

175) 'The Genoese at Rhodes: 1306–1312', in *Oriente e Occidente tra Medioevo ed Età moderna*: *studi in onore di Geo Pistarino*, ed. L. Balletto, 2 (Acqui Terme, 1997), 737–61 = Luttrell, *Hospitaller State*, item I.

176) 'To Byzantio kai oi Joannites Hippotes tes Rodou: 1306–1409', *Symmeikta*, 11 (1997), 189–213.

177) 'Giliberto Abbate's Report on Malta: circa 1241', in *Proceedings of History Week 1993*, ed. K. Sciberras (Malta, 1997), 1–29 = Luttrell, *Christian Malta*, item IX.

178) 'Ordini Militari', in *Enciclopedia dell'Arte Medievale*, 8 (Rome, 1997), 816–20.

179) 'Ospedalieri', ibid., 8, 922–7.

180) 'The Hospitallers and the Papacy: 1306–1314', in *Forschungen zur Reichs-, Papst- und Landesgeschichte: Peter Herde zum 65. Geburtstag*, ed. K. Borchardt and E. Bünz, 2 (Stuttgart, 1998), 595–622 = Luttrell, *Studies*, item V.

181) 'The Latin East', in *The New Cambridge Medieval History*, ed. C. Allmand (Cambridge, 1998), 796–811.
182) 'The Hospitallers' Early Written Records', in *The Crusades and their Sources: Essays presented to Bernard Hamilton*, ed. J. France and W. Zajac (Aldershot, 1998), 135–54 = Luttrell, *Studies*, item III.

183) 'Le Funzioni di un Ordine Militare: gli Ospedalieri a Rodi (1306–1421)', in *I Cavalieri di San Giovanni e il Mediterraneo: I Convegno Internazionale di Studi Melitensi – Taranto 18 febbraio 1996* (Taranto, 1998), 9–22.

184) 'English Contributions to the Hospitaller Castle at Bodrum in Turkey: 1407–1437', in *The Military Orders*, 2: *Welfare and Warfare*, ed. H. Nicholson (Aldershot, 1998), 163–72 = Luttrell, *Studies*, item IX.

185) 'The Military Orders: Some Definitions', in *Milizia Sancti Sepulcri: Idea e Istituzioni*, ed. K. Elm and C. Fonseca (Vatican, 1998), 78–8 = Luttrell, *Studies*, item I

186) 'Margarida d'Erill Hospitaller of Alguaire: 1415–1456', *Anuario de Estudios Medievales*, 28 (1998), 219–49 = Luttrell, *Studies*, item XXII.

187) 'Gli Ospedalieri Italiani: Storia e Storiografia', *Studi Melitensi*, 6 (1998), 73–88.

188) 'The Changing Nature of a Military-Religious Order: the Hospital 1099–1988', *St John Historical Society Proceedings*, 10 (1998), 1–7.

189) 'Gli Ospedalieri a Genova dall'Inchiesta papale del 1373', in *Cavalieri di San Giovanni e Territorio: la Liguria tra Provenza e Lombardia nei Secoli XIII–XVII*, ed. J. Costa Restagno (Bordighera, 1999), 219–33 = Luttrell, *Studies*, item XI.

190) 'Change and Conflict within the Hospitaller Province of Italy after 1291', in *Mendicants, Military Orders, and Regionalism in Medieval Europe*, ed. J. Sarnowsky (Aldershot, 1999), 185–99 = Luttrell, *Studies*, item XV.

191) 'The Hospitallers and their Florentine Bankers: 1306–1346', in *Karissime Gotifride: Historical Essays Presented to Professor Godfrey Wettinger on his Seventieth Birthday*, ed. P. Xuereb (Malta, 1999), 17–24 = Luttrell, *Studies*, item VI.

192) 'Earthquakes in the Dodecanese: 1303–1513', in *Natural Disasters in the Ottoman Empire*, ed. E. Zachariadou (Rethymnon, 1999), 145–51 = Luttrell, *Studies*, item X.

193) 'Crusade', in *Encyclopedia of the Renaissance*, 2 (New York, 1999), 112–14.

194) 'L'oeuvre religieuse des Hospitaliers à Rhodes: 1309–1439', in *Orient et Occident IXe–XVe siècles*: *Histoire et Archéologie – Actes du Colloque d'Amiens 8, 9 et 10 octobre 1998* (Amiens, 2000), 93–103 = Luttrell, *Studies*, item XXIV.

195) 'Templari e Ospitalieri: Alcuni Confronti', in *I Templari, la Guerra e la Santità*, ed. S. Cerrini (Rimini, 2000), 133–52.

196) 'Preface', in A. Calvet, *Les Légendes de l'Hôpital de Saint-Jean de Jérusalem* (Paris, 2000), 5–20 = Luttrell, *Studies*, item IV.

197) 'Rhodes Town: 1306–1356', in *Rodos 2.400 Chronia: É Polé tés Rodou apo tén Idryse tés mexri tén Katalepse apo tous Tourkous (1523)*, 2 (Rhodes, 2000), 309–14.

198) 'The Military Orders: Further Definitions', *Sacra Militia*, 1 (2000), 5–10 = Luttrell, *Studies*, item II.

199) 'From Jerusalem to Malta: the Hospital's Character and Evolution', *Peregrinationes: Acta et Documenta*, 1 (2000), 13–22.

200) 'A Hospitaller *Soror* at Rhodes: 1347', in *Dei Gesta per Francos: Études sur les Croisades dédiées à Jean Richard*, ed. M. Balard, B. Kedar and J. Riley-Smith (Aldershot, 2001), 129–43 = Luttrell, *Studies*, item XXIII.

201) 'Gli Ospedalieri nell'Italia Settentrionale dopo il 1312', in *Riviera di Levante tra Emilia e Toscana: un Crocevia per l'Ordine di San Giovanni*, ed. J. Costa Restagno (Genoa and Bordighera, 2001), 171–88 = Luttrell, *Studies*, item XII.

202) 'Cos after 1306', in *Istoria – Texne – Archaiologia tes Kw* (Athens, 2001), 401–4 = Luttrell, *Studies*, item VIII.

203) 'Gli Ospedalieri a Siena dopo il 1312', in *La Chiesa di San Pietro alla Magione nel Terzo di Camollia a Siena: il Monumento – l'Arte – la Storia*, ed. M. Ascheri (Siena, 2001), 103–20 = Luttrell, *Studies*, item XIII.

204) 'Le Origini della Precettoria Capitolare di Santo Stefano di Monopoli', in *Fasano nella Storia dei Cavalieri di Malta in Puglia*, ed. C. Fonseca and C. D'Angela (Taranto, 2001), 103–20 = Luttrell, *Studies*, item XIV.

205) 'The Hospitallers in Hungary before 1418: Problems and Sources', in *The Crusades and the Military Orders: Expanding the Frontiers of Medieval Latin Christianity*, ed. Z. Hunyadi and J. Laszlovszky (Budapest, 2001), 269–81 = Luttrell, *Studies*, item XX.

206) 'The Hospitaller Commanderies in Roussillon: 1373', in *L'Orde de Malta, el Regne de Mallorca i la Mediterrània* (Palma de Mallorca, 2001), 87–108 = Luttrell, *Studies*, item XIX.

207) 'The Finances of the Commander in the Hospital after 1306', in *La Commanderie: Institution des Ordres Militaires dans l'Occident Médiéval*, ed. A. Luttrell and L. Pressouyre (Paris, 2002), 277–83 = Luttrell, *Studies*, item VII.

208) 'The Crisis in the Bosphorus following the Battle near Ankara in 1402', in *Controllo degli Stretti e Insediamenti Militari nel Mediterraneo*, ed. R. Villari (Rome, 2002), 155–66.

209) 'The Medieval Ager Cosanus', in *Siena e Maremma nel Medievo*, ed. M. Ascheri (Siena, 2002), 27–58.

210) 'Gli Ospedalieri nel Mezzogiorno', in *Il Mezzogiorno Normanno-svevo e le Crociate: Atti delle Quattrodicesime Giornate Normanno-sveve Bari, 17–20 ottobre 2000*, ed. G. Musca (Bari, 2002), 280–300.

211) 'La Orden de San Juan en la Corona de Aragón: siglo XIV', in *La Orden Militar de San Juan en la Península Ibérica durante la Edad Media*, ed. R. Izquierdo Benito, F. Ruiz Gómez and J. Molero García (Alcázar de San Juan, 2002), 11–21.

212) 'The Contribution to Rhodes of the Hospitaller Priory of Venice: 1410–1415', in *Bisanzio, Venezia e il Mondo franco-greco (XIII–XV secolo)*: *Atti del Colloquio Internazionale organizzato nel Centenario della Nascita di Raymond-Joseph Loenertz o.p. – Venezia, 1–2 dicembre 2000* (Venice, 2002), 65–78 = Luttrell, *Studies*, item XVI.

213) 'Iconography and Historiography: the Italian Hospitallers before 1530', *Sacra Militia*, 2 (2002), 19–46 = Luttrell, *Studies*, item XVII.

214) 'Ospedale e Santo Sepolcro in Puglia dopo il 1099', in *Il Cammino di Gerusalemme*, ed. M.S. Calò Mariani (Bari, 2002), 477–84.

215) 'Medieval Malta: Approaches and Reproaches', in A. Luttrell, *The Making of Christian Malta* (Aldershot, 2002), item I, 1–17.

216) 'The Hospitaller Commandery of the Morea: 1366', in *Porphyrogenita: Essays on the History and Literature of Byzantium and the Latin East in Honour of Julian Chrysostomides*, ed. C. Dendrinos et al. (Aldershot, 2003), 291–300 = Luttrell, *Studies*, item XXI.

217) 'The Hospitallers in Twelfth-Century Constantinople', in *The Experience of Crusading*, 1: *Western Approaches*, ed. M. Bull and N. Housley (Cambridge, 2003), 225–32.

218) 'Hospitaller Birgu: 1530–1536', *Crusades*, 2 (2003), 121–50.

219) 'The Island of Rhodes and the Hospitallers of Catalunya in the Fourteenth Century', in *Els Catalans a la Mediterrània Oriental a l'Edat Mitjana*, ed. M.T. Ferrer i Mallol (Barcelona, 2003), 155–65 = Luttrell, *Studies*, item XVIII.

220) 'The Hospitallers' Earliest Statutes', *Revue Mabillon*, 75 = n. s. 14 (2003), 9–22.

221) Review of *L'Antico San Pietro in Asti*, ed. R. Bordone et al., in ibid., 301–2.

222) 'I Cavalieri di San Giovanni di Gerusalemme, Rodi e Malta', in *Monaci in Armi: gli Ordini Religioso-Militari dai Templari alla Battaglia di Lepanto – Storia ed Arte*, ed. F. Cardini (Rome, 2004), 53–62.

223) Review of an edition of the Templar rule, in *Journal of Ecclesiastical History*, 56 (2005), 362.

224) 'Las Órdenes Militares de San Juan de Jerusalén y del Temple', in *Las Órdenes Militares en la Europa Medieval*, ed. F. Novoa Portela and C. de Ayala Martínez (Barcelona, 2005), 45–76 [English version pp. 237–43] = 'Der Johanniter- und der Templerorden', in *Ritterorden im Mittelalter*, ed. F. Novoa Portela and C. de Ayala Martínez (Stuttgart, 2006) 45–76; Portuguese version in *As Ordens Militares na Europa Medieval* (Lisbon, 2005), 45–75; [other translations forthcoming].

225) 'Epilog: Die späteren Kreuzzüge', in *Saladin und die Kreuzfahrer*, ed. A. Wieczorek, M. Fansa and H. Meller (Mannheim, 2005), 127–37.

226) 'Ermengol de Aspa, *Provisor* of the Hospital: 1188', *Crusades*, 4 (2005), 15–19.

227) 'Conclusioni', in *Gli Archivi per la Storia del Sovrano Militare Ordine di Malta*, ed. C. Fonseca and C. D'Angela (Taranto, 2005), 529–34.

228) 'Les Femmes Hospitalières en France Méridionale', in *Les Ordres Religieux Militaires dans le Midi (XIIe–XIVe Siècle) = Cahiers de Fanjeaux*, 41 (Toulouse, 2006), 101–13.

229) with H. Nicholson, 'Introduction: A Survey of Hospitaller Women in the Middle Ages', in *Hospitaller Women in the Middle Ages*, ed. A. Luttrell and H. Nicholson (Aldershot, 2006), 1–42.

230) 'Juan Fernández de Heredia and the Compilation of the Aragonese Chronicle of the Morea' [pp. xiii–lxxxvii, on web at www.xoan.net/morea].

Indexes

compiled by Ditte Gurack

Places

Persons

This index lists names of dynasties, religious orders, peoples, creeds and persons. Brethren and *confratres* of the military religious orders are indicated by abbreviations: H. = Hospitallers, T. = Templars, Teut.= Teutonic Order, SB. = Swordbrethren, Mont. = Order of Montesa